Elements of Shipping

D0220464

BOOKS BY THE SAME AUTHOR

(1984) *Dictionary of Commercial Terms and Abbreviations*, 1st edn (6000 entries), Witherby, London.

(1986) *Elements of Port Operation and Management*, 1st edn, Chapman & Hall, London.

(1988) *Dictionary of English–Arabic Shipping/International Trade/ Commercial Terms and Abbreviations*, 1st edn (4400 entries), Witherby, London.

(1988) *Economics of Shipping Practice and Management*, 2nd edn, Chapman & Hall, London.

(1989) *Import/Export Documentation*, 1st edn, Chapman & Hall, London.

(1990) *Dictionary of Multilingual Commercial/International Trade/ Shipping Terms in English/French/German/Spanish*, 1st edn (over 13 000 entries), Witherby, London.

(1990) *Elements of Export Marketing and Management*, 2nd edn, Chapman & Hall, London.

(1990) *Elements of Import Practice*, 1st edn, Chapman & Hall, London.

(1994) *Export Practice and Management*, 3rd edn, Chapman & Hall, London.

(1995) *Dictionary of Shipping International Business/Trade Terms and Abbreviations (also incorporating Air/Travel/Tourism)*, 1st edn (14 000 entries), Witherby, London.

(1996) *Dictionary of Export/Import/Shipping/Air Documentation – Electronic Data Interchange – Processing Export/Import Consignment*, 1st edn (4000 entries), Witherby, London.

Elements of Shipping

Seventh edition

Alan E. Branch
FCIT, FIEX

International Business Consultant

Senior Lecturer and Chief Examiner in
Shipping/Export Practice/International Marketing,
Basingstoke College of Technology/Reading University/
Central London College UK

and

Visiting Professor,
Institute of Maritime Studies,
Gijon, Spain

CHAPMAN & HALL

London · Weinheim · New York · Tokyo · Melbourne · Madras

Published by Chapman & Hall, 2–6 Boundary Row, London SE1 8HN, UK

Chapman & Hall, 2–6 Boundary Row, London SE1 8HN, UK

Chapman & Hall GmbH, Pappelallee 3, 69469 Weinheim, Germany

Chapman & Hall USA, 115 Fifth Avenue, New York, NY 10003, USA

Chapman & Hall Japan, ITP-Japan, Kyowa Building, 3F, 2–2–1 Hirakawacho, Chiyoda-ku, Tokyo 102, Japan

Chapman & Hall Australia, 102 Dodds Street, South Melbourne, Victoria 3205, Australia

Chapman & Hall India, R. Seshadri, 32 Second Main Road, CIT East, Madras 600 035, India

First edition 1964
Second edition 1970
Third edition 1975
Fourth edition 1977
Fifth edition 1981
Reprinted 1983
Sixth edition 1989
Reprinted 1991, 1992, 1993, 1994, 1995
Seventh edition 1996
Reprinted 1996, 1997

© 1964, 1970, 1975, 1977, 1981, 1989, 1996 Alan E. Branch

Typeset in 10/12 Times by Photoprint, Torquay, Devon
Printed in Great Britain by St Edmundsbury Press, Bury St Edmunds, Suffolk

ISBN 0 412 60460 4

A catalogue record for this book is available from the British Library

Library of Congress Catalog Card Number: 95-71094

∞ Printed on permanent acid-free text paper, manufactured in accordance with ANSI/NISO Z39.48–1992 and ANSI/NISO Z39.48–1984 (Permanence of Paper).

To my wife
Kathleen

Contents

Preface to the seventh edition

Over 30 years has passed since the first edition of this book was published. Today it is regarded as the standard work in the shipping industry and is retailing in over 200 countries. It is used extensively by shipping executives and students globally.

Opportunity has been taken to update not only the contents of the book but also to introduce three new chapters. In so doing the text now takes full account of new disciplines in the industry both currently being developed and those projected to unfold as we enter the next millennium. Accordingly the seventh edition focuses attention on the growing complexity of the industry in an era of great change and opportunity and above all on the need to conduct business on a professional basis. The latest edition features enlarged chapters on containerization, ship types, bills of lading, the international consignment, chartering, international organizations BIMCO and GATT/WTO, plus three new chapters on multi-modalism, seaports and electronic data interchange (computer technology).

Additional illustrations have been provided on containerization, chartering documentation, ship types, cargo handling equipment and logistics.

The seventh edition will be useful specifically for students taking courses sponsored by the Institute of Chartered Shipbrokers, the British International Freight Association, the Institute of Export, the Chartered Institute of Transport, the Institute of Purchasing and Supply, the Chartered Institute of Marketing, Chambers of Commerce, Export Associations/Clubs, the Institute of Marine Engineers, the Institute of Bankers and the Royal Institute of Naval Architects. It will also be ideal for students taking shipping, international trade, maritime transport, international distribution, export, import, transport, seaports, logistics, containerization and international management examinations/research or training courses/seminars at degree/diploma level at universities and colleges not only in the UK but also in Hong Kong, Malaysia, Singapore, Jamaica, Jordan, the USA, Scandinavia, Korea, Australasia, the Middle East, Europe, the Pacific Rim nations and Third World countries. The book remains compulsory reading on the Advanced Certificate Overseas Trade for the subject of International Physical Distribution, the author being one of the four subject specialists responsible for the development of the course in 1975 under the aegis of HM government through the British Overseas Trade Board.

Elements of Shipping treats the subject in a practical, professional way and is an ideal *aide-mémoire* to the shipping/export/seaport/logistics executive. It provides the reader with a basic understanding and knowledge of the international shipping industry with emphasis on the salient economic, political, commercial, operating, management and computerized applications of the subject.

The book reflects the author's many years of experience in ship and port management and international trade including consultancy both in the UK and overseas. In 1993 I was the 'runner up' for the 'World Vision' Award for Development Initiative, presented to encourage British business, through recognition of its achievements, to play an expanding role in supporting economic and social progress in the developing countries of Africa, Asia and Latin America. The award was sponsored by Worldaware Business Awards, an organization which is part of the United Nations.

The reader who wishes to know more about export or import practice should also study the companion volumes *Export Practice and Management* (3rd edn) and *Elements of Import Practice*. Similarly the reader who wishes to know more about ship management techniques should study *Maritime Economics, Management and Marketing* (3rd edn, 1997), while the seaport executive should also consider the book *Elements of Port Operation and Management*.

I am greatly indebted to the various organizations listed in the acknowledgements for the assistance they have so enthusiastically given me. The fact that an increasing number are situated overseas is reflected in the international content and market of the book.

Finally, in common with earlier editions, I would like to acknowledge with grateful thanks the generous secretarial help given by my life-long friends Mr and Mrs Splarn, and Maurice Hicks with proof-reading, and as always my dear wife Kathleen for her forbearance, encouragement and help in this task, especially with proof-reading.

Alan Branch

A.E.B.
November 1995

19 The Ridings	Course Director
Emmer Green	International Trade/Shipping
Reading	Basingstoke College of Technology
Berkshire	Worting Road
RG4 8XL	Basingstoke
Fax: 01734 476291	Hampshire
	RG21 1TN

Acknowledgements

The author wishes to acknowledge the generous assistance provided by the following companies and institutions:

Alcatel
Alsthom
Baltic Exchange
Baltic International Freight Futures Exchange (BIFFEX)
Baltic and International Maritime Conference
British Shipbuilders Ltd
Bureau Veritas
Chamber of Shipping
Club Méditerranée
Denholm Ship Management (Holdings) Ltd
Exportmaster Ltd
Freight Transport Association
Hanjin Shipping
HM Customs and Excise
International Association of Classification Societies Ltd
International Association of Independent Tanker Owners
International Cargo-Handling Co-Ordination Association
International Chamber of Commerce
International Maritime Organization
International Maritime Satellite Organization
Lloyd's Register of Shipping
London Commodity Exchange
Maersk Line (A.P. Møller)
Marine Safety Agency, Department of Transport
MAT Shipping Ltd
Panama Canal Commission
Peninsular and Oriental Steam Navigation Company
P & O Cruises

Port of Rotterdam Authority
Port of Singapore Authority
Sea Containers Ltd
Simpler Trade Procedures Board (SITPRO)
Southampton Container Terminals Ltd
St Lawrence Seaway Authority
Suez Canal Authority
United Nations Conference on Trade and Development
    (UNCTAD)
Wallem Ship Management (Isle of Man) Ltd
World Trade Organization

CHAPTER 1

Introduction

1.1 SCOPE OF THE BOOK

Since this book was first written over 30 years ago the pattern and importance of shipping has changed dramatically as has the strategy adopted by countries/governments and shipowners. Today it is a high profile international business and high tech in its management and operation. Moreover, it conveys some 99% of world trade in volume terms and is a major contributor to the creation and development of global wealth. It also exerts enormous power in trade and political terms. Furthermore, it is highly competitive. For example, there are over 20 operators providing regular liner services from Europe to North America.

This book, now in its seventh edition, is written primarily for the student/international business executive who has limited knowledge of the shipping industry, but wishes to gain a basic and fundamental knowledge of the way it works today and likely future trends. It will deal with the economic, political, commercial, operating and information technology aspects of the subject.

The latest edition will feature electronic data interchange, multil-modalism, the role of seaports in modern ship operation, more extensive evaluation of containerization, a discussion of the land/sea/air bridge concept, the changing pattern of world trade, and more emphasis on ship management and finance.

Overall the book is written in a simple but lucid style and reflects the author's experience in the industry spanning 40 years, which includes not only work and consultancy on a world-wide scale in the industry itself, but also that of lecturer/chief examiner at home and overseas. This has involved overseas governments and multinational industries together with many conferences/ seminars at which he has delivered papers on the subject. This book treats the subject in a pragmatic and professional way. It places particular emphasis on the fact that shipping today is a complex operation and all the ingredients of the subject must be fully understood to ensure the business is conducted both efficiently and profitably. The 'value added benefit' concept is particularly significant whereby the shipper will choose the maritime service which yields the highest benefit both to the exporter and importer.

1.2 FUNCTION OF SHIPPING

The function of shipping is the conveyance of goods from where their utility is low to a place where it is higher. Goods may consist of raw materials conveyed in bulk cargo shipments or purpose-built containers, equipment components/parts for assembly at an industrial plant or on-site capital project like a power station, or the whole range of consumer products many of which are durable and may be shipped in containers, on swap bodies or by an international trucking operation.

The factors influencing the shipper's choice of transport mode has changed dramatically during the past decade. Today it is based on the total product concept embracing all the constituents of distribution. These include reliability, frequency, cost, transit time, capital tied up in transport, quality of service, packaging, import duty, insurance and so on. It favours more strongly multimodalism with sea transport undertaking the major leg of the overall transit. Logistics, just-in-time delivery and distribution centres/'distriparks' play a major role in the decision-making process. All these aspects will be re-examined later as the basis of how the shipowner can best meet the needs of the shipper in the foreseeable future.

1.3 WORLD FLEET AND WORLD SEA-BORNE TRADE

An analysis of the world fleet and world sea-borne trade as featured in Tables 1.1 and 1.2 reveals the following:

(a) The dry cargo tonnage fleet has yielded an annual growth since 1988 and in 1994 stands at 399 million dwt. Likewise the tanker tonnage has grown during the same period following its dramatic decline in the period 1980 to 1988 from 352 million dwt to

Table 1.1 World fleet and world sea-borne trade

Fleet (million dwt)					Seaborne trade (million metric tonnes)			
	Dry cargo	Tanker	Total	1980 = 100		Dry cargo	Tanker	Total	1980 = 100
1980	326	352	677	100	1980	2010	1596	3606	100
1985	372	285	657	97	1985	2134	1159	3293	91
1986	367	264	631	93	1986	2122	1263	3385	94
1987	362	262	624	92	1987	2178	1283	3461	96
1988	358	261	620	92	1988	2308	1367	3675	102
1989	360	262	621	92	1989	2400	1460	3860	107
1990	367	270	637	94	1990	2451	1526	3977	110
1991	383	285	668	99	1991	2537	1573	4110	114
1992	387	294	681	101	1992	2572	1635	4207	117
1993	391	301	692	102	1993	2615	1703	4313	120
1994	399	304	704	104	1994	2720	1755	4475	124

Reproduced by kind permission: Chamber of Shipping.

Table 1.2 World sea-borne trade by cargo 1991–1994

	Million metric tonnes				% of total			
	1991	1992	1993	1994	1991	1992	1993	1994
Crude oil	1200	1305	1345	1380	30	31	31.1	30.8
Oil products	323	330	358	375	8	8	8.3	8.4
Iron ore	352	337	352	380	9	8	8.2	8.5
Coal	360	370	360	370	9	9	8.4	8.3
Grain	180	205	193	185	4	5	4.4	4.1
Other cargoes	1610	1660	1710	1785	40	39	39.6	39.9
Total	4025	4207	4318	4475	100	100	100	100

Reproduced by kind permission: Chamber of Shipping.

261 million dwt, during which time many owners adopted a policy to 'scrap but not replace'.

(b)   The dry cargo trade has grown from 2010 million metric tonnes in 1980 to 2720 million metric tonnes in 1994. This represents an increase of 35% compared with a 22% rise in dry cargo tonnage fleet capacity. Hence the dry cargo fleet capacity utilization is improving.

(c)   The tanker trade has grown by 9% from 1980 to 1994. The tanker fleet in the same period has declined by 16%.

(d)   The dry cargo fleet in 1980 represented 48% of the world fleet compared with 57% in 1994. Likewise the tanker fleet in 1980 represented 52% of the world fleet compared with 43% in 1994. Hence the dry cargo fleet is expanding at a quicker rate than the tanker fleet and this trend is likely to continue.

(e)   The dry cargo sea-borne trade in 1980 represented 55% of total world sea-borne trade. However, by 1994 it had risen to 61%. Conversely during the same period the tanker sea-borne trade fell from 45% of total world sea-borne trade in 1980 to 39% in 1994.

(f)   The structure of world trade is changing. In metric tonnes the volume of grain traded fell in 1993 and 1994 whilst coal returned to its 1992 level. The trade in grain from the former USSR has experienced a fall whilst coal has suffered from changes in the steel industry resulting in reduced demand for coking coal. This must be viewed against a period of expanding world trade.

(g)   Crude oil and oil products have increased annually since 1991. The rise in the shipments of oil products in contrast to crude oil implies that an increasing number of oil producing countries are processing their output before shipment to the eventual market.

1.4 WORLD TRADE FLEET

The following points emerge from an analysis of Table 1.3 covering the world trade fleet and featuring the ten largest trading fleets during the period 1991–1994.

(a)   The last 20 years has seen the share of the world's merchant shipping fleets controlled by developed countries fall from 80% to approximately 55%. Within these figures an increased proportion were registered on open registers such as Liberia, Panama, the Bahamas and the Norwegian International Ship Register. The

Table 1.3 World trade fleet including ten largest fleets (100 GRT and above) 1991–1995

Rank	Register	Number				Million GRT				Million DWT			
		1991	1992	1993	1995	1991	1992	1993	1995	1991	1992	1993	1995
1	Liberia	1546	1566	1532	1550	52.5	55.5	53.5	58.0	93.4	98.1	92.6	95.8
2	Panama	3700	3980	4141	4375	45.7	50.4	55.1	65.0	73.8	80.8	87.7	99.4
3	Greece	1551	1540	1599	1606	23.7	25.2	28.7	30.0	43.7	46.8	53.3	53.6
4	Cyprus	1328	1403	1497	1542	20.1	20.7	22.4	23.2	35.9	36.7	39.4	39.2
5	Japan	5411	5320	5411	5356	24.3	23.9	23.0	20.1	37.3	36.6	34.9	30.3
6	Bahamas	859	933	969	1020	18.2	20.1	20.4	22.2	30.2	33.1	33.1	34.6
7	Norway (NIS)	865	823	745	718	21.8	20.4	19.0	19.8	38.9	35.8	33.0	31.8
8	Malta	715	864	943	1009	8.7	10.9	13.5	15.5	14.8	18.5	23.2	26.2
9	China (People's Republic)	1654	1648	1768	1975	13.0	13.0	14.0	15.3	19.7	19.7	21.3	23.0
10	USA	705	664	643	500	14.4	14.3	13.8	5.5	21.7	21.3	20.2	7.1
	UK & Crown Dependencies	607	508	475	494	5.0	4.9	4.7	5.5	6.6	6.4	6.1	4.2
	USSR	2798	836	110	—	18.2	5.62	0.65	—	23.5	7.27	0.93	—
	Ukraine	—	2	590	—	—	0.01	0.002	—	—	4.35	5.65	—
	Lithuania	—	68	67	—	—	0.39	0.39	—	—	0.46	0.46	—
	Latvia	—	131	133	—	—	1.03	0.93	—	—	1.33	0.93	—
	Russia	—	1743	1866	—	—	10.50	10.70	—	—	13.75	13.89	—

Reproduced by kind permission: Chamber of Shipping.

scale of 'flagging out' suggests that the employment of seafarers from developed countries as a percentage of the world total has fallen rather more than ownership.

(b) The main increase in market share has been enjoyed not by the former USSR or Eastern Europe but by the developed countries, although concentrated in a few such as South Korea, Taiwan, Hong Kong and Singapore. This dispersion of shipping away from the traditional maritime powers and towards developing countries is in line with experience in other industries and it also follows from the huge growth in international sea-borne trade in these countries.

(c) China is emerging as a major growth market and its fleet size continues to increase to cope with its involvement in international trade.

(d) The continuing decline of the UK fleet is due primarily to the fact that UK shipowners feel unable to invest in new and replacement tonnage. The UK flagged fleet carried some 36% of UK international trade by value in 1992, an increase of 1% despite the decline in the fleet size.

(e) The UK fleet size in 1994 of 494 vessels represents about half of all UK-owned tonnage. The rest is registered on other British flag registers (Crown Dependencies), i.e. the Isle of Man, and dependent territories, e.g. Bermuda, Gibraltar and Hong Kong. About a fifth of UK-owned tonnage is registered in non-British registers and about a further quarter is with foreign registers at the more expensive and sophisticated end of the market.

(f) In 1971 the UK fleet totalled 2386 ships with a deadweight tonnage of 41 million, compared with 1019 vessels in 1985 with 20 million deadweight tonnage. In 1995, it was 494 vessels with deadweight tonnage of 4.2 million.

CHAPTER 2

The ship

2.1 MAIN FEATURES OF HULL AND MACHINERY

There are two main parts to a ship: the hull and the machinery.
The hull is the actual shell of the ship including her superstructure,
while the machinery includes not only the engines required to
drive her, but also the ancillary equipment serving the electrical
installations, winches and refrigerated accommodation.

The hull is virtually the shell of the ship and usually designed for
a particular trade in accordance with a shipowner's specification.
A vessel is constructed of a series of transverse frames, which
extend from the fore to aft of the vessel, rising at right angles to
the keel. In reality they form the ribs of the ship. Statutory
regulations exist regarding the distance between each frame. Each
vessel, depending on her classification – passenger, container,
tanker, bulk carrier – must have a number of bulkheads which are
virtually steel walls isolating various parts of the vessel. This is
necessary in the interests of containing a fire or flooding following
a collision. Ocean-going vessels must have at the fore end a
collision bulkhead installed at a distance of not less than 5% of the
ship's length from her bow. The obligatory after-peak bulkhead
function is to seal off the stern tubes through which run the
tailshaft driving the propeller.

The rear portion of the ship is termed the after end or stern.
When moving stern first, the vessel is said to be moving astern.
The front portion of the ship is termed the fore end, whilst the
extreme forward end is called the bows. When moving bow first,
the vessel is said to be moving ahead. Fore and aft are generally
used for directional purposes. The area between the forward and
aft portions of the vessel is called amidships. The maximum
breadth of the vessel, which is found in the amidships body, is
known as the beam.

The engine room houses both the machinery required to drive the vessel and the generators required for lighting, refrigeration and other auxiliary loads. Engines are usually situated aft, thus releasing the amidships space – at the broadest part of the vessel – for cargo and passenger accommodation. The ship's funnel, painted in the shipping line colours, is situated above the engine room. In modern passenger liners, it is specially designed to keep fumes and smuts clear of the passenger accommodation. The propeller shaft, linking the propeller with the engines, passes through a shaft tunnel and is usually a single controllable pitch specification. The ship's anchors and the windlasses used to lower and raise them are found in the bow section. Additional anchors might also be provided on a large ship. All tankers and bulk carriers are constructed of a double hull formation.

Modern tonnage, particularly tankers, container ships and passenger liners, have transverse propulsion units in the bows termed bow thrusters. A number of vessel's have side thrusters situated at the sterm of the ship. Both bow and side thrusters are situated on the port and starboard sides. Their purpose is to give greater manoeuvrability in confined waters, e.g. ports, and so reduce or eliminate the need for tugs. The rudder which enables the vessel to maintain her course is situated aft. Some ships have an additional rudder in the bows for easier manoeuvrability in port. Stabilizers are in appearance similar to the fins of a fish, and are fitted to modern passenger liners and container ships to reduce rolling in heavy seas. They are fitted in pairs, and when in use protrude at right angles from the hull, deep below the water line. Their number depends on the size of the vessel. The provision of a bulbous bow can also improve passenger comfort, as it can reduce pitching in heavy seas and has also been provided in tankers, bulk carriers and modern cargo liners to increase speed when in ballast.

The modern tendency is to have large unobstructed holds with electrically operated hatch covers, for the speedy handling of cargo, and to reduce turn-round time to a minimum.

Their actual design and the number of decks will depend on the trade in which the ship plies. A vessel comprises various decks with the uppermost decks being called the navigational, boat and promenade decks. A continuous deck in a ship would run throughout the length of the vessel from fore to aft.

The transverse bulkheads run from the tank tops or floors of the hold to the deck. The longitudinal framing consists of steel sections running the length of the ship into which are fixed the skin plates forming the hull. Nowadays, with the development of the welded construction, vessels are constructed on the combined system which uses the longitudinal system in the double bottom, and at deck level uses transverse framing for the sides. Basically the combined system is better for welded construction.

Scantlings basically are the dimensions of the structural parts of the ship embracing size of frames, beams, steel plating, bulkheads and decks. A vessel built to the full scantlings would be based on· the maximum draught when the freeboard measured from the loadline to the deckline (the upper side of the continuous main-deck or freeboard deck which is equipped with permanent means of closing all openings to the elements) is at its minimum. Single deck vessels fall within this category such as an ore carrier which needs the strongest type of ship construction to convey such heavy deadweight cargoes with low stowage factors. Such vessels are built to the highest specification of the classification societies such as Lloyd's Register of Shipping, American Bureau of Shipping, Bureau Veritas, etc., as regards strength of the component parts of the structure.

To give access to cargo holds, openings are cut into the deck of the vessel which are termed hatchways and are surrounded by coamings which are like steel walls rising from the deck. The height of these coamings is regulated by statute or classification society regulations.

Each mercantile type vessel has a certain number of various types of tanks for a variety of purposes and the following are the more salient ones:

(a) The forepeak tank is situated in the bows of the vessel between the bows and the collision bulkhead.

(b) Conversely the aft peak tank is situated in the stern of the vessel. It forms the aftermost watertight bulkhead.

(c) The wing tank is located at the side of the holds designed for carrying water ballast. These are found particularly in special-ized bulk carriers.

(d) The deep tanks are situated one in each of the holds at the two ends of the ship. Such tanks are used for carrying water ballast and can be used to carry dry cargo. In modern vessels they are constructed to convey oil, either as bunkers, or wood or palm oil.

A tramp, carrying shipments of coal or ore, will be a single-deck vessel with large unobstructed hatches to facilitate loading and discharge.

The handling of cargo will be mechanized as far as possible with the use of conveyor belts, pallets and containers. The holds of a modern cargo liner are designed to facilitate dealing with such modern methods of cargo handling.

The derricks are the ship's cranes, and are electrically operated. Their lifting capacity can vary from 3 to 50 tonnes. If heavy items such as locomotives or boilers are commonly carried, jumbo derricks capable of lifting up to 120 tonnes are provided (see Fig. 4.3). The decks are strengthened to accommodate such heavy lift cargoes.

A modern vessel called a Combi carrier (see Fig. 4.3) has superseded the 'tween deck tonnage in trades unable to invest in container tonnage and its infrastructure of port facilities and distribution overland network.

The bridge of a vessel is the navigating centre of the ship where her course is determined. Most modern tonnage today has the navigating bridge and machinery situated aft thereby facilitating the naval architect's designing the vessel of the maximum cargo capacity. The engines are bridge controlled and the navigating officer on watch makes use of a bridge computer to steer the vessel, to work out her course, and give position reports etc. More recently vessels use the maritime satellite navigator system explained on pp. 454–62. Included in the navigating bridge accommodation is the helm, and also a large amount of nautical equipment, including radar sets, gyrocompass, radio, direction finder, auto pilot, joystick control, satellite navigator, echo-sounder, weather facsimile, Decca, etc. The bridge is in direct communication with all parts of the vessel.

Crew accommodation on modern cargo ships and tankers is situated aft in close proximity to the machinery. Standards of accommodation are high, and are controlled by various statutory regulations.

In the late 1960s the development of the container ship became evident in many cargo liner trades. Such vessels are usually free of derricks and the fourth generation have a capacity of up to 4000 high capacity ISO containers TEUs (Twenty Foot Equivalent Units). Their speed is between 16 and 22 knots and the more sophisticated type of container vessel is called a cellular ship. Such a vessel is built in the form of a series of cells into which the containers are placed, usually by sophisticated shore-based cranes. The most recent container vessel tends to be multi-purpose in design with ramp facilities for transhipping vehicle cargo. This improves the general cargo mix flexibility of the vessel (see Fig. 3.4 on p. 45).

Passenger accommodation will be either one-class with different. grades of cabin comfort, as on a hotel basis, or two-class, incorporating first class and tourist. This ensures that the most economical use is made of the cubic capacity of the ship. In a cruise passenger liner, it is common to find a swimming pool, cinema, shops, hospital, nursery and numerous other amenities and recreational facilities (see Fig. 4.6 on p. 62).

There are various statutory provisions concerning the quantity and type of life-saving apparatus carried on a vessel. Broadly, it is determined by the type of vessel, crew establishment and passenger certificate (authorized number of passengers permitted to be carried). Life-saving apparatus includes lifeboats, inflatable rubber liferafts, lifebuoys and individual lifejackets.

The draught of a vessel is the vertical distance from the keel to the waterline. The maximum permitted draught varies according to the seasons and waters in which she plies. The markings are given in Fig. 2.1 and all ships must be loaded so that the loadline corresponding to the zone in which they are steaming must not be submerged. The seasons to which the markings apply are Tropical (T), Summer (S), Winter (W) and Winter North Atlantic (WNA). The world has been mapped off into sections showing where those sections apply. These are broadly detailed below:

Tropical Venezuela to Costa Blanco and Rio de Janiero to Walvis Bay, Somalia via Saigon to Guatemala and Diego Suarez via Darwin to Coquimbo.

Summer All areas between the lower line of the foregoing tropical area down to a line passing through Bahia Blanca, Cape Town, Durban, Launceston, Dunedin and Valparaiso.

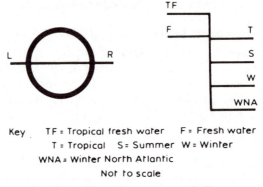

Key TF = Tropical fresh water F = Fresh water
T = Tropical S = Summer W = Winter
WNA = Winter North Atlantic
Not to scale

Fig. 2.1 International loadline of cargo vessel. Passenger and timber vessels have additional lines.

It must be appreciated that some areas change from summer to winter with different dates applying.

Given below is the seasonal situation with details of winter, summer and tropical loadlines.

Bergen to Greenland including the centre of the North Atlantic; Prince Rupert Island and the North Pacific to Yokohama – winter loadlines apply from 16th October to 15th April and summer loadlines from 16th April to 15th October.

All areas below the line between Bahia Blanca, Cape Town, Durban, Launceston, Dunedin and Valparaiso – winter loadlines apply from 16th April to 15th October, and summer loadlines from 16th October to 15th April.

Continent Baltic and North Atlantic – winter loadlines from 1st November to 31st March and summer loadlines from 1st April to 31st October.

Mediterranean and Black Sea – winter loadlines from 16th December to 15th March and summer loadlines from 16th March to 15th December.

Sea of Japan – summer loadlines from 1st March to 30th November and winter loadlines from 1st December to 28–29th February.

Seasonal Tropical (Arabian Sea – above Muscat and Karachi) – tropical loadlines from 1st August to 20th May; summer loadlines from 21st May to 31st July.

Arabian sea, below Muscat and Karachi to a line from Somalia to Colombo – tropical loadlines from 1st December to 20th May; summer loadlines from 21st May to 15th September.

Tropical loadlines from 16th September to 15th October; summer loadlines from 16th October to 30th November.

Bay of Bengal – tropical loadlines from 16th December to 15th April and summer loadlines from 16th April to 15th December.

China sea – tropical loadlines from 16th December to 15th April and summer loadlines from 1st May to 20th January.

The foregoing regulations/zones must be strictly followed as vessels are not permitted to operate submerged above their seasonal loadline marking. Alterations in the zones are made by the timber cargo regulations.

Freeboard is the distance measured amidships from the water line to the main deck of a vessel. This is normally the uppermost continuous deck in a ship with one or more decks. However, in a shelter deck vessel it would be the next deck below.

2.2 TYPES OF PROPULSION

The type and economics of propulsion has changed radically following the escalation in fuel cost in 1973 and 1979. Hitherto there was a trend towards faster vessels but nowadays shipowners have tended to encourage slower and more economical schedules. More emphasis has been placed on improving ship turn-round time, on improving overall transit times and on raising ship utilization performance. Moreover, there has been a tendency to have the type of machinery which burns cheaper fuel. Hence the bulk of the world mercantile fleet is diesel-engine operated. Meanwhile, research continues on both diesel and steam turbines to improve performance not only in fuel consumption terms but also in maintenance costs.

The shipowner has a fairly wide range of propulsion units from which to choose. The steam turbine with its smoothness and reliability of operation is a choice for some large fast passenger liners.

The diesel engine has become increasingly popular for practically all vessels, as its low fuel consumption gives added deadweight and cubic capacity for cargo. It is almost exclusively used in river and short sea trades. A number of ships have also been built with diesel-electric or turbo-electric drive. In these ships the power units, steam turbine or diesel, are used not to drive the propellers directly, but to generate electricity for the driving motor coupled to the shaft. These units have greater flexibility, but against this must be set the increased costs of installation, maintenance and operation.

Today more than 85% of the world fleet is propelled by diesel engines. They have good performance at efficient propeller speeds and can be readily reversed for astern operation. Moreover, it is the most efficient prime mover from the standpoint of overall thermal efficiency. Fuel consumption is lower than with the steamship and consequently less bunker space is required. Additionally, compared with the steamship, it offers a reduction in size/weight ratio which facilitates the diesel machinery being placed aft. Conversely, however, although the diesel engine is less expensive to build, it is more costly to maintain; it creates more vibration and noise and finally tends to have a shorter life compared with the steam turbine engine. The favourable size/weight ratio plus lower fuel consumption which improves the vessel payload potential are very important aspects in favour of diesel propulsion. Moreover, extensive research is being undertaken to lessen the vibration aspect, reduce maintenance and overall to prolong the life of the diesel engine investment. Much has been achieved in these areas during the past ten years.

The choice of the propulsion unit is governed by many factors. These include initial cost; required speed; cost and availability of fuel on the route used; cargo-carrying capacity required; length and duration of voyage and operational expenses.

Improvements in marine engineering and in the efficiency of fuel are constantly reducing costs. For example, many shipowners in recent years have adapted their diesel engines to enable them to use cheaper, heavier boiler oil, instead of the more costly diesel oil for which they were originally designed. Of course, the use of heavy fuel oil for diesel engines raises the cost of maintenance, due to its action on pistons and cylinder linings. Meanwhile, the tendency to produce larger, more powerful diesel engines continues, thereby widening the scope of this type of propulsion in larger tonnages.

Speed is determined by the value set upon it by shippers. A high speed is subject to increasing marginal cost and is only economically possible where the trade can generate the cargo business. On short voyages, higher speeds and consumption are possible because a smaller quantity of fuel has to be carried in fuel tanks and less cargo space is taken up. On long voyages, high consumption would mean more fuel space, and less cargo capacity, so that an engine with a lower consumption is more economic for such voyages. The space required for fuel will also depend on steaming distances between ports where fuel can be replenished at reasonable cost. The modern engine room and wheelhouse is very much automated and the larger vessel is provided with computer facilities to operate at optimum speed and automatic navigation. Such measures aid conservation of fuel cost and lower crew levels.

Factors which will tend to influence a growing movement towards diesel propulsion are given below:

(a) High oil cost.

(b) Lower fuel consumption of the diesel unit compared with steam propulsion. For example, a VLCC powered by steam turbine consumes 170 tons of heavy fuel oil per day. Conversely a diesel-driven equivalent consumes over 100 tons. Hence, not only does consumption fall with diesel propulsion, but also the cost per ton is much cheaper, plus a longer steaming distance before rebunkering.

(c) Technical trends of the 1990s suggest the future propulsion unit will be primarily either the slow or medium/high-speed diesel engine. The cost savings outweigh the advantages of reliability, easy maintenance and compactness usually inherent with the steam turbine.

(d) A growing shift in new tonnage terms from large ships to smaller vessels, and the maximum power of diesel engines offers up to 55 000 bhp with a single slow-speed diesel and 65 000 bhp with two medium speeds.

(e)   A large number of engine transplants took place in the 1980s from steam turbine to diesel propulsion. This includes, for example, container ships being equipped with the slow-speed diesel unit whilst the tanker transplant involves the medium-speed unit. It will be recalled the slow-speed diesel unit is one with less than 250 r/min and is usually better able to cope with low quality bunker fuel. It is usually a two-stroke engine and does not require a gearbox thereby generating more efficiency. Less cylinders are involved and likewise maintenance and lubrication. The medium-speed engine diesel unit is one above 900 r/min and can burn fuel just as low grade as the slow-speed diesel engine.

The future predicts largely an era of diesel propulsion with continuing research into improving the performance of the diesel unit. Nuclear or gas-fired propulsion is unlikely to be developed for a variety of reasons. Long term it looks as though the world mercantile fleet will be largely diesel powered.

2.3 TYPES AND METHODS OF TONNAGE MEASUREMENT

There are five main kinds of tonnage in use in shipping business. These are deadweight, cargo, displacement, gross and net tonnages, now superseded by Tonnage Convention 1994 (2.4).

Deadweight tonnage (dwt) expresses the number of tons (of 2240 lb) a vessel can transport of cargo, stores and bunker fuel. It is the difference between the number of tons of water a vessel displaces 'light' and the number of tons of water a vessel displaces when submerged to her loadline. Deadweight tonnage is used interchangeably with deadweight carrying capacity. A vessel's capacity for weight cargo is less than its total deadweight tonnage.

Cargo tonnage is expressed in terms of a weight or measurement. The weight ton in the US and sometimes in the UK is the American short ton of 2000 lb, or the English long ton of 2240 lb. A measurement ton is usually 40 ft^3, but in some instances a larger number of cubic feet is taken for a ton. Most ocean package freight is taken at weight or measurement (W/M) ship's option. With the growth in use of the metric system the metric tonne of 1000 kg or cubic metre is becoming more widely used. The freight ton is a mixture of weight and measurement tons and can lead to confusion in the collection and analysis of statistics.

Displacement of a vessel is the weight in tons of 2240 lb of the ship and its contents. It is the weight of water the ship displaces. Displacement light is the weight of the vessel without stores, bunker fuel or cargo. Displacement loaded is the weight of the vessel plus cargo, passengers, fuel and stores.

Gross tonnage applies to vessels, not to cargo. It is determined by dividing by 100 the volume in cubic feet of the vessel's closed-in spaces, and is usually referred to as the gross registered tonnage (GRT). The spaces exempt from the measurement include light and air spaces; wheelhouse; galley; lavatories; stairways; houses enclosing deck machinery; hatchways to a maximum of 0.5% of the gross tonnage and open shelter deck. A vessel ton is 100 ft^3. It is used as a basis for pilotage and dry-dock dues, and sometimes tonnage dues. Additionally, it is employed for official statistical purposes, when comparing ship's sizes, and as a basis for Protection and Indemnity club entries.

Net tonnage is a vessel's gross tonnage after deducting space occupied by crew accommodation including facilities for the master and officers; spaces used for navigation; boatswain's store room; water ballast and fresh water spaces including forward and aft peak tanks, deep tanks provided only fitted with manholes and not employable for carriage of liquid cargo; propelling and machinery space which does not represent earning capacity of the ship. A vessel's net tonnage expresses the space available for the accommodation of passengers and stowage of cargo, and is usually referred to as net registered tonnage (NRT). A ton of cargo in most instances occupies less than 100 ft^3: hence the vessel's cargo tonnage may exceed its net tonnage, and indeed the tonnage of cargo carried is almost always greater than the gross tonnage. It is the cubic capacity of all earning space, and it is on this tonnage figure that most harbour dues and other charges are calculated. The aim of the average shipowner is to achieve a low net tonnage consistent with a maximum cubic capacity for cargo and/or passengers.

The Suez and Panama tonnage regulations make it obligatory for vessels to be measured for tonnage if they require to use the canals. The equivalent gross and net tonnage are somewhat lower than the British standard, where one ton equals 100 ft^3. Where vessels proceed to ports in countries which do not accept the British tonnage rules, dues will also be levied on tonnages assessed under local conditions.

2.4 THE TONNAGE CONVENTION 1994

The Tonnage Convention was adopted at a conference held under the auspices of the IMO to introduce a universally recognized system for measuring the tonnage of ships. In merchant shipping, tonnage is basically a measurement of the cubic capacity or volume of the ship. This gives an indication of its cargo-carrying capacity and tonnage is used as a basis for assessing harbour dues, canal dues, pilotage fees and other costs.

Although all existing systems go back to a method devised in 1854 by George Moorsom of the British Board of Trade, considerable differences exist between them and it is quite possible for sister ships to have very different tonnages simply because they fly different flags. The 1969 Convention was intended to eliminate these anomalies by establishing an internationally approved system.

Because of the need to have a system that applied to as many ships as possible, the requirement for entry into force was extremely high (25 states whose combined merchant fleets represent 65% of the world's gross tonnage of merchant ships) and the Convention did not enter into force until 1982. Even then, existing ships (i.e. those built before 1982) were enabled to retain their existing tonnage for a further 12 years, to give shipowners time to phase in the new system as economically as possible.

The Tonnage Convention provides for gross and net tonnages, both of which are calculated independently. The gross tonnage is a function of the moulded volume of all enclosed spaces of the ship. The net tonnage is produced by a formula which is a function of the moulded volume of all cargo spaces of the ship. The net tonnage shall not be taken as less than 30% of the gross tonnage.

The 1994 Convention represents the culmination of more than one hundred years of work on trying to establish an acceptable international method for assessing tonnage. The first conference on the subject was held in 1870 but failed to reach agreement. Further efforts were made by the League of Nations and a draft convention was prepared in June 1939 at a conference in Paris.

Further progress was halted by the outbreak of war and when the IMO met for the first time in 1959 it assumed responsibility for establishing a uniform tonnage-measurement system.

One of the guiding principles of the 1969 conference was that the new system should not adversely affect the economics of shipping and should also be as simple as possible. However, the tonnages of some ship types will increase under the Convention while others will go down. The tonnages of tankers and bulk carriers are expected to decrease slightly while the tonnages of Ro/Ro ships will rise substantially.

This in turn will lead to changes in port dues and other costs which are related to tonnage. Some shipowners are said to have delayed having their ships' tonnages re-calculated, perhaps for this reason, resulting in a substantial backlog of ships building up. Ships whose tonnages have not been assessed in accordance with the Convention could find that their tonnage is assessed by port authorities in foreign countries, possibly at a higher rate than anticipated.

It is expected that the system will be beneficial to shipowners and others involved in the industry. Because tonnages will be calculated in the same way all over the world it should be possible to allow ships to be transferred from one flag to another without having to be re-measured. Tonnage measurement is also quicker to calculate under the new system and can be done by computer.

Despite the overall advantages offered by the Convention, there is some concern about the failure of many shipowners to have their ships re-measured. In March 1993 the United Kingdom sent a note to the Maritime Safety Committee pointing out that many ships would not be re-measured to the requirements of the Convention by the time it entered into force on 18 July 1994.

The note said that 'a problem could well develop world-wide' and the United Kingdom proposed a common approach to the problem through the IMO. The note said: 'Clear guidelines need to be developed on how member states should effectively deal with those shipowners who have not yet applied for re-measurement.'

In response to this concern, at its 38th session (14–18 March 1995) the Sub-Committee on Stability and Load Lines and on Fishing Vessel Safety developed a simplified method of calculating the tonnage of existing ships which have not been measured in accordance with the Tonnage Convention.

A draft circular describing this method was submitted to the Maritime Safety Committee for circulation. It notes that the method only gives good results for normal cargo ships. Ships such as car carriers and passenger ships which have large super-structures should be considered individually.

CHAPTER 3

Ship design and construction

As we approach the year 2000, ship design will focus on a number of specific areas as detailed below:

(a)   Market conditions and how best to respond to the needs of the shipper will be major factors in ship design which will focus on raising standards for the merchant shipper in the form of overall faster transits and the continuing expansion of multi-modalism. The interface between the ship and berthing operations will be much improved thereby speeding up ship turn-round time. This involves quicker and more efficient transhipment techniques both for containerized traffic and the bulk carrier market. A recent example of the lengthened container ship technology demonstrating this point is found in Fig. 3.4 on p. 45.

(b)   The shipowner will continue to extend shipboard efficiency with the aid of continuously improving onboard technology in all areas of operation. The continuing expansion of the INMARSAT shipboard navigation/communication technology (see pp. 457, 462) is bringing in a new era of information technology and communications involving EDI (see Chapter 20) in the global maritime field.

(c)   Ship safety will remain paramount consistent with efficiency and the application of modern technology. The IMO (see pp. 127, 144) is continuing to persuade member states of the need to adopt conventions to raise the safety of ships at sea. This involves especially ship design and specification.

(d)   Ships are now subject to inspection by the registered state maritime agency whilst in port, usually by accredited classification society surveyors or other designated surveyors, to ensure they are seaworthy. Member states subscribing to the IMO Convention have legal powers to detain tonnage which fails to conform to the prescribed standards as found, for example, under MARPOL 90.

(e)   Shipowners, as trade increases, are tending to replace tonnage by larger vessels rather than provide additional sailings.

This lowers nautical tonne per mile costs but places more stress on planning and the total logistics operation at the berth. Accordingly container tonnage has now reached 4000 TEUs and could attain 5000 TEUs by the year 2000. Likewise ferries operating in the cross-Channel and Baltic trades have much increased their capacity from 200 to 450 cars and/or the corresponding combination of road haulage vehicles. It results in vessels having a wider beam, increased length overall, but more especially more decks, increasing the ship freeboard. Such developments require extensive research to evolve/design such tonnage to comply with the strict IMO safety standards.

3.1 GENERAL PRINCIPLES AND FACTORS INFLUENCING DESIGN, TYPE AND SIZE OF SHIP

In his choice of the type of ship to be built, the shipowner must consider primarily the trade in which she is to operate. His decision as to size and propelling machinery will be governed by the factors involved in his particular trade, such as the nature of the cargo mix to be moved, the cost and availability of fuel, the minimum carrying capacity required, the length and duration of the voyages and the required speed. Economic, technical, statutory and safety considerations will all influence his choice.

So far as the building and operating costs are concerned, within certain limits, the larger ship is a cheaper proposition. For example, the cost of the propelling machinery for a 100 000 tonner is less than the cost for two 50 000 tonners developing the same power. The larger ship costs less to crew than two smaller ships and her operating costs per ton are lower. In the bulk trades, where the nature of the cargo calls for large roomy holds, the economics of size alone favour the employment of large ships. However, increased size implies deeper draught, and if a general trader is to be operated economically, she must be able to proceed anywhere where cargo is offered. On one voyage she may be going to Bombay which permits vessels with a maximum draught of 16 m, while her next employment may be in the River Plate where the draught is limited to about 9 m. She may have to load from an ore jetty off the coast of Chile where safety considerations prohibit the large ship. All these considerations have to be balanced, and today the modern tramp has developed into a handy-sized vessel of the

Freedom type of 14 000 dwt with a speed of 14 knots or the Panmax bulk carrier of 66 000 dwt (see Fig. 4.2) capable of passing through the Panama canal.

Recently the cellular container ship has featured more prominently in cargo liner trades. Additionally, more purpose-built tonnage is becoming available for carrying such products as liquefied methane, cement, sugar, wine, bananas, trade cars, etc. Such ships – often owned or on charter to industrial users – are designed for a particular cargo and are frequently involved in a ballast run for part of the round voyage (see pp. 210, 221). Purpose-built tonnage requires special terminals – often situated away from the general port area – frequently involving expensive equipment to ensure quick transhipment. The mammoth oil tanker up to 500 000 dwt with a draught of over 29 m comes within this category. Such vessels together with the OBOs and ore carriers of 100 000 dwt and over are very restricted in their ports of call due to their size, particularly draught. There is every reason that purpose-built tonnage will continue to increase in size subject to economic and technical developments being favourable in particular trades, and it remains to be seen what other types of purpose-built tonnage other than those described elsewhere in this book will reach 100 000 dwt during the next decade. More emphasis is being placed on the multi-purpose vessel to lessen the impact of trade depression as when a market is low the ship can move into one which is more buoyant.

Where the vessel to be constructed is intended for long-term charter to industrial users, as in the case of many oil tankers, ore carriers and other specialized cargo ships, the limits of size are dictated by terminal facilities or by obstacles of the voyage – such as arise, for example, in the Panama canal or St Lawrence Seaway (see p. 114). Such vessels may be sometimes 400 000 dwt which cannot use the St Lawrence Seaway.

Much of the foregoing analysis applies equally to cargo liners, except that flexibility of operation is not so important. A factor tending more to limit their size is the importance of providing frequent sailings which the market can support. The overseas buyer pays for his goods when the seller can produce bills of lading showing that the consignment has been shipped. Under such conditions the merchant demands frequent sailings and, if the shipowner does not provide these, his competitors will! Hence, he must operate a larger fleet of smaller ships, and therefore few cargo liners are as economically large as they might be. This was particularly so with 'tween deck tonnage, but with containerization emphasis is placed on speed coupled with the benefits of quick port turn-round, fewer ports of call, but more reliance on feeder services involving the hub and spoke concept (see p. 411). Such vessels are able to take advantage of economies of scale, thereby permitting the shipowner to operate a more economically sized ship. Moreover, the container shipment is able to offer the combined transport transit embracing rail or road as the collector/distributor with shipping undertaking the trunk haul.

3.2 SAFETY AND OTHER REGULATIONS

Associated with the provision of new tonnage, there is the obligation to comply with statutory regulations, classification society rules and international agreements affecting ship design, and these vary according to the requirements of the different flags, particularly in matters relating to accommodation.

Vessels registered in the UK have to be built to the statutory requirements imposed by the Department of Transport. The regulations concern all life-saving apparatus, navigational aids, the hull and machinery, crew and passenger accommodation, watertight and fireproof bulkheads, gangways, emergency escapes, anchor cable and hawsers, shell plating, ship inspection at the seaport, etc. The basis of these requirements is included in the Merchant Shipping Act of 1894. Various amendments and additions to these regulations have reached the statute book to meet new conditions and developments. These are found in the IMO Conventions on Maritime Safety which include the International Convention for the Safety of Life at Sea (SOLAS) 1960 and 1974 which specifies minimum standards for the construction, equipment and operation of ships compatible with safety; the International Convention on Load Lines 1966, the Special Trade Passenger Ship Agreement 1975, the Convention on the International Maritime Satellite Organization (INMARSAT) 1976, the International Convention on Standards of Training, Certification and Watchkeeping for Seafarers (STCW) 1978 and the International Convention on Maritime Search and Research (SAR) 1979.

All the foregoing have been subject to amendment and protocol as recorded on pp. 134–44.

3.3 STATUTORY REGULATIONS

International conventions, codes and protocols concerning ship safety and marine pollution are agreed by the member states of the United Nations Agency, the International Maritime Organization (IMO – see pp. 127–44). In the past 40 years IMO has promoted the adoption of some 35 conventions and protocols and adopted numerous codes and recommendations. The conventions and codes usually stipulate inspection and the issuance of certificates as part of enforcement. Most member countries and/or their registered shipowners authorize classification societies to undertake the inspection and certification on their behalf. For example more than 100 member states have authorized Lloyd's Register to undertake such inspection and certification.

IMO conventions define minimum standards but member states can instigate national regulations which incorporate IMO standards and apply equally well to their own fleets and visiting foreign ships. Classification societies participate in the work of the IMO as technical advisers to various delegations. Their key function is to provide inspection and certification for compliance and advice on these complex regulations. Various aspects of the IMO conventions are dealt with elsewhere in the book.

Given below are a selection of statutory marine surveys:

(a) *July 1968*. An international load line certificate is required by any vessel engaged in international voyages except warships, ships of less than 24 metres in length, pleasure yachts not engaged in trade and fishing vessels.

(b) *Cargo Ship Safety Construction Certificate*. This is required by any ship engaged in international voyages except for passenger ships, warships and troop ships, cargo ships of less than 500 gross tonnage, ships not propelled by mechanical means, wooden ships of primitive build, pleasure yachts not engaged in trade and fishing vessels. Survey classification ensures the SOLAS 1974 convention is complied with in the areas of hull, machinery and other relevant equipment. For vessels of 100 metres length and over, compliance with damage stability requirements is also required.

(c) *Cargo Ship Safety Equipment Certificate*. This is required by any ship engaged on international voyages except for the ship types detailed in item (b). Survey classification ensures the SOLAS 1974 convention chapters II-1, II-2, III and IV are complied with along with other relevant requirements.

(d) *Cargo Ship Safety Radio Certificate*. This is required by all cargo ships of 300 gross tonnage and upwards and fitted with a radio station and issued with a Safety Radio Certificate under SOLAS 1974 (see pp. 131–44)

(e) *Passenger Ship Safety Certificate*. This is required by any passenger ship under SOLAS Regulation 12(a)(vii) engaged on international voyages except troop ships. A passenger ship is a vessel which carries more than twelve passengers. Pleasure yachts not engaged in trade do not require a Passenger Ship Safety Certificate following compliance with the requirements of the 1974 SOLAS Convention. This includes the survey arrangements for subdivision, damage stability, fire safety, life-saving appliances, radio equipment and navigational aids. It is reviewed annually.

(f) *Carriage of Dangerous Goods – SOLAS Chapter II-2 Regulation 54*. Dry cargo ships which are intended for the carriage of dangerous goods are required to comply with Regulation 54 of Chapter II-2 of SOLAS, except when carrying dangerous goods in limited quantities, and need an appropriate document as evidence of such compliance. Such a Document of Compliance for the Carriage of Dangerous Goods is issued by classification societies at the same time as the Safety Equipment Certificate is issued.

Two examples are found in the IBC and IGC codes. The IMO international code for the construction and equipment of ships carrying dangerous chemicals in bulk (IBC code) provides safety standards for the design, construction, equipment and operation of ships carrying dangerous chemicals. An additional code – the BCH – is applicable to existing ships built before 1 July 1986. A document/certificate termed a Certificate of Fitness is issued by the classification society in accordance with the provisions of the IBC or BCM code and is mandatory under the terms of either the 1983 amendments to SOLAS 1974 or MARPOL 73/78. For national flag administrations not signatory to SOLAS 1974, a statement of compliance would be issued by the classification society in accordance with a shipowner's request.

The other example is found in the IMO international code for the construction and equipment of ships carrying liquefied gases in bulk (IGC code). This requires that the design, constructional features and equipment of new ships minimize the risk to the ship, its crew and the environment. There are additional gas carrier codes applicable to existing ships built before 1 July 1986. A Certificate of Fitness is mandatory under the terms of the 1983 amendments to SOLAS. For national flag administrations not signatory to SOLAS 1974 a statement of compliance would be issued by the classification society in accordance with a ship-owner's request.

(a) International Safety Management Code

In 1993 the International Safety Management (ISM) Code was completed by the IMO. The objectives of the code are to ensure safety at sea, the prevention of human injury or loss of life, and the avoidance of damage to the environment (in particular the marine environment) and property. The functional requirements for a safety management system to achieve these objectives are as follows:

(a)   a safety and environmental protection policy;

(b)   instructions and procedures to ensure safe operation of ships and protection of the environment;

(c)   defined levels of authority and lines of communication between and amongst shore and shipboard personnel;

(d)   procedures for reporting accidents and non-conformities within the provisions of the code;

(e)   emergency response procedures;

(f)   procedures for internal audits and management reviews.

The code effectively supersedes the guidelines in Management for the Safe Operation of Ships and for Pollution Prevention adopted by the IMO Assembly in 1991. Owing to procedural difficulties in developing the necessary amendments to the 1974 SOLAS Convention (see p. 144) and bringing such amendments into force internationally, the IMO adopted the code as an Assembly resolution in the first instance.

It is likely the phases of the ISM Code will become mandatory by June 1998 for passenger ships, tankers and chemical tankers, together with gas carriers and bulk carriers over 500 GRT. This will be followed in 2002 by general cargo ships over 500 GRT and offshore ships such as supply vessels, and in 2004 by all ships over 150 GRT. Overall it will provide an internationally recognized standard for the safe management and operation of ships and for pollution prevention. In these respects it differs from ISO 9000 which is an all-embracing quality assurance system for company management. The need for ISM arose through numerous shipping disasters and pollution incidents, reports into which highlighted crew negligence, sloppiness throughout the company, or plain inexperience. Lack of communication also featured prominently.

To achieve the aims of the ISM Code each company has to establish a safety and environmental protection policy which is complemented and maintained by all staff both ashore and on board ship. To ensure the safe operation of the vessel, companies must appoint a shore-based 'designated person' as a link between ship and shore management. This person must have direct access to the highest level of management whilst being able to effectively communicate with seagoing personnel. Overall, the ISM should not be seen as a means of relegating a Master's responsibility, but rather as a means of endorsing and enhancing the Master's authority/powers.

The scheme for certification to the International Safety Management Code (ISM Code) is a means to demonstrate a shipping company's commitment to the safety of its vessels, cargo, passengers and crew, and to the protection of the environment, in compliance with the ISM Code. Overall it provides for the assessment of a company's safety management systems on board vessels, and as required in shore-based offices. It requires each ship in a company fleet as well as the company's shore-based management systems to be separately certificated. The scheme lays down the assessment procedures which will be followed when either the shipboard systems or the shore-based systems or both are to be assessed for certification, which is usually undertaken by an accredited classification society such as Lloyd's Register. The assessment confirms company policy and central measures in accordance with the ISM Code.

Certification in accordance with the requirements of this scheme should not be taken as an indication that the company or its vessels comply with international or national statutory requirements other than the ISM Code and it does not endorse the technical adequacy of individual operating procedures or of the vessels managed by the company. Overall the certificate will confirm the following:

(a) An appropriate management system has been defined by the company for dealing with safety and pollution prevention on board.

(b) The system is understood and implemented by those responsible for the various functions.

(c) As far as periodic assessments can determine, the key actions indicated in the system are being carried out.

(d) The records are available to demonstrate the effective implementation of the system.

The scheme does not in any way replace or substitute class surveys of any kind whatsoever. The assessment will be undertaken as follows:

1. The company applies for assessment for one or more of its ships. The application is accompanied by evidence of any certificated management system that the company holds.

2. The classification society considers the application and supporting evidence, and communicates any requirement to assess the shore-based management systems directly to the company, with an indication of the likely cost to the company.

3. If the classification society assesses the shore-based organization, this will be done in two stages:

(a) verification of compliance of the documented safety management system;

(b) verification of implementation of the system in the shore-based organization, based on the full commitment and understanding of personnel and evidence of the associated records.

If Category I non-compliances are found in the shore-based operations, no certificate will be issued. One or more follow-up visits may then be necessary, at the company's expense, to assess the revised system.

4. When the classification society is satisfied that the shore-based system is suitably capable of handling, as a minimum, the management controls specified in the ISM Code, the shipboard system will be assessed on each vessel proposed by the company for certification.

5. The shipboard assessment, which is in no sense a technical assessment or inspection, will be carried out by a qualified

assessor. Normally, there will be only one assessor, but this may be increased at the discretion of the classification society.

6. All relevant documentation must be available to the assessor(s) at each location or vessel visited.

7. On completion of the assessment, the assessor will issue a Shipboard Assessment Report detailing the following:

(a) date of assessment;
(b) location (port etc.);
(c) assessor's name and reference;
(d) ship's name
    official number
    classification Society/IMO number
    year of build
    port of registry and flag
    type
    gross tonnage;
(e) company's name and address;
(f) assessment summary:
    confirmation that copies of non-compliance notes and observations are attached;
    total number of non-compliance notes written:
        Number of Category I;
        Number of Category II;
    number of observations;
    brief details of any non-compliance notes not accepted by ship's staff;
(g) recommendation by assessor: should a certificate be issued?
                                                        Yes/No
(h) signature of assessor;
(i) signature and name of ship's master/senior officer.

8. For continued certification to the ISM Code by the classification society, the safety management system will be reviewed to ensure requirements are maintained satisfactorily. This will be carried out by:

(a) an annual partial assessment of the system on each ship – the continuing validity of the company's shore-based certification will be checked at each shipboard assessment;

(b) an annual partial assessment of the shore-based operations;

(c) these partial assessments will take place at approximately twelve month intervals.

3.4 SURVEY METHODS

The traditional way of surveying a vessel was to bring her to a shipyard where items to be surveyed were opened up, cleaned, inspected and reassembled. This method is both time consuming and expensive, but is still practised widely for a variety of reasons. However, a number of alternative survey methods exist today which have been developed by the classification societies and are now very popular. Details are given below:

(a) Voyage survey
The surveyor is in attendance during the ship's voyage, and carries out the required surveys. If requested, he prepares specifications in co-operation with the owner on items to be repaired.

(b) BIS notation
Although docking a vessel is still necessary for a number of reasons, the interval between dockings has been increased considerably. This extended interval may come into conflict with the 'normal' class rules. However, by arranging minor modifications to the hull and its appendages, a notation 'bis' (built for in-water surveys) may be obtained which allows a docking interval of five years.

(c) Continuous survey
Classification Rules require that the surveys of hull and machinery are carried out every four years. Alternatively continuous survey systems are carried out, whereby the surveys are divided into separate items for inspection during a five-year cycle. For the machinery survey the rules provide that certain of these items may be surveyed by the chief engineer. Furthermore, for vessels carrying out machinery maintenance in accordance with a fixed maintenance schedule, this system may replace the continuous machinery survey system, thereby reducing the class survey to an annual survey.

(d) Planned maintenance system
This is subject to a type approval and may thereafter be used as a basis for a special survey arrangement for individual ships at the owner's request.

Today, most cost-conscious shipowners operate advanced planning systems and maintenance procedures in order to meet increasing demand for cost-effective operation.

To avoid unnecessary opening up of machinery and duplication of work, many classification societies have introduced an alternative survey arrangement for the machinery. The arrangement is based on the owner's planned maintenance system already in operation 'on board'. It involves the following sequence of survey programme.

(a) classification society approves the owner's maintenance programme;
(b) initial survey on board by classification society surveyor;
(c) continuous machinery survey to be in operation;
(d) chief engineer to be approved by classification society.

The annual survey inspections carried out by the chief engineer are accepted as class surveys. However, the annual audit survey must be carried out in conjunction with the ordinary annual general survey (AGS). The audit survey is to verify that the arrangement meets agreed procedures. At the annual audit survey, the surveyor reports the class items requested by the owner.

(e) Harmonization of surveys

Hitherto surveys were spread throughout the year indiscriminately and several visits on board were necessary by the surveyor. A number of classification societies have now developed 'harmonization of surveys' whereby the relevant surveys may be harmonized or sychronized with those required by the maritime authorities. Each survey must be carried out with a tolerance time band and there are three categories as detailed below:

(a) annual surveys with a time band of 3 months before and after the due date;
(b) 2 and 2½-year surveys to be undertaken within 6 months before and after due date;
(c) special periodical survey every 4 years with a permitted 1-year extension.

As we progress into the next millennium the implications of the *Estonia* accident, a vessel which sank with the loss of over 900 lives in the Baltic in September 1994, will be manifest through new legislation to reduce the risk of such accidents. The *Estonia* was similar in design to the *Herald of Free Enterprise* which capsized in the port of Zeebrugge in 1987 with the loss of nearly 200 lives, an accident which itself resulted in MARPOL 90 and under review in November 1995. Clearly a major risk area involves the large open car decks with no statutory bulkhead provisions and the risk of sea water entering the bow or stern doors in heavy seas and/or when malfunctioning due to technical or human error. This results in the destabilizing of such ferries which quickly list to starboard or port with no remedy.

3.5 RECENT TRENDS IN SHIP DESIGN

During the past decade the trend has been towards faster vessels of increased size with improved machinery and cargo-handling equipment, while standards of accommodation have been raised for both passengers and crew. However, as we progress through the 1990s more attention in ship design will be given to producing a versatile vessel with optimum capacity and speed – the latter having regard to increasing fuel cost. Additionally, it will reflect the need to reduce crew complement; further extension of high technology in shipboard equipment; increased capacity with cargo liner tonnage; improved maintenance/survey techniques (see Fig. 3.1); development of more computerized techniques in all areas; improved port turn-round time to compensate for slower transits involving combined transport development, and improved marine technology.

Cargo liners have increased in speed from about 15 to 22 knots in the past twenty years mainly because of market forces and the desire to reduce the number of vessels in a fleet by introducing faster ships, particularly container vessels often with rationalized ports of call and dramatically improved, high technology, computerized transhipment arrangements. Similarly tramp owners, conscious of the need to obtain fixtures on liner services where owners seek short-term additional tonnage, have increased both ship size and speed. Long term, due to much higher fuel cost, less enthusiasm will be directed towards high speed ships and more towards economic design and the full integration of shipboard

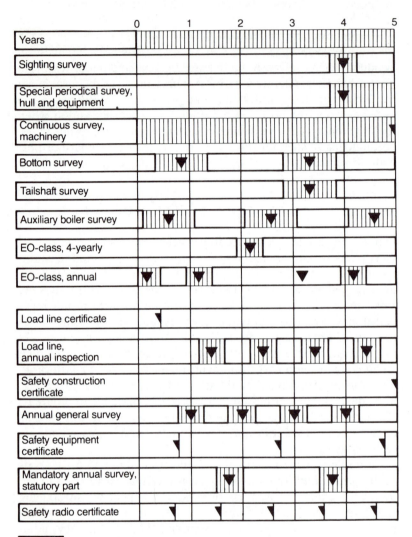

Fig. 3.1 Non-harmonized ship survey programme. (Reproduced by kind permission of Det Norske Veritas.)

efficiency with seaport infrastructure and the overland distribution networks on which it relies.

Extensive use is now made of computers to facilitate the optimum specification in a given set of circumstances having regard to ship type, speed, capacity, draught, beam, length, etc. Ship classification societies frequently feature in such exercises.

The number of specialized vessels has also increased, and this tendency is likely to continue. Moreover, it must be recognized that specialized purpose-built modern cargo tonnage offers the cheapest method of international trade distribution which in itself is one of the paramount reasons for the rapid development of trade since the 1980s.

Nowadays, cargo liners and tramps have their machinery and crew accommodation aft, thereby ensuring that the maximum use is made of the amidships section for cargo. In the case of cargo liners, improved techniques of cargo handling have been introduced, with the object of reducing turn-round time in port to a minimum. These include palletization, conveyor belts and other methods now themselves being superseded by container ships and equipment in many ports. Many of these new cargo-handling techniques have been associated with the introduction of specialized vessels. A good example is the Combi carrier (see Fig. 4.3).

Passenger vessels may be the ferry or the cruise ship (see Fig. 4.6). The tendency during the past two decades has been towards larger vessels, improved standards of passenger accommodation, and a reduction in the number of passenger classes. This has resulted in two-class vessels incorporating first and tourist and, for the cruise tonnage, the development of the hotel concept and a single class as found on the SS *Oriana* (see Fig. 4.6).

Passenger tonnage has increased considerably during the past decade, especially in the ferry division as, for example, in the short sea trades, particularly UK/continental and Baltic trades. The vessels are designed to be as versatile and functional as possible to the market operational requirement and are called multi-purpose ships with vehicular capacity – cars, lorries, trailers, containers and caravans. Many have a passenger certificate of 2000, with about 200 to 300 berths depending on the route. Some have less than 50 cabins on the shorter voyages. The ships are designed for economic operation with both bow and stern ramp loading to facilitate quick turn-round, and a mezzanine deck so that the car/lorry combination capacity can be varied to meet seasonal traffic variations. Such tonnage may have a capacity for 400 cars or 80 lorries/trailers. More recently vessels with two decks of capacity up to 120 lorries/trailers have been introduced. This permits simultaneous loading discharging at either deck, thereby speeding up turn-round time in port. In 1996, the super ferry will be introduced by Stena Sealink. It is five times bigger than existing ferries and operates in cross-channel trades under high-speed schedules. Overall, the new ferry generation has a capacity of 1500 passengers, 375 cars and a speed over 50 knots. The vessel has twin hulls.

As we progress through the 1990s the application of ergonomics to ship design will become paramount particularly in the interest of reducing crew complement. A good example is bridge design and the increasing emphasis on unmanned machinery spaces. This involves the concept of the ship control centre which embraces navigation, ship control and engine and cargo control functions. A further example of the influence of ergonomics involves ship systems concerned with how people get aboard and leave ships and how they move around the ship once aboard. This involves stairways; lifts and hoists; machinery spaces; ladders – fixed and portable; mast and radar platforms; lifeboats; holds and tanks; emergency escapes; watertight doors; stores and workshops; and sick bay and hospital rooms.

During the past few years the global cruise market has significantly increased annually and is now growing at 10% per year. In 1994 the global market totalled four million passengers. Overall it is a very competitive market with a reputation for quality and value for money. Moreover, the cruise tonnage is becoming more sophisticated. Much of it operates on a fly cruise concept with the passenger taking a flight to join the cruise ship. Popular cruise markets are the Mediterranean and Caribbean.

A market leader in the cruise environment is P&O cruises which have been in the business since 1837. P&O cruises currently have 14 cruise liners of which the largest are SS *Canberra*, SS *Sea Princess* and SS *Oriana*. A further two vessels will be delivered in 1997: the SS *Grand Princess*, 100 000 GRT, 2600 passengers, 21 knots; and SS *Dawn Princess*, 77 000 GRT, 1950 passengers, 21 knots. The SS *Grand Princess* will be the world's largest cruise ship and will bring a new level of cruise passenger facilities to the market.

A profile of the most recent delivery, SS *Oriana*, is found in Fig. 4.6 on p. 62. It has the following features: gross tonnage 67 000; service speed 24 knots; overall length 260 metres; breadth 32.2 metres; crew 760; maximum passenger capacity 1975; passenger decks 10, and passenger cabins 914 (594 outside – 118 with balconies, 8 suites, 16 deluxe staterooms, 320 inside cabins, 8 designed for disabled passengers). The SS *Oriana* is the fastest cruise vessel afloat and the first British purpose-built cruise liner. Her technically advanced hull will enable the ship to operate the best and most far-reaching itineraries worldwide and unlike most cruise liners has been specifically designed and equipped to operate round-the-world cruises. Overall the vessel has 14 decks, of which ten are passenger, and was ordered from Meyer Werft Germany in January 1992, undertaking her maiden voyage in April 1995. Passenger facilities include: a 4-deck atrium; 10 passenger lifts; 6 lounges; 9 bars; 2 restaurants; 1 deck restaurant; 3 dance floors; cinema; theatre; nightclub; disco; casino; writing room; library; card room; shops; children and teenagers' rooms; night nursery; 3 swimming pools (including the largest swimming pool on any cruise ship); hair and beauty salon; health spa; gym and sauna; and medical centre.

In sharp contrast Club Méditerranée have recently entered the cruise market with two vessels which occupy a niche market in the competitive cruise business. Club Méditerranée is a high-profile French company offering quality holiday packages throughout their global network of 82 villages extending to over 30 countries. Their two cruise vessels are basically motorized sailing ships operating in the Mediterranean, the Ionian Sea, the Sea of China and the Pacific waters. All cabins are of identical specification. The vessels are 187 m long with a beam of 20 m and eight decks. The ships have five masts with seven sails which can be raised or lowered by computer. Wind surfing, water skiing, sailing, snorkelling and scuba diving are available at the stern of the vessels. The ships have two swimming pools and a golf simulator. Extensive on-board entertainment facilities are also available. The vessels have a small draft to enable easy access to and from ports. Prices are based on cost and market pricing and marks a new venture in the cruise market. Prices are all-inclusive of most shipboard facilities.

Each vessel has some 400 berths and are among the largest sailing cruise vessels afloat. In short, the vessels are unique and offer a high-quality service with excellent cuisine.

Passenger cruise tariffs operate in a very competitive environment and individual cruise operators formulate their own specific pricing strategy which in the main reflects market conditions and cost. The more common basis is to identify the voyage cost of the cruise schedule and break down the cost per passenger relative to a specific load factor, which may be 80% of the berths. A profit margin is added to the voyage cost.

3.6 GENERAL STRUCTURE OF CARGO VESSELS

Cargo vessels can be classified according to their hull design and construction.

Single-deck vessels have one deck, on top of which are often superimposed three 'islands': forecastle, bridge and poop. Such vessels are commonly referred to as the 'three-island type'.

This type of vessel is very suitable for the carriage of heavy cargoes in bulk, as easy access to the holds (with only one hatch to pass through) means that they are cheap to load and discharge.

The most suitable cargoes for single-deck vessels are heavy cargoes carried in bulk, such as coal, grain and iron ore. However, these vessels also customarily carry such light cargoes as timber and esparto grass, which are stowed on deck as well as below, the large clear holds making for easy stowage and the three islands affording protection for the deck cargo. This type of vessel is not suitable for general cargo, as there are no means of adequately separating the cargo.

There are a number of variations in the single-deck type of vessel. Some vessels, for example, may be provided with a short bridge while others have a longer bridge.

The 'tween-deck type of vessel has other decks below the main deck, and all run the full length of the vessel. These additional decks below the main deck are known as the 'tween decks; some vessels in the liner trades often have more than one 'tween deck, and they are then known as the upper and lower 'tween decks.

A vessel with 'tween decks is very suitable for general cargo, as not only is the cargo space divided into separate tiers, but also the 'tween deck prevents too much weight from bearing on the cargo at the bottom of the hold.

An example of a modern products carrier is found in Fig. 3.2. It has an overall length of 182.5 m and a draught of 11.0 m. The service speed is 14 knots. The vessel has a twin-skin double bottom hull structure to give clean, smooth cargo tanks permitting easy and rapid cleaning from one cargo to another with reduced heating and coating maintenance costs; individual tank-mounted cargo pumps which strip the tanks efficiently without the problems of long suction lines thereby obviating the need to have a shipboard pump room; deck-mounted heat exchangers for efficient control of cargo temperature; and versatility of cargoes embracing all of the common oil products and a range of easy chemicals including gasoline, aviation gasoline, jet fuel, naphtha, diesel fuel, fuel oil, caustic soda, ethanol, B-T-X, vegetable oil and molasses. It has a total deadweight tonnage of 47 300 and a cargo capacity of 50 000 m^3 which for example would be sufficient for a 30 000 tonne cargo of naphtha. The vessel has 9 tanks and crew accommodation for 25 persons.

The vessel is suitable for worldwide trading in the bulk product markets. It is called the Tango products carrier. An example of a modern container vessel is found in Fig. 3.3. It has an overall length of 162 m and draught of 9.75 m. It has a total deadweight tonnage of 21 800 and a container capacity of 1739 TEUs. The service speed is 18 knots. It has eight hatches. All are unobstructed to provide full width 40-ft length openings and are closed by lift on/lift off pontoon-type hatch covers. All the holds are designed for 40-ft containers; 20-ft boxes can be stowed using a combination of cell guides, side bars and stacking cones without the use of portable guides or dedicated holds. Three electro-hydraulically operated slimline deck cranes are provided, each of 36 tonnes capacity.

The vessel is suitable for worldwide trading in containerized markets. It is called a Compact containership and is built by British Shipbuilders Ltd in a size range from 600 to 2100 TEUs. Sometimes such tonnage is described as cellular cargo vessels when the holds have been designed to form a series of cells into which the containers are placed.

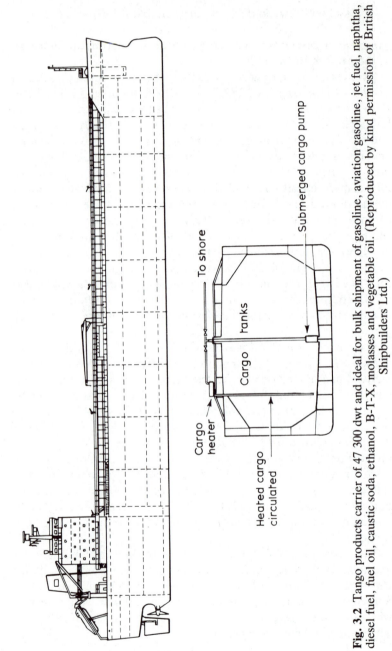

Fig. 3.2 Tango products carrier of 47 300 dwt and ideal for bulk shipment of gasoline, aviation gasoline, jet fuel, naphtha, diesel fuel, fuel oil, caustic soda, ethanol, B-T-X, molasses and vegetable oil. (Reproduced by kind permission of British Shipbuilders Ltd.)

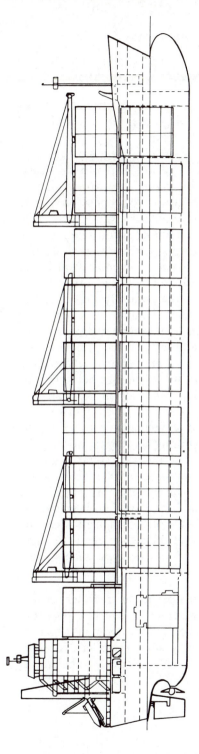
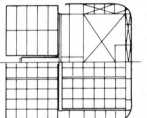

Fig. 3.3 Compact container ship of 21 800 dwt and capacity of 1739 TEUs. The crucial feature is its flexibility and fuel economy as it can hold both 20 ft and 40 ft containers, plus the maximum earning capacity with higher container numbers for the hull envelope. It is ideal for worldwide container trading. (Reproduced by kind permission of British Shipbuilders Ltd.)

3.7 ECONOMICS OF NEW AND SECOND-HAND TONNAGE

The most decisive factors influencing the shipowner's choice between new and second-hand tonnage are the availability of capital and its cost (see also pp. 483, 486).

The economics of new and second-hand tonnage now form an important part of ship management. Moreover, with ship costs continuing to rise, the economics of buying a relatively modern ship of up to 5 years in age proves an attractive proposition despite the conversion cost, especially for countries experiencing hard currency problems. For example, a number of oil tankers have been converted to dry cargo bulk carriers. The cost is modest when related to new tonnage, and particularly when shipyards are hungry for work with a depressed new tonnage order book. Furthermore, it permits the vessel to be quickly introduced to meet the market trade demand. The latter point is very significant in cash flow terms as the vessel starts to earn money sooner than a new one involving up to a 3-year time-scale. If the shipowner has sufficient capital available, he will in all probability prefer new to second-hand tonnage – its most distinct advantage being that he can have a vessel built to his own specification in the matter of type, design and speed.

Among the disadvantages inherent in buying new tonnage is the adequate depreciation of the vessel during her normal working life to provide funds for replacement. At present, in some countries, depreciation is based on initial and not on replacement cost, which because of inflation is likely to be considerably higher. Further disadvantages include the risk of building delays; uncertain costs at time of delivery if the vessel is not being built on a fixed price; and lastly a possible recession in the market when she is ready to trade. Further advantages/disadvantages of buying new tonnage are given below:

(a) The vessel is usually built for a particular trade/service and therefore should prove ideal for the route in every respect, i.e. speed, economical crewing, ship specification, optimum capacity, modern marine engineering technology, ship design, etc. In short, it should be able to offer the optimum service at the lowest economical price.

(b) It usually raises service quality and such an image should generate additional traffic.

(c) It facilitates optimum ship operation particularly if there is a fleet of sister ships aiding minimum stocking of ship spares/ replacement equipment to be provided.

(d) Service reliability should be high.

(e) Maintenance and survey costs should be somewhat lower than older second-hand tonnage, particularly in the early years.

(f) New tonnage presents the opportunity to modernize terminal arrangements, particularly cargo transhipment, cargo collection and distribution arrangements, etc. Overall it should improve the speed of cargo transhipment arrangements and reduce ship port turn-round time to a minimum. This all helps to make the fleet more productive.

(g) A significant disadvantage is the timescale of the new tonnage project which can extend up to 3 years from the time the proposal is first originated in the shipping company to when the vessel is accepted by the shipowner from the shipyard following successful completion of trials. During this period the character and level of traffic forecast could have dramatically adversely changed. In such circumstances it may prove difficult to find suitable employment for the vessel elsewhere.

(h) Annual ship depreciation is substantially higher than the vessel displaced whilst crew complement would be much lower.

With second-hand tonnage, the shipowner has the advantage of obtaining the vessel at a fixed price, which would be considerably lower per deadweight ton in comparison with a new vessel. Furthermore, the vessel is available for service immediately the sale is concluded. Conversely, the shipowner will have to face higher maintenance costs, lower reliability, generally higher operating costs and a quicker obsolescence. It can create a bad image for the service. He is also unlikely to benefit from any building subsidies or cheap loans – available for the new tonnage in certain countries – despite the fact that the shipowner may be involved in a conversion of the second-hand tonnage.

Other significant advantages and disadvantages of second-hand tonnage are detailed below:

(a) On completion of the purchase the vessel is basically available for service commencement. However, usually the new owner will wish to have the ship painted to his own house flag colours and undertake any alterations to facilitate the economic deployment of the vessel. For example, a new section could be inserted in the vessel to lengthen her and increase cargo accommodation. The extent of such alterations will depend on the trade, age and condition of the vessel and capital availability. The paramount consideration will be the economics of the alterations and capital return of the investment.

(b) Second-hand tonnage is ideal to start a new service, enabling the operator to test the market in a low-risk capital situation. In the event of the service proving successful, new tonnage can be introduced subsequently. Likewise, to meet a short-term traffic increase extending over 18/24 months, it may prove more economic to buy second-hand tonnage rather than charter. The advantage of a charter is that the vessel is ultimately returned to the owner to find employment although with some charters one can have an option to purchase on completion of the charter term.

(c) Second-hand tonnage tends to be costly to operate in crewing and does not usually have the ideal ship specification, i.e. slow speed, limited cargo capacity, poor cargo transhipment facilities. Such shortcomings can be overcome by ship modification, but it is unlikely to produce the optimum vessel for the service. Ship insurance premium is likely to be high with older vessels, particularly over 15 years.

(d) The vessel is likely to have a relatively short life and maintenance/survey/operating costs are likely to be high. If the ship registration is to be transferred from one national flag to another, this can prove costly as standards differ. Moreover, it is not always possible to assess accurately the cost involved until conversion work is in progress. Conversely depreciation is likely to be low.

(e) Service quality could be rather indifferent whilst reliabilty/ schedule punctuality could be at risk. For example, the engines may be prone to breakdown and additional crew personnel may be required to keep them maintained to a high reliable standard.

An example of a lengthened third-generation Ro/Ro container ship is provided in Fig. 3.4. It has a draught of 7.75 m, a speed of 20.4 knots and 51 477 dwt.

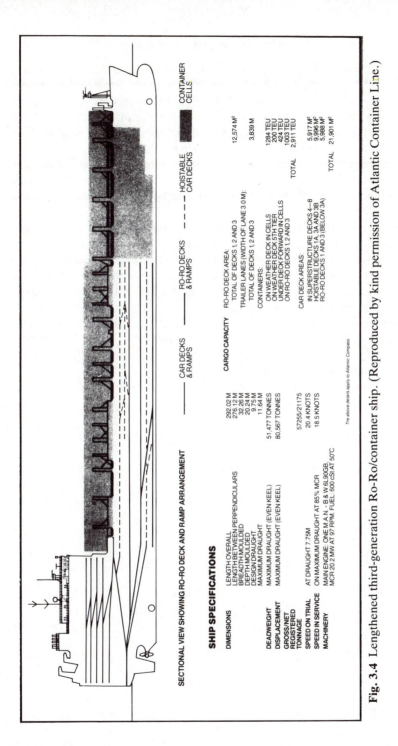

SECTIONAL VIEW SHOWING RO-RO DECK AND RAMP ARRANGEMENT

——— CAR DECKS & RAMPS
——— RO-RO DECKS & RAMPS
- - - HOISTABLE CAR DECKS
▮ CONTAINER CELLS

SHIP SPECIFICATIONS

DIMENSIONS	LENGTH OVERALL	292.02 M
	LENGTH BETWEEN PERPENDICULARS	276.12 M
	BREADTH MOULDED	32.26 M
	DEPTH MOULDED	20.24 M
	DESIGN DRAUGHT	9.75 M
	MAXIMUM DRAUGHT	11.64 M
DEADWEIGHT	MAXIMUM DRAUGHT (EVEN KEEL)	51,477 TONNES
DISPLACEMENT	MAXIMUM DRAUGHT (EVEN KEEL)	80,567 TONNES
GROSS/NET REGISTERED TONNAGE		57255/21175
SPEED ON TRIAL	AT DRAUGHT 7.75M	20.4 KNOTS
SPEED IN SERVICE	ON MAXIMUM DRAUGHT AT 85% MCR	18.5 KNOTS
MACHINERY	MAIN ENGINE: ONE M.A.N. - B & W 6L90GB, MCR 20.2 MW AT 97 RPM. FUEL: 600 cSt AT 50°C	

CARGO CAPACITY

RO-RO DECK AREA:
TOTAL OF DECKS 1, 2 AND 3
TRAILER LANES (WIDTH OF LANE 3.0 M):
TOTAL OF DECKS 1, 2 AND 3 — 12,574 M²
— 3,839 M

CONTAINERS:
ON WEATHER DECK IN CELLS — 1284 TEU
ON WEATHER DECK 5TH TIER — 200 TEU
UNDER DECK FORWARD IN CELLS — 424 TEU
ON RO-RO DECKS 1, 2 AND 3 — 1003 TEU
TOTAL — 2,911 TEU

CAR DECK AREAS:
IN SUPERSTRUCTURE DECKS 4–8 — 5,917 M²
HOISTABLE DECKS 1A, 3A AND 3B — 9,996 M²
RO-RO DECKS 1 AND 3 (BELOW 3A) — 5,988 M²
TOTAL — 21,901 M²

The above details apply to Atlantic Compass

Fig. 3.4 Lengthened third-generation Ro-Ro/container ship. (Reproduced by kind permission of Atlantic Container Line.)

Often when a vessel is uneconomical to operate in one trade, it can be converted for other uses. This may involve lengthening the ship by inserting a portion amidships. In the past decade many oil tankers, too small and slow for the petroleum trade, have been lengthened and converted to ore carriers and other trades. This trend, also involving other cargo tonnage, will continue as the economics of higher capacity ships becomes increasingly attractive. More recently some ore carriers have been fitted with demountable skeleton decks and ramp facilities to convey trade cars.

Finally the ship operator, when conducting the feasibility study of whether to opt for new or second-hand tonnage, must also consider chartered or leased tonnage. Advantages include no long-term commitment or disposal problems but merely its economical operation for the duration of the charter; almost immediate access to the ship to commence operation; the prospect of a wider range of vessels available for fixture; and finally the prospect of a more economical modern-type vessel being available. Many shipowners tend to introduce new services or supplement existing services through chartered tonnage.

Study also Chapter 3 of *Economics of Shipping Practice and Management*.

CHAPTER 4

Ships and their cargoes

4.1 TYPES OF SHIPS

The type of merchant vessel employed on a trade route is determined basically by the traffic carried. Broadly speaking there are three main divisions: liners, tramps and specialized vessels such as tankers.

On occasions, and in particular when merchant vessels in one division are underemployed, a number may be transferred to another division. For example, a tramp may be put on a liner berth to compete for liner cargoes. Conversely, liners may at times carry tramp cargoes, either as full or part cargoes.

During the past decade there has been a trend towards the development of the multi-purpose vessel and the combined transport system. The need for the multi-purpose vessel has arisen to combat trade fluctuations and enable the vessel to become more flexible in her operation. Not only can the vessel vary the cargo mixture capacity on a particular voyage, but also she can switch from one trade to another. Such tonnage, although more expensive to build, should enable the volume of laid-up tonnage to fall. Examples of multi-purpose tonnage are found particularly in the vehicular ferry and container vessel plus an increasing number of combination bulk cargo vessels including the tramp vessels.

During the next few years the global network of containerized services will expand further stimulated by the GATT Uruguay agreement of 1994. Multi-modalism will be an especial feature of this expansion (see Chapter 18). Furthermore, the spot charter in an emergency will be the cellular vessel to maintain a similar profile shipping service. Hence the general cargo tramp ship will not feature in the liner cargo network as it does not fit into such sophisticated logistics.

A vessel type which has emerged in the era of offshore oil development has been the offshore supply ship, an illustration of which may be found in Fig. 4.7 on p. 64.

A description of each division follows.

4.2 LINERS

These are vessels that ply on a regular scheduled service between groups of ports. The student should note that it is this function, and not the size or speed, which defines the liner. Liner services offer cargo space to all shippers who require them. They sail on scheduled dates, irrespective of whether they are full or not. Hence, in liner operation the regular scheduled service is the basis of this particular division, and it is vitally important to the shipowner that everything is done to have punctual sailing and arrival dates, otherwise his prestige will quickly decline. Liner operation involves an adequately sized fleet, and a fairly large shore establishment. Today the modern liner cargo service is multi-modal and very sophisticated in terms of its logistics and computerized operations. Such companies are continuously striving to improve efficiency and overall transit times thereby stimulating trade development and improvement in market share. The liner company therefore tends to be a large concern and in more recent years operating container tonnage on a consortia basis. However, there still remains a very small volume of 'tween-deck break-bulk cargo vessels in service, particularly in the subcontinent, Orient area, the developing countries and Eastern bloc markets.

The cargo liner operation today falls into several distinct divisions but is characterized by a regular service all year round on a fixed route to a group of ports situated in different countries and conveying general cargo in a container or trailer/truck or as break bulk (loose cargo). The vessel sails whether she is full or not. The development of combined transport also involves inland distribution by road/rail through the use of a combined transport bill of lading involving a through-rate door-to-door from warehouse to warehouse. Each type is designed to achieve fast turn-round times and a high level of ship management efficiency. Vessels are completely integrated into the seaport operation which involves purpose-built berths and extensive port and inland infrastructure (see Chapter 17), and include container tonnage, Ro/Ro passenger (road haulage unit/motorist/passenger), Ro/Ro container, Ro/Ro other cargo, general cargo/passenger, general cargo single-deck, general cargo multi-deck, and general cargo/container. The container and Ro/Ro tonnage make up the prime growth sectors as countries worldwide develop their seaports and infrastructure to accept this very efficient and reliable unitized method of global distribution. With the container tonnage much of it is integrated with the seaport overland rail distribution network. More and more liner cargo in all categories of tonnage are being customs cleared inland and away from the former traditional seaport area, and an increasing amount of the port infrastructure operation is computerized (see also pp. 464, 471).

4.3 TRAMPS

The tramp, or general trader as she is often called, does not operate on a fixed sailing schedule, but merely trades in all parts of the world in search of cargo, primarily bulk cargo. Such cargoes include coal, grain, timber, sugar, ores, fertilizers, copra etc., which are carried in complete shiploads. Many of the cargoes are seasonal. The tramp companies are much smaller than their liner cargo counterparts, and their business demands an intimate knowledge of market conditions.

Tramps are an unspecialized type of vessel with two to six holds, each with large unobstructed hatches, and are primarily designed for the conveyance of bulk cargoes. Some ships are built with special facilities particularly suitable to the five main tramp trades: grain, coal, bauxite, phosphates and iron ore.

A typical modern tramp vessel is the SD-14. She has a crew of 30, a speed of 15 knots and has 'tween deck accommodation. The ship is of 9100 GRT, with a NRT of 6100 and a loaded mean draught of 8.84 m. The vessel's length is 140 m and she has a beam of 21 m. Five holds are provided with the accommodation amidship aft. Each hold is served by derricks and total grain cubic capacity exceeds 764 000 ft^3. The total cargo deadweight tonnage is approximately 14 000. This vessel is very versatile both operationally, and to the acceptance of the traditional tramp bulk cargoes, i.e. grain, timber, ore, coal etc.

Another example of a tramp vessel and of Japanese build is the Freedom-type tonnage. This vessel combines the essential features of a single deck bulk cargo carrier with those of a closed shelter deck ship. It is able to operate efficiently in dry cargo trades such as grain, coal, potash, phosphate rock, bauxite and iron ore cargoes, as well as general cargoes, palletized and container cargoes. The vessel has four holds with accommodation aft and crew of 30. She has a speed of 14 knots, an overall length of 145 m, a beam of 21 m and loaded mean draught of 9 m. This ship has a grain cubic capacity of 705 000 ft^3 and a cargo deadweight tonnage of 15 000. Both the SD-14s and 'Freedom'-type vessels are multi-purpose dry cargo carriers.

An example of a modern flexible container/bulk carrier ship is found in Fig. 4.1. It has eight holds and a deadweight tonnage of 45 500 with a draught of 12.2 m. The service speed is 14 knots and the ship's overall length is 194.30 m. The cargo hold grain capacity is 58 700 m^3. Container capacity totals 2127 TEUs of which 1069 TEUs are above deck. It has one single 25 tonnes and two twin 25 tonnes electro-hydraulic deck cranes all of which are fitted with grabs. The crew accommodation complement is 25 of which 9 are officers.

The vessel is suitable for worldwide trading in the bulk carriage of grain, coal, ore, bauxite, phosphates, packaged timber, standard pipe lengths and containers. The vessel is called the Combi King 45 – flexible container/bulk carrier.

Tramp vessels are engaged under a document called a charter party, on a time or voyage basis.

The number of tramp vessels has fallen during the past decade and similarly the number of tramp companies, as such companies, often family-owned, have tended to merge. Nevertheless the total volume of tramp tonnage remains fairly stable as larger capacity vessels are introduced. The trend to have long-term time charters of 5 to 10 years' duration is becoming more popular. The tonnage involved is usually modern, purpose-built, of high capacity such as 100 000 dwt and involves a bulk cargo such as oil, ore, etc. An example of a modern multi-purpose general cargo ship is found in Fig. 4.5 on p. 60.

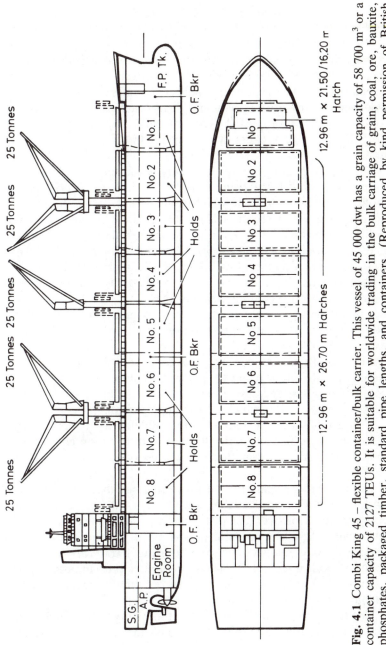

Fig. 4.1 Combi King 45 – flexible container/bulk carrier. This vessel of 45 000 dwt has a grain capacity of 58 700 m³ or a container capacity of 2127 TEUs. It is suitable for worldwide trading in the bulk carriage of grain, coal, ore, bauxite, phosphates, packaged timber, standard pipe lengths, and containers. (Reproduced by kind permission of British Shipbuilders Ltd.)

4.4 SPECIALIZED VESSELS

A number of cargo ships are designed for carrying a particular commodity, or group of commodities. Such specialization is the result of demand, but its provision may also create a new demand depending on the extent of the market. Examples of such specialized vessels are ore carriers and sugar carriers. A description follows of the more usual types of ship, and in view of the preponderance of tankers in this group, these will be examined first.

During the period 1970 to 1978 there was a substantial increase in the world *tanker fleet* rising from 150 million dwt in 1970 to 352 million dwt in 1980 from which time it has started to rapidly decline. The latter trend is likely to continue through a world policy of conservation of energy resources, inflation of oil prices and substantial over-tonnaging of the world tanker fleet. By 1993 it was 301 million dwt or 43% of the world merchant fleet deadweight tonnage. This figure is likely to fall as the world dry cargo fleet grows through containerization (see Table 1.1). Nevertheless, the world tanker fleet will continue to remain very formidable. Some of the world's largest vessels are tankers, a number of which exceed 400 000 dwt.

The world's tanker fleet is divided between tramp operators, which operate under a charter party, and those owned by the oil companies, a fast decreasing number. Most independently owned tankers are on long-term charter to the oil companies.

Crude oil is transported from the oilfields to refineries, and petroleum and fuel oil from refineries to distribution centres and bunkering ports, so that there is worldwide network of tanker routes.

In more recent years the oil producing countries have tended both to own and operate their own tanker fleet thereby having complete control over the distribution arrangements and costs. Moreover, they are shipping it as refined oil and not as they previously did, allowing major importing industrial nations to refine it and re-export it. Their income is thus improved. An example of a high-profile corporation providing chartered tanker tonnage is fully described on p. 309.

The tanker is provided with two or three longitudinal bulkheads and many transverse bulkheads dividing the hull into numerous

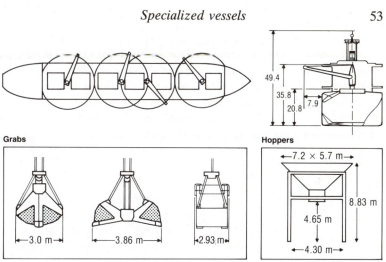

Grabs — Hoppers
Each crane is equipped with a 10 m³ grab of the 4-rope electrical type

Fig. 4.2 Panmax bulk carrier *Maersk Tapah*. Built 1989, 66 000 dwt, length overall 226 m, beam 13.20 m. Seven holds, total grain capacity 2.770 million cu ft. Speed 12 knots laden, 14.5 knots in ballast.

tanks. Each tank has a watertight hatch and ventilator, and is connected by pipeline to pumping rooms. Machinery and crew accommodation are aft together with the navigating bridge. Extensive shore equipment is provided involving pumping apparatus. The tanker would have a double-hull structure – a recent international provision through legislation to improve tanker safety operation and lessen the impact on the environment of any spillage arising from an accident.

(a) Bulk carrier
An example of a bulk carrier is shown in Fig. 4.2, the Panmax carrier MT *Maersk Tapah*. The vessel was built in 1989 and has a speed of 12 knots laden and 14.5 knots when in ballast. Her dwt is 66 000 with a grain cubic foot capacity of 2.770 million spanning seven holds. The ship's overall length is 226 m with a beam of 13.2 m and draft of 13.2 m. Four cranes serve the seven holds as shown in the figure. The vessel is equipped with cranes/grabs and hoppers for self-loading of fuel and discharging operations. In addition Maersk line has 70 000 dwt bulk carriers in their fleet and also convey coal, ore and grain. The vessels are similarly equipped with

their own discharging equipment and are capable of handling up to
25 000 tons per day. Purpose-built terminals are required for this
tonnage and many schedules are on a round voyage continuous
basis with one leg in ballast and one leg fully loaded. Such tonnage
can also discharge/load overside in the port environs into barges
moored alongside the carrier, with transhipment taking place
simultaneously on the port and starboard sides to speed up the
process.

(b) Coasters

These are all-purpose cargo carriers, operating around our coasts.
They are normally provided with two holds, each supplied with
derricks to handle a variety of cargoes. Machinery and crew
accommodation are aft. Coasters are subject to severe competition
from inland transport.

(c) Combi carrier

To cater for the need to improve ship turn-round time, to increase
the versatility of vessel employment and to contain operating cost,
an increasing number of vessels are now being introduced called
Combi carriers as illustrated in Fig. 4.3. Such vessels are a unitized
type of cargo carrier combining container and vehicular shipments
including Ro/Ro.

The Combi vessel in Fig. 4.3 is operated by the DFDS Norland
Line in the US Gulf – US East Coast – Mediterranean/Central
American trade and is called an Omni carrier. The ship has an
overall length of 135 m and beam of 25 m with an NRT of 1714 and
GRT of 4496. Her draught is 6.68 m and dwt (metric) 8000. The
vessel has a container capacity of 516 TEUs with 264 TEUs on
the upper deck, 216 TEUs on the main deck and 36 TEUs on the
lower deck. The ship has a lane capacity of 563 m on the upper
deck, 603 m on the main deck, and 250 m on the lower hold. The
car deck area totals 212 m^2 on the main deck and 293 m^2 in the
lower hold. The cargo conveyed will vary by individual sailing and
be a mixture of containers and vehicle traffic as illustrated in the
figure. This aids flexibility of ship operation and ensures the best
use is made of the available vessel capacity having regard to
market demand.

The vessel is equipped with two derricks of 36 tons and 120 tons
thereby aiding the transhipment of heavy indivisible loads which

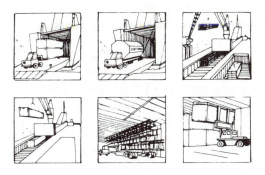

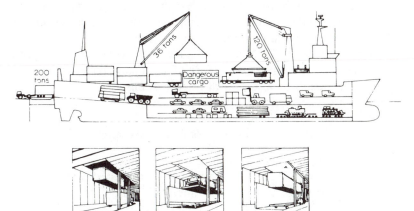

Fig. 4.3 Omni carrier – roll-on/roll-off, lift-on/lift-off and side-loading Combi carrier.

are much on the increase. By using a medium/heavy duty mobile crane on the quay it is possible to load and discharge at the same time with the vessel using its own gear for loading/discharging through the lift hatch. Loading of containers or other cargo is through the aft hatch. A high capacity fork lift is available for stowing on the main deck. The vessel has a crew of 30.

The stern ramp is 14 m long and has a flap of 4.2 m. The width of the ramp is 8.5 m at the shore-based end. It can be used for fast loading/discharging of containers on trailers or by heavy fork lifts operating with 20-ft containers athwartships.

The spacious main deck may be used for awkward shaped goods, e.g. building cranes, offshore and refinery equipment, prefab building components etc. The clear height of 6.3 m on the main deck allows double stacking of containers each up to 9 ft 6 in high.

Special suspension hooks underneath the lift provide an additional lifting facility of 60 tons for the transfer of units onto trailers. Containers are placed on trailers for transfer by lift to the lower hold. The lift hatch when required serves as a third point of access for loading/discharging cargo by use of the shore crane.

A side door of 7.5 × 4.0 m width is provided which allows simultaneous operation by two fork lifts handling palletized cargo. The wide side door also allows truck loading or the discharge of large items. Containers of 20 ft length can also be handled through the side door.

Advantages of the Combi carrier can be summarized as follows:

(a) It has a versatile cargo mixture permitting a variation of unitized cargo to be conveyed plus awkward shaped cargo. This is a major advantage in the cargo liner field where more consignments are indivisible loads.

(b) The range of cargo transhipment facilities on the vessel, i.e. derricks, stern ramp, side doors etc., aid quick transhipment and is virtually independent of quay transhipment facilities. This improves the ship's versatility particularly in ports where cargo transhipment facilities are virtually non-existent. It also reduces the cost of using port equipment.

(c) Good shipboard cargo transhipment facilites quicken the ship turn-round time and improve ship utilization/efficiency.

(d) The vessel specification, i.e. draught, beam, length, is an optimum ideal for a wide range of ports and thereby generates versatility of ship employment and operation worldwide.

(e) The vessel is able to convey a wide variety of cargo at economical cost including particularly ease of handling.

(f) The ship's specification facilities reduce port congestion as the vessel is independent with her own handling equipment.

Furthermore, for example, the 200 ton capacity stern ramp requires only 30 m of quay space.

The foregoing explanation of the Combi carrier specification as illustrated in Fig. 4.3 demonstrates the versatility of the vessel and undoubtedly it will become more common as we progress through the 1990s, particularly in the liner cargo deep-sea trades involving less-developed nation's seaboards.

(d) Container vessels
These are becoming increasingly predominant in many cargo liner trades and such tonnage has been described in Chapter 4 together with Fig. 3.3. The merits of containerization are described in Chapter 16. There is no doubt that this type of tonnage which permits complete integration with other forms of transport, thereby offering a door-to-door service, will become more popular annually and by the year 2000 some 97% of the tonnage on liner cargo services will be containerized.

A modern container vessel today would have a capacity of 2000 containers of which 60% would be conveyed under deck and the residue on deck. A substantial proportion of the containers may be refrigerated for which under-deck hold accommodation facilities would be provided. The vessel would be of 33 300 tonnes and have an overall length of 250 m with a beam of 33 m. Her draught would be 12 m and service speed 22 knots.

More recently the multi-purpose type of container vessel has been developed with an integral ramp being provided as part of the ship's equipment. This permits both container and vehicular cargo to be conveyed and enables flexibility of berth/port operation as no portal is required. In 1995, there were 1617 container vessels.

(e) Fruit carriers
These are similar in design to refrigerated vessels. Cool air systems are installed in the holds to keep the fruit from over-ripening. Such vessels convey apples, oranges and bananas, and may be owned by the cargo owners. Fast voyage times are essential, otherwise the fruit over-ripens and deteriorates. In 1995, there were 1483 reefer vessels.

(f) Gas tanker
An example of a gas tanker is illustrated in Fig. 4.4, the LPG/C *Hans Maersk* which was built in 1993 of 23 257 dwt. The tanker's overall length is 159.98 m with a beam of 25.6 m and draft of 8.78/ 10.90 m depending on cargo type. The vessel has four bilobe tanks under deck with a pipeline system connected so that two different grades can be cooled simultaneously with two different uncooled grades. The tanks are constructed for loading and carrying cargoes with a temperature down to − 48°C. A cargo heater/vaporizer is provided. Cargo can be heated by means of a heat exchanger using sea water. The vessel is equipped with a fixed methanol washing system and methanol storage tank with a capacity of 40 m³. The tanker can carry anhydrous acids, ammonia, butane, propane, butadiene, propylene, isoprene, monomer propylene oxide, vinyl chloride monomer, methyl chloride and others. By 1995 there were 950 liquified gas carriers and the growth trend will continue.

(g) Multi-purpose general cargo ship
An example of a modern multi-purpose general cargo ship is shown in Fig. 4.5. It has four holds and a deadweight tonnage of 21 500 with a draught of 10.75 m. The vessel's overall length is 155.5 m and the service speed is 15.3 knots. The cargo hold grain capacity is 30 340 m³ and bale capacity 27 950 m³. The container capacity is 746 TEUs of which some 408 TEUs are above deck. The crew complement is 25 of which 9 are officers. The vessel has two single 25 tonnes and one twin 25 tonnes electro-hydraulic deck cranes.

The vessel is suitable for worldwide trading in general cargoes, dry bulk, long steel products, grain cargoes and containers. The vessel is called the Multi King 22 – multi-purpose general cargo ship.

(h) OBO
Ore/bulk/oil ships are multi-purpose bulk carriers designed for switching between bulk shipments of oil, bulk grain, fertilizer and ore trades. They were first introduced in the mid-1960s and many of them exceed 200 000 dwt. This type of vessel with engines aft is growing in popularity and will have a profound effect on tramping as it will probably bring a new and more profitable era to this

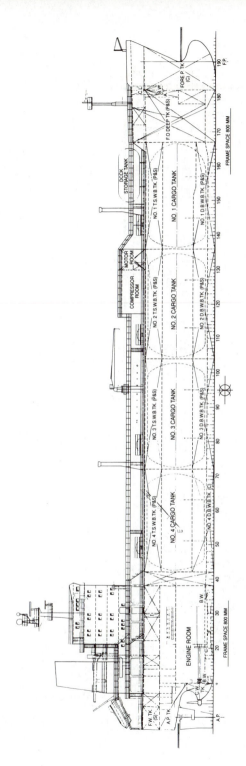

Fig. 4.4 LPG/C gas tanker *Hans Maersk*. Built 1993, 23 257 dwt, length 159.98 m, beam 25.6 m, draft 8.78/10.90 m depending on cargo type. Four bilobe tanks under deck connected by a pipeline system so that two different grades can be cooled simultaneously.

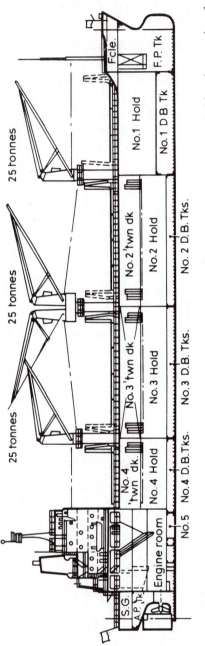

Fig. 4.5 Multi King 22 – multi-purpose general cargo vessel. The vessel is of 21 500 dwt with a cargo hold grain capacity of 30 340 m³, a bale capacity of 27 950 m³ or container capacity of 746 TEUs. The vessel is suitable for world-wide trading in general cargoes, dry bulk, long steel products, grain cargoes and containers.

important shipping division. A typical vessel would have an overall length of 280 m, draught of 17 m and 270 000 dwt. Her dry cargo capacity would be 170 000 m^3 whilst her oil capacity totals 224 000 m^3. Cargo space is provided in eleven holds to carry oil of which seven can ship dry cargo or ore as an alternative shipment. Crew accommodation and machinery – much automated – is situated aft. Such vessels although of high initial cost are very flexible in their use, keeping ballast voyages to a minimum and are of course ideal for modern-day requirements in international trade, which demand high capacity (optimum-sized) vessels to move world bulk shipments at a very low cost per ton. The development of the combination bulk carrier is likely to continue through the 1990s.

Ore carriers are provided with long wide hatches over the self-trimming large holds. By using longitudinal bulkheads, wing holds or tanks are provided which are used for water ballast when the vessel is returning light to the loading areas. The depth of the double-bottom tanks is greater than in other vessels, so as to raise the centre of gravity, because a low centre of gravity will give a 'stiff' effect in heavy seas. The machinery is situated aft, together with crew accommodation and navigation bridge. Cargo-handling gear is not provided, as loading and discharging is undertaken by mechanical shore-based gear. This may be in the form of conveyor belts (self-unloaders), magnetic loaders, or grabs. These vessels are particularly renowned for speedy loading and discharging, permitting a quick turn-round. Today some of the largest ships afloat are ore carriers and frequently exceed 100 000 dwt. Specialized terminals are required which are frequently away from the general port area or situated at a private terminal. Such vessels are often integrated with an industrial process programme demanding a reliable regular shipment schedule, without which industrial production is jeopardized; at modern terminals they can be loaded at the rate of 3500 tons per hour. In 1995 there were 239 OBOs.

(i) Parcel tankers

This type of ship is designed to carry shipments including chemicals, petroleum products, edible oils and molasses. Vessels of this type vary in size but have a capacity range between 30 000 and 80 000 dwt.

Fig. 4.6 SS *Oriana* passenger cruise liner. (Reproduced by kind permission of P&O.)

(j) Passenger vessels

These fall into two distinct divisions. There are those which operate in the short sea trade and have limited cabin accommodation. They also convey motorist and Ro/Ro (roll-on/roll-off) units. This type of vessel of up to 9000 GRT is described on p. 35.

The other division concerns the cruise market where vessels of up to 100 000 GRT are found. Such passenger liners are designed with each passenger allocated a cabin or berth. Adequate lounges, entertainment, restaurant, etc. facilities are provided. Italy has the largest passenger fleet. An example of a modern passenger cruise liner built in 1995 is the SS *Oriana*; she has a capacity of 1975 and is illustrated in Fig. 4.6 (see also pp. 36, 37).

(k) Platform supply vessels

The A.P. Møller Group including the Maersk Shipping Company is a market leader in the provision of platform supply vessels for the offshore oil and gas industry. Their fleet exceeds 40 vessels of different types. Platform supply vessels handle the transportation of all necessary equipment such as pipes, cement, tools and provisions to such destinations as the North Sea platforms and

drilling rigs. Other tonnage includes multi-purpose anchor handling tug supply vessels, and advanced multi-purpose offshore
support ships. The total support vessels tow drilling rigs, handle
anchors, work as fire-fighting vessels and are equipped to assist in
restraining oil pollution.

An example of an advanced multi-purpose offshore support
vessel is shown in Fig. 4.7 featuring the MS *Maersk Pacer*. It was
built in 1991 and has a speed of 16.6 knots. The overall length is
73.6 m, beam 16.4 m and draft 6.85 m. The vessel has extensive
versatile equipment including a continuous bollard pull of 180
tonnes, and towage and very extensive anchor-handling equipment including stoppers, shackles, chaser, grapnel, hydraulic
guide pins of triangular type, winch, triplex shark jaws and rig
chain lockers. The bridge equipment/manoeuvring facilities
include joystick control, autopilot, gyro compass, repeators,
radars, speed log, Decca and Satnav Shipmates, echo sounder,
rapid direction finder facsimile, Navtex and VHF direction finder.
Cabin accommodation is provided for six officers and six ratings
and there are twelve berths for passengers. A hospital is provided
equipped to British and Norwegian standby rules. The vessel is
also equipped for safety/standby duties for 200 survivors according
to Norwegian Rules.

The MS *Maersk Pacer* is low on consumption of heavy fuel and
is able to carry deck cargo. For towing/anchor handling, she has a
high-speed 4-drum winch and deep-water anchoring capability, as
well as an emergency helicopter landing area, oil recovery capacity, high bow and high freeboard, dry cargo hold, superior station
keeping, safe environment for crew, large aft deck, high deck
strength, high discharging rates, two powerful bow thrusters and
standby/rescue facilities.

(1) Product/chemical carrier
The MT *Rasmine Maersk* featured in Fig. 4.8 was built in 1986 and
is 27 350 dwt with a US barrel capacity of 195 000. Her gross
tonnage is 16 282 and length overall 170 m with a beam of 23.10 m
and draft of 11.41 m. Special features of the vessel include a
double hull, bow thruster, stern thruster, a hydraulic hose-
handling crane of 10 tonne capacity, an aft crane for stores/
provisions of 5 tonne capacity, an inert gas generator, nitrogen
topping-up, a closed loading system with vapour return, stern

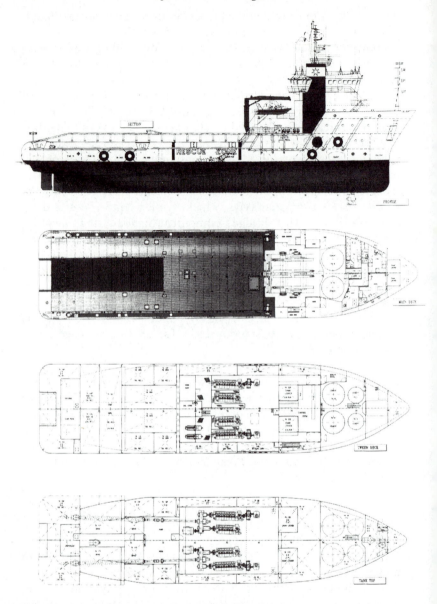

Fig. 4.7 Advanced multi-purpose offshore support vessel MS *Maersk Pacer*. Built 1991, 2651 dwt, overall length 73.6 m, beam 16.4 m, draft 6.55 m. Speed 16.6 knots.

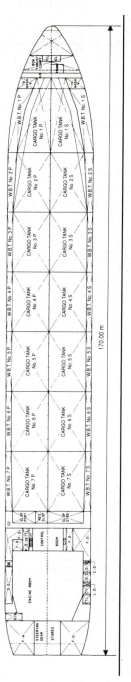

Fig. 4.8 Product/chemical carrier MT *Rasmine Maersk*. Built 1986, overall length, 170 m, beam 23.10 m, draft 11.41 m. Fourteen tanks.

discharge, crude oil washing and protective location ballast tanks. The carrier has seven twin cargo tanks situated on port and starboard side and one twin slop tank. The vessel is equipped to convey all petroleum products, crude oil, vegetable oils, molasses, etc. as well as selected IMO class 2 and 3 cargoes. Overall up to eight grades are acceptable and each is provided with true line/double valve separation. This type of carrier is very versatile and ideal for many trades.

(m) Pure car and truck carriers (PCTC)
This type of tonnage is designed for the conveyance of cars, lorries/trucks and other wheeled units. A modern PCTC has thirteen decks and can convey between 5500 and 5800 cars or a permutation of 3200 cars and 600 trucks. Such tonnage can also convey containers on 20 ft (6.10 m) or 40 ft (12.2 m) long Mafi trailers. A major operator in this field is Wallenius Lines Ltd which has a 19-vessel fleet of PCTC providing a worldwide service embracing the Far East, North America and European markets.

(n) Refrigerated vessels
These are designed for the carriage of chilled or frozen meat, butter or eggs. Such vessels operate on liner cargo services, and are provided with large insulated holds with refrigerating machinery to maintain the cargo in good condition. (See Fruit Carrier, item (e).)

(o) Ro/Ro vessels
A Ro/Ro type of vessel was designed for the conveyance of road haulage vehicles and private cars. It is often called a multi-purpose ship, and is described on p. 35.

Ro/Ro combination is now found in the container vessel field as shown in Fig. 3.4 on p. 45 and described on p. 44.

Another example of a Ro/Ro (roll-on/roll-off) – Lo/Lo (lift-on/lift-off) vessel is one of 17 000 dwt, with an overall length of 140 m. The moulded breadth is 23 m and she has a speed of 16 knots. The ship has a Ro/Ro lane capacity of 1300 m and 600 TEUs container capacity. Hold capacity totals 27 000 m^3. The vessel has a stern ramp, internal fixed ramps, electro-hydraulic cranes, and hydraulically operated hatch covers. Liquid cargoes (latex or similar) can be conveyed in the foretanks. Such a vessel offers a high cargo mix versatility. Hence such a cargo combination could include general break bulk cargo which could be palletized, bulk cargo, containers, trailers, cars and Ro/Ro cargo.

A further example of the Ro/Ro development in the deep sea sector and of a combination carrier, is the 33 000 dwt Ro/Ro ship operative in the Canadian/Japanese trade. The vessels convey packaged timber from Canada whilst Japanese cars are conveyed on the return leg. The vessels have a 3600-car capacity.

All the three vessels types are likely to increase significantly in many liner cargo trades in the next decade.

(p)   Sugar ships
These are designed with self-trimming longitudinal subdivisions with wing holds, the latter being used for ballast purposes. Such vessels are served by special mechanical shore gear incorporating grab equipment capable of handling up to 20 tons per minute, which ensures quick turn-round. The engines are situated aft to provide additional cargo space, and also to prevent the sugar drying out in after-holds due to heat from machinery spaces.

(q)   Timber carriers
These are provided with large unobstructed holds and large hatches to facilitate cargo handling. They are frequently called three-island vessels and incorporate a raised forecastle, bridge and poop, thereby facilitating stowage of deck cargo which is now packaged.

(r)   Train ferries
These have been aptly described as floating moveable bridges. In design, they are in many ways similar to the Ro/Ro type of vessel, except, of course, that they carry railway passenger and freight rolling stock. Railway track is provided on the main deck. At each terminal a link span is provided, which enables the rolling stock to be propelled on or drawn off the vessel. This eliminates cranage and facilitates a quick turn-round. Additionally, it permits through-transits, dispenses with cargo handling and reduces damage and pilferage to a minimum.

(s)   Very large crude carriers (VLCCs)
An example of a modern VLCC, MT *Estelle Maersk*, is shown in Fig. 4.9. It was built in 1994 and has a dwt 299 700 and US barrel

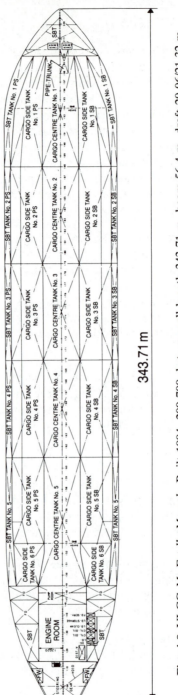

Fig. 4.9 VLCC *Mt Estelle Maersk*. Built 1994, 299 700 dwt, overall length 343.71 m, beam 56.4 m, draft 20.06/21.32 m depending on cargo type. Five centre tanks and six sets of wing tanks.

capacity of 2.144 million. The carrier's length is 343.71 m with beam of 56.40 m. The international gross tonnage is 159 000 and draft of 20.06/21.32 m depending on cargo type. The Suez net tonnage is 149 000. The vessel has five centre tanks and six sets of wing tanks. The system is arranged for carrying up to three different cargoes with double valve segregation. Overall the ship has a highly flexible cargo system and can convey the following oil products – Arabian heavy, Arabian medium, Arabian light, Iranian light, Oman, Muran and Zakum. Special features of the carrier include a double hull, fully computerized cargo handling, multiple double-valve segregation, remote cargo tank level indicators, remote-controlled hydraulically operated cargo system valves, flush bulkheads in wing tanks and flush tank tops, crude oil washing, stripping wells, inert gas system and no ballast lines in cargo tanks. The carrier cleaning system offers hot and cold. The vessel is equipped with fixed fully automatic tank cleaning machines. Segregation of the slop tank is possible in case of two different cargoes for crude oil washing, enabling the process to be started earlier.

The VLCC is a very specialized vessel and to be efficient must operate in a high-volume oil trade market to maximize her loadability on a continuous basis. Specialized terminals are required with an adequate tank farm infrastructure at the oil terminal environs.

Our study of ship types would not be complete without mention of the hovercraft, hydrofoil and jetfoil type of craft which are primarily orientated towards the passenger market involving the estuarial and short sea trades.

(t)   The hovercraft
This was developed in the early 1960s and operates on a cushion of air above the water. Early versions were primarily confined to estuarial services and land/river exploration work. As technical improvements were realized, general operational reliability improved and the craft became of larger capacity. Particular attention has been given to improving the skirt of the hovercraft.

(u)   The hydrofoil
This was developed in the early 1960s and is propelled by water jet with fully submerged foils and an automatic control system to

provide a jet-smooth ride at 40 knots even in rough water. A modern craft would have two decks with an overall passenger capacity of 300 and speed of 50 knots. Many operate between the Greek islands.

(v) The jetfoil
This craft emerged in the early 1970s as a commercial craft. It is an advanced design high-speed hydrofoil. Basically it is a ship whose weight is supported by foils which produce lift by virtue of their shape and forward velocity through the water in the same manner as an airplane wing. There are two types of hydrofoils: those with surface-piercing foils and those with fully submerged foils. The surface-piercing foil has inherent stability but it is greatly affected by wave disturbances. The fully submerged foil is affected to a much smaller degree by wave disturbances and produces a much more comfortable ride as a result.

The passenger capacity can range from 150 to 400 passengers depending on the craft range. On a 36-mile schedule the capacity would be 260 passengers falling to 190 passengers on a 100-mile route.

Present indications suggest that the hovercraft is not likely to improve on its operational performance in terms of faster schedules, whilst the hydrofoil could attain a speed of up to 60 knots. However, new generations of the hovercraft should produce more simple design, much increased capacity and substantially reduced overall operating cost. Reliability should also be much improved. A recent innovation is the Seacat operated by the Stena Line in the Irish Sea.

4.5 CALIBRATED AUTOMATIC PILOTING SYSTEM

It is perhaps appropriate to conclude our examination of ships of the previous three chapters by looking at the calibrated automatic piloting system (CAPS). It enables ships and other floating vessels to follow a set track or to keep on station with high accuracy. It also provides computer-aided control functions.

The control system is based on state-of-the-art automatic control engineering techniques. An optimized track is first computed, allowing for all ship-originated constraints. A complete model of the ship and propulsion system is then used to evaluate the effect of a series of command vectors on the displacement of the vessel relative to the optimized track. Finally, the vessel is piloted on the basis of selected command vectors in real time, and with continuous interaction with the immediate positioning data input. The use of models, which include non-linear variations of the system parameters, enables the autopilot to operate under a wide range of conditions without operator intervention.

The performance of a given ship and propulsion system is greatly improved, and high accuracy of tracking or station-keeping is achieved.

With this system it is also possible to keep control of the ship after complete loss of position data, during the time necessary to introduce emergency procedures in all safety.

The dynamic positioning can be fitted with all kinds of position reference sensors: taut wires, acoustic radio, radio navigation, satellite or inertial navigation systems.

CAPS also provides: continuous calculation of the most favourable heading in station-keeping mode; a control system for manoeuvres in manual-assisted mode, with forces and moment instructions input to the console; and automatic checks facilitating maintenance procedures. This system has been developed by Alcatel.

CHAPTER 5

Manning of vessels

5.1 INTRODUCTION

The manning of vessels is an extensive subject, and this chapter is intended only to cover its most important aspects. Ship manning today forms a very important part of the shipping industry complex in an increasingly competitive cost-conscious situation. New technology is being introduced whilst economic change is continuous. Moreover, seafarers' standards both in ship accommodation terms and navigation/engineering/catering techniques are rising. Overall seafarers' shipboard living standards are improving. Basically there are important costs which can vary between maritime nations: the effective cost of capital, the flag state's regulating requirements (the country to which the vessel is registered), and finally crew cost which we will now examine.

A major factor influencing manning cost is the change in the disposition of the world mercantile fleet as Table 1.3 (see p. 5) and the market share held by each maritime fleet of world trade reveals. It confirms the rapid rise of the Liberian, Panamanian, Bahamian and Cypriot fleets all of which are open registers, and the Norwegian International Ship Register.

A major problem internationally is the differing wage scales offered to seafarers worldwide which makes it very difficult to compete on equal crew cost terms. An example is given in Table 5.1 based on an all-UK crew of officers and ratings for a bulk carrier.

The cost of employing seafarers of a particular nationality is in the first instance related to the general level of wages and cost of living in that country. Accordingly, as Table 5.1 demonstrates, the Far East nationals' skilled seafarers have lower salary levels and shipowners are clearly advantaged in their crewing costs when compared with crews of European origin such as from the UK, Germany or Holland. Moreover, such reduced crew costs places

Table 5.1 Comparison of crew costs based on all UK crew of officers and ratings being 100 index of a bulk carrier

Crew description	Annual crew cost index	Daily crew cost index
UK officers: UK rating	100	100
UK officers (offshore rates): Filipino ratings	65	65
UK/Indian officers: Filipino ratings	54	54
UK/Indian officers: Hong Kong/China ratings	53	53
Filipino officers: Filipino ratings	42	42
Indian officers: Indian ratings	50	50

such shipowners in a favourable position to offer lower rates and develop markets.

To counter this an increasing number of shipowners from the UK, Japan, Greece, Norway, Sweden, the US and Germany are flagging out their fleets, that is they are transferring the flag to a national register which has lower crew cost and fringe benefits plus overall tax benefits to the shipping company. This tends to counter the very high competitive crew cost in high labour cost maritime fleets. An example is Hapag-Lloyd decided in 1995 to flag out one-third of its container fleet and yielded annual savings of DM30 million in crew costs. Such offshore registries are situated in the Isle of Man, Bermuda, Gibraltar or Hong Kong. The UK shipowner then either negotiates 'offshore' agreements with the British seafarers' unions through foreign associate companies or hands over the manning of his ships to international manning agencies. By the end of 1995 over 50% of UK tonnage was registered to offshore registries.

Some governments such as those of the Netherlands and Sweden have introduced measures to reduce the cost of employing national seafarers by granting relief on personal taxation and social security. These remove some or all of the burden of substantial 'on cost' for the employer reducing the gap between Western and third-world crew costs. Some governments have also established 'international' or 'second' ship registers which either incorporate tax exemptions for national seafarers as in Denmark, or allow the employment of foreign seafarers at third-world pay levels as in Germany and Norway. A further partial solution is being sought by some industrial nations through reduced manning levels, but the scope is limited and one must bear in mind the continually rising standards in seamanship competency certification. This is demonstrated by the agreement reached by the IMO as detailed on p. 84 to raise the number of certificated crew personnel. An example occurred in 1978 when the IMO adopted the Convention on Standards of Training, Certification and Watch-keeping for seafarers (see pp. 82, 85). Such international regulations ensure the man on the ship meets the standards required of him. The Convention received worldwide support and is further evidence of measures designed to raise seafaring navigation standards. The manning levels and duties for UK registered tonnage are contained in the Merchant Shipping Acts 1970 and 1979.

In attaining such crew complement reductions, one must also remember that vessels have tended to increase in size/capacity and resources. Today, we have computerized engine room/navigation aids. On the catering side many owners are using pre-prepared foods to aid catering crew reduction. These factors have tended to favour maritime nations who can finance new tonnage as such crew reductions can only be attained without impairing safety standards. Moreover in some industrial maritime nations' fleets studies are being conducted in the field of ship maintenance, with a view to transferring the ship maintenance functions which were previously done ashore to an onboard activity. This aids improved ship utilization, less time spent in port, more productive use of the crew and overall lower cost to the shipowner. Additionally the need to encourage more crew diversification continues. This has tended to eliminate the traditional demarcation lines found in the engineering, catering and deck departments. This is very common in modern container tonnage and foreign-going tankers. Moreover, the Chamber of Shipping has revised the designation of certain rating personnel to raise productivity and status as described on p. 77.

Many more operators now have up to three crews assigned to a vessel and fly out and back crew personnel to all ports of the world to ensure the ship is in continuous operation. Modern ships have accommodation for wives to accompany their officer husbands. Again all these factors add to crew cost in an era of rising living standards.

In an era when shipowners are endeavouring to reduce their crew costs the following options exist other than flagging out as earlier described:

(a) Reduction of the crew to the minimum number required under legislation. This increases the workload on remaining crew personnel but ship maintenance and operation may suffer as a result. Further training to ensure the crew are familiar with automation can also be undertaken with a subsequent reduction in crew numbers.

(b) Increased ship utilization involves shorter turn-round time in port and shorter leave periods, both of which factors can improve crew utilization. This is particularly relevant to western-ized tonnage crews. It can also extend to lower fringe benefits leaving it to the seafarer to make his own arrangements for medical insurance and pension contributions.

(c) An increasing number of shipowners are employing more low cost non-domiciled seafarers with their European crews. Often the officers would be European and the ratings Filipinos or North Koreans. Hence a vessel may have a ratings crew of 1.1/1.2 compared with an officer crew of 1.5/1.8 enabling favourable cost reductions to be achieved (see pp. 72, 73).

(d) The process of greater integration of crew personnel duties is likely to accelerate in the 1990s as the need to reduce crew cost becomes more significant and shipboard automation further de-velops. The duties of the ship Master and first mate, and chief engineer and second engineer could be integrated on tonnage where circumstances so allow.

In conclusion one must bear in mind the lower the crew complement and number of crews per ship, plus the longer the voyage length, the greater the cost savings. This applies to fringe benefits especially.

In studying this chapter one must bear in mind the foregoing arises at a time when it is vital for shipping costs to remain competitive to aid international trade development: crew cost has a vital role to play in this situation.

5.2 DUTIES AND RESPONSIBILITIES OF THE MASTER

It is a common but very wrong belief that the person in charge of a vessel is the Captain. This term is simply a naval rank. The correct term to be applied to the person in absolute charge of the vessel, which may be a large passenger liner like the *Oriana* or a relatively small cargo ship engaged in our coastal trade, is the Master.

The Master's duties and responsibilities are many, varied and extensive. He is the owner's personal representative, and bears the ultimate responsibility for the safe navigation of his vessel and for the efficient loading, stowage and discharge of cargo. Furthermore, he has the power to act as a lawyer, a doctor and even to bury people. The Master may arrest members of the crew or passengers, if they constitute a nuisance during the voyage. In certain circumstances, particularly if the person is dangerous to other members of the ship, the Master may place the individual under restraint. In the event of any mutiny, any act of the Master is regarded as one entirely of self-defence, and he has the power to call on persons on board to render assistance. Similarly, if the ship is imperilled in any way, the Master may call upon all persons on board to give assistance.

Wide authority is vested in the Master and, under maritime law, acts done within the scope of his authority are binding on his owners. Under very rare circumstances, he is empowered by a 'bottomry bond' to pledge the vessel, and likewise by a 'respondentia bond' her cargo, so that funds may be secured to permit the voyage to proceed.

It is therefore readily apparent that the Master's responsibilities and duties are very diverse. To hold the position of a Master, especially on a large passenger liner, is a much coveted appointment, and is the culmination of years of sea experience. The Master is required to hold a Master's Certificate (see p. 81), which is obtained by examination, and issued by the Department of Transport. Furthermore, in common with the deck officers from which department he is promoted, he must be thoroughly competent in navigation matters including the use of such navigational aids as the gyrocompass, radar, direction finder, echo-sounding device, and position-fixing device.

In the 1990s the traditional watch-keeping crew manning system will change radically as is evident in many modern maritime fleets today. The present modern tonnage provides automation in the engine room coupled with extensive computerization and minimum of crew personnel. This reduces crew costs especially in the engineer and deck departments. A further significant aspect is that the departmental system of deck and engineers will become more integrated and more productive in manpower, especially in deep-sea tonnage.

An example of an integrated crew manning system is given below and involves the 16-man complement of a Danish registered 'Omni carrier' vessel of 8000 dwt operating on the route Gulf of Mexico/US East coast-Mediterranean-Caribbean/Central America/Mexico.

Master	Second engineer
Chief mate	Third engineer
First mate	Electrician
Second mate	Purser
Radio officer	Cook
Chief engineer	Four trainees
First engineer	

The ship has a total container capacity of 516 TEUs and vehicular deck space of 1416 m^2; heavy lifting gear for loads up to 120 tonnes is also provided.

An integrated crew is especially common with Scandinavian and German registered tonnage crews.

A brief description of the departments, responsibilities and composition follow, but it is stressed that this manning system is becoming less and less common as integration takes place to attain more productive use of the crew.

5.3 SHIP'S OFFICERS AND CREW MANNING

(a) Deck department

The running of this department is the responsibility of the chief officer or first mate who supervises the handling of cargo and is responsible for the upkeep of the ship and her equipment, excluding the engine room and auxiliary power gear. In addition, he also acts as a semi-chief of staff to the Master. He is assisted by two, three or more mates on larger vessels. These deck officers have to be duly certified by Department of Transport examination after the appropriate qualifying sea time has been completed. There are five certificates of competency for deck officers as fully described on p. 80. It is the practice in many vessels for both the chief and second officers to hold Master's Certificate of competency command endorsement. The statutory requirements for British vessels are fully described on p. 80.

The deck department also includes chief petty officer (deck), petty officers (deck) and a carpenter, together with a number of deck-hands, including junior seamen, seamen grade II and seamen grade I. The duties of the bosun are such that he acts as a foreman of the deck-hands. The carpenter's responsibilities include attendance at the forward windlass during berthing and unberthing operations. In common with the officers, the seamen grades I and II are watch-keepers, taking their turn at steering and look-out duties, while the remaining deck-hands are day workers employed at sea in general duties. The deck department in port usually works cargo watches in 8-hour stretches.

In the case of a large passenger liner, it is the frequent practice to have a Staff Captain, who is primarily responsible for looking after passengers' administration.

(b) Radio officers

Statutory provisions stipulate under SOLAS 1974 that all cargo vessels of 300 tons gross and upwards must be fitted with a radio station and issued with a safety radio certificate (see p. 26). For keels laid before February 1995 the radio station should be either a radio telephone station (only applicable for ships of 300 to 1599 gross tonnage), a radio telegraph station or a Global Maritime Distress and Safety System (GMDSS) for operation in specific sea areas. For keels laid after 31 January 1995 a GMDSS must be fitted. The radio officer requirements are contained in the Merchant Shipping (Radio Installations) Regulations 1992. This outlines the number of radio officers required for different vessels and the need for a valid certificate of competency. Overall the role of the radio officer has changed significantly following the emergence of GMDSS.

(c) Engine room department

The engine room is the charge of the chief engineer, who is responsible to the Master both for the main propulsion machinery and for auxiliaries comprising electrical plant, cargo winches, refrigerating machinery, steering gear, ventilating system, etc. He is also responsible for fuel, maintenance and repairs. He is assisted by a number of engineer officers, according to the size of the vessel. For example, a motorship requires more engineers than a steamship of equivalent power, while a turbo-electric or diesel-electric ship would require more electricians. Minimum manning scales of certified marine engineer officers are given on p. 81.

The ratings of the engine room department comprise junior motorman, motorman grade II, motorman grade I, petty officer (motorman) and chief petty officer (motorman). The complicated machinery of the modern ship has made the engine room department a very important one and much of it is computerized in modern tonnage.

(d) Catering department

This department is under the control of the chief steward, or catering officer, who is responsible for catering and the galley, for galley stores and for ship's linen. He is assisted by cooks, bakers and assistant stewards. In deep sea passenger ships and those engaged in multi-purpose passenger tonnage in the short sea trades, this is a very large and important department. As such it is usually in the charge of the Purser. Many passenger vessels are now manned as a floating hotel.

(e) Manning

'Manning scales' are laid down for vessels flying the British flag, and every vessel must carry a minimum number of duly certificated deck officers and engineers, while more detailed requirements are often agreed jointly between employers and unions.

The number of personnel in each of the various departments depends on the type and size of vessel, and the trade in which she is engaged. For instance, a cargo vessel of 10 000 dwt would have a very small catering department compared with a vessel engaged in deep-sea cruising carrying 750 passengers.

The Merchant Shipping Act 1970 introduced new regulations regarding the certification of deck officers and marine engineer officers. They are contained in the Merchant Shipping (Certification of Deck and Marine Engineer Officers) Regulations 1977, which became operative from 1 September 1981.

This involves UK-registered ships of 80 gross register tonnage or over and passenger ships in carrying a specified number of deck officers determined according to the tonnage of the ship and the voyage to, from or between locations in specified trading areas in which it will be engaged. Similar requirements are prescribed for ships registered outside the UK which carry passengers between places in the UK, or between the UK and the Channel Islands or Isle of Man or on voyages which begin or end at the same place in the UK and call at no place outside the UK. Provision is made for the exceptional circumstance when one deck officer cannot be carried because of illness. Special requirements are prescribed for tugs and sail training ships. Certificates of competency will be issued to deck officers who satisfy the requisite standards of competency as determined by the Department of Transport Additional training is required for certain deck officers in ships carrying bulk cargoes of specified dangerous chemicals or gases. The same applies to certain marine engineer officers. Overall the new standards of certification reflect broadly the outcome of discussions at the IMO.

The minimum number of deck officers to be carried is prescribed in the Merchant Shipping (Certification of Deck Officers) Regulations 1977. These must be regarded as the minimum manning scales and this equally applies to the marine engineer officers. From January 1988, the syllabuses for Classes I and II Deck Officer Certificates of Competency, combined into a single syllabus examined at the Class II stage, came into effect.

Differing scales apply to passenger vessels which are much higher.

The Regulations specify trading limits. The 'Near Continental' is any location within the area bounded by a line from a point on the Norwegian coast in latitude 62° North to a point 62° North 02° West; thence to a point 51° North 12° West; thence to Brest, but excluding all waters which lie to the east of a line drawn between Kristiansand, Norway and Hanstholm lighthouse on the north Danish coast.

The 'Middle Trade' is any location not within the Near Continental trading area but within an area (which includes places in the Baltic Sea) bounded by the Northern shore of Vest Fjord (Norway) and a line joining Skemvaer lighthouse to a point 62° North 02° West; thence to a point 58° North 10° West; thence to a point 51° North 12° West; thence to a point 41° 9' North 10° West; thence to Oporto. Basically the unlimited trading area is any location not within the Middle Trade or Near Continental trading areas.

The five classes of Certificate of Competency (Deck Officer) is such that Class I is the Master Mariner level. In broad terms the new Class I certificate is equivalent to the Master Foreign Certificate as prescribed under the Merchant Shipping Act 1894. Likewise a First Mate Foreign-Going certificate and Second Mate Foreign-Going certificate is equivalent to the new Classes II and III respectively.

Differing Certificates of Competency and Command Endorsements exist for tugs. With regard to the regulations of marine engineer officers these involve UK-registered ships having registered power of 350 kW or more, including all sail-training ships with a propulsion engine. It embraces the voyage to, from or between locations in specified training areas. Similar requirements are prescribed for a specified number of engineer officers for ships registered outside the UK, which carry passengers between places in the UK or between the UK and the Channel Islands or Isle of Man or on voyages which begin and end at the same place in the UK and call at no place outside the UK. Provision is made for the exceptional circumstance when one engineer officer cannot be carried because of illness or incapacity. Special requirements are prescribed for sail-training ships.

Overall there are four classes of Certificate of Competence and related to the First Class Engineer Certificate as prescribed under the Merchant Shipping Act 1894 it will be the Marine Engineer Officer Class 1. Certificates of Competency of Class 1, 2 or 4 shall be issued for motor or steam machinery, or for combined motor and steam machinery. Class 3 certificates shall be issued for motor machinery only.

In an attempt to raise the status of ratings both in the deck and engineer departments, plus the need to facilitate the productivity and diversification of rating workload on UK vessels, a new structure has been introduced to a number of posts. Brief details are given below of the new structure:

Deck department *new designation*	*Marine engineer department* *new designation*
Junior Seaman	Junior Motorman
Seaman Grade II	Motorman Grade II

Seaman Grade I	Motorman Grade I
Petty Officer (Deck)	Petty Officer (Motorman)
Chief Petty Officer (Deck)	Chief Petty Officer (Motorman)

Similar restructuring has taken place on the catering side.

In the late 1990s, it is likely the concept of crew manning will further change to reflect the greater technology now found in modern tonnage. Radical changes could emerge in manning scales, particularly in the increased number of certificated personnel (see pp. 83–5). These become operative from 1st February 1997 following the IMO Conference on 7th July 1995 described below. It will change much of the analysis on pp. 77–82.

5.4 IMO CONVENTION ON STANDARDS OF TRAINING, CERTIFICATION AND WATCHKEEPING (STCW) ADOPTED 1984

A two-week long conference to amend the most important treaty dealing with the standards of training, certification and watchkeeping of the world's seafarers was successfully concluded on 7 July 1995 at the International Maritime Organization. The treaty is the International Convention on Standards of Training, Certification and Watchkeeping for Seafarers (STCW), 1978, which so far has been accepted by 112 countries whose fleets represent 93.53% of world tonnage of merchant ships.

The Convention has for some time been generally regarded as technically out of date and in need of revision. The conference adopted a series of amendments including a restructuring of the existing treaty. It is expected that the amendments will enter into force on 1 February 1997 under the Convention's 'tacit acceptance' procedure (see p. 132).

Until 1 February 2002, however, parties may continue to issue, recognize and endorse certificates which applied before that date in respect of seafarers who began training or seagoing service before 1 August 1998. The Conference was attended by 480 delegates from 71 parties and eight non-parties.

The revision of the STCW Convention represents the conclusion of a major effort by IMO and its member governments. IMO agreed in December 1992 that the Convention should be amended and in May 1993, decided to prepare the draft text under a specially accelerated programme. The original date for completing the revision at sub-committee level was 1996, meaning that the revision conference would probably not have been held until 1998.

The target was achieved by holding extra sessions of the Sub-Committee on Standards of Training and Watchkeeping, forming inter-sessional working groups and using a number of consultants and maritime training institutes to work on the text.

One of the major features of the revision is the adoption of a new STCW Code, to which many technical regulations have been transferred. Part A of the code is mandatory while Part B is recommended. Dividing the regulations up in this way makes administration easier and it will also make the task of revising and updating them more simple: for procedural and legal reasons there is no need to call a full conference to make changes to Codes.

Some of the most important amendments adopted by the conference concern Chapter I (General Provisions). They include the following:

- Parties to the Convention will be required to provide detailed information to IMO concerning administrative measures taken to ensure compliance with the Convention, education and training courses, certification procedures and other factors relevant to implementation (Regulation 7).

  This information will be used by the Maritime Safety Committee (MSC), IMO's senior technical body, to identify parties that are able to demonstrate that they can give full and complete effect to the Convention. Other parties will then be able to accept that certificates issued by these parties are in compliance with the Convention.

  This regulation is regarded as particularly important because it means that governments will have to establish that they have the administrative, training and certification resources necessary to implement the Convention.

  No such proof was required in the original Convention, leading to complaints that standards differed widely from country to country and certificates could therefore not always be relied on. Further regulations dealing with this aspect are contained in the mandatory Part A of the STCW Code.

Parties will be obliged to investigate incidents in which incompetence or negligence is alleged against seafarers to whom they have issued certificates. Administrations wishing to recognize certificates issued by another state for use in their ships will be required to ensure that the standards concerned are in accordance with the Convention.

- Enhanced procedures concerning the exercise of port state control under Article X of the Convention have been developed to allow intervention in the case of deficiencies deemed to pose a danger to persons, property or the environment.

  This can take place if certificates are not in order or if the ship is involved in a collision or grounding, if there is an illegal discharge of substances (causing pollution), if the ship is manoeuvred in an erratic or unsafe manner, etc.

- Technical innovations, such as different working practices and the use of simulators for training purposes have been recognized. Simulators will become mandatory for training in the use of radar and automatic radar plotting aids.

- Special requirements have been introduced concerning the training and qualifications of personnel on board ro-ro passenger ships. This was done in response to proposals made by the panel of experts set up to look into ro-ro safety following the capsize and sinking of the ferry *Estonia* in September 1994. Previously, the only special requirements concerned crews on tankers. Crews on ro-ro ferries will have to receive training in technical aspects and also in crowd management and human behaviour.

  Parties will be required to ensure that training, certification and other procedures are continuously monitored by means of a quality assurance system (Regulation 8).

- A reference is made in Regulation 14 to the International Safety Management (ISM) Code, which was adopted by IMO in 1993 and was made mandatory under the May 1994 amendments to the International Convention for the Safety of Life at Sea (SOLAS), 1974. The Regulation details further company responsibilities for manning, certification, etc. See also pp. 27–30.

The remaining chapters contain Regulations that concern specific departments and ranks. Chapter II, for example, deals with the master and deck department and Chapter III with the engine department.

Regulations regarding alternative certification have been included in a new Chapter VII. This involves enabling crews to gain training and certification in various departments of seafaring rather than being confined to one branch (such as deck or engine room) for their entire career. Although it is a relatively new concept, the Conference was anxious not to prevent its development. At the same time, the new Chapter is intended to ensure that safety and the environment are not threatened in any way.

Measures have been introduced for watchkeeping personnel to prevent fatigue. A new Chapter VIII requires Administrations to establish and enforce rest periods for watchkeeping personnel and to ensure that watch systems are so arranged that the efficiency of watchkeeping personnel is not impaired by fatigue.

In addition to the amendments and the Code, the conference also adopted a number of resolutions which deal with such subjects as:

- training in crisis management and human behaviour for personnel on board ro-ro passenger ships and training of personnel on passenger ships;
- monitoring the implications of alternative certification;
- development of international standards of medical fitness for seafarers;
- promotion of technical co-operation and the contribution of the World Maritime University; and
- promotion of the participation of women in the maritime industry.

5.5 ENGAGEMENT AND DISCHARGE OF THE CREW

We have already established that the person in sole charge of the vessel is the Master. The conditions of employment of seamen are the subject of statutory legislation and regulations under the Merchant Shipping Act 1970. A voyage is still a venture subject to many hazards and difficulties. To complete the venture successfully, relative rights, duties and restraints must be enforced on all who share the venture. These special circumstances have given rise to legislation in most countries to restrict and protect seamen in their employment.

The Merchant Shipping Act 1970 brought into effect the first major change for many years in the legislation relating to the employment of seamen. It repealed parts of the 1894 and 1906 Merchant Shipping Acts. The Act deals with crew agreements; crew lists; engagement and discharge of crew; seamen's documents; discipline; wages and accounts; seamen left behind abroad; deceased seamen; and medical treatment and expenses. The more salient aspects are now examined.

The contract of employment is made between the shipowner and the crew. It is called a crew agreement, and a number of clauses are taken directly from the Merchant Shipping Act 1970 whilst other derive from National Maritime Board agreements. The shipowner is the contracting party, but seamen must sign the crew agreement prior to the intended voyage. It is not necessary for the superintendent or proper officer to be present during the signing on or discharge but in some Commonwealth countries this practice is obligatory under their legislation involving shipping masters/superintendents.

A standard form of crew agreement is provided by the Department of Transport, or non-standard editions as prepared by employers and approved by the Department of Transport may also be used. The crew agreement contains a voyage clause giving the geographical limits of the voyage, and notice/termination clauses which vary by the trade in which vessel engaged, i.e. foreign-going voyage or home trade. If a seaman wishes to terminate his employment in contemplation of furtherance of an industrial dispute, 48 hours' notice must be given to the Master, when the vessel is securely moored at a safe berth in the UK.

It will be recalled that in many maritime countries the employment agreement between the seamen and shipowner is called the articles of agreement. Indeed it is still referred to as such in UK tonnage rather than the 'crew agreement' and applies to individual crew members.

The ship's Master is required to maintain a crew list which must be produced on demand to the Registry of Shipping and Seamen as required under the Merchant Shipping Act 1970 and the Merchant Shipping (Registration etc.) Act 1993. The crew list embraces reference; name of seaman; discharge book number or date/place of birth; mercantile marine office where registered; name of ship in which last employed – if more than 12 months since last ship, actual year of discharge; address of seaman; name of next of kin; relationship of next of kin; capacity in which employed; grade and number of certificate of competency; date of commencement of employment on board; date of leaving ship; place of leaving ship; rate of wages; if discharged – reason for discharge; signature of seaman on engagement; and signature of seaman on discharge.

The crew list remains in being until all the persons employed under the crew agreement have been discharged. A copy must be kept with all the changes by the UK shipowner, and any change in the crew list must be notified to a superintendent or proper officer within two days of the change.

Before seamen are engaged on a new crew agreement and before they are added to an agreement which is already current, at least 24 hours' notice must be given to the appropriate super-intendent or proper officer. The notice of engagement must include name of ship; port of registry; official number; whether a new crew agreement is to be made or whether a person(s) is to be added; and the capacity in which each person to be engaged is to be employed.

When a seaman is present at his discharge it must be before (a) the Master, or (b) the seaman's employer, or (c) a person so authorized by the Master or employer. The person before whom the seaman is discharged must enter in the official log book the place, date and time of the seaman's discharge and in the crew list the place, date and reason for the discharge. The seaman must sign the entry in the crew list. In the event of the seaman not being present at the time of discharge, similar entries must be made in the official log and in the crew list. All entries in the official log must be signed by the person making the entry and by a member of the crew. The seaman can request a certificate either as to the quality of his work or indicating whether he has fulfilled his obligations under the agreement.

The detailed requirements of seamen's documents are contained in the Merchant Shipping (Seamen's Documents) Regulations (Statutory Instrument 1972 No. 1295). This embraces a British seaman card valid for five years, and a discharge book.

The Act also deals with discipline and covers stowaways and their prosecution, aiding and abetting stowaways, and the Master's power of arrest. This indicates that where the Master considers it necessary for any person on board to be placed under restraint in the interest of safety or for the preservation of good order or discipline on board the ship, the Master is empowered to do so.

The Act makes provision for payment of seamen's wages including at the time of discharge. Additionally provision is made for an allotment of his wages to up to two persons and not more than 50% of his income both of which may be varied only in exceptional circumstances. This arrangement is concluded at the time when the crew agreement is signed.

The Act also places on the employer the primary responsibility and the cost of providing for the relief and repatriation of seaman left behind. This covers the following relating to the responsibilities of the employer or his agent to the seaman:

(a) Maintenance and cost of repatriating seamen who are left behind.

(b) Provision of their surgical, medical, dental and optical treatment.

(c) Provision of their accommodation.

(d) Making arrangements for their repatriation.

(e) Applying, if necessary, to the proper officer for the issue of a conveyance order.

Basically the regulations relating to the relief and repatriation of seamen are found in the Merchant Shipping (Repatriation) Regulations 1979 (SI 1977 No. 97). Shipboard disciplinary procedures (ss. 23–25) are contained in the Merchant Shipping Act 1979 but have not yet been introduced except for s. 23.7. This repealed the discipline arrangements in the Merchant Shipping Act 1970 and was brought into force by statutory instrument SI 1985 No. 1827.

The Merchant Shipping Act 1988 amended the law relating to crew agreements to bring the payment of seamen into line with that for other categories of employee.

5.6 THE CHAMBER OF SHIPPING

Consequent to an organizational restructuring the General Council of British Shipping was redesignated the Chamber of Shipping in 1992 – a name it bore on its inception as a holding company in 1873.

The Chamber of Shipping is based in London and is the trade association and employers' organization for British shipowners and ship managers. It promotes and protects the interests of its member companies both nationally and internationally. It also represents British shipping to the government, Parliament, international organizations, unions and the general public. Overall, it covers all issues which have a bearing on British shipping ranging from fiscal policy and freedom to trade, through to recruitment and training, maritime safety and the environment, navigational aids and pilotage. The Chamber is structured to represent six commercial sectors trading at sea: deep-sea bulk; short sea bulk; deep-sea liner; ferry; cruise; and offshore support. In 1994 it had 121 member companies which own or manage 562 trading ships totalling 16.85 million deadweight tonnes, excluding some managed for foreign owners.

Associated with the Chamber of Shipping is the Merchant Navy Training Board. It is a voluntary body representing the industry, unions, colleges and government departments concerned with the training and education of seafarers. It provides a forum for interested parties to formulate and oversee policy concerning entry standards and the training of seafarers.

The Board is representative of ship owners who are nominated by the Chamber of Shipping.

5.7 THE INTERNATIONAL SHIPPING FEDERATION (ISF)

This organization is a federation of national shipowners' organizations on the same basis as the International Chamber of Shipping. It is, however, administered by the Chamber of Shipping.

Founded in 1909, much of its work at that time was concerned with indemnifying shipowners for losses incurred through labour disputes and it was exclusively a European organization.

The creation of the International Labour Office in 1919 radically altered both the membership and the practical scope of the Federation. It became and remains a worldwide organization and is concerned primarily with the whole and ever-widening field of industrial relations for shipping. It is a consultative and advisory organization and in no way infringes national autonomy. Its present membership consists of the national organizations of shipowners of the following 19 countries:

Australia	Greece	Norway
Belgium	India	Portugal
Canada	Italy	Spain
Denmark	Japan	Sweden
Finland	Netherlands	United Kingdom
France	New Zealand	United States of
Germany		America

Since 1919 the principal function of the International Shipping Federation has been to give shipowners of different countries an opportunity to exchange views upon all social and personnel problems affecting the shipping industry. In particular it acts as a medium of preparation for international labour (maritime) conferences and provides the secretariat of the shipowners' group. It acts in the same way for the shipowners' side of the Joint Maritime Commission of the ILO (International Labour Organization). The ISF also works closely with BIMCO on a number of issues and also with the British Shipping Federation.

CHAPTER 6

Customs house and ships' papers

6.1 INTRODUCTION

One must bear in mind that Customs entries are necessary for the following reasons:

(a) To provide a record of exports and imports, and so enable the government to assess and thereby control the balance of trade.

(b) To ensure that no dutiable goods enter the country without paying duty.

(c) To bring all imports 'to account' by perfected entries prepared by importers or their agents.

(d) In so far as dutiable cargo is concerned, to provide a valuable form of revenue through the imposition by the government and European Union of certain duties and levies on certain goods imported into a country.

During the past 20 years there has been a mood in many countries to harmonize and simplify their customs procedures in order to facilitate trade development. This has been particularly self-evident in the European Union, NAFTA, ASEAN and other trading blocs worldwide. In the UK we have seen gradual changes in the pattern of control exercised by the Customs and Excise department. We have seen a number of relaxations introduced to facilitate the clearance of imported cargo, the ongoing expansion of computerization to process cargo through customs, the encouragement of the clearance of cargo at the trader's premises for both imports (LIC) and exports (LEC), and the emergence of the Single Market on 1 January 1993 which allowed for the freedom of movement of merchandise within the European Union. Overall the role of HM Customs & Excise embraces five areas: landing and shipping; warehousing; excise; value added tax; and preventive duties.

6.2 CUSTOMS TARIFF – HARMONIZED SYSTEM (HS)

All products exported or imported are identified by the use of numerical codes as listed in the customs tariff. For statistical purposes and in connection with the enforcement of export licences, there must be a formal declaration of all commercial exports to the Customs authorities showing the tariff code of the product concerned. Each item has only one correct classification under the harmonized tariff system which has been adopted by 85% of the world's trading nations. It follows that the code used by the exporter should be the same (at either four- or six-digit level) as that used by the importer. If exporters use an incorrect code, they can mislead customers who may well pay more or less duty than is legally due.

The foregoing data is found in the customs tariff published in three volumes by HM Customs. It includes a full list of goods with their various rates itemized. A supplement to the tariff is regularly issued in the form of an HM Customs notice. Overall the tariff includes 15 000 headings, set out in 97 chapters broken down into sections, headings and sub-headings. The tariff is not used for intra-EU trade.

The present tariff is based on the harmonized system. It should be noted the system adopted for collecting intra-EU trade statistics is called 'Intrastat' and, unlike the HS has no value thresholds.

6.3 INTRASTAT

The introduction of Intrastat is a consequence of the European Union Single Market whereby the imposition of cross-frontier controls relative to goods were withdrawn on 1 January 1993. This involved the elimination of customs duties between member states and customs declarations thereby permitting the virtual free flow of goods without any physical examination and barrier to trade. Overall it reduced distribution costs by up to 5%.

Intrastat is the system for collecting statistics on the trade in goods between European Union countries. It came into operation on 1 January 1993, replacing customs declarations as the source of trade statistics within the community. Intrastat is a community-wide system, so requirements are similar in all EU countries.

Only movements which represent trade in goods are covered by Intrastat. In general these movements equate to supplies (and corresponding acquisitions) under the arrangements for intra-EU VAT and are to be recorded using the same rules.

Commodities covered by the Intrastat system include goods bought and sold; goods transferred within the same legal entity; merchandise which has been or will be processed or repaired; goods supplied as part of a contract for services; items to be installed or used in construction; goods supplied free of charge; and finally goods on long-term hire, loan or operational lease. Items excluded from Intrastat include movements not regarded as by way of trade; certain commercial samples provided free of charge; and certain purely temporary movements where the goods are to be returned to the original EU country within two years, and there is to be no change of ownership.

The processing of the export consignment is explained on pp. 438–47.

6.4 EXPORT CONTROLS

There are three main reasons for controlling the exportation of goods and persons from the UK. These are as follows.

(a) Revenue interest
These interests (and the economy) may suffer if the following types of transactions are not controlled:

(a) Transhipment goods – should these goods not be transhipped, there is the possibility of loss of revenue.
(b) Goods for re-exportation after temporary importation.
(c) Goods exported from a bonded warehouse.
(d) Goods exported from an excise factory.
(e) Goods exported on drawback.
(f) Cars supplied free of VAT to overseas residents.
(g) Goods exported for processing and subsequent re-importation.

Should these types of transactions not be controlled, there is a strong possibility of loss of revenue through dishonest traders claiming that goods had been exported etc. when in fact they had found their way onto the home market. The insistence on proper documentation for these transactions ensures that the revenue is safeguarded.

(b)   Prohibitions and restrictions
The regulations regarding prohibitions and restrictions change periodically. This involves export licences, the Intervention Board for Agricultural Produce (IBAP) and prohibitions on the exportation of certain animals and drugs.

(c)   Trade statistics
The introduction of the Intrastat system has important implications for the publication of trade statistics (see p. 91).

6.5 CUSTOMS HANDLING OF IMPORT AND EXPORT FREIGHT (CHIEF)

CHIEF is the new entry processing computer system introduced in November 1992 by HM Customs to replace the Departmental Entry Processing System (DEPS).

The system enables exporters/importers/agents to input into the system electronically. It covers pre-shipment and post-shipment information; full pre-shipment declaration; low value pre-shipment advice; non-statistical pre-shipment advice; abbreviated entry (AE) pre-shipment messages and completed entries; and simplified clearance procedure (SCP) post-shipment declaration (prior approval required). When a pre-shipment advice or pre-shipment declaration is input to CHIEF a paper advice or declaration (on plain paper or preprinted but conforming to the SAD) must also be provided to the place where the goods are being declared for export.

The abbreviated entry
The abbreviated entry (AE) facility will allow the build-up of an electronic entry on CHIEF. The AE is a two-part entry consisting of the input of a pre-shipment message and the build-up of information leading to the input of the completed entry (see p. 98).

The AE will require minimal information. In electronic data interchange (EDI) transactions (see Chapter 20) the user will be able to use the local system (e.g. a PC package) to build up the complete AE entry before submitting it to CHIEF. Using Human Computer Interface (HCI) on the completed entry that cannot be completed it may be stored until final details are available to the declarant.

Both the pre-shipment message and the completed entry must be input to CHIEF. The information required for the pre-shipment message must be input and the hard copy produced to customs at the place of export before the goods are shipped. The completed entry must be input no later than 14 days after shipment from the UK.

The AE cannot be used for goods which are dutiable or restricted, e.g. goods which are exported from bonded warehouses or which are subject to export or specific licensing requirements.

6.6 CUSTOMS RELIEFS

Inward processing relief

A range of duty reliefs is available for goods imported into the UK the availability of which is dependent on the goods being re-exported under control of customs authorities. An example is the inward processing relief (IPR) whereby the goods may be processed or assembled in a componentized basis and subsequently re-exported. The customs regulations and procedures are stringent and adequate documentation must be provided to substantiate the imported merchandise. An increasing number of goods are now being treated in this way as global manufacturing strategies change.

Outward processing relief and standard exchange relief

Outward processing relief (OPR) permits partial or total relief from duty on goods that are exported for processing and subsequently re-imported. The regulations and procedures laid down by Customs are stringent and prior arrangements must be made with them. Another relief system is the standard exchange relief (SER). This permits duty relief on items imported as replacements.

Returned goods relief

Another form of customs relief is the returned goods relief. It arises when goods which are exported for other purposes can also be relieved of duty if re-imported under the returned goods relief provisions, provided the re-importation takes place within three years of export (or within an extended time limit negotiated with the Customs authorities), and the goods have not undergone any process whilst outside the EU other than running repairs.

6.7 ATA CARNETS

Carnets are permits which allow goods to be temporarily exported without payment of duty or VAT on entry to the country or countries visited or on the re-importation of the goods into the country of original export. They also remove the need for the normal customs documentation. It covers samples and goods for exhibition and professional equipment only and is issued, under international agreements, by Chambers of Commerce. Security for duty may be required before an ATA carnet is issued at a rate varying according to the goods covered and the countries to be visited.

6.8 TIR CARNETS

The UK is a party to the Customs Convention on the International Transport of Goods under Cover of TIR carnets (TIR Conventions 1959 and 1975) which is designed to facilitate the international transportation of goods on road vehicles by simplifying customs requirements. It covers road vehicles, trailers, semi-trailers and containers – road or rail borne, including those of demountable body type.

The association which issues the TIR carnet guarantees the duty payable on the goods carried under cover of the carnet. The TIR carnets in the UK are issued by the Freight Transport Association on behalf of their members. Road vehicles and containers must be approved by a competent authority before they may be used for the transport of goods under cover of a TIR carnet. The competent authority must be satisfied that the vehicles or containers comply with the technical annexes to the Convention before such approval will be granted. On all TIR journeys, approved vehicles must have with them a valid certificate of approval issued by a competent authority, such as the Department of Transport, the Bureau Veritas, the American Bureau of Shipping, etc.

A TIR carnet gives no right to operate; it is purely a customs facility which enables goods in customs-sealed vehicles and customs-sealed containers to transit intermediate countries with the minimum of customs formalities. TIR carnets cannot be used for journeys wholly within the territory of the EU. TIR carnets, however, continue to be used for journeys which start and finish outside the EU.

Countries which are party to the Convention include Afghanistan, Albania, Australia, Belgium, Bulgaria, Canada, the Czech Republic, Denmark, Finland, France, Germany, Greece, Hungary, Iran, Ireland (Republic of), Israel, Italy, Japan, Jordan, Liechtenstein, Luxembourg, Morocco, the Netherlands, Norway, Poland, Portugal, Romania, Slovakia, Spain, Sweden, Switzerland, Turkey, the United State of America, the United Kingdom and Yugoslavia.

6.9 CUSTOMS WAREHOUSING AND FREE ZONES

Customs warehousing allows imported goods to be stored free of duty and VAT. Entering goods to a customs warehouse prior to export can also provide benefits to the exporter. Such entry often satisfies the conditions to discharge a relief such as IPR, and could allow the exporter to build up sufficient goods to consolidate into an economic consignment to a particular customer without the risk of exceeding any time limit by keeping them in free circulation.

Those countries with which the EU has negotiated preferential trading terms include Iceland, Norway, Liechtenstein, Switzerland – together with the Mediterranean countries of Cyprus, Israel and Malta.

6.10 LOCAL EXPORT CONTROL

Local export control (LEC) allows approved exporters who regularly ship goods as unit loads e.g. in secure containers or vehicles, in specialized aircraft containers, on pallets, on open roll-on/roll-off vehicles or on rail ferry wagons, to have their goods cleared for exportation at their own premises provided that certain specified conditions are satisfied. A prescribed volume of traffic must be achieved before approval is given and the exporter must give advance notice of intended packing.

6.11 IMPORTATION AND EXPORTATION OF GOODS

Commercial importations

Customs procedures for commercial importations vary according to the type of traffic involved but the principles remain broadly the same:

(a) goods may be imported legally only through places approved by customs;

(b) ships and aircraft must lodge a report, including a cargo list, with customs on arrival (usually before unloading begins);

(c) all goods must be properly 'entered' and any duty (or levies on goods subject to the Common Agricultural Policy (CAP)) and other charges due must normally be paid before they are released from customs control; this usually takes place at a wharf or aiport of importation but the requirements can be completed at inland clearance depots or at the importer's premises under a local import clearance scheme (see p. 99);

(d) customs officers have the right to examine all goods to confirm that they correspond with the 'entry' made for them.

Import entry procedure

The importer is responsible for preparing an 'entry' for all the goods he is importing. The 'entry' is a document on which he declares the description, value, quantity, rate of duty and various other details about the goods. When presented to customs it is normally accompanied by supporting documents such as copies of commercial invoices and packing lists to provide evidence of the nature and value of the goods, but frequently also by an official document to prove their status for duty purposes; this involves the appropriate customs declaration document. In the case of goods which may be imported only under a licence issued by a government department (e.g. the Department of Trade and Industry), the licence must normally accompany the entry. Detailed descriptions of goods for duty and statistical purposes necessary for the preparation of an entry are shown in HM Customs Tariff published by HM Stationery office (see p. 92). The importer or his agent presents the completed entry with its supporting documents to the appropriate customs office. In all UK seaports the system is fully computerized and many major importers and agents have on-line access to the customs network CHIEF (see p. 94). A large number use the simplified procedure for goods transported by sea. It is checked for accuracy and any duties or other charges due are then paid, or deferred under special arrangements (see item 1. below).

A number of consignments are selected for examination; in these cases it is the responsibility of the importer or his agent to produce the goods for examination as required by the officer. Much of the information given on the entry is also used in compiling the overseas trade statistics.

Variations in entry procedure include the following:

1. *Suspension of duty and reliefs.* There are procedures for suspending the payment of duty or for relieving goods of duty provided that certain conditions are met and, usually, that the goods remain under customs control. One example is where goods are moved to an approved warehouse; other examples include goods imported under a variety of temporary importation reliefs, and goods imported by certain traders to undergo an authorized process before being re-exported. Goods being transhipped (i.e. imported for re-export either from the port of importation or from another port) are also relieved of duty.

2. *Local import control (LIC).* Traders who regularly import repetitive traffic and who can satisfy specific conditions may make entry of their goods locally and have them cleared at their premises. Many such traders operate under the computerized CHIEF customs arrangements (see p. 94).

3. *Period entry (imports).* Traders who use computers for stock control and accounting purposes and whose import trade is repetitive and on a large scale may apply to submit a simplified entry at the time of import supplemented by periodic schedules in a computer medium such as magnetic tape.

4. *Sea traffic.* The system of direct trader input has also been introduced at all seaports and inland clearance depots.

5. *Postal consignments.* Goods imported by post are subject to the same duties, taxes, prohibitions and restrictions as other imports. Postal packages enter the country through postal depots where they are subject to customs scrutiny. In most cases any charges due are assessed on the basis of the customs declaration by the sender and/or examination and are collected by the postman when he delivers the package.

6. *Inward processing relief.* See p. 95.

7. *Free zones*. HM Customs and Excise is also responsible for the control and administration of the free zones which have been set up at a number of ports and airports. A free zone is an enclosed area into which goods may be moved without payment of customs duty and similar import charges, including value added tax charged at importation. Such charges become payable only if goods are brought out of the zone into the UK market or are consumed within the zone. In addition, duty (but not VAT) is payable if goods are processed other than for export outside the EU.

Export entry procedure

Goods may be exported only through approved wharves, airports, inland clearance depots, etc. Exporters must declare their goods for export and these declarations are examined by customs to check that all details required are included. The export declarations are used both for control purposes and for the compilation of external trade statistics. Regular exporters may register to use a simplified clearance procedure under which a commercial document may be presented at the time of exportation and the entry submitted retrospectively. For entries submitted retrospectively there is a similar system to that available at import whereby traders are able to input their entries electronically through CHIEF (see p. 94).

Entries required to be received before exportation are sent to the officer at the place of loading who is responsible for ensuring that the goods are actually exported and that reliefs have been claimed correctly or that levies due have been properly declared. Finally, the shipping company (or airline) submits a manifest detailing all the cargo loaded.

Local export control is an option (see p. 97).

Period entry (exports) enables appropriate traders to submit periodic schedules of their exports instead of individual export declarations for each consignment.

Report (or entering in) and inward clearance

On arrival of a ship in a UK port from a place outside the UK, it is necessary for the vessel to be 'entered in' with HM Customs in accordance with the provisions found in ss 35 and 64 of the

Customs & Excise Management Act 1979. This is the responsibility of the Master or his appointed agent who must report to the customs house or other designated place.

The report must embrace the following:

(a) *Form C 13 – Master declaration.* This gives general information about the ship, the voyage, and details of ships stores including duty free stores. It must be signed by the Master.

(b) *Form C 142 – Crew declaration.* This form gives details of goods owned by crew members including the ship's Master for presentation and clearance by customs. It will have regard to prohibited and restricted goods.

(c) *A declaration of cargo.* A complete declaration of cargo on board the vessel. It can be undertaken in four ways as under:

    (i) On a cargo manifest giving details of each consignment and embracing the following:

        – the maritime transport document reference, e.g. the bill of lading number;

        – the container identification/vehicle registration number;

        – the number, kind, marks and numbers of the packages;

        – the description and gross weight/volume of the goods;

        – the port or place where the goods were loaded on to the ship;

        – the original port or place of shipment for goods on a through maritime transport document.

    (ii) If there is no manifest or other suitable document, customs will accept a cargo declaration on the model form produced by the International Maritime Organization.

    (iii) If the vessel is carrying a single commodity bulk cargo, details can be given in box 13 of form C 13 of the Master declaration.

    (iv) Most UK ports now operate a computerized inventory control system termed Direct Trader Input, in which case the Master must endorse form C 13 in box 13 that the cargo declaration will be undertaken in this manner.

(d) *Form SUR 238.* Declaration of deck tonnage if applicable.

(e) *PAS 15 (arrival).* Passenger return – if applicable.

The customs officer may visit the vessel on arrival in which case the report will be submitted to him/her. If such a visit does not take place, the report must be submitted not later than 3 hours after the vessel has reached its place of loading or unloading, or 24 hours after arrival within port limits.

Customs require to have details of passengers disembarking and crew members being paid off. Passengers must not be allowed ashore until they have been cleared by an immigration officer or under local arrangements approved by an immigration officer. The latter would include passenger ports where immigration procedures are undertaken ashore. All relevant immigration documents must be completed.

When the foregoing has been completed, the vessel may commence discharge and/or loading.

Entry outwards and outward clearance

For a vessel sailing outwards the following procedure applies.

The Master or his appointed agent must report to the customs house or other designated place and present the following:

(a) *Form C 13* – Master's declaration detailing cargo on board the vessel. Additionally customs require the following – if applicable.

(i) The cargo declaration copy – form C 13 which was submitted at the time of ship's arrival under inward clearance. Customs require to have details of any imported goods remaining on board for export.

(ii) Details of any clearance given previously at a UK port for the same voyage.

(b) *Form SUR 238* – declaration of deck cargo tonnage if applicable.

(c) *PAS 15 (Departure)* – passenger return if applicable.

Additionally customs will check the following ship's papers to confirm they are valid and correct:

(a) *International load line certificate* – required by any vessel engaged on international voyages (see pp. 11–13, 25). It complies with the International Convention on Load Lines 1966.

(b) *Cargo ship safety construction certificate* – required under the International Convention for Safety of Life at Sea (SOLAS) 1974 (see pp. 25–6).

(c) *Cargo ship safety equipment certificate* – required under SOLAS (see p. 26). This document is mandatory except for ships in possession of a cargo ship safety construction certificate (see (b) above).

(d) *Passenger ship safety certificate* – required for any passenger ship carrying more than twelve passengers engaged in international waters (see p. 26).

(e) *Ship's register or certificate of registry.*

(f) *Lights certificate* – to confirm any light dues which fall for payment have been paid.

When all these formalities have been completed the ship may sail on her voyage.

6.12 SHIP'S PAPERS

UK registered ships, where so required, should carry the following documents, including those required by international regulations, and it is obligatory for the Master to produce them to any person who has authority to inspect them.

1. Charter party or bills of lading.
2. Cargo manifest. This contains an inventory of cargo carried on board the vessel giving details of cargo description, consignee/consignor, destination port, container number, etc. The data are despatched by telex/airmail/fax/e-mail to the ship/port agent by the shipowner to give details to port authority importers, customs,etc. It enables the agent to prepare for the ship's arrival.
3. List of dutiable stores.
4. Load line certificate or load line exemption certificate.
5. Cargo ship safety equipment construction certificate ship licence (if less than 500 tons gross).
6. Safety certificate.
7. Passenger certificate (if a passenger ship), or cargo ship safety radio certificate or exemption certificate (if 300 tons or more).
8. Ship's register or certificate of registry. This is the ship's official certificate of registration and is issued by the authorities of the country in which the ship is registered. It gives the registration number, name of vessel, port of registry, details of the ship and

particulars of ownership. The UK body responsible is called the Registry of Shipping and Seamen (RSS) and is based in Cardiff. Legislation is found in the Merchant Shipping (Registration etc.) Act 1993.

9. Official log.

10. Radio log book if required.

11. De-ratting certificate in accordance with Regulation 19 of the Public Health (Ships) Regulations 1970.

12. Deck log book.

13. Oil record book.

14. Crew list.

All these documents have been described elsewhere in this book, with the exception of the official log. This is in reality the ship's diary, and is required to be compiled in a form laid down by the Department of Transport. Entries found in the official log include any births, deaths and marriages; a record of the crew's conduct, wages and any fines; any unusual incident or mishap to the ship (such as going to the aid of another vessel in distress); fire in the engine room; adverse weather conditions causing the ship to reduce speed or even shelter in an estuary; and so on. All entries in the log book are admissible as evidence in a court of law. Furthermore, all entries recorded must be made as soon as practicable after the actual incident and signed by the Master and by a senior member of the ship's crew on duty at the time of the occurrence. Apart from the official log, ships also keep deck, engine and radio logs.

6.13 SHIP'S PROTEST

The Master, on arrival at the port, may decide to make a protest before a consul or notary public, declaring that he and his officers have exercised all reasonable care and skill during the voyage to avoid damage to ship and cargo, and that any actual loss is due to extraordinary circumstances beyond their control. Protest is a formality, but in cases where damage or loss has occurred, extending protest is made within six months of noting, and sworn declaration may be supported by members of the ship's crew. In the UK there is no legal necessity to note protest, but noting of protest assists the defence against claims by consignees. In other countries protest is necessary before certain legal remedies can be obtained.

In the event of any casualty to the ship, the Master and/or his officers would be required to give depositions under oath before a receiver of wrecks, who is a senior customs officer.

CHAPTER 7

Maritime canals and inland waterways

7.1 INTRODUCTION

The geographical position and economic importance of artificial waterways must be considered by all concerned in the shipping industry. In fact it is a subject of growing importance in the shipping industry with the development of multi-modalism.

The real economic importance of maritime international canals has, however, changed in recent years, due in the main to the introduction of larger capacity vessels with deeper draught, such as the mammoth oil tankers and container ships. Maritime canals must therefore keep pace with new tonnage developments, otherwise ships will follow alternative routes due to the sheer inability of the canal to accommodate their draught, beam or length. One must therefore judge individual maritime canals in terms of their economic importance, seen in the light of their physical ability to accept modern tonnage currently or potentially available such as in the Suez and Panama Canals.

A study of the international trade patterns and the disposition of the world maritime fleet (see pp. 2–6) will confirm radical changes in the last decade. The growing development of containerization/multi-modalism and the decline of traditional tramp cargoes such as grain and coal have opened up new opportunities for the enterprising international entrepreneur. It has placed more emphasis on the shipper's needs and moved away from the seaport-to-seaport operation, encouraging instead the provision of pre-shipment and post-shipment capabilities overland. This facilitates the development of intermodalism and improved transit times. It has contributed to the decline of the liner conference system (see pp. 203–9) and witnessed the emergence of round-the-world services, and the decline of the fleets of the developed countries and the emergence of those of Taiwan, South Korea, China, Singapore and Hong Kong – all Far East based and focused.

A glance at a map will indicate the vital importance of the Suez Canal not only to those countries with a Mediterranean coastline, or bordering on the Arabian Sea, but also to the countries of North West Europe – the UK, Holland and Germany – which have extensive and long-established commercial connections with countries of the Far East.

Other considerations in an owner's mind when routing his vessel are the price and availability of fuel at the alternative bunkering ports, and the complexities of the International Loadline Regulations (varying with the time of year) which limit the amount of both freight-earning cargo and bunkers. With regard to fuel cost, which now forms a substantial portion of the daily operating expense of a vessel, the bunker savings realized by choosing the canal route will have a major bearing on the evaluation.

A liner operator has the same basic problem of routing to face, but additional consideration has to be given to the amount of cargo likely to be shipped to and from the intermediate ports of call on the alternative routes. Thus a liner company in the Australian trades can participate also in trade with Egypt, the Red Sea, and Colombo if their ships proceed via Suez. Otherwise, if they sail via South Africa they can also carry cargo between such ports and Australia. Of course, the schedule of liner services is complicated by the fluctuations in cargo offerings and the profitability to those operators concerned.

7.2 EUROPEAN INLAND WATERWAYS

Inland waterway networks play a major role in the economic development of Europe. The Maritime Euro Region is focused particularly on the Ports of Rotterdam, Hamburg, Antwerp and Dunkerque and their connecting inland waterway systems which penetrate southwards. Such ports have up to 30% of their transhipment cargoes conveyed on the inland waterway network and the market is fast growing. It extends not only to bulk commodities, but also to an increasing volume of containerized goods and vehicular merchandise.

A major development emerged in 1992 with the opening of the Rhine–Main–Danube (RMD) canal which is predicted to carry up to 20 million tonnes annually by the year 2000. Its length is 3500 km between the North Sea and the Black Sea and serves nine East and West European countries. The RMD route runs through Holland and Germany to Mainz and up the Main to Bamberg, the Northern Canal entrance. On the other side of the Franconian Jura, the canal joins the Danube at Kelheim. That river flows through Austria, clips the former Czechoslovakia and continues south through Hungary and former Yugoslavia. Turning east again, it forms the border between Bulgaria and Romania before turning north to touch in Romania, the southern tip of the CIS and finally empties itself into the Black Sea.

One of the services which commenced with the opening of the RMD was the Danube Container Service (DCS) between Rotterdam and Vienna. Ports of call include Frankfurt, Main, Regensburg, Linz and Krems. There is a sailing every Friday from all the terminals in Rotterdam and the transit time to Vienna is about nine days. The containers are stacked two high and the vessel capacity ranges from 50 to 70 TEUs.

Further examples of RMD traffic include iron ore from Rotterdam to Linz and Krems. Other cargoes include bricks, animal feed and fertilizer. Nepa Shipping BV transport aluminium, sugar and structures from Rotterdam to Budapest and Mohacs, while the return cargoes are agricultural products, sunflower seeds, canary grass and dried peas.

Indivisible loads are also conveyed on the RMD together with heavy and bulky loads.

Rotterdam port is a focal point in the extensive network of inland waterway services and features strongly in the 'just in time' strategy adopted by the shippers who use it. The area is served by 30 terminals in the Rhine. Apart from cost savings achieved through the large-scale barge operation, the additional logistics benefits are paramount. These include flexibility of services and the close proximity of the terminals to the shipper's premises.

The barge network acts as a feeder service to the ports of Rotterdam, Antwerp and Amsterdam. An example is the container terminal of Nijmegen on the River Waal and the barge terminal at Born on the River Maas between Maastricht and Roermond. At Born the catchment area extends beyond the borders of South Lumburg and includes container movements from the neighbouring industrial areas of Germany, Belgium and the more distant markets of Luxembourg. The containers are moved by barge in units of four operated by a push boat and generate an overall capacity of 360 TEUs.

A container movement which has grown considerably in the lower region of the Rhine is operated by the consortium Haeger & Schmidt, Haniel Reederei and Rhine-container. Each vessel has a capacity of 156 TEUs and there are 19 sailings per week between Rotterdam and Duisburg. The sailings run from Rotterdam and Antwerp to Nijmegen, Emmerich, Duisburg, Neuss, Stuizeberg, Dusseldorf, Cologne and Leverkusen.

7.3 THE SUEZ CANAL AUTHORITY

The Suez Canal links the Mediterranean Sea to the Red Sea and was opened for international navigation in 1869. The Suez Canal is a level canal though the height of the tide differs slightly being 50 cm in the north and 2 m in the south. Overall the canal's length is 195 km from Port Said to Ismailia to Port Tewfik. The maximum permitted draught of ships is 53 feet. It is the longest canal without locks in the world and is navigable both day and night. The canal is run in a convoy system to transit at a fixed speed and a fixed separation distance between two passing ships. Three convoys pass through the canal daily, two southbound and one northbound. Pilotage is compulsory and speed limits vary from 13 to 14 km per hour according to the category and tonnage of ships. It takes a ship 12 to 16 hours to transit the canal permitting about 76 ships per day to pass through. The width of the canal has been doubled in four areas which are passing loops. These are located at Port Said bypass, Ballah bypass, Timsah bypass and finally Deversoir bypass and the Bitter Lanes area. The canal operates an electronic vessel traffic management system using a radar network to ensure safety of transit for vessels. There are eleven signal stations situated on the western bank of the canal, each of which is about 10 km apart. These offices are to control traffic and facilitate pilotage operations. The maximum sized vessel able to go through the Canal is called a 'Suezmax'.

The geographical position of the Suez Canal has made it the shortest navigable route between the East and West as compared with the route round the Cape of Good Hope. It shortens the

Table 7.1 Voyage reductions via the Suez Canal (in miles)

From	To	Round Africa	Through canal	Difference
Rotterdam (North West Europe)	Bombay (India)	10 850	6 337	4 513
Piraeus (Greece)	Jeddah (Red Sea)	11 410	1 320	10 090
New York (USA)	Singapore	12 430	10 169	2 261

distance between countries situated to the north of the canal and those situated to the south, thus offering considerable savings in operating costs, voyage time and bunkers. Details of the distance variations are given in Table 7.1.

Traffic continues to increase annually and in 1993 17 317 vessels passed through the canal, an increase of 4.1% over 1992. Total net tonnage increased to 316.6 million tons, an increase of 7.2%. Tankers totalled 137.9 million tons, bulk carriers 66.7 million tons, container ships 101 million tons and car carriers 31 million tons. A total of 66 passenger ships daily passed through the canal in 1993. Overall 12% of vessels were Liberian, 11% Panamanian and 8% Greek.

Tables 7.2 and 7.3 provide details of the areas to the north and south from which goods were exported or imported and passed through the canal in 1993. From the top ten countries to the north, goods amounting to 162 343 000 tons, representing 54.8% of the total goods passing through from that area, were distributed as shown in Table 7.4. From the top ten countries to the south, goods amounting to 163 992 000 tons, representing 55.3% of the total passing through from that area, were distributed as in Table 7.5.

The Suez Canal Authority has a continuous modernization plan which currently includes increasing the west cross-section bringing it up to a maximum draught of 56 feet instead of 53 feet. This will permit vessels of 180 000 dwt fully loaded to transit the canal. Currently the limit is 150 000 dwt. Larger and more powerful tugboats for escort, towage and fire- and pollution-fighting operations will be introduced. Finally, a major navigation control project is underway providing radar coverage for the whole canal

Table 7.2 Goods from areas north of the canal – 1993

Region	Quantity (000 tons)	%
North and West Europe and UK ports	116 383	39.2
Baltic Sea ports	7 746	2.6
North Mediterranean ports	52 754	17.8
East and South East Mediterranean ports	40 693	13.7
West and South West Mediterranean ports	30 900	10.4
Black Sea ports	26 634	9.0
American ports	17 719	5.9
Other areas	4 085	1.4
Total	296 914	100.0

Table 7.3 Goods from areas south of the canal – 1993

Region	Quantity (000 tons)	%
Red Sea ports	62 714	21.1
East African ports and Aden	3 700	1.2
India, Pakistan, Burma and Sri Lanka ports	22 858	7.7
Arabian Gulf ports	41 433	14.0
South East Asia ports and Sunda Islands	37 023	12.5
Far East ports	115 806	39.0
Australian ports	13 315	4.5
Other areas	65	—
Total	296 914	100.0

and INMARSAT communication and other facilities to ensure the continuing safe transit of ships through the canal.

7.4 THE PANAMA CANAL

The Panama Canal was opened in August 1914 and is 50 miles long from deep water in the Atlantic to deep water in the Pacific. It runs

Table 7.4 Distribution of goods from north of the canal – 1993

Country	Quantity (000 tons)	Proportion to the total (%)
1. Turkey	32 146	10.8
2. Italy	30 165	10.2
3. Russia	15 444	5.2
4. USA	15 325	5.2
5. Holland	14 418	4.9
6. Greece	12 396	4.2
7. France	11 690	3.9
8. Belgium	11 274	3.8
9. Spain	11 215	3.8
10. Morocco	8 270	2.8
Total	162 343	54.8

Table 7.5 Distribution of goods from south of the canal – 1993

Country	Quantity (000 tons)	Proportion to the total (%)
1. Saudi Arabia	49 124	16.5
2. China	20 069	6.8
3. Iran	19 153	6.5
4. India	17 727	6.0
5. Singapore	13 806	4.6
6. Australia	9 964	3.4
7. A.R.E.	9 830	3.3
8. Thailand	8 917	3.0
9. Indonesia	8 599	2.9
10. Malaysia	6 803	2.3
Total	163 992	55.3

from northwest to southeast with the Atlantic entrance being 38.5 miles north and 27 miles west of the Pacific entrance. It is open 24 hours per day throughout the year and an average vessel takes about 8 to 20 hours passage time out of a total of 24 hours in canal waters. In 1993 over 12 000 ocean going vessels passed through the canal conveying 158 million long tons of cargo. The maximum sized vessel able to go through the canal is called a Panamax.

The canal linking the Atlantic and Pacific Oceans is a relatively inexpensive passageway and has greatly influenced world trade patterns, spurred growth in developed countries and has been the primary impetus for economic expansion in many remote parts of the world. For example, a vessel laden with coal sailing from the east coast of the United States to Japan via the Panama Canal saves about 3000 miles versus the shortest alternative all water route, and for a vessel laden with bananas sailing from Ecuador to Europe the distance saved is about 5000 miles.

The Panama Canal serves a number of important world trades, including East Coast US–Asia; Europe–West Coast US/Canada; East Coast US–West Coast South America; Europe–West Coast South America; and East Coast US–West Coast Central America. Cargo moving on these routes includes important shipments of grain, coal, phosphates, containerized cargo, chemicals and petroleum products from the US to Asia; manufactures of iron and steel, automobiles, and containerized cargo from Asia to the US; lumber and products, coal and petroleum coke from the US and Canada to Europe; and containerized cargo and manufactures of iron and steel from Europe to North America. Leading exports from West Coast South America to the US consisted of petroleum and petroleum products, refrigerated foods, ores and metals, minerals and agricultural commodities. Important commodities from Europe destined for West Coast South America included containerized cargo and fertilizers. The principal cargo moving from the US to West Coast Central America consisted of grain, petroleum and products, and phosphates, and from Central America to the US agricultural products and minerals.

By far most of the traffic through the canal moves between the east coast of the United States and the Far East, while movements between Europe and the West Coast of the United States and Canada comprise the second major trade route at the waterway.

Improvements to operational procedures have also been instituted to increase the efficiency and safety of the canal. A transit reservation system allows customers to schedule a guaranteed day of canal transit for a nominal fee; major upgrading of the computerized traffic management system provides for more controlled movement of vessels through the canal; vessel accident investigation procedures have been simplified; state-of-the-art weather monitoring and reservoir management equipment provide accurate current data on weather conditions, lake levels and watershed inflows; and channel improvement projects provide increased manoeuvrability, navigation safety and visibility in the canal channel.

In 1992 the scheme to introduce two-way passage of the Gaillard Cut totalling eight miles commenced and when completed will provide virtually unrestricted two-way passage of all vessels throughout the waterway.

In 1994 the Panama Canal introduced a new tonnage measurement system to comply with the 1969 International Convention on Tonnage Measurement of Ships (see pp. 16–20).

7.5 THE ECONOMIC EFFECT OF CANALS AND THE LEVEL OF DUES CHARGED – THE ST LAWRENCE SEAWAY

A good example of the economic effect a canal may impose on a region is the St Lawrence Seaway. Opened in 1959, the St Lawrence Seaway is formed by a natural waterway via the St Lawrence River, the Great Lakes and their connecting channels, stretching more than 3700 km from the Atlantic Ocean to the heartland of North America. Overall there are fifteen twin locks accommodating vessels of a beam of 23.8 m and length of 225.5 m. It is an international waterway thus serving the industrial and agricultural heartland of North America.

The St Lawrence Seaway, in opening the mid-continent's inland lakes to ocean traffic, added an important new route to the world's established trading patterns. The exposure of inland cities to the major seaports of the world has contributed to increased efficiency and convenience, eliminating in many cases the necessity for cargo transhipment.

Prior to the completion of the seaway, export and import commodities flowing between the continental interior and the nations of the world had to be transported by a combined water–land route involving both handling and re-handling procedures en route to various destinations. Now, vessels plying this route can move a tonne of bulk cargo from Chicago to Liverpool for less cost than the overland freight charges to East Coast transhipment ports. Machines, tools, automobiles and a host of other goods are now shipped directly between the mid-continent and trading destinations in Europe and elsewhere – requiring, in most cases, only one loading from departure point to destination and offering important savings in shipping costs.

In addition to those with Europe, the mid-continent is building strong trading links with other continents. Each year more ships are plying their way to Africa, South America, Australia and Asia. Surprisingly, there is often a saving in distance to even these far-off areas of the world. Here again, significant cost savings make this traffic attractive to both shipper and receiver.

Some 80% of the seaway traffic is made up of bulk cargoes such as grain, iron ore, coal, chemicals and oil. The residue is manufactured goods much of which is containerized. The seaway is closed between late December and early April due to the cold winters.

The St Lawrence Seaway commercial strategy in 1995 was to offer an incentive toll programme in three areas as detailed below.

(a) New business discounts

Qualifying cargo will receive an immediate cargo toll discount of 50%. An imported or exported commodity can qualify if it has not moved between one of five geographic regions within the seaway system and a particular country in quantities totalling 5% or more of the total traffic between the two locations based on seaway statistics for the prior three seaway navigation seasons. The five geographic regions are: the Gulf of St Lawrence to St Lambert Lock at Montreal; St Lambert Lock to Cape Vincent on the St Lawrence River, Lake Ontario and the Welland Canal; Lake Erie, Lake Huron and connecting waters; Lake Michigan; and Lake Superior and St Mary's River. A minimum of 1000 tonnes per transit of the specified commodity is required.

Example: A shipment of 26 000 tonnes of bulk cargo transiting the entire seaway that qualified for a new business discount would save $17 875.

(b)   Volume rebates

Shippers of downbound cargo (cargo moving out of the system) or receivers of upbound cargo (cargo moving into the system) will be eligible for a 50% cargo toll rebate for a commodity if they ship or receive that commodity in an amount that exceeds by 25 000 tonnes their own highest annual tonnage for the prior three years.

Example: If a shipper or receiver moved grain through the seaway in a quantity that exceeded by 25 000 tonnes the party's highest annual seaway tonnage of the prior three years, the party would receive a 50% rebate on cargo tolls paid for each tonne over its previous high. If the party exceeded the tonnage by 1 million tonnes, the rebate for using the Seaway System would be $530 000 (1 000 000 × $1.06 × 50%).

(c)   Alternative laker use discount

General or containerized cargo shipped aboard a bulk laker vessel will pay the lower grain cargo toll rate if the Seaway Authority is given a written notification prior to vessel transit. The cargo toll reduction for a complete transit of the seaway is a near 65% saving on general cargo and a 25% saving for containerized cargo.

Example: 12 000 tonnes of general cargo moved in a US or Canadian bulk laker would ordinarily be charged $2.88 per tonne – for a total of $34 560. Under this programme, the same shipments would qualify for the grain toll of $1.06 – a saving of $21 840.

7.6 THE INFLUENCE OF CANALS ON SHIP DESIGN

The construction of artificial waterways, and any necessary locks, is very costly and therefore the size of ships which can use them is often restricted. Bearing such limitations in mind, the ship designer therefore limits the dimensions of the vessels so that they are able to navigate the particular waterways likely to be used. Such limitations affect the draught in the case of many canals, and length and beam in respect of locks, while, to deal with overhead obstructions, retractable top masts and removable funnel tops may be needed.

To get the longest possible sized vessel through various locks the designer uses all his skill, sometimes resulting in the compromise of vessels with inferior sea-keeping qualities and added cost per deadweight tonne.

Canal authorities charge their dues on the tonnage of the vessels using their waterways; major canals such as Suez and Panama have their own system of tonnage measurement.

The development in recent years of inland waterways in certain European countries has fostered the development of major ports such as Antwerp, Rotterdam, Hamburg, Dunkerque and Calais.

7.7 CANAL AREAS AS POINTS OF ECONOMIC GROWTH

Not all ships pass directly through canals; the ports at their entrances become important transhipment ports through the regular services traversing the waterway. Other activities concerned with shipping such as bunkering also develop. Such areas offer flat land with excellent port facilities for private quays and a position on the ocean trade routes; all these are very important factors in the location of modern large-scale industry.

This final aspect is observed more in those artificial waterways as yet hardly mentioned – those which lead to an important trade centre or industrial area. Ports like Dunkerque and Rotterdam can only be reached by ocean vessels through their own canals, and it is on the banks of these that modern industrial installations are constructed, with all the benefits arising from deep water quays on the actual site. Refineries, iron and steel works, paper mills and chemical installations all come into this category.

7.8 INLAND WATERWAYS

Shipping is becoming more integrated with inland waterways as the concept of the combined transport system develops. The provision of LASH, BACO and SEABEE liner concepts are facilitating such developments, primarily in African markets. Other types of tonnage exploiting the combined transport system include containers, Combi carriers, train ferries and Ro/Ro vessels. Such ships rely primarily on rail and road as a distributor.

In considering inland waterways one must give particular emphasis to the role they play in many less developed and developing countries. The infrastructure in such countries tends to be inadequate in many areas especially in the area of transportation/distribution to and from the ports. Inland waterway barge distribution acting as a port feeder service is long established in many developing and less developed countries. Examples are found in the markets of Africa, the sub-continent and the Far East and in the ports of Bangkok, Klang and Dar-es-Salaam which permit overside loading thereby speeding up the turn-round of vessels.

Hence lighterage remains an important distributor especially of primary products and other non-containerized cargoes. It is economical and aids the quicker port turn-round of vessels. Moreover, it reduces the level of congestion in the port/quay.

7.9 THE CHANNEL TUNNEL (EURO TUNNEL)

In 1994 the Euro Tunnel opened linking the British rail network with the European rail system which extends to 150 000 miles. The Euro Tunnel is a 31-mile subterranean rail tunnel between Folkestone (UK) and Frèthun near Calais (France). It is built below the seabed in the English Channel and comprises three tunnels, two of which are 7.6 m diameter to convey trains and one of 3.3 m which is a service tunnel. Terminals with road and rail access are provided at both portals (Ashford and Calais).

7.10 THE SCANLINK PROJECTS

Finally the Oresund fixed transport link between Denmark and Sweden is planned for completion in the year 2000. It involves a 16 km long tunnel and bridge link between Malmo and Copenhagen. Four contracts are involved – a tunnel, two artificial islands and other bridges to link the new structure with the Swedish mainland.

Work on the other Scanlink route, the tunnel and bridge link across Denmark's Store Belt between Zealand and Funen, was well advanced by 1995. Both projects will improve substantially the infrastructure of the Scandinavian markets and have significant economic and social implications.

CHAPTER 8

Services performed by principal shipping organizations

This chapter focuses attention on a wide range of both national and international shipping and trade organizations which exist to facilitate the development of international shipping and promote professionalism at all levels and in all activities. Understandably the number of organizations annually tend to increase and existing ones change their focus to respond to a changing international shipping and trade scene embracing technology, political, economic and commercial factors. Safety remains paramount in the conduct and operation of a maritime fleet and its interface operations. Attention is focused in this chapter on the WTO and former GATT Uruguay round of trade negotiations.

8.1 INTERNATIONAL ASSOCIATION OF CLASSIFICATION SOCIETIES

The International Association of Classification Societies (IACS) is an association representing the world's major classification societies and was founded in London in 1968. Its main objectives are to promote the highest standards in ship safety and the prevention of marine pollution. Over 90% of the world's merchant fleet in terms of tonnage is covered by the standards of IACS' eleven members for hull structure and essential engineering systems which are established, updated, applied and monitored on a continuous basis. IACS works closely with the IMO and with the world's maritime industries and international organizations.

Compliance with the various IMO international conventions on safety is mandatory for the issue of statutory safety certificates by any of the states signatory to the conventions. Without such certificates ships cannot legally operate internationally. Statutory safety certification under these conventions is conditional on a ship's hull structure and essential shipboard engineering systems being satisfactory in all respects, but the only recognized authoritative rules for these are set by the major classification societies.

Compliance with the rules of the major classification societies is therefore the only practical basis for essential statutory certification. To ensure adequate implementation worldwide over one hundred IMO member states have delegated statutory surveys to the IACS member societies.

IACS has held consultative status with the IMO since 1969 and is the only non-governmental organization with such status at the IMO process of formulating developing rules/regulations in consultation with interested parties. These rules, implemented by its member societies, are accepted by the maritime community as the technical standards. In areas where the IMO intends to establish detailed technical and procedural requirements, IACS with its expertise endeavours to ensure that these requirements are easily applicable and as clear and unambiguous as possible.

IMO representatives have routinely attended IACS Council meetings and IACS representatives participate as observers at the meetings of the Assembly of the Maritime Safety Committee, the Marine Environment Protection Committee, and the many subcommittees and working groups of the IMO.

IACS also liaises with international organizations for exchange of views and information on matters of mutual interest. This ensures that the views of industry are taken into consideration in IACS' work. Examples of such organizations are international marine insurers, the International Chamber of Shipping, the Oil Companies, International Marine Forum, the Society of International Gas Tanker and Terminal Operators Ltd, the International Standarization Organization, CIMAC and Intertanko.

The need for unified standards remains paramount and informal steps by classification societies towards unification of specific technical standards began in the mid-1950s. The formation of IACS accelerated progress; the Council has since agreed on a wide range of unified requirements and unified interpretations of international conventions and codes. Typical examples of IACS unified requirements are as follows.

(a) Minimum longitudinal strength standard.
(b) Enhanced hull surveys of oil tankers and bulk carriers.

(c) Landing and guidance information.
(d) Use of steel grades for various hull members.
(e) Hull and machinery steel castings.
(f) Cargo containment on gas tankers.
(g) Prototype testing and test measurements on tank containers.
(h) Inert gas generating installations on vessels carrying oil in bulk.
(i) Fire protection of machinery spaces.
(j) Survey of hatch covers and coamings.
(k) Various requirements on diesel engine and propulsion shafting.

Additionally IACS' work is focused on its working groups/parties and details of their general terms of reference are given below:

(a) To draft unified classification requirements between member societies.
(b) To prepare responses to requests made by the IMO and evaluate unified interpretations of conventions, codes, resolutions and guides.
(c) To identify problems related to the working group's area of activity and propose IACS actions.
(d) To monitor the work of organizations related to the expertise of the working group.

The granting of membership status – or continuation as a member – requires audited compliance with a set of formal requirements and possession of a valid IACS QSCS (certificate of conformity). It is based on the requirements of ISO 9001, the sets of rigorous standards to create and maintain uniformity and consistent quality of members societies' internal operations. It covers classification of ships and offshore installations in respect of design, construction and operation, together with the statutory work carried out on behalf of national maritime administrations. The Society Certificate of Conformity is valid for three years and subject to intermediate audits.

IACS offers an extensive technical advisory service and undertakes research and development. It currently has eleven members and two associate members. Members include the Bureau Veritas, Germanischer Lloyd, Det Norske Veritas, Lloyd's Register of Shipping, Register of Shipping (CIS) and Palski Rejestr Statkow.

Circumstances do arise when a shipowner decides to change/transfer the class of a vessel from one ship registration society to another, such as from the Korean Register of Shipping to Lloyd's Register of Shipping. It arises often through a transfer of ownership of a vessel. Details of the IACS procedure relating to the transfer of class are:

(1) Change of class request.
(2) Exchange of vessel survey status data.
(3) Exchange of statutory reports.
(4) Exchange of calculations.
(5) Report declassing vessel.
(6) Report classing vessel.

The most recent development operative from January 1996 is that a vessels classification certificate will be automatically suspended if an owner fails to carry out the regular five-year survey of his vessels. Moreover, if repair or maintenance work which has been ordered to be completed by a set date is not done, a vessels certificate will also be suspended. Additionally, vessels can only change societies when all overdue work has been completed.

Undoubtedly IACS will continue to make a major impact on raising ship safety and lessening marine pollution.

8.2 INTERNATIONAL ASSOCIATION OF INDEPENDENT TANKER OWNERS

The International Association of Independent Tanker Owners (Intertanko) with headquarters in Oslo is an association of tanker owners from all major maritime nations. Today Intertanko's membership comprises of some 400 members and associate members between them controlling about 2000 tankers – 80% of the world independent tanker fleet. Only independent tanker owners are eligible for full membership but many oil company and government-owned ships are entered as associate members.

Intertanko existed in London since the 1930s but principally traces it history back to its establishment in Oslo in 1970 by a group of independent tanker owners.

Intertanko's Executive Committee consists of a chairman, four vice-chairmen and six executive members who propose policy recommendations to the Council of some 70 full members elected by country of registration. Administratively the association operates with the secretariat in the Oslo office headed by the managing director.

The association is a non-profit organization whose aims are to further the interests of independent tanker owners, to promote a free and competitive tanker market and to work for safety at sea and the protection of the marine environment. The scope and objectives are to promote internationally the interests of its members in matters of general policy, to co-operate with other technical, industrial or commercial interests or bodies on problems of mutual concern to its members and to such interests, and to take part in the deliberations of other international bodies.

Intertanko's vigorous participation in international fora has produced its reputation for effective promotion of the interests of independent owners and the association works closely with the following organizations.

(a) IMO

Intertanko is represented at all relevant IMO meetings. It has stressed the problem of lack of shore reception for oily wastes; promoted further ratification of MARPOL – particularly by the oil exporting countries – to ensure a fair division of liability for oil pollution compensation between cargo and shipowning interests; supported the IMO's Civil Liability Convention and Fund Convention adding compensation for oil spill compensation and promoted the ratification of the latest (1992) Protocols to that Convention; promoted in the IMO the enhanced survey programme for classification societies' special surveys of tankers (adopted at the IMO's meeting at Rapello in 1991); taken an active role in discussions of guidelines for application of the ISM Code; generally promoted the principle of internationally agreed regulation of shipping against the pressure for unilateral national legislation (for example the Oil Pollution Act of 1990 in the USA).

(b) OECD

Intertanko has supported the OECD's measures to reduce subsidies on shipbuilding which has over the years contributed to a surplus of tonnage and thereby continued to depress freight markets. Intertanko's position has underlined its policy of promotion of free competition without government interference.

(c)   The Worldscale Associations

Close links are maintained between Intertanko and the Worldscale Associations. There is a continuos dialogue on both basic principles and updating freight schedules. Intertanko's Port Office provides crucial information for the updating of freight schedules.

(d)   UNCTAD

Based on sound economic facts which taken together reveal the benefits of free competition, Intertanko has firmly resisted past measures in UNCTAD to promote protectionism, cargo sharing in the bulk trades and elimination of open registries. It is an indication of the strength of Intertanko's arguments that UNCTAD's pressure for these measures has largely subsided.

Over the past four years much of Intertanko's activity has involved accommodating the Oil Pollution Act of 1990 in the United States, which Intertanko opposed in principle as undermining the fundamental reasoning of the international compensation regimes, by removing charterer's liability for oil spill compensation. Intertanko has also vigorously shown that the potential unlimited liability which could arise from application of the Oil Pollution Act cannot be sustained by the tanker industry or the insurance industry. However, Intertanko has always taken a constructive role in discussions regarding practical application of rules raised by the US Coast Guard under the OPA and has as a service to its members assisted them in planning and formulating their modes of compliance with these rules. Further, Intertanko has called for action by US authorities to improve the safety and pollution prevention situation in the other contributory agencies to shipping operations, namely ports and terminals, pilotage, vessel traffic, navigation support systems in rivers and confined waters, etc.

Calls in recent years for greater access to information regarding ship quality and conditions have been met by Intertanko which has supported methods of 'opening up' records on tanker inspections and tanker conditions generally. For example, Intertanko has cooperated closely with the oil companies and with the OCIMF in the establishment of their 'Sire' system for exchanging inspection reports, and has worked to promote more thorough and efficiently conducted ship inspections.

Intertanko places much emphasis on the quality of the services that it offers to its members and these include:

(a) *Port Information Office.* Members receive monthly bulletins including the latest data on port conditions and costs. Intertanko's comprehensive service includes prompt action on behalf of members where over-charging is demonstrated, and expert advice on port costs, agency arrangements, freight taxes, etc.

(b) *Freight and Demurrage Information Pool.* This is a service designed to combat the growing problem of late or non-payment by charterers and oil traders. The Pool succeeded in collecting or speeding up settlement of over US$55 million in its first nine years of operation.

(c) *Charter party conditions.* Intertanko has produced model clauses and documents for all forms of tanker chartering. Its experts provide members with practical advice on chartering problems and publish commentaries on other charter party forms.

(d) *Market research.* Intertanko's market research provides an independent view on basic trends in tanker supply and demand. A number of research publications are produced by Intertanko from time to time.

(e) *Commercial/safety information.* Intertanko members regularly receive bulletins providing the latest data on port and bunker costs, charter party news, market trends, information on regulatory developments affecting the operation of tankers and safety at sea, and other vital information.

In the last two years, Intertanko has also developed a higher profile in promoting positive aspects of the independent tanker owner's image, which has taken a battering with increased attention on high-profile tanker casualties. This has included the production of a series of leaflets demonstrating the importance of the tanker in delivering energy oil and chemicals, the comparatively good record of the tanker industry with regard to safety and pollution prevention, and developments and progress regarding even greater contributions to safety. Intertanko has made significant breakthroughs in contact with environmental groups, for example Green Peace and Friends of the Earth, and takes part in environmental conferences relating to the reduction of maritime pollution.

Intertanko's activities for tanker owners are not limited by any means to oil tankers only. A growing number of independent chemical tanker owners are also in membership of Intertanko and a Chemical Tanker Owners Advisory Group operates to assist and support those members.

8.3 INTERNATIONAL CARGO HANDLING CO-ORDINATION ASSOCIATION

The aim of the International Cargo Handling Co-ordination Association (ICHCA) is to promote efficiency and economy in the handling and transportation of goods by all transport modes, at all stages of the transport chain and in all regions of the world. It was founded in 1952. Overall it is completely independent, non-political and non-profit-making. Its international membership extends to 76 countries with a network of 17 National Sections. The ICHCA is based in London.

The ICHCA provides a technical enquiry and cargo-handling information service to its members. It provides advice on any aspect of cargo operation and problem-solving. A unique and comprehensive ICHCA database of cargo-handling information is available to members utilizing modern computerized techniques. Access is also available to a panel of experts on the widest range of cargo-handling related topics including health and safety, containerization, bulk cargoes, intermodalism shipping, combined transport and air cargo.

The ICHCA liaises and consults with a wide range of national and international organizations. These include the IMO, ILO, Chamber of Shipping, UNCTAD, EU, IRU, IAPH, ICC, ICS, World Bank and UNCITRAL. International biennial conferences are held as are regular regional conferences. The ICHCA Cargo ware conducts international specialist seminars. An extensive programme of locally organized national and regional events are also conducted. Membership of ICHCA includes corporate members featuring companies, individuals seeking to develop their professionalism in the cargo-handling industry and students. The ICHCA is very active in the publication field. Publications include *Cargoware International* published monthly, an ICHCA quarterly bulletin, the world of cargo handling ICHCA annual review and national section newsletters. Corporate members also receive the *Containerization International and International Bulk* journal.

There is no doubt in the next decade, as multi-modalism develops, the role and influence of the ICHCA will increase globally.

8.4 INTERNATIONAL CHAMBER OF SHIPPING

Formed in 1921 as the International Shipping Conference, and re-named as the International Chamber of Shipping (ICS) in 1948, this body is an association of national organizations representing predominantly private shipowners in over 25 countries.

Through these organizations, membership of the ICS embraces some 50% of the world's active trading fleets.

ICS deals with shipping policy in its broadest sense, primarily in the technical and legal spheres; it is not concerned with personnel relations, which are handled by the International Shipping Federation.

The objects of the ICS as set out in its constitution are:

(a) To promote internationally the interests of its members in all matters of general policy.

(b) With that end, to exchange views and frame policies for international and national application by way of representations through the governments of the countries represented in the ICS or otherwise.

(c) To co-operate with other technical, industrial or commercial interests or bodies on problems of mutual concern to its members and to such interests.

(d) To take part in the deliberations of other international bodies so far as it may be necessary for the achievement of its objectives.

8.5 INTERNATIONAL MARITIME ORGANIZATION

The International Maritime Organization (IMO) is a specialized agency of the United Nations concerned solely with maritime affairs. Its interest lies mainly in ships used in international services. Altogether 131 states are members of the IMO including ship-owning nations, countries which use shipping services and countries in the course of development.

The objectives of the IMO are to facilitate co-operation among governments on technical matters affecting shipping, particularly from the angle of safety of life at sea, and the prevention of marine pollution from ships. This entails providing an extensive exchange of information between nations on technical maritime subjects and the concluding of international agreements.

The industrial revolution of the eighteenth and nineteenth centuries and the upsurge in international commerce which resulted led to the adoption of a number of international treaties related to shipping, including safety. The subjects covered included tonnage measurement, the prevention of collisions, signalling and others.

By the end of the nineteenth century suggestions had even been made for the creation of a permanent international maritime body to deal with these and future measures. The plan was not put into effect, but international co-operation continued in the twentieth century, with the adoption of still more internationally developed treaties.

By the time the IMO came into existence in 1958, several important international conventions had already been developed, including the International Convention for the Safety of Life at Sea of 1948, the International Convention for the Prevention of Pollution of the Sea by Oil of 1954 and treaties dealing with load lines and the prevention of collisions at sea.

The IMO was made responsible for ensuring that the majority of these conventions were kept up to date. It was also given the task of developing new conventions as and when the need arose.

The creation of the IMO coincided with a period of tremendous change in world shipping and the Organization was kept busy from the start developing new conventions and ensuring that existing instruments kept pace with changes in shipping technology. It is now responsible for 35 international conventions and agreements and has adopted numerous protocols and amendments.

(a) Adopting a convention
This is the part of the process with which the IMO as an organization is most closely involved. The IMO has six main

bodies concerned with the adoption or implementation of conventions. The Assembly and Council are the main organs, and the committees involved are the Maritime Safety Committee, the Marine Environment Protection Committee, the Legal Committee and the Facilitation Committee. Developments in shipping and other related industries are discussed by member states in these bodies, and the need for a new convention or amendments to existing conventions can be raised in any of them.

Normally the suggestion is first made in one of the committees, since these meet more frequently than the main organs. If agreement is reached in the committee, the proposal goes to the Council and, as necessary, to the Assembly.

If the Assembly or the Council, as the case may be, gives the authorization to proceed with the work, the committee concerned considers the matter in greater detail and ultimately draws up a draft instrument. In some cases the subject may be referred to a specialized sub-committee for detailed consideration.

Work in the committees and sub-committees is undertaken by the representatives of member states of the organization. The views and advice of intergovernmental and international non-governmental organizations which have a working relationship with the IMO are also welcomed in these bodies. Many of these organizations have direct experience in the various matters under consideration, and are therefore able to assist the work of the IMO in practical ways.

The draft convention which is agreed upon is reported to the Council and Assembly with a recommendation that a conference be convened to consider the draft for formal adoption.

Invitations to attend such a conference are sent to all member states of the IMO and also to all states which are members of the United Nations or any of its specialized agencies. These conferences are therefore truly global conferences open to all governments who would normally participate in a United Nations conference. All governments participate on an equal footing. In addition, organizations of the United Nations system and organizations in official relationship with the IMO are invited to send observers to the conference to give the benefit of their expert advice to the representatives of governments.

Before the conference opens, the draft convention is circulated to the invited governments and organizations for their comments.

The draft convention, together with the comments thereon from governments and interested organizations is then closely examined by the conference and necessary changes are made in order to produce a draft acceptable to all or the majority of the governments present. The convention thus agreed upon is then adopted by the conference and deposited with the Secretary-General who sends copies to governments. The convention is opened for signature by states, usually for a period of 12 months. Signatories may ratify or accept the convention while non-signatories may accede.

(b)   Entry into force
The adoption of a convention marks the conclusion of only the first stage of a long process. Before the convention comes into force – that is, before it becomes binding upon governments which have ratified it – it has to be accepted formally by individual governments.

Each convention includes appropriate provisions stipulating conditions which have to be met before it enters into force. These conditions vary but, generally speaking, the more important and more complex the document, the more stringent are the conditions for its entry into force. For example, the International Convention for the Safety of Life at Sea 1974 provided that entry into force requires acceptance by 25 states whose merchant fleets comprise not less than 50% of the world's gross tonnage; for the International Convention on Tonnage Measurement of Ships 1969, the requirement was acceptance by 25 states whose combined merchant fleets represent not less than 65% of world tonnage.

When the appropriate conditions have been fulfilled, the convention enters into force for the states which have accepted – generally after a period of grace intended to enable all the states to take the necessary measures for implementation.

In the case of some conventions which affect a few states or deal with less complex matters, the entry into force requirements may not be so stringent. For example, the Convention Relating to Civil Liability in the Field of Maritime Carriage of Nuclear Material 1971 came into force 90 days after being accepted by five states; the Special Trade Passenger Ships Agreements 1971 came into force six months after three states (including two with ships or nationals involved in special trades) had accepted it.

For the important technical conventions, it is necessary that they be accepted and applied by a large section of the shipping community. It is therefore essential that these should, upon entry into force, be applicable to as many of the maritime states as possible. Otherwise they would tend to confuse rather than clarify shipping practice since their provisions would not apply to a significant proportion of the shipping they were intended to deal with.

Accepting a convention does not merely involve the deposit of a formal instrument. A government's acceptance of a convention necessarily places on it the obligation to take the measures required by the convention. Often national law has to be enacted or changed to enforce the provisions of the convention; in some case, special facilities may have to be provided; an inspectorate may have to be appointed or trained to carry out functions under the convention; and adequate notice must be given to shipowners, shipbuilders and other interested parties so they make take account of the provisions of the convention in their future acts and plans.

At present IMO conventions enter into force within an average of five years after adoption. The majority of these instruments are now in force or are on the verge of fulfilling requirements for entry into force.

(c) Amendment
Technology and techniques in the shipping industry change very rapidly these days. As a result, not only are new conventions required but existing ones need to be kept up to date. For example, the International Convention for the Safety of Life at Sea (SOLAS) 1960 was amended six times after it entered into force in 1965 – in 1966, 1967, 1968, 1969, 1971 and 1973. In 1974 a completely new convention was adopted incorporating all these amendments (and other minor changes) and was itself modified (in 1978, 1981, 1983, 1988, 1990 and 1991).

In early conventions, amendments came into force only after a percentage of contracting states, usually two-thirds, had accepted them. This normally meant that more acceptances were required to amend a convention than were originally required to bring it into force in the first place, especially where the number of states which are parties to a convention is very large.

This percentage requirement in practice led to long delays in bringing amendments into force. To remedy the situation a new amendment procedure was devised in the IMO. This procedure has been used in the case of conventions such as the Convention on the International Regulations for Preventing Collisions at Sea 1972, the International Convention for the Prevention of Pollution from Ships 1973 and SOLAS 1974, all of which incorporate a procedure involving the 'tacit acceptance' of amendments by states.

Instead of requiring that an amendment shall enter into force after being accepted by, for example, two-thirds of the parties, the new procedure provides that an amendment shall enter into force at a particular time unless, before that date, objections to the amendment are received from a specified number of parties.

In the case of the 1974 SOLAS Convention, an amendment to most of the Annexes (which constitute the technical parts of the Convention) is 'deemed to have been accepted at the end of two years from the date on which it is communicated to Contracting Governments . . .' unless the amendment is objected to by more than one-third of contracting governments, or contracting governments owning not less than 50% of the world's gross merchant tonnage. This period may be varied by the Maritime Safety Committee with a minimum limit of one year.

As was expected the 'tacit acceptance' procedure has greatly speeded up the amendment process. The 1981 amendments to SOLAS 1974, for example, entered into force on 1 September 1984. Compared to this, none of the amendments adopted to the 1960 SOLAS Convention between 1966 and 1973 received sufficient acceptances to satisfy the requirements for entry into force.

(d)   Enforcement

The enforcement of IMO conventions depends upon the governments of member parties. The Organization has no powers in this respect.

Contracting governments enforce the provisions of IMO conventions as far as their own ships are concerned and also set the penalties for infringements where these are applicable.

They may also have certain limited powers in respect of the ships of other governments.

In some conventions, certificates are required to be carried on board ship to show that they have been inspected and have met the required standards. These certificates are normally accepted as proof by authorities from other states that the vessel concerned has reached the required standard, but in some cases further action can be taken.

The 1974 SOLAS Convention, for example, states that 'the officer carrying out the control shall take such steps as will ensure that the ship shall not sail until it can proceed to sea without danger to the passengers or the crew'.

This can be done if 'there are clear grounds for believing that the condition of the ship and its equipment does not correspond substantially with the particulars of that certificate'.

An inspection of this nature would, of course, take place within the jurisdiction of the port state. But when an offence occurs in international waters the responsibility for imposing a penalty rests with the flag state.

Should an offence occur within the jurisdiction of another state, however, that state can either cause proceedings to be taken in accordance with its own law or give details of the offence to the flag state so that the latter can take appropriate action.

Under the terms of the 1969 Convention Relating to Intervention on the High Seas, contracting states are empowered to act against ships of other countries which have been involved in an accident or have been damaged on the high seas if there is a grave risk of oil pollution occurring as a result.

The way in which these powers may be used are very carefully defined, and in most conventions the flag state is primarily responsible for enforcing conventions as far as its own ships and their personnel are concerned.

The majority of conventions adopted under the auspices of the IMO or for which the Organization is otherwise responsible fall into three main categories.

The first group is concerned with maritime safety, the second with the prevention of marine pollution, and the third with liability and compensation, especially in relation to damage caused by pollution. Outside these major groupings are a number of other conventions dealing with facilitation, tonnage measurement, unlawful acts against shipping and salvage.

Details of IMO Conventions are provided in Table 8.1.

Table 8.1 IMO Conventions as at 1 January 1994

Title	Year of adoption	Requirement for entry into force*	Entry into force	Contracting parties + % world tonnage
Maritime safety				
International Convention for the Safety of Life at Sea (SOLAS)	1974	25 states whose combined merchant fleets constitute not less than 50% of world gross tonnage	25 May 1980	122 + 97.11%
Amendments and Protocols				
Protocol	1978		1 May 1981	82 + 91.46%
Amendments	1981	Tacit acceptance	1 Sept 1984	As parent Convention
"	1983	"	1 July 1986	"
"	1987	"	30 Oct 1988	"
"	April 1988	"	22 Oct 1989	"
"	Oct 1988	"	29 April 1990	"
"	GMDSS 1988	"	1 Feb 1992	"
Protocol	1988	15 states + 50% world gt	—	12 + 9.01%
Amendments	1989	Tacit acceptance	1 Feb 1992	As parent Convention
"	1989 (IBC Code)	"	13 Oct 1990	"
"	1990	"	1 Feb 1992	"
"	1990 (IBC Code)	6 months after entry into force of 1988 SOLAS and LL Protocols	—	"
"	1990 (IGC Code)	"	1 Jan 1994	"
"	1991	"	(1 Oct 1994)	"
"	May 1992	"	(1 Oct 1994)	"
"	Dec 1992	"	(1 July 1994)	"
"	Dec 1992 (IBC Code)	"	(1 July 1994)	"
"	Dec 1992 (IGC Code)	"	(1 July 1994)	"

Instrument	Year	Entry into force requirements	Entry into force	Ratifications + tonnage
International Convention on Load Lines (LL)	1966	15 states including 7 with not less than 1 m gt	21 July 1968	130 + 98.02%
Amendments and Protocols				
Amendment	1971	2/3 contracting parties (87)	—	50
"	1975	"	—	45
"	1979	"	—	43
"	1983	"	—	26
Protocol	1988	15 states + 50% world gt	—	13 + 9.48%
Special Trade Passenger Ships Agreement (STP)	1971	3 states (including at least 2 in whose territory are registered ships engaged in special trades or whose nationals are carried in ships engaged in these trades)	2 Jan 1974	15 + 25.75%
Amendments and Protocols				
Protocol	1973	10 states	2 June 1977	14 + 23.81%
International Convention for Safe Containers (CSC)	1972	Tacit acceptance	6 Sept 1977	57 + 63.91%
Amendments and Protocols				
Amendment	1981	Tacit acceptance	1 Dec 1981	"
"	1983	"	1 Jan 1984	"
"	1991	"	1 Jan 1993	"
"	1993	"	(4 Nov 1995)	"

Table 8.1 continued

Title	Year of adoption	Requirement for entry into force*	Entry into force	Contracting parties + % world tonnage
Convention on the International Regulations for Preventing Collisions at Sea (COLREG)	1972	15 states with not less than 65% of world fleet by number of ships or gt of vessels of 100 gt and over	15 July 1977	120 + 95.81%
Amendments and Protocols				
Amendment	1981	Tacit acceptance	1 June 1983	"
"	1987	"	19 Nov 1989	"
"	1989	"	19 April 1991	"
"	1993	2/3 of contracting parties		
Convention on the International Maritime Satellite Organization (INMARSAT) Operating Agreement	1976	States representing 95% of initial Investment shares	16 July 1979	71 + 87.67%
Amendments and Protocols				
Amendment	1985	2/3 of contracting states representing 2/3 investment shares	13 Oct 1989	"
"	1989	"	—	26
Torremolinos International Convention for the Safety of Fishing Vessels (SFV)	1977	15 states with not less than 50% by number of world fishing fleet of 24 m in length and over	—	18 + 12.21%
Protocol	1993		—	—

Convention	Year	Entry into force requirement	Date	States + %
International Convention on Standards of Training, Certification and Watchkeeping for Seafarers (STCW)	1978	25 states with not less than 50% of world gt	28 April 1984	101 + 92.79%
Amendments and Protocols				
Amendments	1991	Tacit acceptance	1 Dec 1992	—
International Convention on Maritime Search and Rescue (SAR)	1979	15 states	22 June 1985	48 + 44.43%

PREVENTION OF MARITIME POLLUTION

Convention	Year	Entry into force requirement	Date	States + %
International Convention Relating to Intervention on the High Seas in Cases of Oil Pollution Casualties (INTERVENTION 69)	1969	15 states	6 May 1975	60 + 64.30%
Amendments and Protocols				
Protocol (INT PROT 69)	1973	—	30 March 1983	29 + 44.01%
Amendment	1991	Tacit acceptance	24 July 1992	
Convention on the Prevention of Marine Pollution by Dumping of Wastes and Other Matter (LC)	1972	15 states	30 Aug 1975	71 + 66.31%

Table 8.1 continued

Title	Year of adoption	Requirement for entry into force*	Entry into force	Contracting parties + % world tonnage
Amendments and Protocols				
Amendment	Disputes 1978	2/3 of contracting parties	—	18
"	Incineration 1978	Tacit acceptance	11 March 1979	—
"	Substances 1980	"	11 March 1981	—
"	1989	"	19 May 1990	—
"	1993	"	(20 Feb 1994)	—
International Convention for the Prevention of Pollution from Ships, 1973 as modified by the	1973 (Conv)	15 states with not less than 50% of world gt of merchant shipping	—	
Protocol of 1978 (MARPOL 73/78)	1978 (Prot)	As above	2 Oct 1983	83 + 92.01%
Annex I	—	"	2 Oct 1983	"
Annex II	—	"	6 April 1987	"
Annex III (optional)	—	"	1 July 1992	60 + 56.42%
Annex IV "	—	"	—	51 + 41.01%
Annex V	—	"	31 Dec 1988	65 + 66.51%
Amendments and Protocols				
Amendment	1984	Tacit acceptance	7 Jan 1986	As parent Convention
"	1985 (ANNEX II)	"	6 April 1987	"
"	1985 (PROTOCOL I)	"	6 April 1987	"
"	1987 (ANNEX I)	"	1 April 1989	"

Convention	Date of adoption	Conditions for entry into force	Date of entry into force		
"	March 1989 (IBC CODE)	"	13 Oct 1990		"
"	March 1989 (BCH CODE)	"	13 Oct 1990		"
"	March 1989 (ANNEX II)	"	13 Oct 1990		"
"	1989 (Annex V)	"	18 Feb 1991	—	"
"	1990 (HSSC)	6 months after entry into force of 1988 SOLAS and LL Protocols	—		"
"	1990 (IBC CODE)	"	—	—	"
"	1990 (BCH CODE)	"	—	—	"
"	1990 (Annex I + V)	Tacit acceptance	17 March 1992		"
"	1991 (Annex I)	"	4 April 1993		"
"	1991 (Annex V)	"	4 April 1993		"
"	1992 (Annex I)	"	6 July 1993		"
"	1992 (IBC)	"	(1 July 1994)		"
"	1992 (BCH)	"	(1 July 1994)		"
"	1992 (Annex II)	"	(1 July 1994)		"
"	1992 (Annex III)	"	(28 Feb 1994)		"
International Convention on Oil Pollution Preparedness, Response and Co-operation (OPRC)	1990	15 states	—		10 + 6.07%

Table 8.1 continued

Title	Year of adoption	Requirement for entry into force*	Entry into force	Contracting parties + % world tonnage
LIABILITY AND COMPENSATION				
International Convention on Civil Liability for Oil Pollution Damage (CLC)	1969	8 states including 5 with not less than 1 million gt of tanker tonnage each	19 June 1975	81 + 84.99%
Amendments and Protocols				
Protocol (CLC PROT 76)	1976	"	8 April 1981	43 + 62.73%
" (CLC PROT 84)	1984	10 states including 6 with not less than 1 million gt of tanker tonnage each	—	9 + 4.36%
Protocol (CLC PROT 92)	1992	10 states including 4 with not less than 1 million units of gross tanker tonnage	—	—
Convention relating to Civil Liability in the Field of Maritime Carriage of Nuclear Material (NUCLEAR)	1971	5 states	15 July 1975	14 + 24.41%
International Convention on the Establishment of an International Fund for Compensation for Oil Pollution Damage (FUND)	1971	8 states, which have received at least 750 m tons of contributing oil during previous calendar year	16 Oct 1978	57 + 62.55%

Amendments and Protocols

Protocol (FUND PROT 76)	1976	"	—	22 + 46.23%
Protocol (FUND PROT 84)	1984	8 states + 600 million tons of contributing oil	—	4 + 2.10%
Protocol (FUND PROT 92)	1992	8 states + 450 million tons of contributing oil	—	—
Athens Convention relating to the Carriage of Passengers and their Luggage by Sea (PAL)	1974	10 states	28 April 1987	16 + 32.72%

Amendments and Protocols

Protocol	1976	"	30 April 1989	13 + 32.46%
"	1990	"	—	2 + 0.73%
Convention on Limitation of Liability for Maritime Claims (LLMC)	1976	12 states	1 Dec 1986	22 + 44.52%

Table 8.1 continued

Title	Year of adoption	Requirement for entry into force*	Entry into force	Contracting parties + % world tonnage
OTHER MATTERS				
Convention on Facilitation of International Maritime Traffic (FAL)	1965	10 states	5 March 1967	71 + 55.90%
Amendments and Protocols				
Amendment (Convention)	1973	2/3 of contracting parties	2 June 1984	"
Amendment (Annex)	1969	Tacit acceptance	12 Aug 1971	"
"	1977	"	31 July 1978	"
"	1986	"	1 Oct 1986	"
"	1987	"	1 Jan 1989	"
"	1990	"	1 Sept 1991	"
"	1992	"	1 Sept 1993	"
"	1993	"	(1 Sept 1994)	"
International Convention on Tonnage Measurement of Ships (TONNAGE)	1969	25 states with not less than 65% of world gt of merchant ships	18 July 1982	101 + 96.11%

Convention for the Suppression of Unlawful Acts Against the Safety of Maritime Navigation (SUA)	1988	15 states	1 March 1992	23 + 23.61%
Amendments and Protocols Protocol (SUA PROT)	1988	3 states (but not before Convention)	1 March 1992	21 + 23.42%
International Convention on Salvage (SALVAGE)	1989	15 states	—	` 8 + 4.21%

Instruments which are in force or applicable but which are no longer fully operational because they have been superseded by later instruments.

PREVENTION OF MARINE POLLUTION

International Convention for the Prevention of Pollution of the Sea by Oil (OILPOL)	1954	10 states including 5 with not less than 500 000 gt of tanker tonnage	26 July 1958	69
Amendments and Protocols Amendment	1962		28 June 1967 and 18 May 1967	
"	1969		20 Jan 1978	
" Great Barrier Reef	1971	46 acceptances	—	25
" Tank size 1971		"	—	25

Table 8.1 continued

Title	Year of adoption	Requirement for entry into force*	Entry into force	Contracting parties + % world tonnage
MARITIME SAFETY				
International Convention for the Safety of Life at Sea (SOLAS)	1960	15 states including 7 with not less than 1 million gt of merchant shipping each	26 May 1965	96
Amendments and Protocols				
Amendment	1966	64 (+ conditions)	—	46
"	1967	"	—	36
"	1968	"	—	37
"	1969	"	—	26
"	1971	"	—	18
"	1973 (general)	"	—	9
"	1973 (grain)	"	—	10
International Regulations for Preventing Collisions at Sea	1960	Individual Acceptances	Applied from 1 Sept 1965	72

*Tacit acceptance is given where this option is available. It is the amendment process normally used but in all conventions other procedures are possible.
N.B. Entries in parenthesis represent the provisional date of entry into force.

8.6 COUNCIL OF EUROPEAN AND JAPANESE NATIONAL SHIPOWNERS' ASSOCIATIONS

The Council of European and Japanese National Shipowners' Associations (CENSA) comprises the National Shipowners' Associations of thirteen major maritime nations, namely Belgium, Denmark, Finland, France, Germany, Greece, Italy, Japan, the Netherlands, Norway, Spain, Sweden and the UK.

Individually these associations are concerned with all aspects of shipping policy, whether in the liner, tramp, bulk carrier or tanker sectors. Collectively the work of CENSA also extends to these areas.

The primary objective of CENSA is the promotion and protection of the interests of its membership through the development of sound shipping policies including in particular:

(a) the elimination of restriction on, and interference with, international transport and trade;

(b) the promotion of a system free, so far as possible, from governmental discrimination or regulation and which preserves for shippers the freedom of choice of vessel;

(c) the development of a system of fair trading between providers and users of shipping services on the basis, as far as possible, of self-regulation.

8.7 LLOYD'S REGISTER OF SHIPPING

Lloyd's Register of Shipping was founded in 1760 and reconstituted in 1834. It is the world's leading ship classification society and classes around 96 million gross tonnage of shipping comprising more than 6700 ships. Today Lloyd's Register is no longer solely concerned with shipping but all kinds of marine, offshore and industrial survey and advisory services, improving quality, enhancing safety and protecting the environment.

Through its constitution Lloyd's Register is directed 'to secure for the benefit of the community high technical standards of design, manufacture, construction, maintenance, operation and performance for the purpose of enhancing the safety of life and property both at sea and on land'. For more than two centuries safety and reliability have been assured through Lloyd's Register quality survey of materials, workmanship and construction. As a non-profit-distributing organization, it is financially independent using the income from fees to improve technical services. It operates independently of any government or other body and assures absolute commercial impartiality.

Lloyd's Register is headed by a General Committee representing the main interests of the international maritime community, and a Technical Committee consisting of representatives nominated by marine and industrial institutions. They are supported by 17 Area and National Committees located in those areas of the world most prominent in shipbuilding and marine affairs. The Lloyd's Register Board, elected by the General Committee from its own members, directs the organization, while the Management Committee, which is responsible to the Board, provides the impetus and management control essential to Lloyd's Register.

Over 3900 people, of whom half are experienced engineers, work solely for Lloyd's Register throughout more than 255 offices worldwide – a degree of exclusive coverage unmatched by any other classification society. Three principal divisions exist within Lloyd's Register: the Ship Division, the Industrial Division and the Offshore Division. They are supported by two technical groups – Engineering Services and Advisory Services – which also provide specialist services directly to clients. Qualified accounting, administrative and computing staff ensure the organization operates smoothly. A commentary on each of the Divisions/Groups now follows.

The Ship Division is made up of four elements: Classification, Statutory Certification, Specification Services and Safety Emergency Response Services.

Ship classification has been a principal activity for Lloyd's Register for over 200 years. Classification sets and maintains standards of safety and reliability by establishing requirements for the design, construction and maintenance of ships. It applies to all kinds of ships, floating docks, yachts and small craft. Lloyd's Register classification is an internationally recognized standard and helps shipowners negotiate favourable insurance rates and charter arrangements. It also assures third parties such as underwriters/shippers that the ship maintains recognized standards. The Lloyd's Register classification demands that the materials structure, machinery and equipment are of the required quality. In shipyards throughout the world, construction is surveyed to ensure proper standards of workmanship are adhered to.

Quality inspection during construction is essential. Upon completion, Lloyd's Register issues the appropriate classification certificate (see pp. 25–30) from which the shipowner, charterer, crew and underwriter can be confident that the ship has been surveyed to the standards of safety and quality required by Lloyd's Register rules: standards that will enhance the vessel's reliability during service life. Classification applies to all kinds of ships and floating structures, and extends to equipment and machinery designed for a specific purpose, including propulsion and electrical control systems, floating docks, passenger liners, mechanical lifts, liquefied gas containment systems, international racing class yachts and mobile drilling units. Shipowners are assured that design, materials, construction and workmanship meet recognized standards. Lloyd's Register provides impartial technical authority respected by owners, manufacturers and builders.

Maintenance of Lloyd's Register class necessitates regular surveys of both the hull and machinery involving inspection of several hundred individual items. Lloyd's Register CLASSDATA, a free confidential on-line computer service, keeps owners of Lloyd's Register classed ships up-to-date with their fleet's survey status. Classification surveys can be synchronized with the survey requirements of the International Maritime Organization (see pp. 31–3).

The Statutory Certification coverage embraces international conventions, codes and protocols concerning ship safety and marine pollution as laid down by the IMO (see pp. 127–44). Lloyd's Register performs statutory surveys covering international conventions relating to load lines; cargo ship construction; safety equipment; fire protection, detection and extinction; radio equipment; passenger ship safety; grain loading; collision; pollution prevention; tonnage measurement; chemical and liquefied gas carrier construction; and crew accommodation.

The Specification Services involve an independent project management team MARSPEC – the Marine Specification Services Department. It is a technical group which offers advisory and survey services to the marine industry worldwide. It covers all types and size of vessel and marine construction. It covers new building/conversion; sale and purchase; ship repair; condition assessment studies; and miscellaneous services relating to proposed or existing ship designs.

Finally the Safety Emergency Response Service (SERS) provides a 24-hour service which in the event of a casualty gives subscribers to SERS relevant technical information based on computer simulations to evaluate how the stricken vessel will respond to rescue options.

Lloyd's Register is a major certification and verification authority for the offshore industry and has been extensively involved in over 700 major offshore projects. It provides certification for all types of fixed and mobile offshore structures and associated equipment, and undertakes formal safety assessments.

The Industrial Division embraces the oil, chemical, petrochemical, power, civil and general engineering industries worldwide. It provides independent technical appraisal, inspection, testing and certification; quality assurance; reliability and risk analysis with safety assessment; environmental assurance; contract co-ordination; and in-service inspection and structural analysis. Overall the Industrial Division provides independent advisory consultancy and inspection services for all types of industrial plant, machinery and engineering projects.

Lloyd's Register Advisory Services can develop and improve management systems for safety (e.g. the ISM Code), quality and the environment and has access to a wide range of advice and technical auditing services.

Lloyd's Register Engineering Services are very extensive, providing a wide range of specialist technical services covering the complete engineering spectrum embracing marine, industrial and offshore installations. Specialist activities include field measurement and analysis; materials laboratory facilities; FOBAS – an advisory fuel oil bunkering analysis service; LOS – a lubricating oil analysis and advisory service; BQS – a bunker quantity service; a drug and alcohol screening programme for the marine industry; performance technology; engineering calculations using in-house computer facilities and advanced software programs; information technology services; and a type approval scheme. Such engineering resource services are provided against the background of Lloyd's Register's continuous programme of research and development.

For example, Lloyd's Register Fuel Oil Bunker Analysis and Advisory Service embraces all aspects of marine fuel oils, their efficient use, and associated problems derived from an in-depth analysis. This can include monthly reports. Similarly, the lubricant quality scan provides an independent assessment of oil performance, on-site technical investigations and a lubrication information service.

Lloyd's Register also provides a Register of Ships which contains authoritative details of the world's merchant fleet covering some 78 000 ships. Similar registers, statistical publications and three supplementary books give details of shipowners, shipbuilders, docks and offshore craft. Example pages are shown in Fig. 8.1.

Finally Lloyd's Register has a number of subsidiary companies, including Lloyd's Register Quality Assurance Ltd which provides a quality assurance management systems approval and product conformity certification service, and Marine Offshore Management Ltd which provides asset integrity management to the offshore and petrochemical industries. A joint venture exists between Lloyd's Maritime Information Services Ltd and Lloyd's of London Press which supplies the world's largest source of commercially available shipping information.

There is no doubt that Lloyd's Register will continue to remain a market leader in the global maritime service sector.

8.8 BUREAU VERITAS

Bureau Veritas (BV) is a ship classification society long-established and of world repute based in Paris. It has attained quality assurance standard ISO 9000 as audited by the Marine Division Services of the International Association of Classification Societies and the International Safety Management (ISM) Code introduced by the International Maritime Organization. By 1993 there were some 7702 ships in the Bureau Veritas Register representing 12.9% in number of the world's maritime fleet.

Bureau Veritas has a broadly based portfolio of services covering research and development on a wide variety of maritime and industrial projects; technical assistance; quality and safety inspection services for buildings and engineering structures: transport and logistics services, particularly with regard to the carriage of

These pages present fictitious data of a typical entry in the *Register of Ships*, together with the corresponding entries in other LR publications to provide an example of the breadth of information available and the way in which it is cross-referenced.

Register of Ships entry

LR No.	Ship Name & Owners		Tonnages	Classification		Hull Details			
8590346	CAMELLIA TRADER		13 627	+100A1	ss 2/93	1987 - 12 Kita Minami Zosen K K - Tokumizu			
7YRP	ex Xebec Sailor - 93		7 504	Ice Class 3					(442)
705341	ex Mexania - 90		18 532			166.24	(BB)	24.09	10.062
Df Esd	Camellia Naviera S.A.		T/cm	+LMC	UMS	150.43		23.73	13.53
Gc Pfd	Speciality Services Ltda		32.3	+Lloyd's RMC		P 19.3	F 20.4	2dk	
Rdr RT				EL (G+) 577.5/70.0 U2		rf nil			
	Playa Marina	San Patricio			FN 5605				
	SatCom: 2958663/CAMT								

Entries in other Publications

List of Shipowners, Managers and Managing Agents

CAMEL CARRIERS	(2483425)
Camel Carriers (Pte) Ltd	
See ARABIAN SHIPMANAGEMENT	

CAMELLIA NAVIERA	(5037626)
Camellia Naviera S.A.	
See SPECIALITY SERVICES	

CAMENORI NAVIGAZIONE	(1538655)
Camenori Navigazione s.p.a.	
Via della Nostra	

List of Shipowners, Managers and Managing Agents

Speciality Services (3555001)
Speciality Services Ltda
Pino 1, Edificio Florida,
Avenida Liberlador Carlos O'Reilly 43,
Playa Marina 1043, San Patricio.
Telephone: (041) 248395
Facsimile: (041) 248396
Telex: 24839 specs

As **Managers** for the following:

gc	AMARYLLIS TRADER (Amaryllis Naviera S.A.)	84	10023
bu	BLUEBELL TRADER (Bluebell Naviera S.A.)	85	20524
gc	CAMELLIA TRADER (Camellia Naviera S.A.)	88	13627
gc	DANDELION TRADER (Dandelion Naviera S.A.)	88	13627
bv	EDELWEISS TRADER (Edelweiss Naviera S.A.)	82	19053
bv	FUSCHIA TRADER (Fuchsia Naviera S.A.)	83	19053
gc	GLADIOLUS TRADER (Gladiolus Naviera S.A.)	87	13544
fc	HIBISCUS TRADER (Hibiscus Naviera S.A.)	86	9887
fc	IPOMOEA TRADER (Ipomoea Naviera S.A.)	86	9887
bu	JONQUIL TRADER (Jonquil Naviera S.A.)	89	21886
bu	KUDZU TRADER (Kudzu Naviera S.A.)	90	21886
gc	LOBELIA TRADER (Lobelia Naviera S.A.)	92	10546
gc	MESEMBRYANTHEMUM TRADER	92	10546
	(Mesembryanthemum Naviera S.A.)		

Maritime Guide
Listing of Shipbuilders and Ships built by them

KITA-MINAMI ZOSEN K.K
Tokumizu, Tokumizu Pref
Orania

ta	ARIATA MARU NO.18	(434)	86	110
ta	ARIATA MARU NO. 38	(435)	86	110
gc	YUNG LO	(444)	87	856
gc	YUNG LU	(445)	87	858
gc	CAMELLIA TRADER	(442)	87	13627
gc	DANDELION TRADER	(443)	88	13627
gc	TIKARAMA STAR	(446)	88	6853
gc	RYUGATAKE MARU NO 1	(447)	88	1508
gc	RYUGATAKE MARU NO 2	(448)	89	1510
bu	CHIN FUNG	(451)	89	20053
bu	CHIN FENG	(452)	90	20053

P-Z Volume of Register of Ships
Index of Former Names

Xanadu Explorer	4384	BRILLIANT EXPORTER
Xanadu Reefer	8667	CHRYSANTHEMUM REEFER
Xanten	1599	FIRANICE
Xanthi	343	PITTS TRADER
Xanthi River	37867	BAUXITE EXPORTER
Xanthippe	584	PISA ESPRESSO
Xanthippe 1	584	PISA ESPRESSO
Xebec	606	XEBEC 1
Xebec Trader	13627	DANDELION TRADER
Xebecca	193	PRIDE OF MISTLEY
Xema	12843	UFALES
Xenonia	14732	LEXIUS
Xerafin	499	SAO HERMINIAO
Xeren Exporter	4327	SHERRY EXPORTER
Xerestar	1204	LUNG YI
Xi Feng Qiao	10544	ORIENTAL ECSTASY
Xi Feng Xing	10545	ORIENTAL FANTASY
Xi Qing Yang	48523	GIANT CARRIER
Xicun	143	GIANT CARRIER

Fig. 8.1 Extracts from Lloyd's Register of Shipping. (Reproduced by permission of Lloyd's Register Maritime Publications.)

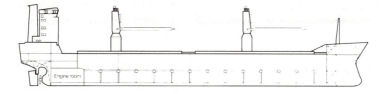

Ship Type & Cargo Details	Machinery	Further details and codes

M General Cargo
Ref

4 Ho   39.5   25.0   33.5   19.J   ER   4 TWD
G20   732   B20   193   ln. 4 027   HeCls. B
TEU 644
C.Ho   340/20' (40') C.Dk 304/20' (40')
incl. 50 ref C.
6 Ha (stl) (12.7 x 12.7) (26.0 p&s 18.60 p&s
17.5 p&s x 8.2) ER
Cr 2(30)

Koyuboshi   K7YBO5/173A
Oil 2SA 6Cy. 720 x 1270
10 332bhp (7 600kW)
Koyuboshi Diesel K.K.   Iyoda
Aux B (o.f.) 8.7 Kgf/cm (8.6 bar)
Aux B (ex.g) & rcv 10.1 kgf/cm (9.9 bar)
rcv 8.3 Kgf/cm (8.2 bar)
Gen 1x1 200 KW 3 x 712 KW 390V 50 Hz a.c.
Controllable pitch propeller
Thw. thrust Contr. pitch propeller fwd
Fuel 400.0t (d.o.) 1 226.0t (hvf)   12.75kn

The Key to all the details and codes shown in a
Register of Ships entry is situated at the beginning
of each volume. For easy reference field titles and
positions are shown on the multi-lingual header
cards inside the A-G volume.

World Shipowning Groups

A/S WILH KARLING   3013
Group Fleet: 35 Vessels
Founded: 1976
Address: Wilhelmogaton 24, Postbus 172, 8 Zwickerstadt, Normany
Tel: (83) 5131 29   Fax: (83) 5131 30   Telex: 45131 wKarl
Cable: KARLINGZWICK
Managing Director: Ing. Edvard M Korndorff.

1979 New Continent Carriers Inc.
7490128   New Continent 1   bu   1976   18956   32131   LR   LUB

1984 Delios Shipping Co Inc.
8277226   Delios Legend   gc   1984   2675   4113   RE   SPT
8277238   Delios Myth   gc   1985   2674   4138   RE   SPT

SPECIALITY SERVICES LDA
Founded: 1989
Address: Piso 1, Edificio Florida, Avenida Liberlador,
Carlos O'Reilly 43, Playa Marina 1043, San Patricio
Tel: (041) 248395   Fax: (041) 248396   Telex 24839 specs

1990 Amaryllis Naviera S.A.
8355290   Amaryllis Trader   gc   1984   10023   13521   LR   SPT

1990 Camellia Naviera S.A.
8590346   Camellia Trader   gc   1987   13627   18532   LR   SPT

1990 Dandelion Naviera S.A.
8590358   Dandelion Trader   gc   1988   13627   18532   LR   SPT

Maritime Guide
Listing of Shipbuilders and Engine Builders etc.

ORANIA

IYODA, KOYUBOSHI PREF.
Koyuboshi Diesel K.K   **DE**
3-1 Saha-cho 3-chome, Chiyoda-ku, Iyoda,
Koyuboshi Pref.
Tel: (0273) 85-4343   Fax: 85-4334

TOKUMIZU, TOKUMIZU PREF
Tokumizu Zosen K.K.
8-12 Urata-Cho 1-chome, Yoi-ku, Tokumizu,
Tokumizu Pref.
Tel: (0556) 96-3452   Fax: 96-3458

Maritime Guide
Ports and Harbours Section

SAN PATRICIO

12 53 N, 77 37 W
Admiralty Chart(s): ECB205, ECB 207
Tel: (041) 353494
Fax: (041) 353499

EMPRESA PORTUARIA SAN PATRICIO

Load	Breadth	Draught	Dwt
250.00	-	15.00	-

AFO	BBK	BUN	CAR	COA CON
	DBK	FER	GEN	LIF
ORE	STE	TIM	TOW	TUG

Maritime Guide
Call Sign Index

7YR1	BLUEBELL TRADER	20524
7YRJ	DELIOS LEGEND	2675
7YRK	DELIOS MYTH	2674
7YRL	YAXMUN	6895
7YRM	DEKTA L	998
7YRN	LEKTA L	998
7YRP	CAMELLIA TRADER	13627
7YRQ	DANDELION TRADER	13627
7YRR	KIWI BLOSSOM	675
7YRS	LEVANTINE HERO	1009
7YRT	EDELWEISS TRADER	19053
7YRU	FUSCHIA TRADER	19053
7YRV	GLADIOLUS TRADER	13544
7YRW	QUICK SHIPPER	18349

Fig. 8.1 continued

dangerous goods and specialized forms of transport; aeronautics and space involving promotion, technical assistance and construction surveys; and building inspection services for the construction industry to reduce operating risk. All these activities are undertaken on a global basis. Additional activities include BIVAC which involves supervision of exports and imports covering, for example, the pre-shipment inspection certificate scheme; TECH-ITAS which provides technical economic consultancy services and studies; VERIDATAS which covers information technology services and consultancy; and Veritas Automobile which covers motor vehicle testing.

In 1994 Bureau Veritas developed a new classification approach involving on line class. The following points are relevant to the scheme.

Ship classification is necessary to ensure the ship is built and maintained appropriately for the hazards and risks involved in maritime trading activities. This fundamental mission was translated into the existing traditional classification scheme by means of the following features:

(a) Standards, or rules, are defined for the design, construction and service of a ship.

(b) The design and construction are controlled to assure compliance with the rules. A certificate of conformity is issued.

(c) To assess ship seaworthiness periodical inspections are carried out and their results are compared to the applicable in-service rules.

(d) With the requirements of the rules met, the certificate of conformity is renewed with a certain degree of authority and credibility, thus providing reassurance to users of the ship/trade service.

The methodology of the scheme may be analysed as in Table 8.2.

The classification is therefore mainly a linear process where each stage of a ship's life is treated separately from the others. Once the standard is met one passes to the next stage. It is a process where the only possible output is a statement of compliance or non-compliance with the rules.

At each stage there are plans, documents, reports or more generally records which are filed and preserved for the whole life of a ship. Additionally there is a computerized system to manage

Table 8.2 Bureau Veritas on-line classification methodology

	(1) Input	(2) Stage	(3) Assessment	(4) Standard	(5) Records	(6) Output
Phase						
One	Plans from client	Design	Design review	Design rules	Calculation notes and plans	Stamped plans
Two	Stamped plans	Construc-tion	Construc-tion survey	Construc-tion rules	Construc-tion reports	Original certificate
Three	Original certificate	Service	Periodical inspection	In-service rules	Survey reports	Certificate renewal

NB: Phase three is continuously reported.

class status of all registered ships. This system keeps on record when surveys are due and remarks which are pending. Once solved they are no longer useful and then deleted.

The new classification embraces two new elements:

(a) Hull design review by direct engineering analysis involving the provision of additional class notation embracing RSD – Rational Ship Design.

(b) Systematic estimation of the evolution of the ship's hull condition involving the provision of additional class notation including STAR – System of Traceability and Analysis of Records.

The main objective is to offer owners and shipyards advanced techniques to improve the design and maintenance of ships. These two notations will constitute the core of an optional new classification approach, the main features of which are as follows:

(a) Direct engineering analyses, allowing for a better distribution of steel weight and more homogeneous definition of safety factors.

(b) The issue of a 'hot-spot map' of the ship's structure as the conclusion of the design review process, including explicit indication of corrosion margins.

(c) A comprehensive and permanent computerized database for each ship covering design, construction and service phases.

(d) A computerized system for the acquisition of survey data in liaison with the ship's databases.

(e) A systematic evaluation of the evolution of the ship's hull condition delivered at each special survey, or whenever desired, assisting the maintenance strategy decisions of the owner.

Undoubtedly the new on-line ship class system will become popular as the scheme develops and shipowners' have experience of the benefits.

8.9 ORGANIZATION FOR ECONOMIC CO-OPERATION AND DEVELOPMENT

The Organization for Economic Co-operation and Development (OECD) is based in Paris, France and is a unique forum permitting governments of the industrialized democracies to study and formulate the best possible policies in all economic and social spheres. It has 25 member countries.

Issues addressed by the OECD in the mid-1990s are wide ranging and include the creation of employment, economic growth and rising living standards through fiscal, monetary and structural economic policies; managing competition among nations in an era of the globalization of production and of the continuing opening of borders to trade and investment; consolidating and advancing reform in agricultural policies; protecting the environment; addressing the potential effects of global warming; the swelling tide of migration around the world; the improvement of life in cities and in the countryside; the enhancement of the human capital of nations through education and training; improving the efficiency of government and the quality of public sector spending and taxation; strengthening the scientific and technological base of nations; assuring the security of energy supplies; and trade facilitation such as through the certification of agricultural seeds.

The OECD differs from other inter-governmental organizations in three respects:

(a) It has neither supranational legal powers nor financial resources for loans or subsidies – its sole function is direct co-operation among the governments of its member countries, the principal industrialized countries of the world. These include Australia, Austria, Belgium, Canada, Denmark, Finland, France, Germany, Greece, Iceland, Ireland, Italy, Japan, Luxembourg, Mexico, the Netherlands, New Zealand, Norway, Portugal, Spain,

Sweden, Switzerland, Turkey, the United Kingdom and the United States. Additionally there are some 33 countries classified as partners in the transition programme. This co-operation is carried out directly by governments through the framework of committees.

(b) Co-operation among nations is realized through domestic policies where these interact with those of other countries, in particular through trade and investment. Co-operation usually means that member countries seek to adapt their domestic policies to minimize conflict with other countries with compliance assured either by informal mutual review or sometimes by legally binding agreements that provide follow-up procedures to monitor and encourage progress.

(c) The OECD approach to specific issues benefits in particular from the multi-disciplinary dimension applied through the broad expertise of the various OECD Directorates and member governments. The organization deals with both the general macro-economic and other more specific or sectoral issues.

As we progress towards the millenium the OECD will retain its global role. The central aim of governmental work through the OECD has always been to enable the major players in the world's economy co-operatively to devise and set policies that strengthen the market economy and improve the efficiency of markets both nationally and internationally. These include policies that minimize distortions and abuses thereby assuring opportunity to all, together with a responsibility for the sustainable development of human and natural resources. This will continue to be the main theme of OECD work, but within a changing context in which the possible impairments to market efficiency loom with more force and develop more rapidly than in the past.

What is changing is the intensity of competition. The progressive liberalization of international trade and investment over nearly half a century has opened national economies across the globe progressively to worldwide competition. Today, under the influence of a process of globalization given further impetus by the new information technologies, truly worldwide competition is developing both in services as well as goods.

As competition puts pressure on producers to adapt more and more rapidly, speed of adjustment and mobility, including that of production units, have become essential for survival. Yet the less adaptable still raise cries for protectionism or domestic anti-competitive barriers, thus bringing policies affecting domestic production into confrontation with the imperatives of the world-wide production of goods and services. This calls for more vigilance in maintaining competitive markets and this increasingly requires internally agreed disciplines that affect domestic policies, similar to those agreed through the forum of the OECD over the years.

The trend towards regional integration can be a powerful force for opening markets to international competition and is counter-balanced to some extent by the overall trend to economic globalization. But regional development should not be allowed to weaken the multi-lateral approach to trade embodied in the OECD Convention, even if some of the OECD countries at present and in the future participate in regional groupings.

8.10 BALTIC EXCHANGE

The Baltic Exchange is the only international shipping exchange in the world and a major earner of foreign currency for Britain.

Its origins can be traced to the seventeenth century, when shipowners and merchants met in London coffee houses. Foremost among these were the Jerusalem Coffee House and the Virginia and Maryland Coffee House (known from 1744 as the Virginia and Baltic as the cargoes dealt with came from the American colonies or from the countries on the Baltic Seaboard). The proprietors provided newspapers and commercial information for their customers as well as refreshments, and cargoes were auctioned there.

In 1810 larger premises were acquired at the Antwerp Tavern in Threadneedle Street which was renamed the Baltic. Membership of the 'Baltic Club' was limited to 300, and a committee was set up to control its affairs in 1823. From this moment onwards the importance and membership of the Baltic increased.

In 1900 the Baltic amalgamated with the London Shipping Exchange and became the Baltic Mercantile and Shipping Exchange Limited. Shortly afterwards in April 1903, a site was purchased in St Mary Axe. After the Second World War an adjoining site was acquired and the foundation stone for a new wing was laid by Sir Winston Churchill on 2 March 1955. The building was opened by Her Majesty the Queen on 21 November 1956 and today it is called the Baltic Exchange. In September 1993 a terrorist bomb destroyed the Baltic Exchange. It was temporarily relocated in nearby premises, and in the following year celebrated 250 years – 1744–1994 – serving world shipping. In April 1995 the Baltic Exchange was relocated to a new building at 38 St Mary Axe, London. The new building will provide an opportunity for the Baltic Exchange to expand its activities, especially in the hybrid areas, and thereby keep pace with the expansion in the market for global shipping centred on London.

The Baltic Exchange provides a unique professional market for cargo interests, shipowners, shipbrokers, port operators, agents and all those involved in international freight transport by sea. Overall it is a marketplace which is self-regulated with strict business ethics. It deals with cargoes for ships, ships for cargoes, buying and selling ships, commodities and aircraft chartering.

Associated with the bulk transport of goods by sea is the intermediary, the shipbroker, who seeks to find gainful employment for his owner's ships, or a vessel to move the iron ore, coal or grain he has contracted to supply. Working on a commission-only basis, brokers arrange the worldwide movement of bulk goods. When times are good and there are emerging markets like China importing steel and iron ore, cement and grain, the broker engages in frenetic activity and welcomes the profits. But when the price of oil rockets up and the major owners lay up their ships in the Norwegian fjords and pay off the seafarers, commissions are few and far between, and times are tough.

Much of the world's shipbroking is focused on the ancient institution of the Baltic Exchange in London. It is of world renown and its shipbroking services are fully integrated into the City of London maritime/insurance/financial markets and the hybrid activities/entities remain indisputable market leaders. The rationale for this situation is that the brokers on the Baltic Exchange still provide the most timely, market sensitive and reliable information worldwide. Throughout the Baltic, the broker has a reputation for integrity, for speed and for maintaining at the forefront of his or her mind the interest of the client above all else. The key to all of this is the standards of the market. Members of the Baltic Exchange meet to do business and operate under a code of practice built on trust over the many years since its inception. The broker's word is his bond. The Baltic Exchange has demonstrated that self-regulation by peers and through elected members serving on the board of directors is successful. International bulk freight and the acquisition and disposal of ocean-going vessels are complex businesses. The business ethics of the Baltic – 'Our word is our bond' – remain as vital today as they did a century ago.

The modern Baltic Exchange increasingly relies on electronic communications. Today there are some 400 chartering and brokering firms on the Baltic in London together with about 150 sale and purchase operations. The agents acting for the Greek shipowning community in London employ altogether some 3000 brokers, though not all are Baltic Exchange members.

Traditionally the Baltic Exchange has seen its membership drawn from those based in the City of London. Increasingly modern telecommunications has meant that there are those who can operate in the market without a physical base in the City. To respond to this, the Exchange in 1994 offered a new category of membership for those based outside the United Kingdom. Such overseas members will be subject to all the business ethics of the Baltic including the Baltic Code. Those from areas associated with international freight, even if they are not members themselves, are now admitted.

The services provided by the broker are wide ranging. Nowadays modern communications relying on computers and VDUs enable brokers to keep abreast of current developments/opportunities, but the tradition of meeting face to face continues. On a Monday lunch time in St Mary Axe, London, around 400 brokers congregate at the Exchange. They are there to renew their daily and weekly contacts with their colleagues. A constant barrage of calls echoes round the floor from the top-hatted Superintendent as booking offices seek to make contact with their representatives on the floor with a new order or a response to an enquiry they had put out to New York an hour earlier. In the main they are dealing with major foods and dry raw materials – grain, coal, iron ore, fertilizers, sugar, cement and steel. In the back offices wet cargo brokers are handling 300 000 tonnes of crude from Kuwait to Rotterdam for refining in the knowledge that by the time the oil reaches the port it will have been sold and resold tens of times, so that the final buyer will need a clear understanding of the cost of ocean transport, to the negotiation of which he was not a party. Tanker brokers use a sophisticated system of standardized cost called worldscale (see p. 124) which allows flexibility in a fast-moving trading environment. Some two-thirds of all tanker broking is carried out through the London market excluding, of course, those cargoes which are shipped in the major oil companies' own vessels – a decreasing number as oil companies are opting out of ownership.

Brokers also are engaged in the process of buying and selling ships. Such London-based broking firms handle most of the world's sale and purchase deals. These deals may be related to a new contract for the shipment of a base commodity such as coal or liquefied natural gas, but more often than not are speculative ventures for the charter industry. An acceptable price must be found for a new building, probably located in the Far East, China or Eastern Europe, with a delivery date which allows the vessel to be integrated into the fleet to meet the new commitment. Lawyers and financiers are brought in to complete the deal and contracts are signed to work to a delivery date. Alternatively a shipowner may dispose of an ageing vessel in the second-hand market for deployment by another owner. At the end of their lives ships get recycled and the sale and purchase broker needs to get the best possible price for the scrap and arrange the voyage to the grave yard.

Situated on the Baltic Exchange is BIFFEX, the Baltic International Freight Futures Exchange index (see p. 161). The Exchange calculates daily from a panel of its brokers the Baltic Freight Index (BFI), and by this means displays the rapidly varying cost of transporting by sea the major dry commodities of the world. This is indeed a business where skilled interpretation of what the market will do next is vital for success. Against this background investors are prepared to risk their capital tied up in a tanker worth US$80 million, or even a small second-hand bulk carrier at US$15 million. Rates of return can fluctuate by 30% in one quarter of the year, and likewise can swing violently from one year to the next.

There is no doubt that the Baltic Exchange will make an increasing contribution to world shipping and in so doing facilitate the development of international trade and rising living standards. The latest WTO (see p. 170) will stimulate this development and undoubtedly the Institute of Chartered Shipbrokers have played a significant role in attracting and training adequately professionally qualified shipbrokers worldwide.

8.11 BALTIC INTERNATIONAL FREIGHT FUTURES EXCHANGE

The Baltic International Freight Futures Exchange (BIFFEX) was opened in 1985 in London and provides a means by which the many elements of the international freight and shipping industry can protect themselves against adverse price movements. Overall, it provides the essential economic function of offering members of the international shipping and commodity trading communities embracing shipowners, operators and charterers a viable, effective and consistent means of reducing the risk inherent in fluctuating freight rates. Trade participants buy and sell Baltic Freight Index Futures to offset their exposure of forward commitments, transferring the price risk to other trade participants with opposing viewpoints and to speculators who are willing to assume these risks in pursuit of profit.

Risk control using futures trading is called 'hedging'. Broadly defined it is taking a position in a futures market as a substitute for a forward cash transaction. For example, using BIFFEX, a charterer who has sold a commodity forward is concerned that freight rates will rise, eroding or eliminating his trading profit. To protect himself against this he buys BIFFEX futures contracts. If freight rates do rise the loss incurred in the 'cash' shipping market, when he actually secures a ship, will be offset by a profit on BIFFEX.

A shipowner's risk is the exact reverse of the charterer's risk, hence he sells BIFFEX futures to protect himself against the market falling by the time he actually fixes his ship on a charter.

By using BIFFEX it is possible to hedge forward freight rates at the level of the futures price traded for up to eighteen months forward. Future prices are broadcast through data vending companies worldwide and are obtainable from futures brokers.

With an index-based futures contract it is not possible to deliver a cargo or ship in settlement of a futures position. All contracts traded on BIFFEX that remain open on the last trading day are settled in cash, based on the average of the BFI over the last five

Table 8.3 Baltic Freight Index (BFI)

Route No.*	Cargo size/voyage	Weighting (%)
1.	55 000 light grain USG/ARA (US Gulf to Continent)	10.0
1a.	Panmax T/S round T/C (Trans-Atlantic Round)	10.0
2.	52 000 heavy grain USG/JPN (US Gulf to Japan)	10.0
2a.	Panmax trip FE T/C (time charter)	10.0
3.	52 000 grain NOPAC/JPN (North Pacific to Japan)	10.0
3a.	Panmax PAC round T/C (time charter)	10.0
6.	120 000 coal HR/RBAY-JPN (Hampton Roads or Richard Bay to Japan)	7.5
7.	110 000 coal HR/RDAM (Hampton Roads to Rotterdam)	7.5
8.	130 000 coal QLD/RDAM (Queensland to Rotterdam)	7.5
9.	Panmax trip back T/C (time charter)	10.0
10.	135 000 ore TUB/RDAM (Tubarao to Rotterdam)	7.5
		100.0

*Routes 4 and 5 have been deleted.

business days of the settlement month. Cash settlement is the most convenient method of settling futures contracts.

BIFFEX is situated on the Baltic Exchange. It was formed in 1954 and merged the major soft commodity future trade associations to form a single Recognized Investment Exchange under the Financial Services Act 1986. Over the years, the exchange has adapted to meet the ever-changing nature of the international marketplace. Today, it is recognized as Europe's primary centre for the trading of soft commodity futures and options contracts, including cocoa, coffee, sugar, wheat, barley, potatoes and BIFFEX.

Given below is the BIFFEX contract specification while Table 8.3 specifies the individual route indices and their weighting system.

BIFFEX – Contract Specification

Unit of trading	Baltic Freight Index valued at $10 per full index point.
Trading months	The current month, the following two consecutive months and January, April, July, October for up to eighteen months forward.
Settlement	Each month.
Settlement day	The first business day after the last trading day of the settlement month.
Last trading day	The last business day of the settlement month with the exception of December which will be 20 December (if that day is not a business day then the immediately preceding business day).
Tick size	One full index point equivalent to $10 per lot.
Settlement price	The average of the index on the last trading day and the four previous working days of the settlement month.
Trading hours	10.15–12.30 and 14.30–16.30 London local time.

Basically the futures market is a centralized trading operation. Overall, futures prices move in parallel with freight. Moreover, it is a barometer of various opinions. Factors influencing BIFFEX futures prices include information about the underlying freight market, the market users' expectations of physicals and futures, and the technical interpretation of futures prices.

The London Clearing House is an independent organization owned by the major UK clearing banks which guarantees financial performance on each futures contract. The Clearing House operates between shipowner and charterers as a middleman to all trades, covering client 1 – broker 1 – London Clearing House – broker 2 – client 2. This may be compared with the chartering process which covers client 1 – broker 1 – broker 2 – client 2.

(a)   Sell hedge

An owner may have a number of his ships coming free over the next half-year or year but is unable to find suitable business on the freight market for those forward positions. The BIFFEX futures prices are being traded at a level which the owner considers to be a satisfactory relationship to the current BFI and he wishes to lock in this level of income. He calculates the amount of freight he wishes to cover (freight rate × cargo quantity) and divides it by the contract value (Index × $10.00) to give the number of lots to sell.

Subsequently, as his ships are actually fixed he then buys back the lots he had sold. If the freight market has fallen in comparison with the price at which he originally sold he will have reduced earnings on his ship but will have made a profit on his futures contract, and vice versa, i.e. his loss or profit on his physical ship transaction will be offset by his profit or loss on his futures transaction.

This method of hedging is completely flexible as, if at any time the owner finds suitable contract or timecharter employment, he can fix the business and buy back his sold futures contracts thus cancelling his futures position(s).

(b)   Buy hedge

A shipper makes a sale on CFR terms for delivery north Europe from the US Gulf area of one cargo per quarter over one year. The shipper does not wish an exposure to the forward freight market.

To protect himself and to lock in his freight costs he should identify the forward prices on BIFFEX and relate them to the current freight market (the BFI) to see what premium or discount is being applied to the four freight futures positions that he wishes to trade. He calculates the amount of freight he wishes to cover and divides by the contract value to give the number of lots to buy (in exactly the same way as the owner calculates the amount of cover needed to sell).

Subsequently, he sells the lots he bought (for each position) as he fixes a ship to carry each cargo. Any loss or gain in the physical ship market will be offset by a compensating gain or loss in his future contracts.

In addition to the price protection gained from the futures market, the shipper retains maximum logistical flexibility and is not constrained by specific cargo size or origin/destination.

A number of factors can affect freight rates and these are given below:

(a)   Ship draught restrictions that are temporary in nature – seasonal or unusual weather conditions, siltation or obstructions – at major ports.

(b)   Changes in the price of bunker fuel for ships.

(c) Changes in international currency values – the US dollar is the dominant currency for freight and changes in its relative value to other major currencies will affect the cost of running ships and operating them in international trades.

(d) Changes in the cost of port expenses and in major canal transits.

(e) War and acts of aggression may affect the level of confidence in world economic conditions and cause shortages of raw materials and finished products. Disruptions in patterns of supply and demand can cause increases or decreases in the costs of transportation.

(f) Strikes and other disruptions in the supply of labour or services will affect the volume of cargo that can be handled and produce a temporary aberration in shipping markets.

(g) Severe weather conditions can cause reductions in the supply of material and in the amount of cargo a ship can carry.

(h) Seasonal variations in commodity demand and production – the world's grain harvests are seasonal and the demand for coal energy will be highest in winter months.

(i) Political events.

(j) Commodity production and its movement.

(k) Fleet size including vessels under construction.

(l) Moving averages/trends.

(m) Market anticipation.

(n) Technical interpretation of future prices.

(o) Market users' expectation of physicals and futures.

The Baltic Freight Index is formulated as follows:

(a) The routes are chosen based on the frequency of spot voyage and time charter fixtures per commodity, geographic origin, tonne-mile contribution and the balance of ship capacity relative to available cargo.

(b) The BFI reflects the movements in the voyage and time charter fixtures market covering a mixture of the gross cost of moving cargo and net earnings to the owner.

(c) It has ten panel members who report daily freight rates for the BFI. These include shipbrokers Fearnleys A/S (Norway) and Banchero Costa & Co. SpA (Italy), the remainder being based in the UK: H. Clarkson & Co. Ltd, Eggar Forrester Ltd, Galbraith's Ltd, E.S. Gibson Shipbrokers Ltd, Howard Houlder & Partners

Ltd, Howe Robinson & Co Ltd, Lambert Bros Shipbroking Ltd and Simpson, Spence & Young.

(d)   Formal significance of BFI with respect to BIFFEX and any cash settlement.

(e)   The BFI is an index of voyage and time charter rates in the dry bulk shipping market composed of dry cargo routes, averaged and weighted according to a predetermined formula.

In Table 8.3 there are seven routes in the Panmax group and four in the Cape size group. The correlation between the Panmax and Cape size groups varies according to market conditions between the BFI routes within the index. They are grouped together by ship size, irrespective of type of cargo, load and discharge area, voyage or time charter. The individual route indices are averaged and then compared to the BFI.

8.12 FREIGHT TRANSPORT ASSOCIATION INCORPORATING THE BRITISH SHIPPERS' COUNCIL

The Freight Transport Association is the only UK trade association which exists to safeguard the interests of and provide services for trade and industry as operators and users of all forms of freight transport. It is accordingly recognized in this capacity by both central and local government and by other public bodies. This recognition extends to the EU and indeed worldwide involving international agencies.

Full FTA membership is open to all companies concerned with the movement of goods as an ancillary part of their main trade or business, whether as operators of their own goods vehicles or as users of services provided by others such as road hauliers and railway authorities.

Overall the Association has two main functions. The prime function is to represent members' interest as operators and users of freight transport and to provide services for the benefit of members and associate members alike. The second function is to represent British shippers through the British Shippers' Council.

The British Shippers' Council was formed in 1955 to further the interests of importers and exporters in the UK in all matters concerning the overseas transport of their goods, whether by sea or air. In 1979 it merged with the Freight Transport Association but retained its identity.

The main emphasis of the Council's work has been with the problems and costs of the carriage of goods by sea but in recent years more attention has been given to the interests of the air shipper and multi-modalism/containerization.

The Council has been closely involved with the EU and the European Shipper Council to develop trade and safeguard the interests of the shipper in all areas of the business. This includes not only the sea leg but also the 'on carriage'. It includes multi-modalism and the emerging development of rail-borne business through the Channel Tunnel.

The Council also has had a long-standing dialogue with the deep-sea liner cargo operators, including those which remain in the liner conference system. Relationships with liner conferences have been at the centre of the Council's work for many years.

The Council plays a significant role in the field of air freighting but here circumstances are notably different from those which attach to the carriage of goods by sea.

The third most important role lies in the field of trade documentation and procedures. Here the Council works closely with SITPRO and other agencies.

Finally, the Council acts as the focus of the shippers' viewpoint in determining changes to international conventions and other legislation affecting the carriage and insurance of goods by sea and air. Worldwide national shippers' councils play an important role in the process of representing the shippers' interests in the movement of goods internationally.

8.13 UNITED NATIONS CONFERENCE ON TRADE AND DEVELOPMENT

UNCTAD was established in 1964 to affirm the United Nations General Assembly's conviction that international co-operation in trade and development is vital for world economic growth and the economic development of developing countries.

With a membership of 187 states, UNCTAD, based in Geneva, is a permanent inter-governmental body and a principal organ of the General Assembly. The inter-governmental machinery comprises the Conference, the Trade and Development Board (TDB) and its subsidiary bodies serviced by a permanent secretariat. It is committed to accelerating international trade and development through co-operation, negotiation and partnership. It is distinctive not only for what it has achieved, but also because it is the only United Nations body dealing with economic issues in holistic terms, going beyond sectors to include their interactions and interlinkages. Its special quality is its concern with change as the hallmark of development.

UNCTAD's objectives are detailed below:

(a) To encourage concensus in favour of changes in the world trade system to foster economic development.

(b) To formulate pragmatic principles and policies on international trade and development and facilitate their application.

(c) To promote the international trade and economic development of developing countries.

(d) To introduce a development dimension into international economic policies.

(e) To promote appropriate natural policies, particularly in developing countries, supporting market orientation, entrepreneurship, transparent decision-making, efficient practices and good economic management.

(f) To promote trade and economic co-operation among developing countries whatever their stage of development or economic and social systems.

(g) To provide special help for the poorest developing countries which are usually the least able to take advantage of the benefits of trade for their economic development.

UNCTAD Conferences – the organization's highest policy-making body – are held every four years. They formulate major policy guidelines and decide on the programme of work. Eight conferences have been held so far: Geneva, Switzerland, 1964; New Delhi, India, 1968; Santiago, Chile, 1972; Nairobi, Kenya, 1976; Manila, Philippines, 1979; Belgrade, Yugoslavia, 1983; Geneva, Switzerland, 1987; and Cartagena de Indias, Colombia, 1992.

The turning point of UNCTAD development emerged at UNCTAD VIII held in Cartagena de Indias, Colombia, 1992. It was helped by a new impetus for global co-operation in response to the threats to economic and human security arising from economic and social frustrations and tensions in developing countries and economies in transition. The concept of development had also evolved significantly. From a narrow focus on economic growth and capital accumulation, development came to be widely understood as a multi-dimensional undertaking and a people-centered process in which the ultimate goal of economic and social policies is to improve conditions for all members of society. Emphasis was placed on economic interpendence and the shared responsibility of all countries to take supportive actions. Greater recognition was given to the needs for improved policy coordination, the importance of interlinkages between the external environment and domestic policies and the contributions of the public and private sectors.

UNCTAD VIII took a giant step towards laying to rest the reciprocal misgivings of developed and developing countries which had caused deadlock in the economic co-operation dialogue during the 1980s. In the Cartagena Commitment adopted at UNCTAD VIII, all participants pledged a 'new partnership for development' and established the spirit of Cartagena expressing their political will to translate words into reality. UNCTAD became a focal point for facilitating and implementing the new development consensus. It gave priority to the following areas:

(a) *A new partnership for development.* The central focus of UNCTAD's work is on giving high quality concrete and pragmatic content to the new partnership for development by:

(i) suggesting and supporting national and international efforts to ensure greater participation in the world economy of developing countries and economies in transition;

(ii) improving the quality, scope, depth and themes of international co-operation for development.

(b) *Global interdependence.* The chief aim of UNCTAD work is now on strengthening interdependence and reducing global economic imbalances by focusing on:

(i) the international implications of macro-economic policies;

(ii) the evolution of the world trading, monetary and financial systems;

(iii) good management at the international level;

(iv) the impact of enlarged economic spaces and regional integration processes.

Undoubtedly the Cartagena UNCTAD VIII will manifest itself as we progress through the 1990s, especially through WTO.

In the development of shipping and ports UNCTAD has played a significant role in the area of rules covering international shipping. A Committee on Shipping was set up in 1965 to focus on international shipping legislation and such development issues as the establishment and expansion of national merchant marines. It was later expanded to include multi-modal transport bulk cargo markets and the registration of ships. Several binding and non-binding codes have been agreed in these areas. Details of new areas emerging at UNCTAD VIII are as follows:

(a) Promotion of transparent and competitive maritime services, particularly the development of infrastructure including ports;

(b) Analysis and monitoring of developments in multi-modal transport, including technological development and containerization;

(c) Further work on maritime legislation and strengthening human resources development.

UNCTAD VIII called for increased involvement of the various actors of the port industry in UNCTAD work. An inter-governmental group of experts on ports in 1992 began to process the under-mentioned two main tasks:

(a) Port organization, including issues relating to privatization, commercialization, deregulation and legislation.

(b) Port management, including issues relating to human resourses, development, strategic planning, marketing, sustainable development and investment.

This involved the following areas being addressed in the work programme in shipping, ports and multi-modal transport:

(a) Promoting transparency: (i) collect and disseminate information on technological and structural changes in shipping, ports and multi-modal transport, and on the balance between supply and demand for maritime services; and (ii) collect and disseminate information on measures including laws and regulations affecting access to markets for international shipping and multi-modal transport, and affecting port services.

(b) Fostering competitive maritime transport services: (i) undertake comparative analysis of the shipping sector and related policies in different countries with a view to determining factors contributing to or impeding the development of competitive national shipping industries; (ii) assess the impact of progressive liberalization on the development of shipping services; (iii) monitor and report on changes in national practices covering shipper/ocean carrier relations; (iv) identify and examine possible activities and policies aimed at enhancing co-operation in the field of shipping, ports and multi-modal transport; (v) study prevailing ship financing arrangements and their adequacy; (vi) undertake comparative analysis of the port sector and related policies in different countries; (vii) assess competition between ports and potential for increased regional co-operation.

A number of other areas are being likewise examined in maritime legislation and the development of multi-modal transport, technology and containerization.

Overall the foregoing programme will be a lengthy process to determine and implement, and involves liaising with other international agencies such as ICC/ILO/IMO/WTO/UNCTRAL, but the effect will be profound (see p. 124).

8.14 WORLD TRADE ORGANIZATION AND THE GENERAL AGREEMENT ON TARIFFS AND TRADE

The General Agreement on Tariffs and Trade (GATT) was formed in 1947 with a membership of 23 countries. It came into being as result of successive conferences held between 1946 and 1948 in London, New York and Havana and which were intended to result in the establishment of the international trade organization. Today it has some 108 member countries, with more than 30 associate members which apply GATT rules and objectives to their trading operations and, in return, are afforded equal treatment by the contracting parties. Over 80% of world trade is conducted under GATT; it is based in Geneva.

The General Agreement comprises 38 general articles which contain provisions relating to both tariffs and non-tariff barriers to trade. The underlying objective is to ensure the observance by every GATT contracting party of its tariff obligations and to exclude the use of non-tariff barriers to trade except in the limited circumstances permitted. The General Agreement has four underlying discernible principles detailed below:

(a) Non-discrimination. The most favoured nation clause (MFN) of the GATT obliges each contracting party to grant all other signatories equal treatment in their trade policies.

(b) Reliance upon tariffs, as opposed to other less transparent commercial policy measures, where protection is considered necessary for domestic industry.

(c) The effective provision of a stable and predictable environment for trade through the 'binding' of tariffs.

(d) The settlement of trade disputes through an ongoing process of consultation and conciliation.

In pursuit of its aims, the GATT functions on two complementary levels:

(a) As a body of rules comprising the General Agreement itself and various additional legal instruments which have been negotiated under its aegis.

(b) As a permanent institution to monitor trade developments, to organize negotiations to remove or reduce trade barriers, and to resolve trade disputes.

Also of considerable importance is the preferential status given to developing countries, in particular under Part IV of the General Agreement. Developing countries have participated in the GATT since its inception, when they comprised 10 of the 23 founding members. During the course of successive negotiations, they have been released from certain obligations of membership. Thus, during the Uruguay Round, developing countries were not expected to make concessions which were potentially inconsistent with their individual development, financial and trade requirements.

In addition, by promoting multi-lateral, as opposed to bilateral, trade the GATT allows small and medium sized countries, together with LDCs, to play a positive role in determining trade policy and to benefit from the trade deals negotiated with major nations. Hence, GATT is both a body of rules and a forum for conciliation and negotiation.

There have been some eight series of trade negotiations and details are given below:

1947 Geneva – 23 countries – drafting Havana charter.

1949 Annecy – ongoing tariffs cuts.

1950/51 Torquay – ongoing tariff cuts.

1955/56 Geneva – ongoing tariff cuts. Overall, between 1949 and 1956 some 45 000 tariff cuts and concessions were agreed, especially with major trading nations.

1961/62 Geneva – Dillon Round – 4400 tariff concessions and of special relevance to formulation of EC in 1957 with resulting tariff concessions.

1963/1967 Geneva – Kennedy Round – adoption of new tariff negotiating methods, comprising multi-lateral across-the-board cuts for industrial products. Overall average tariff reductions of 35% agreed and adoption of anti-dumping code.

1973/79 Geneva – Tokyo Round – continuing tariff reduction agreed and inception of a series of supplementary agreements known as codes on a wide variety of subjects. They include technical standards, import licensing procedures, dumping, subsidies, government procurement, and certain commodity areas such as beef and dairy products.

1986/94 Uruguay – This round was the most complex and ambitious trade liberalizing negotiations ever undertaken by the contracting parties to the General Agreement. It stemed from the two-part format of the Punta del Este declaration.

The basic aims of the negotiations, as agreed at Punta del Este, were fourfold:

(a) To achieve further liberalization and expansion of world trade for the benefit of all countries, especially less developed countries.

(b) To strengthen and improve the role of GATT and bring about a wider coverage of world trade under agreed, effective and enforceable multilateral disciplines.

(c) To increase the responsiveness of the GATT system to the evolving international economic environment, notably through closer co-ordination between GATT and other international bodies and by taking account of changes in trade patterns and prospects.

(d) To foster concurrent co-operative action at national and international levels to strengthen the ties between trade and other economic policies affecting growth and development.

In order to achieve these objectives, it was agreed that the negotiations would be conducted in as transparent a manner as possible and that balanced concessions would be sought within broad trading areas in order to avoid unwarranted cross-sectoral demands. Above all the contracting parties agreed that the principle of special and differential treatment of developing countries would apply unequivocally to the new Round.

Thus, developed countries had no right to expect or demand reciprocity of concessions from the LDCs in the Round. Special attention was also to be given to the particular problems of the less developed countries and to measures to facilitate an expansion of their trading opportunities.

The Uruguay round covered the following areas.

(a) *Tariffs and non-tariff barriers.*

(b) *Safeguards, notification and surveillance and dispute settlement.*

(c) *Agriculture protectionism and subsidies* (especially relevant to the EU and USA).

(d) *Services.* This embraces a wide range of services and seeks to determine some broad concepts on which to base the principles and rules for trade in services, including possible disciplines for individual sectors, and covers consultancy, accountancy, advertising, health, education, banking, telecommunications, insurance and so on.

(e) *Intellectual property and counterfeiting.* The aim is to introduce new multilateral rules and disciplines in order to reduce distortions and impediments to international trade in patents, trade marks, copyright, trade secrets and industrial design.

(f) *Trade-related investment measures.* This involves a wide variety of requirements and the current practice of limitation on foreign investment, and covers local content, export performance, trade balancing requirements, technology transference and so on.

(g) *Textiles and clothing.* This involves reviewing the Multi-Fibre Agreement (MFA) which was adopted in 1974 and renewed on three occasions, the last being in 1986.

The objectives stated in the preamble to the MFA are to ensure the expansion of trade in textile products, particularly for the developing countries, and progressively to achieve the reduction of trade barriers and the liberalization of world trade in textile products. At the same time, it seeks to avoid disruptive effects in individual markets and on individual lines of production, both in importing and exporting countries. In practice, the MFA permits participating countries to impose selective quotas against disruptive textile imports in prescribed circumstances in derogation from the GATT. Parties may also negotiate bilateral agreements when there is perceived to be a real risk of market disruption. The arrangement applies to textiles and clothing made from cotton, wool and man-made (synthetic or regenerated) fibres.

The Final Act of the Uruguay round was signed in Marrakesh on 15 April 1994 by some 124 countries and the EU. It also established the World Trade Organization (WTO). Overall it contained some 28 agreements and GATT economists estimate that it will add some US$755 billion to world exports and raise incomes by some $235 billion annually, excluding China and the CIS. A number of other countries signed the new Government Procurement Code that was negotiated in parallel with the Uruguay Round and three other plurilateral agreements on dairy products, bovine meat and civil aircraft.

Details of the trade expansion predicted by 2002 involving world income gains of US$235 billion annually and trade gains of $755 billion annually are as follows:

(a) A major increase in ability to enter overseas markets without trade barriers hitherto in existence through higher levels of tariff bindings (on industrial products from 78% to 99% in developed countries and from 22% to 72% in developing countries).

(b) Emerging from tariffication and bindings has produced 100% security for agricultural products.

(c) A 38% overall reduction in developed countries' tariffs on industrial products from 6.3% to 3.9%.

(d) An increase from 20% to 43% in the value of imported industrial products that receive duty-free treatment in developed countries together with a decline from 7% to 5% in the proportion of imports subject to peak tariffs.

(e) Considerable progress in reducing 'tariff escalation' which should benefit developing economies seeking to export more processed versions of primary products.

(f) Above-average tariff cuts for many products of export interest to developing economies.

(g) A significant number of commitments in service areas, including especially tourism and travel, and business and financial services.

Salient details of the Uruguay Round are given below as notified at Marrakesh.

(a) Agriculture

There are four main elements: the concessions and commitments members are to undertake on market access, domestic support and export subsidies; the agreement in sanitary and phytosanitary measures, and the ministerial decision concerning least developed and net food importing developing countries. Overall the results of the negotiations provide a framework for the long-term reform of agricultural trade and domestic policies over the years to come. It also includes provisions that encourage the use of less trade-distorting domestic support policies to maintain the rural economy. In the area of market access non-tariff border measures are replaced by tariffs that provide substantially the same level of protection.

(b) Sanitary and phytosanitary

This involves food safety and animal and plant health regulations. It recognizes that governments have the right to take sanitary and phytosanitary measures but that they should be applied only to the extent necessary to protect human, animal or plant life or health and should not arbitrarily or unjustifiably discriminate between members when identical or similar conditions prevail. In order to harmonize sanitary and phytosanitary measures members are encouraged to base their measures on international standards, guidelines and recommendations where they exist.

(c) Textiles and clothing

This involves the eventual integration of the textiles and clothing sector – where much of the trade is currently subject to bilateral quotas negotiated under the MFA – into the GATT on the basis of strengthened rules and disciplines. A textiles monitoring body will be established to oversee the implementation of commitments and to prepare reports for the major reviews.

(d)   Technical barriers to trade
This extends and clarifies the agreement on technical barriers to trade reached in the Tokyo Round. It seeks to ensure that technical negotiations and standards as well as testing and certification procedures do not create unnecessary obstacles to trade. However, it recognizes that countries have the right to establish protection at levels they consider appropriate.

(e)   Trade-related aspects of investment measures (TRIM)
This recognizes that certain investment measures restrict and distort trade. A TRIM list has been agreed which features measures which require particular levels of local procurement by an enterprise (local content requirements) or which restrict the volume or value of imports such an enterprise can purchase or use to an amount related to the level of products it exports (trade balancing requirements).

(f)   Anti-dumping
This provides the right to contracting parties to apply anti-dumping measures, i.e. measures against imports of a product at an export price below its 'normal value' (usually the price of the product in the domestic market of the exporting country), if such dumped imports cause injury to a domestic industry in the territory of the importing contracting party. A new provision requires the immediate termination of an anti-dumping investigation in cases where the authorities determine that the margin of dumping is *de minimis* (which is defined as less than 2% expressed as a percentage of the export price of the product) or that the volume of dumped imports is negligible (generally when the volume of dumped imports from an individual country accounts for less than 3% of the imports of the product in question into the importing country).

(g)   Customs valuation
This provides customs administrations the right to request further information from importers where they have reason to doubt the accuracy of the declared value of imported goods.

(h)   Pre-shipment inspection (PSI) (see p. 446)
The agreement recognizes that GATT principles and obligations apply to the activities of pre-shipment inspection agencies mandated by governments. The obligations placed on PSI user governments include non-discrimination, transparency, protection of confidential business information, avoidance of unreasonable delay, the use of specific guidelines for conducting price verification and the avoidance of conflicts of interest by the PSI agencies. The agreement establishes an independent review procedure – administered jointly by an organization representing PSI agencies and an organization representing exporters – to resolve disputes between an exporter and a PSI agency.

(i)   Rules of origin (including certificate of origin – see p. 445)
The agreement aims at long-term harmonization of the rules of origin other than rules of origin relating to the granting of tariff preferences, and to ensure that such rules do not themselves create unnecessary obstacles to trade. The agreement sets up a harmonization programme to be completed within three years.

(j)   Import licensing procedures
The agreement strengthens the discipline on the users of import licensing systems and increases transparency and predictability. In particular it requires parties to publish sufficient information for traders to know the basis on which licences are granted.

(k)   Subsidies and countervailing measures
The agreement is an extension of earlier agreements and establishes three categories of subsidies: prohibited subsidies are to be subject to a new dispute settlement procedure which embraces an expedited timetable for action by the dispute settlement body; actionable subsidies are those which it is stipulated that no member should cause through the use of subsidies adverse effects to the interests of other signatories; non-actionable subsidies which could either be non-specific subsidies or specific subsidies involving assistance to industrial research and pre-competitive development activity, assistance to disadvantaged regions, or

certain types of assistance for adopting existing facilities to new environmental requirements imposed by laws and/or regulations.

The other part of the agreement features the use of countervailing measures on subsidized imports and outlines the regulatory environment in which the countervailing measures would function, investigations by national authorities, and rules of evidence to ensure that all interested parties can present information and argument. Certain disciplines on the calculation of the amount of a subsidy are outlined as is the basis for the determination of injury to the domestic industry.

(l) Safeguards
The agreement breaks new ground in establishing a prohibition against so-called 'grey area' measures and in setting a sunset clause in all safeguard actions. It stipulates that a member should not seek, take or maintain any voluntary export restraints, orderly marketing arrangements or any other similar measures on the export or import side. Any such measure in effect at the time of entry into force of the agreement would be brought into conformity with this agreement or would have to be phased out within four years after entry into force of the agreement establishing the WTO. The agreement establishes a Safeguards Committee which would oversee the operation of its provisions and be responsible for the surveillance of its commitments.

(m) Trade in services
The agreement is in three parts and covers basic obligations for all member countries, the specific conditions in individual sectors, and national schedules of commitments containing specific further areas which will be the subject of a continuing process of liberalization, e.g. capital movement for investment, the development of tourism. It features the most favoured nation obligation and embraces all the service sectors such as banking, education, tourism, telecommunications, air and maritime services. In regard to maritime services it embraces three sectors – international shipping, auxiliary services and access to and use of port facilities. Overall the aim is to eliminate restrictions within a timescale. Eighteen countries plus the EU have announced their intention to take part in these negotiations on a voluntary basis. The liberalization of trade services in this sector was an important element in the

Uruguay Round and by April 1994 participants, including the European Union as a single market, had submitted a list of 89 commitments. The effect is likely to be very profound.

(n) Intellectual property rights (including trade in counterfeit goods)

The agreement recognizes that widely varying standards in the protection and enforcement of intellectual property rights and the lack of a multilateral framework of principles, rules and disciplines dealing with international trade in counterfeit goods have been a growing source of tension in economic relations. Rules and disciplines are needed to cope with these tensions. Accordingly the agreement addresses the applicability of basic GATT principles and those of relevant international intellectual property agreements; the provision of adequate intellectual property rights; the provision of effective enforcement measures for those rights; multilateral dispute settlement; and transitional arrangements. The agreement embraces compliance with the Berne Convention for the protection of literary and artistic works in its latest version (Paris, 1971). This covers computer programs and sound recordings. It also includes trade marks and service marks under industrial design, and integrated circuits as trade secrets. The agreement establishes a Council for Trade-Related Aspects of Intellectual Property Rights to monitor the operation of the agreement and government compliance with it.

Overall a major aspect of the agreement is the global reduction of tariffs by 40% and the achievement of wider open markets.

The World Trade Organization (WTO)

The WTO was established on 1 January 1995 and brought a new era of global economic co-operation, reflecting the widespread desire of member countries to operate a fairer and more open multilateral trading system for the benefit and welfare of their peoples. It was set up to facilitate the implementation and operation of all the agreements and legal instruments negotiated in connection with the Uruguay Round, including the plurilateral trade agreements (trade in civil aircraft, government procurement, trade in dairy products and bovinement); to provide a forum for all negotiations; and to administer the understanding on rules and procedures governing the settlement of disputes and trade policy (TPRM). It co-operates with the International Monetary Fund and the International Bank for Reconstruction and Development to ensure greater coherence in global economic policy-making.

CHAPTER 9

Passenger fares and freight rates

9.1 THEORY OF PASSENGER FARES

Passenger fares are normally dictated by the nature of the voyage, the class of ship and the accommodation offered. The Italians have the largest deep-sea passenger fleet. The docking expenses of the passenger vessel on an international voyage involving the disembarkation of passengers is costly and many cruise operators rely on passenger tenders (launches) to convey passengers to and from the vessel situated in outer harbour. Shipboard operating costs are high, since food and service must be provided. Product differentiation is an outstanding factor, since the service and comfort of different cruise lines and vessels by class of cabin accommodation vary greatly.

Generally speaking, the cruise shipowner will charge a fixed rate per day depending on the accommodation offered. The technique of market pricing has been introduced on some cruise markets, differing fares being charged according to demand; for example, during off-peak periods a lower tariff would be offered.

9.2 THEORY OF FREIGHT RATES AND EFFECT OF AIR COMPETITION ON CARGO TRAFFIC

Freight is the reward payable to the carrier for the carriage and arrival of goods in a mercantile or recognized condition, ready to be delivered to the merchant.

The pricing of cargo ships' services, like all pricing, is dependent on the forces of supply and demand, but the factors affecting both supply and demand are perhaps more complicated than in the case of most other industries and services. As with all forms of transport, the demand for shipping is derived from the demand for the commodities carried, and is, therefore, affected by the elasticity of demand for these commodities.

The demand for sea transport is affected both by direct competition between carriers and, because it is a derived demand, by the competition of substitutes or alternatives for the particular commodity carried. On any particular route, the shipowner is subject to competition from carriers on the same route, and also from carriers operating from alternative supply areas. The commodities carried by the latter may be competitive with the commodities from his own supply area and, to that extent, may affect the demand for his services. On some routes there is also competition from air transport for high value to low weight ratio consignments, and in the coasting trade there is also competition from inland transport.

The elasticity of demand for shipping services varies from one commodity to another. In normal times, an important factor affecting elasticity of demand for sea transport services is the cost of transport in relation to the market price of the goods carried. Although it can be negligible, the cost of sea transport and associated expenses is often a considerable element in the final market price of many commodities. It may be between 8 and 15%.

The price eventually fixed depends largely on the relationship between buyers and sellers. Where both groups are numerous, and have equal bargaining power, and where demand is fairly elastic, conditions of relatively perfect competition prevail. Under these circumstances, prices are fixed by the 'haggling of the market' and are known as contract prices. The market for tramp charters operates under such conditions, and the contract is drawn up as an agreement known as a charter party.

The contract may be for a single voyage at so much per tonne of the commodity carried, or it may be for a period at a stipulated rate of hire, usually so much per tonne of the ship's deadweight carrying capacity. The charter rates are quoted on a competitive basis, in various exchanges throughout the world. Foodstuffs and raw materials in particular are traded in a highly competitive world market, and their movement is irregular, depending upon demand and supply conditions. It is quite usual for cargoes of these commodities to be loaded and actually marketed during transit, the charterers instructing the ship to proceed to a certain range of ports and determining the port of discharge while the ship is en route. In the case of very long-term charters, tankers or ore carriers, the rate of hire is fixed to give the owner a reasonable return on his investment.

Under these conditions, the rate structure for tramps is a very simple product and emerges from competitive interplay of supply and demand. From the economist's point of view, rates made in this way represent the most efficient methods of pricing, for where price is determined under conditions of perfect competition, production is encouraged to follow consumers' wishes, and price itself does not deviate to any great extent from average total cost. In this way the customer is satisfied and production capacity most usefully employed. Detailed below are the factors influencing the formulation of a fixture rate:

(a) Ship specification which would also embrace the type of vessel, i.e. bulk carrier, containership, oil tanker.

(b) The types of traffic to be conveyed.

(c) General market conditions. This is a major factor and generally an abundance of available ships for charter tends to depress the rate particularly for voyage and short-term charters.

(d) The daily cost to be borne by the charterer. This basically depends on the charter-party terms. In a favourable shipowners' market situation the shipowner would endeavour to negotiate a rate to cover not only direct cost, which, depending on the charter-party terms, covers fuel, crew, etc., but also a contribution to indirect cost such as depreciation and mortgage repayments. In so doing the shipowner would strive to conclude a profitable fixture rate. Some shipowners under demise time charter terms insist on retaining their own master for a variety of reasons, and this cost is borne by the charterer. This could be extended to include chief engineer.

(e) The duration of the charter. Generally speaking the longer the charter, the less it is influenced by the market situation relative to the availability of ships and the demand for them.

(f) The terms of the charter. It must be remembered that the shipowner and charterer are free to conclude a charter party of any terms. Usually, however, a charter party bearing one of the code names for a particular trade, i.e. Cementvoy for cement, is used when practicable. It is frequently necessary in such circumstances to vary the terms of the charter party by the deletion or addition of clauses to meet individual needs.

(g) The identity of cost to be borne by the charterer and shipowner must be clearly established. For example it may be a gross form charter or FIO charter or net form (see p. 333).

(h) Responsibility for the survey costs of the vessel must be clearly defined as to whether they are for the charterer's or shipowner's account.

(i) The urgency of the charter. If a charterer requires a vessel almost immediately there tends to be less haggling on fixture rates and this favours the shipowner.

(j) The convenience of the charter to the shipowner. If the broker negotiates a charter which terminates and places the vessel in a maritime area where demand for tonnage is strong, it will tend possibly to depress the rate. In such circumstances the shipowner will have a good chance to secure another fixture at a favourable rate with no long ballast voyage.

(k) The BIFFEX criteria (see pp. 163–4).

The importance of each of the foregoing points will vary by circumstances.

The tramp industry can be regarded as a pool of shipping, from which vessels move in accordance with world demand to the employment in which they are most valued by the consumer. Freight fixtures for tramp charters are recorded daily in such shipping publications as *Lloyd's List*, which students are recommended to study. The Chamber of Shipping publishes a quarterly issued statistical brief covering VLCC (worldscale) Arabian Gulf–West, the Baltic Freight Index (dry cargo) and the Tramp Trip Charter Index with a 1985 = 100 base year and March 1995 recording of 305. Data is also available on fixture rates for the the Suezmax, Aframax and Panamax sectors. Such data are ideal as a measure of the state and trends of the world tramp market.

In the liner trades, the shipowners control fairly large concerns, and although some of their shippers may be very large firms, the bulk of their traffic comes from the numerous small shippers. In these conditions, it is more convenient for the shipowner to estimate how much his customers are prepared to pay, and fix his own rate. Such prices are known as tariff prices. As liner rates are relatively stable, merchants can quote prices (including freight) in advance of sailings. A declining number of liner cargo shipowners operate under liner conference terms who formulate the tariffs (see p. 198).

Liner rates are based partly on cost, and partly on value. Many freight rates are quoted on a basis of weight or measurement at ship's option. This means that the rate quoted will be applied either per metric ton of 1000 kg (2205 lb) or per tonne of 1.133 m³, whichever will produce the greater revenue. The reason for this method of charging is that heavy cargo will bring a vessel to her loadline before her space is full, while light cargo will fill her space without bringing her down to her maximum draught. To produce the highest revenue a vessel must be loaded to her full internal capacity, and immersed to her maximum permitted depth. Therefore charging by weight or measurement is a cost question. In most trades, cargo measuring under 1.133 m³ per tonne weight is charged on a weight basis, whilst cargo measuring 1.133 m³ or more per ton is charged on a measurement basis. With the spread of the metric system, most freight rates are quoted per 1000 kg or m³ (35.33 ft³).

Liner tariffs quote rates for many commodities which move regularly. These rates are based on the stowage factor (rate of bulk to weight), on the value of the cargo and on the competitive situation. Many tariffs publish class rates for general cargo not otherwise specified. Some tariffs publish class rates whereby commodities are grouped for charging into several classes. On commodities of very high value *ad valorem* rates are charged at so much per cent of the declared value. When commodities move in large quantities, and are susceptible to tramp competition, tariffs often employ 'open rates', i.e. the rate is left open, so that the shipping line can quote whatever rate is appropriate.

To illustrate the calculation of the freight rate an example is given below. It involves the conveyance of electrical goods from Birmingham to Bilbao involving a maritime movement and the alternative road vehicle transit throughout – all items are packed in wooden cases.

16 cartons:	120 × 80 × 60 cm
Weight of each carton:	75 kg

Freight rates by sea/road (assume US\$1.5 = £1):

Sea:	US\$175 per tonne W/M
Road:	US\$350 per 1000 chargeable kg

Chargeable weight/volume ratios for each mode (CBM = cubic metre):

Sea:	1 CBM = 1000 kg
Road:	3 CBM = 1000 kg

Sea rate per tonne (1000 kg): US$175

Rate sterling per tonne:	US$175 ÷ 1.5 = 116.66
Rate sterling per kg:	£116.66 ÷ 1000 = £0.11

Volumetric rate:

$$\text{1 carton} = \frac{120 \times 80 \times 60}{1000} \text{ kg}$$

$$\text{16 cartons} = \frac{16 \times 120 \times 80 \times 60}{1000} \text{ kg} = 9216 \text{ kg}$$

Sea freight rate	=	£0.11 per kg
	=	£0.11 × 9216
	=	£1013.76

Rate by weight:

1 carton	=	75 kg
16 cartons	=	16 × 75 kg = 1200 kg
Sea freight rate	=	£0.11 per kg
Total sea freight rate	=	1200 kg × £0.11 per kg
	=	£132

In some trades the rate would be based on the nearest tonne in which case the volumetric rate would rise from 9216 kg to 10 000 kg and yield £1166.60, and the weight from 1200 kg to 2000 kg to produce £220.

Road rate per chargeable 1000 kg: US$350

Rate sterling per chargeable 1000 kg:	US$350 ÷ 1.5 = £233.33
Rate sterling per kg:	£233.33 ÷ 1000 = £0.23

Volumetric rate:

$$\text{1 carton} = \frac{120 \times 80 \times 60}{3000} \text{ kg}$$

$$\text{16 cartons} = \frac{16 \times 120 \times 80 \times 60}{3000} \text{ kg} = 3072 \text{ kg}$$

Road freight rate   =   £0.23

Total road frcight rate   –   3072 × £0.23

                                =   £706.56

Rate by weight:

   1 carton   =   75 kg

   16 cartons   =   16 × 75 kg = 1200 kg

   Road freight rate   =   £0.23

   Total road freight rate =   1200 × £0.23

                                  =   £276

In some trades the rate would be based on the nearest tonne in which case the volumetric rate would rise from 3072 kg to 4000 kg and yield £933.32, and the weight from 1200 kg to 2000 kg to produce £466.66.

Accordingly the carrier would charge the volumetric or weight rate which will yield the highest income:

Sea volumetric: £1166.60

Road volumetric: £933.32

In recent years there has been a tendency in an increasing number of liner cargo trades to impose a surcharge on the basic rate and examples are given below of the types which emerge:

(a) Bunkering or fuel surcharge. In an era when fuel costs now represent a substantial proportion of total direct voyage cost – a situation which has arisen from the very substantial increase in bunkering expenses from 1973 and 1979 – shipowners are not prepared to absorb the variation in fuel prices. They take the view that price variation of bunker fuel tends to be unpredictable bearing in mind it is usually based on the variable dollar rate of exchange and it is difficult to budget realistically for this cost to reflect it adequately in their rate formulation. Moreover, an increase in the bunkering price erodes the shipowner's voyage profitability.

(b) Currency surcharge. This arises when the freight rate is related to a floating currency such as sterling. For example, if the rate was based on French or Belgian francs which both operate fixed rates of currency, the sterling rate of exchange in January would be probably different to the situation in the following July. For example, when sterling is depressed, sterling would probably

Table 9.1 Currency adjustment factor scale

When charges are to be paid in French francs: French francs to £1	Surcharge in French francs (%)
10.82 to 11.04	5
10.59 to 10.81	4
10.36 to 10.58	3
10.13 to 10.35	2
10.02 to 10.12	1
No surcharge 9.78 to 10.01 (void area)	Nil

When charges are to be paid in Sterling	Surcharge in French francs (%)
9.66 to 9.77	1
9.43 to 9.65	2
9.20 to 9.42	3
8.97 to 9.19	4
8.74 to 8.96	5

earn more French and Belgian francs per £1 in January than in the following July. Accordingly a currency surcharge is imposed to minimize losses the shipowner would incur bearing in mind the shipowner would obtain less sterling equivalent in French or Belgian franc-rated traffic, whilst at the same time the port expenses in Belgium and France would be more expensive due to the depressed sterling rate of exchange.

An example of a currency surcharge scale is given below. It involves the Anglo/French trade. The freight tariff is sterling based calculated as 9.90 French francs to £1 and the rate per tonne is £20 or 198 French francs.

The percentage of surcharge will be determined each week by reference to the average rate as published in *Le Monde* and *The Financial Times* on Saturdays, i.e. Friday's closing prices.

(i)	Payment in sterling – exchange rate 9.18 French francs to £1	£
	10 tonnes merchandise at £20 per tonne	200
	4% surcharge based on exchange rate of 9.18 Ffr	8
	Total	£208

(ii)	Payment in French francs – exchange rate 11.02 Ffr to £1	Ffr
	10 tonnes at 198 French francs per tonne	1980
	5% surcharge based on exchange rate of 11.02Ffr	99
	Total French francs	2079

(c)   Surcharges are usually raised for heavy lifts such as indivisible consignments and on excessive height or length of Ro/Ro rated traffic, together with any other traffic where special facilities are required.

For livestock and dangerous classified cargo special rates apply to reflect the additional facilities the shipowner must provide to convey such traffic. The dangerous cargo classified traffic normally attracts a 50% surcharge above the general rated traffic. Such traffic requires extensive prebooking arrangements and a declaration signed by the shipper of the cargo contents. This is extensively dealt with in Chapter 7 of my book *Export Practice and Management*.

It is important to note that a substantial volume of general merchandise cargo now moves under groupage or consolidation arrangements. This involves the freight forwarder who originates the traffic from a number of consignors to a number of consignees and despatches the compatible cargo in a container or international road haulage vehicle. The freight forwarder in consultation with another freight forwarder in the destination country operates on a reciprocal basis. The rate includes the collection and delivery charges, usually undertaken by road transport. The freight forwarders operate from a warehouse which may form part of some leased accommodation at a container base with inland clearance depot facilities. The latter will permit the cargo to move under bond to and from the port. The rates are based on a weight/

measurement (W/M) basis whichever produces the greater revenue to the freight forwarder and is described in detail on p. 186. A cargo manifest accompanies the consolidated consignment throughout the transit and the merits of groupage are described on p. 231. It is usual for the freight forwarder to prebook shipping space involving the container or road vehicle on specified sailings to thereby offer a regular assured service to the shipper.

Rate making is affected by such factors as susceptibility of the cargo to damage or pilferage, nature of packaging, competition, transit cost and convenience of handling. A properly compiled tariff should encourage the movement of all classes of cargo, to ensure the best balance between revenue production and the full utilization of vessels.

It is important to note than in liner trades cargo is received and delivered into transit sheds or onto the quay, so that loading and discharging expenses are met by the shipowner and covered by the rate of freight quoted. Therefore, the efficiency of ports and their labour and equipment has a direct influence on rate making.

As indicated elsewhere in this book, liner cargo trades are becoming containerized and, whilst the factors relating to rate making tend to remain virtually unchanged, it should be noted that the tariff is now being based on the container as a unit or commodity based for the LCL cargo (see p. 378). It does of course vary by ownership, distance, route, size and type. Many containers are consigned on a through-rate basis from the inland point of despatch to the destination with the maritime transit intervening.

A market which has developed extensively in recent years is project forwarding. It involves the despatch/conveyance arrangements which stem from a contract award such as a power station project. The contract is usually awarded to a consortium and the freight forwarder undertakes all the despatch/conveyance arrangements. This involves the freight forwarder negotiating with the shipowner special rates for the merchandise conveyed and the associated prebooking and shipment arrangments. Often such shipments require special arrangements and purpose-built equipment being provided for which a comprehensive rate is given, usually on a cost plus profit basis.

Another market is antiques. It may be a valuable painting, collection of furniture, etc. Such goods require specialized packing undertaken by professional packers. Pre-shipment arrangements are extensive including security and documentation. Two types of antiques market exist: one as just described, the very valuable art treasure of national prestige, and the other involving the much larger market of antiques. The rates of the former market are negotiated with the shipowner and have regard to various provisions including security and the cost thereof. Much of such traffic travels by air freight. The latter market of less valuable antiques is usually containerized as found in the Anglo/North American trade. Standard rates for the range of antiques exist which are subject to strict conditions of shipment such as to be professionally packed.

An additional method of freight rate assessment is found in Ro/Ro services. It is based either on the square footage occupied by the vehicle on the ship's deck, or on a linear footage basis calculated at so much per foot depending on the overall length of the road vehicle. The rate usually remains unchanged irrespective of type of cargo shipped in the road vehicle. Rates vary in whether the vehicle/trailer is empty or loaded, accompanied or unaccompanied. Concessionary rates sometimes apply in certain trades when the vehicle uses the same route for the return load. Generally speaking, air competition has so far not made any serious inroads in cargo traffic – certainly not to the same extent as has been experienced in the passenger trade. Nevertheless, the tendency has been for certain types of traffic which have a relatively high value and low weight ratio or demand a fast service, due to the nature of the cargo or urgency of the consignment, to be conveyed by air transport. Such competition has not been felt very much in tramping, but has had a more significant effect on liner cargo services and in some markets the sea/air bridge has been developed (see pp. 424–6). The liner operator is very conscious of such competition, and to help combat the situation; vessels of higher speeds have been introduced.

It must be recognized as mentioned earlier that most of the world's most important liner cargo routes are now containerized on an intermodal basis (see Chapter 16), offering much faster services through the provision of faster ships and rationalization of ports of call. The rates are often from the inland terminal such as a container base, to a similar facility in the destination country. Many of the container shipments for the general cargo-covered type of container are mixed cargoes, each individually rated by commodity classification. The more specialized form of container has individual rates formulated by classified container type.

The continuous expansion of maritime containerization has adversely tempered the further growth of air freight. However, the world's airlines are beginning to devote more resources to develop increased air freight capacity through wide-bodied aricraft and increase marketing effort, including developing the sea/air bridge (see pp. 422–6). Such developments will marginally abstract traffic from the consolidated ISO container market of high value to low weight ratio high cube commodities in distance markets. Currently some 10% of the world's trade by value is conveyed by air transport.

In recent years the CABAF technique has been introduced which is the currency adjustment and bunkering adjustment factor. When shipping companies calculate their freight rates, they take account of the exchange rate level and fuel costs. In so doing they can use rates applicable at the time the freight rate is compiled or the market forecasts of currency exchange rates and bunker costs operative at the time the new freight rate is introduced on the service/trade. For example, if the shipowner is calculating their rate in deutschmarks, and an exporter is paying for freight in sterling, in the event of the deutschmark rate rising the shipowner will want more sterling for the freight and an adjustment factor will be added to the freight invoice. If the price of bunker fuel is also likely to vary similarly a surcharge is likely to be imposed relative to the increased cost. In some trades they are called simply currency and fuel surcharges and their application varies. The bunker surcharge is usually consolidated into the rate as soon as new rate levels are introduced which in many trades is every six or twelve months depending on the level of inflation operative. See pp. 187–9.

9.3 RELATION BETWEEN LINER AND TRAMP RATES

In general, liner and tramp rates fluctuate in the same direction. But liner rates are more stable than tramp rates, which are particularly sensitive to short-term supply and demand conditions. Comparisons are not easy, however, since published data on liner rates are fragmentary, and no index of liner rates is available to set against the quarterly issued tramp rate indices (see p. 184).

Nevertheless, although tramps provide liners with only limited competition, the world tramp fleet is a factor to be taken into account, and, in times of falling tramp rates, liner rates must inevitably be influenced in the same direction by fear of such competition in some markets. Conversely, when tramp rates rise, liner operators will feel able to follow in the same direction, particularly if costs are rising. Generally speaking, liner rates are less sensitive to changes in market demand and more sensitive to changes in cost than tramp rates. The student should note that the increasing specialization in the range of container types (see pp. 378–93) may remove tramp competition from some commodities and routes, so that rates for such commodities may remain outside the influence of competition. During the past decade the correlation between liner and tramp rates has been greatly reduced, especially with the development of multi-modalism, and this trend is likely to continue.

9.4 RELATION BETWEEN VOYAGE AND TIME CHARTER RATES

A voyage charter is a contract for specific voyage, while a time charter is a contract for a period of time which may cover several voyages. Therefore, the voyage charter rate is a short-term rate, while the time charter rate is often a long-term rate. When trade is buoyant and voyage rates are rising, charterers, in anticipation of further rises, tend to charter for longer periods to cover their commitments; when rates are expected to fall, they tend to contract for shorter periods. Therefore, the current time charter rate tends to reflect the expected trend of voyage rates in the future. If rates are expected to rise, it will tend to be above the current voyage rates; if they are expected to fall, it will tend to be below the current voyage rates. Generally speaking, the two rates move in the same direction but because time charter rates depend on market expectations, they tend to fluctuate more widely than voyage rates. When conditions are improving, long-term rates tend to rise more rapidly than voyage rates; when conditions are deteriorating, voyage rates tend to fall more rapidly. Students are urged to study the tramp rate indices mentioned on p. 184 and the market conditions determincing their variation.

9.5 TYPES OF FREIGHT

This study of freight rates would not be complete without an examination of the types available. The true test of the shipowner's right to freight is whether the service in respect of which the freight was contracted to be paid has been substantially performed, or, if not, whether its performance has been prevented by any act of the cargo owner. Freight is normally payable 'ship lost or not lost'. Details of the various types are given below:

(a) *Advance freight* is payable in advance, before delivery of the actual goods. This is generally regarded as the most important type of freight, and is extensively used in the liner cargo trades and tramping. It must not be confused with 'advance of freight' which may be a payment on account of disbursements or an advance to the Master, in which case the charterer would be entitled to a return of the monies advanced. Such a payment is really in the nature of a loan.

(b) *Lump sum freight* is the amount payable for the use of the whole or portion of a ship. This form of freight is calculated on the actual cubic capacity of the ship offered, and has no direct relation to the cargo to be carried. Lump sum freight is payable irrespective of the actual quantity delivered.

(c) *Dead freight* is the name given to a damage claim for breach of contract by, for example, the charterer to furnish a full cargo to a ship. Such a situation would arise if the charterer undertook to provide 500 tonnes of cargo, but only supplied 400 tonnes. The shipowner would, under such circumstances, be entitled to claim dead freight for the unoccupied space. Alternatively, a shipper may fail to provide all the cargo promised and for which space has been reserved on a particular sailing, in which case the shipowner would again claim dead freight for the unoccupied space. The amount of deadfreight chargeable is the equivalent of the freight which would have been earned, less all charges which would have been incurred in the loading, carriage and discharge of the goods. It will therefore be seen that, as it is a form of compensation, the shipowner is not entitled to make more profit by deadfreight than he would by the actual carriage of the goods. He must make an allowance for all expenses which have not been incurred. There is no lien on deadfreight, but by express agreement in the contract a lien may be extended to other cargo for the payment of dead-freight.

(d) *Back freight* arises when goods have been despatched to a certain port, and on arrival are refused. The freight charged for the return of the goods constitutes back freight.

(e) *Pro-rata freight* arises when the cargo has been carried only part of the way and circumstances make it impossible to continue the voyage further. For example, ice formation may exist at the original port of delivery, and the owner may decide to accept delivery of the cargo at an intermediate port. The point then arises whether the freight calculated *pro rata* for the portion of the voyage actually accomplished becomes payable. It will only do so when there is a clear agreement by the cargo owner to pay.

(f) *Ad valorem freight* arises when a cargo is assessed for rate purposes on a percentage of its value. For example a 2% *ad valorem* rate on a consignment value at £10 000 would raise £200.

Other forms of freight rates exist. These include Ro/Ro (pp. 191–2); dangerous cargo (pp. 280–95); livestock (p. 189); antiques (pp. 190–91); project forwarding (p. 190); personal effects (p. 190); weight/measurement (W/M) ship's option (pp. 185–7); groupage/consolidated (p. 231) fixture (pp. 183–5); FAK (freight all kinds) (pp. 190–91); indivisible loads (pp. 221–2); deferred rebate (pp. 201–3); trade vehicles (pp. 66–7); pallets (pp. 270–71); and commodity rates (p. 202).

CHAPTER 10

Liner conferences

10.1 LINER CONFERENCE SYSTEM

The liner conference is an organization whereby a number of shipowners offer their services on a given sea route on conditions agreed by the members. Conferences are semi-monopolistic associations of shipping lines formed for the purpose of restricting competition between their members and protecting them from outside competition. Conference agreements may also regulate sailings and ports of call, and in some cases arrangments are made for the pooling of net earnings. Conferences achieve their object by controlling prices and by limiting entry to the trade. Their chief policy is to establish a common tariff of freight rates and passenger fares for the trade involved, members being left free to compete for traffic by the quality and efficiency of their service. The organization of a conference varies from one trade to another. It may consist of informal and regular meetings of shipowners at which rates and other matters of policy are discussed, or it may involve a formal organization with a permanent secretariat and prescribed rules for membership, together with stipulated penalties for violations of agreement. Members are often required to deposit a cash bond to cover fines in respect of non-compliance with their obligations.

The Europe–East Africa conference has eleven members including P & O containers, Ellerman Lines, Thos. & Jas. Harrison, Jadroplor International Maritime Transport, Ignazio Messina, POL, DSR Senator Lines, Consortium Hispania Lines, Kenya National Shipping Line, MSC and West European Container Lines. Ports served in East Africa include Durban, Maputo, Beira, Nacala, Dar es Salaam, Mombasa, Mogadishu, Berbera, Djibouti and Asmera.

In some conferences there exists a pooling agreement whereby traffic or gross or net earnings in the trade are pooled, members receiving agreed percentages of the pool. Under the gross earnings arrangements, each shipowner bears all his operating/investment cost and pools all the gross revenue. With a net earnings situation each operator pools only his net earnings. Hence under the latter arrangement the more efficient low-cost shipowner operating within the pool is penalized by the more expensive and less efficient operator. It arises as each operator has no control on other operators' expenditure and this tends to favour the less efficient shipowner as there is no real incentive for him to contain his costs as indirectly they will be borne by other members of the pool. The object of such an arrangement is to guarantee to members a certain share of the trade, and to limit competition. It leads to the regulation of sailings and may in some circumstances enable the trade to be rationalized. Pools are becoming more common, where shipowners normally prefer to establish an agreed tariff and permit competition in quality of service. An excess of tonnage in a particular trade may very likely lead to an agreed reduction in the number of sailings and poolings of receipts. Often when the conferences perform special services, such as lifting unprofitable cargo or resorting to chartering to cover temporary shortages of tonnage, they pool the losses or profits on such operations.

A further example of a liner conference agreement is where each member agrees to operate a percentage of the sailings and thereby have an identical percentage of the total pooled income. Hence one may have four operators and two may each undertake 20% of the sailings and receive 20% of the pooled revenue. The other two may provide 30% of the sailings and likewise receive 30% of the pooled receipts. Each operator would be responsible for his costs.

The objects of the liner conference are to provide a service adequate to meet the trade requirements; to avoid wasteful competition among members by regulating loading; to organize themselves so that the conference can collectively combat outside competition; and to maintain a tariff by mutual agreement as stable as conditions will permit.

10.2 ADVANTAGES AND DISADVANTAGES

The main advantages claimed for the conference system are as follows:

(a) Avoidance of wasteful competition through over tonnaging.

(b) The reasonable assurance that members have a good chance of realizing a profit, and no rate wars as freight rates are determined by the conference.

(c) Stability of rates which enables manufacturers and merchants to make forward contracts for goods and so diminishes undesirable risk and uncertainty in international trade.

(d) Regular and frequent sailings which enable the shipper/exporter to plan his supplies to overseas markets and avoid the need to carry large stocks with the risk of obsolescence and commodity deterioration, and the operator to maximize the use of his vessels.

(e) Equality of treatment, i.e. the rate quoted applies to all shippers whether they are large or small.

(f) Economies of service which enable operators to concentrate on providing faster and better ships.

The disadvantage from the shipper's point of view arises from the fact that, if he is tied to a particular conference, he cannot take advantage of tramp tonnage when rates are low or switch to no conference line tonnage without being penalized (see p. 182). Moreover, if he is a large shipper he often cannot use his superior bargaining power to obtain lower rates. Carriers who are not members of a conference object to the system because it prevents their competing successfully with conference vessels.

In the mid 1970s, UNCTAD introduced a liner conference code and these were subsequently made in a General Assembly resolution. It was substantially different from the European Code which sought to bind shipping conferences by convention and international law, and to involve governments in the consultative process. This is not generally favoured by the Western maritime nations who prefer the minimum of governmental interference in liner conference activity. Conversely the developing countries seek a system which gives their national shipping line rights of entry into conferences serving their country's trade and of a larger share of that trade. Moreover they favour some form of inter-governmental regulation of conference freight rates.

A significant factor of the UNCTAD Liner Conference Code is that some 40% of the cargo will be reserved for each of the maritime countries participating in the trade with the residue of 20% to the established liner conference operator operating in the cross trade or other operators. The 40/40/20 conference code is strongly opposed by Western countries who have been established for many years as liner conference operators within such cross trades. They take the view that such a policy is one of trade protectionism thereby reserving a substantial volume of the trade (import and export) for their own maritime fleets irrespective of the commercial considerations involved. This situation is particularly relevant to third world developing countries who are anxious to sustain and in some cases inaugurate their own maritime fleets to save hard currency and develop their maritime fleets many of which are subsidized. Moreover, such developing countries wish to have a greater influence on liner tariffs and by operating their own fleets are able to control them more directly. A further point is that Western countries regard the UN code as non-commercial competition and prefer the voluntary commercial principles as found in the ESC/CENSA code.

To enable the UN code to become international requires an international convention. This involves ratification by 24 states representing 25% of world liner tonnage. However, in June 1979 the UNCTAD V conference was held in Manila which discussed the UN Code of Conduct for liner conferences involving the 40/40/20 rule. This involved the trading partner country having the right to carry 40% generated by their own trade. The remaining portion would be available for third flag carriers. The code actually allows considerable flexibility in reaching agreements on cargo shares and was adopted in 1983.

The following points emerged from a UN Liner Code review conference held in Geneva, November 1988.

The scope of the convention must be defined

(a) The Code should apply only to conference pier-to-pier services between contracting parties. The clause should relate only to liner services.

(b)   National line membership rights in conferences does not relate to membership of consortia.

(c)   The existing definition of 'shipper' under the Code should be maintained.

(d)   Care should be taken in case attempts are made to 'tighten up the Code'. This does not refer to attempts to remove ambiguities of language (which are acceptable) but to efforts to widen the areas of shipping to which the Code should relate (for example, an attempt to bring non-conference lines within the scope of the Code). These efforts should be opposed. Equally, there may be attempts to introduce a cargo reservation system for the bulk trade.

Conferences must operate without government intervention

(a)   Cargo reservation: the current Code limitation should be maintained with no derogation.

(b)   Sailing and loading rights: implementation of trade participation agreements should be left to conference member lines.

(c)   Day-to-day operation of conferences: there should be no 'back door' regulation of conferences using Article 47.

(d)   Fixing of freight rates: governments should have no role in deciding the timing and level of changes in freight rates; the fifteen month rule should be deleted, and periods of notice of freight rate changes left to commercial negotiation.

(e)   Consultation: the joint recommendation of CENSA and the European Shippers' Council should be used as the pattern for consultation.

(f)   Admission of new members etc., national lines: there should be no admission to conference membership as a result of government directive.

Conferences must be subject only to fair competition
Any proposals for multilateral regulation of outsiders which preserve shares in the whole liner trade for national lines and regulate rates for commercially competing outsiders should be opposed.

The Review Conference was reconvened in 1991 and following guidelines accepted:

(a) Slot charterers should not be excluded from becoming conference members.

(b) The trade-share provision should apply to the sea leg of multi-modal transport.

(c) The trade-share provision should apply to transhipped cargoes, including those from landlocked countries.

(d) Governments may seek consultations with one another over issues of concern relating to implementation of the Code.

(e) National shippers' organizations from more than one country may participate in consultations.

(f) States and contracting parties may take such measures as are necessary to implement the convention.

The UN forum featured three divisions: Group 77 represents the developing nations; Group B represents the industrialized countries; and Group D the former socialist countries of East Europe.

Finally, the Conference called for non-contracting parties to sign the Convention and for a further review to take place in 1996. Today some 75% of containerized trade moves on routes either between non-contracting parties such as the US and Japan or as in the case of EU countries which have ratified the Convention but with the Brussel's Package exemption. Hence the 1996 review will be critical as many believe it could lead to the eventual break-up of the conference system since containership operators are no longer pure shipping companies which can make use of the conference system, but are logistics companies involved in door-to-door transportation.

10.3 DEFERRED REBATE AND CONTRACT SYSTEMS

Associated with liner conferences are the deferred rebate and contract systems.

The deferred rebate is a device to ensure that shippers will continue to support a conference. A shipper who ships exclusively by conference vessels can, at the end of a certain period (usually six months), claim a rebate, usually 10% of the freight money paid by him during the period. Hence the shipper has an inducement to remain loyal to the conference in so far as he stands to lose a rebate by employing a non-conference vessel. The deferred rebate system has tended to become less popular in some trades in recent years due to the high cost of clerical administration. Accordingly, it has been substituted – under the same code of loyalty conditions – by the immediate rebate system. This is a somewhat lower rebate – maybe 9½% – but granted at the time freight payment is made and not some six months later as with the deferred rebate system. Such a lower deferred rate is termed a nett rate. The level of deferred rebate varies by individual conference.

A further way of retaining the shipper's patronage of a conference is by the contract or special contract agreement systems. The contract system is for a shipper who signs a contract to forward all his goods by conference line vessels either in the general course of business, or perhaps associated with a special project over a certain period. The particular contract concerned may be associated with a large hydroelectric scheme, for example, and the goods would then probably be special equipment. Under this system the shipper would be granted a cheaper freight rate than a non-contract shipper. In addition there are the special commodity agreements which are specially negotiated between the trade and conference to cover goods shipped in large quantities and often for short duration. The shipper may be forwarding a commodity such as copper, tea, rubber, foodstuffs or cotton in considerable quantities.

The shippers' criticism of the deferred rebate system is that it enables conferences to build up monopolies tending to keep rates at a high level. Furthermore, the shipper is reluctant to use outside tonnage for fear of loss of rebate and the system thus restricts his freedom of action. Another point is that a record must be kept of all freight paid subject to rebate to enable claims to be made in due course. This involves clerical expenses, and moreover the shipper contends that he is out of pocket to the extent of the interest on the rebate while it is in the carrier's hands. So far as the carrier is concerned, the retention of the rebate for the appropriate period has the added advantage of an automatic deterrent to shippers using non-conference vessels. In fact, it can be a very strong weapon, as the carrier is the sole arbiter in deciding whether or not any shipper's rebate should be forfeited. The carrier also finds it easy to maintain rebate records in his manifest freight database and, by virtue of the amount of work involved, finds it convenient to have a small rebate department. He maintains that there is no compulsion on the shipper to remain with the conference, although of course if he chooses to ship outside it, the shipper will forfeit his rebate. A shipper who forfeits his rebate has, after all, had the benefits of conference shipment which later he discards for something he considers better.

10.4 HARMONIZATION CONFERENCES

A development in recent years has been the formulation of harmonization conferences amongst liner cargo operators, some of which may be members of a number of different conferences.

The situation may emerge in a particular trade whereby the bulk of the cargo operators are anxious to avoid rate wars and keen to concentrate on providing a quality service at a reasonable competitive tariff. The services are likely to be indirectly in competition with each other, operating from different ports and each having a varying voyage time and distance. The individual rates would be different.

The object of the harmonization conference is to move in harmony with any rate increases and agree on the level of rebate and its code of application. Other matters of mutual concern are similarly discussed such as documentation, the basis of the constituents of the freight rate, currency/fuel surcharges etc.

Such harmonization conferences are entirely voluntary and often involve shipowners of differing nationality. This type of conference is likely to increase in its application.

10.5 FACTORS INFLUENCING THE DECLINE OF THE LINER CONFERENCE SYSTEM AND LIKELY FUTURE TRENDS

The liner conference system emerged in 1875 – the Calcutta Conference – in an era of international trade which was very different compared with today. The concept and application of the liner conference system remained *in situ* up to the emergence of containerization. Throughout this period, despite being the subject of 'commissions of inquiry', it has broadly remained unscathed on the basis that it provided a quality service at a reasonable price, offering reliability, frequency of sailings and impartiality of treatment amongst shippers. This quality of service provided by modern tonnage has had to be sustained through the loyalty of shippers generating adequate income from freight rates to fund new investment. There is no doubt that the liner conference system made an enormous contribution to the development of world trade and this is still the case today.

Containerization has brought a new era to the development of world trade both for the FCL and LCL movements and in reality has brought markets closer together. Moreover it is multi-modal, and has accelerated a movement away from the port-to-port operation on which the liner conference system was conceived to the warehouse-to-warehouse or door-to-door transit involving NVOCCs or NVOCs. In consequence it involves carriers outside the sea leg including the road haulier and railway operator, plus of course the seaport authority playing a major role of co-ordination and facilitation. It has seen the emergence of logistics as a major skill in aiding/counselling the shipper to decide on the most advantageous distribution network (see pp. 428–31). Moreover, INCOTERMS 1990 and ICC No. 500 have emerged favouring multi-modal operation coupled with the combined transport bill of lading providing a single document with one rate and common code of liability throughout transit. Hence the international agencies in the form of ICC, UNCTAD and UNCITRAL have recognized that the future of liner cargo trades lies in the multi-modal network and accordingly have, through their various committees and leadership, devised the commercial and legal framework for it to develop under conditions of confidence and professionalism involving total commitment and adherence by the member states which represent about 90% of trading nations.

Against this background one must examine the developments which have emerged to the international distribution infrastructure. Information technology involving EDI (see pp. 448–79) have transformed many markets. It crosses international boundaries without demur and eliminates time zones and culture barriers. This has opened up markets and quickened the decision-making process. Meanwhile customs have encouraged the movement away from the port to examine goods and devised LIC/LEC (see pp. 97–9). Seaports have devised districentres and distriparks and developed the trading port concept (see Chapter 17). Moreover, FTZ and CFS facilities (see pp. 409–10) have been set up. Railway authorities in many countries have joined forces with the container ship operator and port authority to develop the dry port concept (see pp. 391–3). Additionally, in North America we have seen the development of the landbridge concept involving container shipments from the Far East being transhipped at the West Coast port and conveyed by rail to industrial centres within the USA or to the East Coast ports in double stack container trains. Such developments have reduced costs by 35% and transit times by 40% using dedicated services.

To conclude our analysis one can see that the liner cargo market has seen a radical change which is gaining momentum as we enter the next century. Indeed, one can say without hesitation that countries/markets which are not on the global international container network offering multi-modalism networks will be seriously disadvantaged in the development of their external trade.

Given below are the salient factors influencing the decline of the liner conference system and observations on future developments.

(a) The inflexibility of the rating system and lengthy procedures and timescale to negotiate a discounted rate are major factors.

(b) The rigidity of liner conference strategies reflects their historical background and failure to take advantage of the market development inherent in multi-modalism.

(c) The emergence of round-the-world container operators such as the Taiwanese-owned Evergreen Liner container service. By 1995 it operated a weekly eastbound round-the-world schedule involving twelve vessels of 3500/4000 TEU capacity. In the westbound direction, sailings are every six days with eleven vessels of 3500/4000 TEUs. Evergreen relies on feeder services. A major aspect of the Evergreen Liner strategy is a streamlined organization enabling quick decisions to be taken. The company is driven on a global basis. Conversely the liner conference system involves consulting numerous shipping companies to obtain a decision, a process which is tedious and frustrating to the shipper. Moreover, the liner conference shipping consultation procedure and individual shipping company structure is complex and does not aid quick decisions but relies more on consultative committee procedures.

(d) The emergence of consortia. Consortia generally combine the concepts of vessel cost-sharing and cargo pooling. Participants in consortia commit themselves to the cost-sharing venture whereby, in effect, all vessels become a joint responsibility. The responsibility for providing capital normally rests with the individual participants and serves as an important means of retaining corporate identity. Members usually carry each other's containers on each other's vessels under mutual slot charter or other space-sharing arrangements. The essence of a consortium agreement therefore is that the parties accept limitations upon their own autonomy as individual companies within the framework of agreed co-operation. The motives for the creation of a consortium are the sharing of capital costs; the sharing of facilities in order to improve operating efficiency; the joining of capacity in order to improve competitiveness with larger lines; and the institution of multi-modal operations, i.e. to provide joint operations which include the inland movement of containers. The consortium does of course offer flexibility in the rate structure and a quick decision-making process. It has a strong empathy with shippers and has become very popular in many liner trades.

(e) Conferences have lost the advantage that they possessed over newcomers in the age of conventional transport as a result of their many years of experience and the quality of their cargo handling. Today the importance of cargo handling has been largely neutralized by the container.

(f) A number of shipping conferences operate in too intro-verted a manner. Their concentration on the conference internal pool has sometimes impaired their ability to see changes in market behaviour.

(g) Various shipping organizations have criticized the behav-iour of the liner conference system but this has little effect on the overall price/performance ratio. The basic aim has been to encourage change in the system under which liner shipping operates in the container age in view of the growing intermeshing of sea transport with pre- and post-shipment transport on land.

(h) International liner transport has undoubtedly been in the process of radical change for some time as a result of technological developments, and this naturally has also had a substantial impact on its organization, operational process, structures and the systems that have been customary up to now. Such times of change – in which things long-established come to be questioned but the full consequences of the new developments do not seem to have been clearly recognized – can easily lead to illusions about the possibilities offered by these developments. The liner conference falls into this category.

(i)   It is difficult to identify what would be an acceptable liner conference system operative in the next decade. The widely differing expectations of the shippers make it difficult to judge what innovative elements should now be incorporated into co-operative liner shipping models in order to get widespread approval rather than criticism. The situation is complicated by a further divergence of opinion relating to an extremely important field with potential for development: the linking of sea transport with pre- and post-shipment transport (from the factory to the port of loading and from the port of discharge to the receiver). One faction expects the carriers or groups such as conferences to provide increasingly efficient and complete door-to-door transport chains as part of the shippers' logistics and distribution systems. The other faction aims more at restricting the activities of the conferences to pure sea transport in order to operate pre- and post-shipment on their own account and manage without a door-to-door transport chain in the hands of a single operator.

(j)   In today's era the vessels themselves are no longer the largest expenses in the carriers' cost structures. Computer systems and container imbalance and positioning now stand out as the major cost items. Such an environment drives the container operator to adopt flexibility of pricing and quick decision-making to aid efficiency and generate profitability.

(k)   The movement in market share of the world trading liner cargo fleet away from the traditional maritime powers and increasingly towards developing countries such as South Korea, Taiwan and the developed markets of Hong Kong and Singapore have undermined the liner conference system (see Table 1.3 and p. 5).

(l)   The Council of the European Union through Regulation 4056/86 of December 1988 provided the maritime transport sector with the detailed procedures for the application of the competition rules laid down by the Treaty of Rome. They comprise the following:

> (i) rules on applying Community competition law are similar to those laid down for other sectors by Regulation No. 17/82;

    (ii) a particularly liberal set of rules on competition under which conferences benefit from a block exemption for a period of unlimited duration.

The EU Commission endeavours to maintain the balance of these rules which are based in practice on an open-ended block exemption offset by the need to comply with specific conditions. The conditions relate to the following:

    (i) on the one hand, to the conferences themselves, non-discrimination, availability of tariffs, user consultation, loyalty arrangements, etc.;

    (ii) on the other hand, to the environment in which conference operates, size and role of outsiders.

The Commission has taken steps to ensure that conferences remain subject to effective competition and the latter is tangible rather than hypothetical. Overall the EU regards that the role played by conferences in stabilizing trade has been eroded and that the time had come for the Commission to look for more suitable instruments to ensure protection of competition in a changing technical and commercial environment.

The foregoing will have a profound impact on the development of the liner conference system within the European Union sector.

Finally, in concluding our analysis, one should record that the decline of the liner conference system is due primarily to the development of containerization, which emerged as serious competition from the 1970s. Conferences were forced to build a different type of fleet, to buy containers and equipment, to restructure their organizations, to move inland and establish freight stations and depots, to change conference structures, especially tariffs, rules and regulations, and finally to join forces with competitors in the form of new companies or consortia. New operators and shipowners such as Evergreen entered the field with no allegiance to liner conferences. With the development of new strategies such as round-the-world services and larger vessels, this led to over-tonnaging, coupled with fierce rate wars. The emergence of inter-modal services and pricing undermined tariff structures and the high fixed cost of containerization accelerated freight tariff erosion.

Today the market power of conferences has virtually disappeared and they are faced with ever increasing commercial requirements from shippers and shippers' councils and regulatory demands from governments. A critical stage will emerge in 1996 when the UN Code of Conduct 40/40/20 is reviewed (see pp. 199–201). The possibility of the dismantling of conferences does bring the discussion forward on to how competition might be influenced by other regulatory mechanisms such as subsidies and, in the case of developing nations, countervailing measures such as those adopted to implement the Code. Vision, empathy with the shipper and pragmatism are the ingredients of the liner conference system of the future. By 1995 non-conference vessels carried nearly 80% of liner cargo compared with 5–10% in the 1970s.

CHAPTER 11

Ship operation

11.1 FACTORS TO CONSIDER IN PLANNING SAILING SCHEDULES

In planning a vessel's sailing schedule it is of the utmost importance that she should be fully employed while she is available. She earns no money for the shipowner when laid up – whether for survey, general maintenance or due to lack of traffic – and such periods must be kept to an absolute minimum.

This is particularly important in shipping, because of the large amount of capital invested in a ship which itself has heavy annual depreciation charges. Furthermore, a ship has only a limited life, and when she is ultimately withdrawn from service it may fairly be asked what profit she has earned. It is obvious that the owner who has secured full employment for the vessel is more likely to realize a larger profit than one who has been content to operate the vessel only during peak periods, and made no effort to find additional employment at other times. In this latter case, where the vessel might be involved in a few months' uneconomic service a year, it might be worth while reducing the size of the fleet to give the owner a more reasonable opportunity for improved utilization.

There comes a time, however, when the cost of increasing the size of the fleet exceeds the additional revenue thereby gained, and so the operator sustains a loss. If such is the case, the project should be abandoned unless there are compelling reasons, e.g. social, political, or even commercial, to the contrary. The optimum size of fleet is that where the minimum number of vessels is earning the maximum revenue. It should also be remembered that the owner is not normally able to have a standby vessel available, as the amount of capital tied up in any one vessel is considerable.

Today an increasing number of vessels are multi-purpose in their design and accordingly permit flexibility of operation which is particularly advantageous in times of international trade depression. It enables the vessel to switch from one trade to another, or carry a variety of cargoes as distinct from one specialized cargo. Examples are found in the multi-purpose container ship capable of carrying containers and vehicles; the Ro/Ro vessel capable of shipping all types of vehicular traffic; the OBO ship able to convey oil or ore, and the very versatile multi-purpose dry cargo carriers found in the SD-14 and Freedom-type tramp tonnage. Such tonnage is better able to combat economically unequal trading.

There are basically two types of service: the regular and those operated according to a particular demand. The first type of vessel is primarily associated with liner cargo trades, whilst the latter is mostly confined to tramps.

Liner cargo vessels may be cellular container ships, dual purpose vessels having accommodation for both container and conventional cargo, Ro/Ro vessels, and conventional break bulk ships. The tramp vessel may vary from the Freedom-type vessel to modern bulk carrier of 90 000 tonnes. Additionally there exists a significant volume of world trade which is moved by specialized – often purpose-built – bulk cargo tonnage on charter to industrial companies conveying their raw material for industrial processing. Such services are often scheduled to meet an industrial production programme and operate from specialized purpose-built berths.

The number of passenger vessels engaged in deep-sea schedules today is very few. In the main they are engaged in all-the-year cruising which remains a buoyant market. The cruise vessel operates on a sailing schedule prepared many months in advance on a particular itinerary. A number are linked to the fly-cruise concept whereby the passenger is flown to the port to join the passenger cruise liner.

A significant volume of tonnage is now found in the short sea trade such as UK/Europe involving multi-purpose vessels but on the Dover/Calais trade this could now be in decline as the Channel Tunnel begins to make an impact (see p. 118). These vessels of up to 10 000 GRT are capable of conveying passengers, coaches, accompanied cars and Ro/Ro vehicles. Such schedules are fully integrated with the port operating arrangements and a dominant feature is the quick port turn-round of such tonnage. Some vessels primarily convey Ro/Ro vehicles and operate a year-round schedule with little variation. Overall, such services carry substantial quantities of passengers, coaches and accompanied cars, and tend to vary their sailings to meet varying market demands with the sailings being greatly increased in the peak summer months. A new era could emerge with the super ferry of twin hull construction and speed of over 50 knots (see p. 36).

With the cargo liner, the frequency of sailings is predetermined and published months in advance, and agreed within the consortium where such conditions apply. Many cargo liners operate outside the liner conference system (see pp. 196–209). Cargo traffic attracted to a liner service includes a wide variety of commodities and consumer goods such as machinery, chemicals, foodstuffs, motor vehicles, and so on. At certain times and in various trades, there is, of course, a need for increased sailings to cater for seasonal traffic variations, and these are sometimes obtained by chartering additional tonnage. This has the advantage of ensuring that the additional tonnage required is available only in peak periods, and not throughout the year when traffic considerations could not justify it. Surveys and overhauls are again undertaken when practicable outside peak periods. In many container liner trades, vessels are on continuous survey to ensure the frequency and time spent in dry dock is kept to a minimum. This also applies to modern specialized bulk carriers.

A variety of specialized bulk carrier tonnage now exist. These include the mammoth oil tankers and ore carriers, very large crude carriers, liquefied natural gas carriers, bulk carriers, car carriers and so on. Such tonnage sometimes under charter requires extensive planning of schedules which are designed to maximize ship utilization. They have to be integrated with production/supply areas at the point of cargo despatch and dove-tailed in with the industrial processes and/or storage capacity at the destination port. Many of the terminals are situated off shore to meet the excessive draught of such vessels which can exceed 65 m. The schedules and type of ship may permit cargo to be conveyed in only one direction, such as with crude carriers, with the return voyage in ballast and frequently at slightly faster speed. The development of unidirectional cargo shipments has been partially overcome by the oil bulk ore (OBO) carrier which also allows such tonnage to be switched from one trade to another when market demands so dictate. This is a very flexible situation operationally.

The tramp operator has no regular sailing schedule, but plies between ports throughout the world, where cargo is offered. As was established earlier in the book, the extent of advanced sailing schedules varies from weeks, days or, in extreme cases, a matter of hours, to many months, depending on market and trading conditions.

So far we have reviewed the background against which schedules are compiled. Given below are the various factors influencing the formulation of sailing schedules:

1. The overall number of ships and their availability.

2. The volume, type and any special characteristics of the traffic.

3. Traffic fluctuations such as peak demands.

4. Maintenance of time margins where services connect. For example, with multi-modalism involving container tonnage and the dry port concept involving dedicated rail networks (see pp. 417–26) port turn-round time is crucial.

5. Availability of crew and cost. In particular, the impact of STCW applicable from February 1997 (see pp. 82–5).

6. Arrangements for relief measure which may arise in cases of emergency.

7. Climatic conditions. Some ports are ice-bound throughout certain periods of the year, which prevents any shipping calling at these particular ports.

8. Competition. This arises when conference and non-conference tonnage, for example, operate schedules alongside each other and compete in the same market place.

9. Time necessary for terminal duties at the port. This will include loading and/or discharging, customs procedure, bunkering, victualling, etc.

10. Voyage time.

11. The actual types of ship available and in particular their size, incorporating the length, beam and draught, together with any special characteristics. For instance, some may be suitable for cruising. Other vessels, by virtue of their size, can only operate between ports that have deep-water berth facilities. Hence, a large fleet of small vessels has more operating flexibility than a small fleet of large vessels which are restricted to a limited number of

ports having adequate facilities to accommodate them. Another vessel may require special equipment for loading and discharging her cargo.

12. Any hostile activities taking place or envisaged in any particular waters.

13. Location of canals such as the Suez and Panama as alternative routes.

14. Actual estimated voyage cost and expected traffic receipts.

15. Political actions such as flag discrimination, bilateral trade agreements causing unbalanced trading conditions.

16. General availability of port facilities and dock labour, and any tidal restrictions affecting times of access and departure.

17. Plying limits of individual ships, and for liner tonnage, any condition imposed by liner conference agreements.

18. With multi-purpose vessels conveying road haulage vehicles, passengers and accompanied cars, the number of cars and road haulage vehicles shipped can vary according to the time of year and/or period of the day.

The schedule ultimately devised in liner cargo trades should help the operator to increase his market share of the trade, having particular regard to the need to operate a profitable service. To the container operator the number of containers available for shipment, their type (40′ reefer or 20′ steel flat rack) have to be predetermined coupled with the number of containers and their specification to be discharged at a particular port. This data has to be reconciled with the ship specification. Computers therefore now play a major part in ship planning and stowage.

Variations in demand on trade vehicle or ferry operators are accommodated by the use of vehicle decks controlled by means of hydraulically operated ramps. Thus the vessel which for one sailing may accommodate 50 cars and 30 large road haulage vehicles can on another occasion carry as many as 300 cars exclusively.

Thus it is apparent that sailing schedules are based primarily on commercial considerations with political, economic, operating and, to some extent, the technical capabilities of the ship all playing their role as contributory factors. In the container operation, it is multi-modal.

11.2 PROBLEMS PRESENTED TO SHIPOWNERS BY FLUCTUATIONS IN TRADE AND UNEQUAL BALANCE OF TRADE

The problem of unused capacity in ocean transport is largely caused by secular or long-term fluctuations in world trade. The position is further aggravated by the fact that shipping capacity, in common with all forms of transport, cannot be stored and is consumed immediately it is produced.

An unequal balance and fluctuation in trade is common to all forms of transport, and particularly difficult to overcome satisfactorily in shipping. It is caused by economic, social or political factors. In all, there are nine main sets of circumstances in which unbalanced trading arises in shipping:

1. One of the largest streams of unbalanced trading is found in the shipment of the world's oil. Tankers convey the oil outwards from the port serving the oilfield, whilst the return voyage is in ballast.

2. An abnormal amount of cargo in a particular area can give rise to unequal trading. Such a glut tends to attract vessels to the area for freight, the majority of which often arrives in ballast. The situation may arise due to an abnormally heavy harvest. Conversely, a country may be in a state of famine or short of a particular commodity or foodstuff. This tends to attract fully-loaded vessels inward to the area whilst on the outward voyage the ship is in ballast.

3. Government restrictions might be imposed on the import and/or export of certain goods. This may be necessary to protect home industries, restricting certain imports to help maintain full employment. Additionally, this restriction may be introduced due to an adverse balance of trade caused by a persistent excess of imports over exports. Such restrictions may be short term or permanent, depending on the circumstances in which they were introduced.

4. Climatic conditions such as ice formation restrict the safe navigation of rivers, canals and ports to certain periods of the year.

5. The passenger trades are, of course, subject to seasonal fluctuations, which present to the shipowner the problem of filling the unused capacity during the off-peak season.

6. Political influence can also cause unequal balance of trade. This can be achieved by flag discrimination which in effect is pressure exerted by governments designed to divert cargoes to ships of the national flag, regardless of commercial considerations normally governing the routeing of cargo. Flag discrimination can be exercised in a number of ways, including bilateral trade treaties, import licences and exchange control. Bilateral trade treaties include shipping clauses reserving either the whole of the trade between the two countries, or as much of it as possible, to the ships of the two flags. Brazil, Chile and India have all used the granting of import licences to ensure carriage of cargoes in ships of the national flag. Exchange control also offers endless means of making shipment in national vessels either obligatory or so commercially attractive that it has the same effect. Brazil, Colombia, India, Poland and Turkey have all indulged in this method of control in the interest of their national fleets.

7. The growing fleet of the People's Republic of China (see Table 1.3) and the former Easter Bloc mercantile fleet, especially the CIS tonnage, are strongly favoured by their national governments, particularly for the importation of goods, and thereby practise flag discrimination. Such fleets have low-cost crews and charge rates up to 30% below those of established liner cargo operators.

8. The practice of trade protectionism in many parts of the world is much on the increase. It finds itself in the UN Liner Conference cargo code with the 40/40/20 cargo-sharing formula (see pp. 198–201).

9. Another example of trade protectionism is found in the US government policy. It takes the view that government supervision and control is in the interest of the public and US commerce. Conversely European liner cargo operators involved in the North American trade consider that generally the best results are achieved by self-regulation, competition and the minimum amount of government involvement. The US government is keen to impose policies which would assume a certain percentage of various trades are shipped in US cargo vessels.

To counteract unequal trading, it is necessary for the liner and tramp operators to take measures to obtain the maximum loaded capacity of the vessel and reduce ballast runs to an absolute minimum. The development of OBO type of tonnage has partially countered the problem of unequal trading in modern bulk carrier tonnage. Moreover, there is the growing tendency to develop multi-purpose vessels to permit operating flexibility and counter trade imbalance in liner trades.

The larger the fleet the more flexible it is to combat unequal trading problems. The operator of a large fleet is generally in a number of different trades and is thus able to switch his vessels to the trades where the demand is greatest. Hence in particular trade 'A', due to seasonal variations, demand for shipping may be light, whilst in another trade 'B' the demand may be exceptionally heavy. The prudent operator would accordingly arrange to transfer some of his vessels from trade 'A' to 'B'.

Cargo liners are more vulnerable to unequal trading inasmuch as normally they must stick to the berth and not jump from one trade into another, as in tramp operating. To combat this, a liner may return, for instance, from the Pacific coast of North America as a tramp vessel. This necessarily involves a short ballast haul to link up with one of the tramp trades. Alternatively, the liner can change her berth. This system, which is very satisfactory, operates where a liner goes out on one berth and then at some time changes to another berth within another trade, possibly within a group of companies. Hence the vessel may operate independently for one company but co-ordinate with other companies within the group, thereby ensuring that the maximum use is made of the vessel in various parts of the world. Such a system is very flexible.

A further method of combating unequal trading is to have dual-purpose vessels. Thus a ship may be equipped to carry either oil or ore. Another example is a vessel which can convey either refrigerated or general cargo. Ships of this type, which are more expensive to build, are flexible to operate as the shipowner can vary the trades in which they ply.

The liner cargo containerized market is acutely aware of the imbalance of trade and the need to reposition containers to meet market needs. Hence more attention is now being given by container operators to designing/developing container types to cope with unequal trading patterns. Sea Containers is a market leader in this area and has developed successfully the platform flats, flat racks and sea-deck sea-vent container types (see pp. 376–93).

Major container operators are under heavy pressure to continue to enhance their services through quality and improved transit operations. Imbalance of trade is a continuing problem and its solution hinges on the marshalling of containers (see pp. 376–8). However, the current trend is to rationalize long-haul services and to develop the hub port concept with fewer direct calls and increased regional or inter-regional transhipment services. This is termed the 'hub and spoke system' (see pp. 420–22) and overall should improve ship capacity utilization and lessen the impact of imbalance of trade. It is a highly computerized operation.

The tramp operator obtains much of this trade through a shipbroker who is a member of the Baltic Exchange. His vessel is chartered by the shipper, who is responsible for providing the cargo, on a voyage or time-charter basis. When the charter has been fixed, the prudent operator will endeavour to obtain a further fixture. By adopting these tactics, coupled with the most favourable rate offered, the operator will plan the movement of his vessels as far in advance as possible and reduce ballast hauls to a minimum.

Since the 1980s, modern technology has developed various techniques – in particular modern processing and storage plant – which have permitted the seasonal nature of international bulk foodstuff distribution in certain trades to be spread over a longer period. This has helped counter the problem of unequal trading by extending the period over which such shipments are made, and has largely been facilitated by the range of hardware available in the international distribution system. This includes an ever-increasing range of container types, the computerized temperature-controlled warehouses found at major trading ports such as Rotterdam, Singapore and Hong Kong, and major technical developments in the agricultural industry in all areas of their business.

Finally, on the cargo side, an era of more vision and co-operation amongst carriers, consolidators, distributors, importers, exporters, railway operators, customs, road hauliers, governments, seaports and airports has emerged with the sole purpose of developing international trade. It has greatly facilitated the growing network internationally of multi-modalism. This has encouraged forward planning amongst shippers and carriers to make the best use of available carrier capacity. This in turn aids efficiency and lowers costs to acceptable market levels. A major development is the expansion of the sea/air/land bridge concept. Examples are to be found from Singapore and Dubai to Europe and the USA (see pp. 422–6). Such development stimulates trade and brings markets closer together.

On the passenger side, however, the problem of unused capacity during off-seasons is largely solved by the organization of cruises but in many markets such an opportunity does not exist. Cruising is now confined to purpose-built tonnage operating in all the year round schedules (see pp. 36–7).

11.3 THE RELATIVE IMPORTANCE OF SPEED, FREQUENCY, RELIABILITY, COST AND QUALITY OF SEA TRANSPORT

There are five factors that influence the nature of a shipping service: speed, frequency, reliability, cost and quality.

Speed is important to the shipper who desires to market his goods against an accurate arrival date and to eliminate banking charges for opening credits. This can be achieved by selecting the fastest service available and thereby obtaining the minimum interval between the time the goods are ordered/despatched and the date of delivery at their destination. Speed is particularly important to manufacturers of consumer goods as it avoids expense and the risk of obsolescence to the retailer carrying large stocks. In the case of certain commodities, and especially fresh fruit and semi-frozen products and fashionable goods, a regular and fast delivery is vital to successful trading. The need for speed is perhaps most felt in the long-distance trades where voyage times may be appreciably reduced and the shipper given the benefit of an early delivery and frequent stock replenishment. These various needs are fully recognized by the liner operator, to whom speed is expensive both in terms of initial expenditure on the marine engines and the actual fuel cost. His aim is to obtain the optimum and provide a vessel with the maximum speed at the minimum cost which will fulfil the requirements of the shipper. These aspects have partially precipitated the development of container services in liner cargo trades offering faster transits.

Speed is not so important in the world tramp trades where generally lower-value cargoes are being carried and where many trades are moving under programmed stockpile arrangements. In this category are included coal, mineral ores, timber, bulk grain and other cargoes which normally move in shiploads and have a relatively low value: these demand a low transport cost.

Frequency of service is most important when goods can only be sold in small quantities at frequent intervals. Here the liner operator will phase his sailings to meet shippers' requirements, whilst the vessels must be suitable in size, speed and equipment for the cargoes offered. The shipper of perishable fruit and vegetables also relies on frequent, as well as fast, ships to obtain maximum benefit from the season's crop. Fashionable goods and replacement spare stock also benefit from frequent service.

To the tramp charterer, frequency of sailings is not of paramount importance. He must not, of course, allow his stocks to run down too far, but he will have a margin within which he can safely operate and will come in to buy and ship when conditions suit him.

Reliability is an essential requirement to the shipper engaged in the liner service which is usually multi-modal, whose goods are sold against expiry dates on letters of credit and import licences. Furthermore, the liner shipper relies upon the operator to deliver his traffic in good condition. To the shipper, therefore, reliability infers that the vessel will sail and arrive at the advertised time; the shipowner will look after the cargo during pre-shipment, throughout the voyage and after discharge on carriage; and, finally, the operator can be relied upon to give adequate facilities at the terminal, usually inland (ICD/CFS), and at his offices to enable the appropriate documents and other formalities to be satisfactorily completed. In short, prestige in the liner trade goes with the reliance which the shipper can place on any particular multi-modal service.

The tramp shipper marketing goods of relatively low value must seek the lowest possible transport charge, as the freight percentage of the total value may have a direct bearing on the saleability of the commodity. He has thus a prime interest in the availability of tramp shipping space at any particular time by reason of the fact that freight and chartering rates will reflect variations in the economic forces of supply and demand. In a market situation where there are plenty of vessels the shipper will be able to charter at a rate which will be only marginally above the operating costs of the vessel. In the opposite situation he will be forced to pay more but there is a limiting factor in the price of the commodity at the point of sale to the rate which the shipowner may receive. In these conditions the premium returns are earned by the operators of the most efficient ships. In weak market conditions their relative efficiency ensures a small profit while others just break even. Where the market is strong the proven reliability shown before will ensure that the services of such vessels will be sought out before other opportunities are taken up.

In the liner trades the freight costs are more stable and controlled; the shipowner is able to hold the rate at a fair level to show a profit margin, but he must be careful not to hold his rates so high that they price the goods out of the market; at this point there is need for joint consultation between shipper and carrier and other parties to the multi-modal operator. It can be argued that the liner shipper should pay a higher transport charge to compensate for the liner service which in itself is expensive.

Quality of service is especially important in the competitive world of shipping and international trade today. The service provided must be customer-oriented with emphasis being placed on providing a reliable service and handling the goods and documentation in an efficient way.

The foregoing analysis relative to liner cargo shipments involving frequency, cost, reliability, speed and quality must be reconciled with the increasingly discerning needs of the shipper. Today all these factors are absolutely essential for international trade to operate under conditions of business confidence, competition and market/product development. Liner cargo services must strive to be competitive in all areas of the business, a situation which has been stimulated by the development of logistics involving multi-modalism (see pp. 428–31). Many companies operate on the 'just in time' concept and review regularly their international distribution network on the basis of the value added concept, the value added to the product by using a particular distribution network and the total cost of the service.

11.4 INDIVISIBLE LOADS

A market which has grown in recent years is the movement of the indivisible load. It may be a transformer or engineering plant with a total weight of up to 250 tonnes.

Such a product requires special arrangements and the freight forwarder specializing in such work usually has a project forwarding department to handle such transits. The following points are relevant in the movement internationally of the indivisible load.

(a)　The ports of departure, destination and any transhipment areas need to be checked out to ensure they can handle such a shipment, especially regarding the availability of heavy lift equipment.

(b)　The shipowner needs to have a plan and specification of the shipment to evaluate the stowage and handling arrangments, as well as to identify the weight distribution.

(c)　The transportation of the indivisible load to and from the ports requires pre-planning with regard to route and time-scale. Usually such goods may only move at night under police escort and subject to police and/or Department of Transport permission.

(d)　The rates are usually assessed on a cost plus profit basis. The cost can be very extensive for any heavy-lift equipment and special arrangements to transport the goods overland to and from the ports. Freight forwarders tend to work closely with the correspondent agent in the destination country. Transhipment costs can be much reduced if a MAFI type six-axle trailer is used as in the Ro/Ro tonnage.

The advantages of the indivisible load shipment to the shipper/buyer/importer include lower overall transportation cost; quicker transit; much reduced site assembly cost; less risk of damage in transit; lower insurance premium; less technical aid, i.e. staff resources, required by the buyer as there is no extensive site assembly work; equipment tested and fully tested operationally in the factory before despatch; no costly site assembly work; less risk of malfunctioning equipment arising; earlier commissioning of the equipment which in turn results in the quicker productive use of the equipment with profitable benefits to the buyer overall.

CHAPTER 12

Bills of lading

When a shipowner, or another authorized person, for example an agent, agrees to carry goods by water, or agrees to furnish a ship for the purpose of carrying goods in return for a sum of money to be paid to him, such a contract is a contract of affreightment and the sum to be paid is called freight. Shipment of the goods is usually evidenced in a document called a bill of lading.

The bill of lading has been defined as a receipt for goods shipped on board a ship, signed by the person (or his agent) who contracts to carry them, and stating the terms on which the goods were delivered to and received by the ship. It is not the actual contract, which is inferred from the action of the shipper or shipowner in delivering or receiving the cargo, but forms excellent evidence of the terms of the contract.

12.1 CARRIAGE OF GOODS BY SEA ACTS 1971 AND 1992

Before examining the salient points, function and types of bills of lading, we will first consider two Acts which play an important part in the role and function of this document, namely the Carriage of Goods by Sea Act 1971 which succeeded the Carriage of Goods by Sea Act 1924, and the Carriage of Goods by Sea Act 1992 which repealed the Bills of Lading Act 1855.

The bill of lading starts its life as (in almost all cases) containing or evidencing the contract of carriage between the carrier and the shipper, under which the carrier and the shipper promise that the goods will be carried from the port of loading and safely delivered at the port of discharge.

During the voyage the ownership of the goods will be normally transferred from the original seller to the ultimate receiver who will take delivery of the goods from the ship. There may in exceptional cases be 100 or more buyers who (or whose banks) will pay for the goods and then receive payment from the next buyer in the chain. During this process the goods are, of course, not in the possession of any of the parties. They are, or should be, safely on board the ship, steadily crossing the ocean. Neither the buyer of an unascertained portion of a bulk nor an endorsee after discharge had rights against the carrier.

The defect at the heart of the Bills of Lading Act 1855 was considered to be the linkage between property in the goods and the right to sue on the bill of lading contract. Under the 1992 Act this was removed.

The 1992 Act provides that any lawful holder of the bill of lading has the right of suit but that *only* he/she has the right (thus preventing more than one claimant for the same breach of contract). If, as can arise, the actual loss has been sustained by someone other than the holder of the bill of lading, the holder must account for the damages to the person who has suffered the actual loss.

The Act also recognizes the rights of suit of someone who became holder of the bill of lading after discharge of the cargo, provided that he did so under arrangements made before that date (thereby preventing trading in bills relating to goods known to be damaged – in effect, trading in causes of action).

Finally, the Act recognizes the rights of parties interested in two forms of shipping documents which are commonly used today but which do not appear within the 1855 Act. The consignee under a sea waybill and the holder of a ship's delivery order will both have rights to sue on the contract in question.

It will affect the P & I Clubs who can no longer take unmeritorious defences based on lack of title to sue. Those involved in the bulk commodity trades will gain rights they did not previously have, as will the consignees named in a waybill. Less obvious is the new feature in which the banks who finance international trade will now be able to enforce the bill of lading rights in their own name.

In examining other legislation in relation to maritime transport, it is relevant to mention that international conventions set out minimum terms and conditions out of which carriers cannot contract to the detriment of merchants. Carriers can, of course, accept terms more favourable to merchants. Generally speaking, international conventions aim to regulate international carriage and, in most cases, national carriage is allowed freedom of contract, although in most countries there are standard trading conditions which are usually applied.

The Hague Rules were agreed at an international convention at Brussels in 1924 and govern liability for loss of or damage to goods carried by sea under a bill of lading. They are officially known as the 'International Convention for the Unification of Certain Rules relating to bills of lading' and were signed in Brussels on 25 August 1924 and given effect in the UK by the Carriage of Goods by Sea Act 1924.

The Rules apply to all exports from any nation which ratified the Rules. This is virtually universal wherever they have not been superseded by the Hague Visby Rules (p. 226), either by the application of law or by contractual incorporation into the terms and conditions of the relevant bill of lading.

The main features of the Hague Rules are as follows:

1. Minimum terms under which a carrier may offer for the carriage of all goods other than live animals, non-commercial goods including personal and household effects, experimental shipments and goods carried on deck where the bill of lading is claused to indicate such carriage.

2. The carrier has to exercise due diligence to provide a seaworthy vessel at the voyage commencement, and this cannot be delegated. Additionally, the goods must be cared for adequately during the transit. Provided the carrier complies with these requirements, if loss or damage still occurs, he can rely on a number of stated defences. The majority of these elaborate on the general principle that the carrier is only liable for loss or damage caused by his own negligence, or that of his servants, agents or subcontractors. However, the carrier remains protected in three situations where the loss or damage has been caused by negligence as detailed below:

(a) negligence in navigation;

(b) negligence in the management of the vessel (as opposed to the care of the cargo);

(c) fire, unless the actual fault or privity of the carrier.

Liability in the UK is £100 per package before the Hague-Visby Rules superseded the Hague Rules. Other nations have set alternative limits: USA, US $500; Japan Y100 000; and Greece DR8000.

In 1968 at an international conference the Hague Rules were revised primarily in the area of limitation. The amended rules, the Brussels Protocol, was signed on 23 February 1968. They are more popularly known as the Hague-Visby Rules and are reflected in the UK Carriage of Goods by Sea Act 1971.

Limitation was amended to provide a weight/package alternative and originally the limits were set in Poincare Francs – a fictitious currency. This proved unacceptable and, accordingly, the 1979 Special Drawing Rights (SDR) Protocol was adopted in February 1984. Currently there are 15 member countries, primarily European and including the UK. Limitation in terms of SDRs is now the greater of SDR 666.67 per package or unit, or SDR 2 per kilo.

The Brussels Protocol embracing the Hague-Visby Rules became operative in 1977 and has 24 contracting member states including the UK, Japan and some European countries (see p. 228). The Visby amendment applies to all bills of lading in the following situations:

(a)   the port of shipment is in a ratifying nation, or
(b)   the place of issue of the bill of lading is in a ratifying nation, or
(c)   the bill of lading applies Hague-Visby Rules contractually.

At a Committee of Maritime Lawyers international conference in June 1990 the question of greater uniformity of the law of carriage of goods by sea was debated with the conclusion to allow to remain undisturbed the current Hague-Visby Rules.

In March 1978 an international conference in Hamburg adopted a new set of rules, termed the Hamburg Rules. These radically alter the liability which shipowners have to bear for loss or damage to goods in the courts of those nations where the Rules apply. The main differences between the new Rules and the old Hague-Visby Rules are given below:

1. The carrier will be liable for loss, damage or delay to the goods occurring whilst in his charge unless he proves that he, his servants or agents took all measures that could reasonably be required to avoid the occurrence and its consequences. The

detailed list of exceptions set out in the Hague and Hague-Visby Rules is no longer available to the carrier. In particular, the carrier is no longer exonerated from liability arising from errors in navigation, management of the ship or fire.

2. The carrier is liable for delay in delivery if 'the goods have not been delivered at the port of discharge provided for under the contract of carriage within the time expressly agreed upon or in the absence of such agreement within the time which it could be reasonable to require of a diligent carrier having regard to the circumstances of the case'.

3. The dual system for calculating the limit of liability, either by reference to package or weight as found in the Hague-Visby Rules, has been readopted, but the amounts have been increased by 25% to SDR 835 per package and SDR 2.5 per kilo. The liability for delay is limited to an equivalent to two and half times the freight payable for the goods delayed, but not exceeding the total freight payable for the whole contract under which the goods were shipped. In no situation would the aggregate liability for both loss/damage and delay exceed the limit for loss/damage.

4. The Hamburg Rules cover all contracts for the carriage by sea other than charter parties, whereas the Hague/Hague-Visby Rules apply only where a bill of lading is issued. The Hamburg Rules are therefore applicable to waybills, consignment notes, etc.

5. It covers shipment of live animals and deck cargo, whereas the Hague/Hague-Visby Rules may not.

6. It applies to both imports and exports to/from a signatory nation, whereas the Hague/Hague-Visby Rules apply only to exporters.

The Hamburg Rules became operative in November 1992, involving the requisite minimum 20 nations. It features strongly African nations, but only two European states, namely Hungary and Austria. The adoption of the Hamburg Rules destroys the uniformity which currently obtains with the Hague and Hague-Visby Rules thereby creating a third force in the market.

The liability of the Carrier under any of the above sea carriage conventions is, of course, always subject to the overriding application of the provisions of the Merchant Shipping Acts relating, *inter alia*, to limitation of liability. The current UK Act is the Merchant Shipping Act 1979, which implemented the 1976

International Convention on Limitation of Liability for Maritime Claims (LLMC) with effect from December 1986 (see pp. 141–2). This new convention applies a virtually unbreakable right to claim with increased levels of limitation as follows:

(a) In respect of loss of life or personal injury (other than passengers for whom a separate Fund applies).

(i) 333 000 units of account (SDRs) for a vessel with a tonnage not exceeding 500 tons;

(ii) for a vessel with tonnage in excess thereof, in addition:
- for each ton from 501 to 3000 tons: 500 SDRs;
- for each ton from 3001 to 30 000 tons: 333 SDRs;
- for each ton from 30 001 to 70 000 tons: 250 SDRs;
- for each ton in excess of 70 000 tons: 167 SDRs.

(b) In respect of any other claims:

(i) 167 000 SDRs for a vessel not exceeding 500 tons;

(ii) for a ship with a tonnage in excess thereof, in addition:
- for each ton from 501 to 30 000 tons: 167 SDRs;
- for each ton from 30 001 to 70 000 tons: 125 SDRs;
- for each ton in excess of 70 000 tons: 83 SDRs.

The balances of unsatisfied loss of life or personal injury claims (a) can participate *pari passu* along with the other claims (b). Accordingly total limitation where loss of life and/or personal injury claims are involved in conjunction with other claims is found by adding the amounts produced by formulae (a) and (b) together.

By 1994 the convention had been ratified by 24 countries, including the UK, Japan and many European nations.

Finally, in an age of global trading development in 1995 the maritime/legislative position of two particular nations needs special mention – China and the USA.

China has never ratified any international convention, but introduced on July 1993 an extensive Maritime Code covering many aspects of maritime law as detailed below:

(a) contracts of carriage of goods by sea (broadly based on Hague-Visby Rules but with some Hamburg features);

(b) contracts of carriage of passengers by sea;

(c) contracts of chartering ships;

(d) contracts of towage;

(e) collision of ships;
(f) general average;
(g) limitation of maritime claims;
(h) contracts of marine insurance;
(i) time limits; and
(j) legal relationships with foreign parties.

Many of these codes are based on existing international conventions and this provides a degree of consistency with most trading partners.

The US Maritime Law Association is attempting to produce a compromise between the requirements of merchants and carriers based on the Hague-Visby Rules but with certain Hamburg amendments to replace the US Carriage of Goods by Sea Act 1936.

12.2 SALIENT POINTS OF A BILL OF LADING

The salient points incorporated in a bill of lading can be conveniently listed as follows:

1. The name of the shipper (usually the exporter).
2. The name of the carrying vessel.
3. Full description of the cargo (provided it is not bulk cargo) including any shipping marks, individual package numbers in the consignment, contents, cubic measurement, gross weight, etc.
4. The marks and numbers identifying the goods.
5. Port of shipment or dry port/CFS.
6. Port of discharge or dry port/CFS.
7. Full details of freight, including when and where it is to be paid – whether freight paid or payable at destination.
8. Name of consignee or, if the shipper is anxious to withhold the consignee's name, shipper's order.
9. The terms of the contract of carriage.
10. The date the goods were received for shipment and/or loaded on the vessel.
11. The name and address of the notified party (the person to be notified on arrival of the shipment, usually the buyer).
12. Number of bills of lading signed on behalf of the Master or his agent, acknowledging receipt of the goods.
13. The signature of the ship's Master or his agent and the date.

12.3 TYPES OF BILLS OF LADING

There are several types and forms of bills of lading and these include the following:

(a) Shipped bill of lading

Under the Carriage of Goods by Sea Act 1971 (Hague-Visby Rules), the shipper can demand that the shipowner supplies bills of lading proving that the goods have been actually shipped. For this reason, most bill of lading forms are already printed as shipped bills and commence with the wording: 'Shipped in apparent good order and condition.' It confirms the goods are actually on board the vessel.

This is the most satisfactory type of receipt and the shipper prefers such a bill as there is no doubt about the goods being on board and, in consequence, dispute on this point will not arise with the bankers or consignee, thereby facilitating earliest financial settlement of the export sale.

(b) Received bill of lading

This arises where the word 'shipped' does not appear on the bill of lading. It merely confirms that the goods have been handed over to the shipowner and are in his custody. The cargo may be in his dock, warehouse/transit shed or even inland such as dry port/CFS/ICD, etc. The bill has, therefore, not the same meaning as a 'shipped' bill and the buyer under a CIF or CFR contract need not accept such a bill for ultimate financial settlement through the bank unless provision has been made in the contract. Forwarding agents will invariably avoid handling 'received bills' for their clients unless special circumstances obtain.

(c) Through bills of lading

In many cases it is necessary to employ two or more carriers to get the goods to their final destination. The on-carriage may be either by a second vessel or by a different form of transport (for example, to destinations in the interior of Canada). In such cases it would be very complicated and more expensive if the shipper had to arrange on-carriage himself by employing an agent at the point of tranship-ment. Shipping companies, therefore, issue bills of lading which cover the whole transit and the shipper deals only with the first carrier. This type of bill enables a through rate to be quoted and is growing in popularity with the development of containerization. Special bills of lading have to be prepared for such through-consigned cargo.

(d)   Stale bills of lading

It is important that the bill of lading is available at the port of destination before the goods arrive or, failing this, at the same time. Bills presented to the consignee or his bank after the goods are due at the port are said to be stale. A cargo cannot normally be delivered by the shipowner without the bill of lading and the late arrival of this all-important document may have undesirable consequences such as warehouse rent etc.

(e)   Groupage and house bills of lading

A growth sector of the containerized market is the movement of compatible consignments from individual consignors to various consignees usually situated in the same destination (country/area) and forwarded as one overall consignment. The goods are consolidated into a full container load and the shipping line issues a groupage bill of lading to the forwarder. This is the ocean bill of lading and shows a number of consignments of groupage of a certain weight and cubic measurement in a cargo manifest form. The forwarder issues a house bill of lading cross referring to the ocean bill of lading. It is merely a receipt for the cargo and does not have the same status as the bill of lading issued by the shipowner. Shippers choosing to use a house bill of lading should clarify with the bank whether it is acceptable for letter of credit purposes, and ideally ensure it is stipulated as acceptable before the credit is opened. Advantages of groupage include: less packing; lower insurance premiums; usually quicker transits; less risk of damage and pilferage; and lower rates when compared with such cargo being dispatched as an individual parcel/consignment.

(f)   Transhipment bill of lading

This type is issued usually by shipping companies when there is no direct service between two ports, but when the shipowner is prepared to tranship the cargo at an intermediate port at his expense.

(g) Clean bills of lading

Each bill of lading states: 'in apparent good order and condition', which of course refers to the cargo. If this statement is not modified by the shipowner, the bill of lading is regarded as 'clean' or 'unclaused'. By issuing clean bills of lading, the shipowner admits his full liability for the cargo described in the bill under the law and his contract. This type is much favoured by banks for financial settlement purposes.

(h) Claused bills of lading

If the shipowner does not agree with any of the statements made in the bill of lading he will add a clause to this effect, thereby causing the bill of lading to be termed as 'unclean', 'foul' or 'claused'. There are many recurring types of such clauses including: inadequate packaging; unprotected machinery; second-hand cases; wet or stained cartons; damaged crates; cartons missing, etc. The clause 'shipped on deck at owner's risk' may thus be considered to be claused under this heading. This type of bill of lading is usually unacceptable to a bank.

(i) Negotiable bills of lading

If the words 'or his or their assigns' are contained in the bill of lading, it is negotiable. There are, however, variations in this terminology, for example the word 'bearer' may be inserted, or another party stated in the preamble to the phrase. Bills of lading may be negotiable by endorsement or transfer.

(j) Non-negotiable bills of lading

When the words 'or his or their assigns' are deleted from the bills of lading, the bill is regarded as non-negotiable. The effect of this deletion is that the consignee (or other named party) cannot transfer the property or goods by transfer of the bills. This particular type is seldom found and will normally apply when goods are shipped on a non-commercial basis, such as household effects.

(k) Container bills of lading

Containers are now playing a major role in international shipping and container bills of lading are becoming more common in use. They cover the goods from port to port or from inland point of departure to inland point of destination. It may be an inland clearance depot, dry port or container base. Undoubtedly, to the shipper, the most useful type of bill of lading is the clean, negotiable 'through bill', as it enables the goods to be forwarded to the point of destination under one document, although much international trade is based on free carrier (named place) FCA, free-on-board (FOB), cost, insurance, freight (CIF), and carriage and insurance paid (to named point of destination) (CIP) contracts (see pp. 435–8).

(l) Bill of lading in association with a charter party
With the development of combined transport operations, an increasing volume of both liner cargo trade and bulk cargo shipments will be carried involving the bill of lading being issued in association with a selected charter party. An example is found in the Combined Transport Bill of Lading 1971 – codename 'Combi-conbill' issued with selected charter parties (see pp. 350–56).

The combined transport document rules are found in the ICC Rules for a Combined Transport Document (brochure no. 298). They are widely used by major container operators and reflects the earlier Tokyo-Rome Rules, the Tokyo Rules and TCM Convention (see p. 241).

(m) Straight bill of lading
An American term for a non-negotiable bill of lading (i.e. a waybill) governed by the US Pomerene Act. This is known more correctly as the Federal Bills of Lading Act 1916 and provides the law in the USA in relation to bills of lading in interstate and foreign commerce. It allows the consignee to enforce the rights of the merchant against the carrier. Its provisions enable the holder of the bill of lading not to surrender it to secure delivery of the goods. Overall, it applies to straight bills of lading involving US exports and interstate traffic only and is not applicable to US imports.

(n) Negotiable FIATA combined transport bill
This document is becoming increasingly used in the trade and is a FIATA bill of lading (FBL), employed as a combined transport document with negotiable status. It has been developed by the International Federation of Forwarding Agents Associations and

acceptable under the ICC Rules on the Uniform Customs and Practice for Documentary Credits (ICC publication no. UCP 500 – revision 1994). The FIATA bill of lading should be stipulated in letters of credit where the forwarders' container groupage service is to be utilized and a house bill of lading is to be issued.

FIATA states that a forwarder issuing a FIATA bill of lading must comply with the following:

(a)   The goods are in apparent good order and condition.

(b)   The forwarder has received the consignment and has sole right of disposal.

(c)   The details set out on the face of the FBL correspond with the instructions the forwarder has received.

(d)   The insurance arrangements have been clarified – the FBL contains a specific delete option box which must be completed.

(e)   The FBL clearly indicates whether one or more originals have been issued.

The FIATA FBL terms create more shipper obligations in the areas of packing, general average, payment of charges and description of goods. Additional rights are also conferred on the forwarder in the areas of lien, routeing of cargo and stowage, handling and transport of consignments.

12.4 FUNCTION OF THE BILL OF LADING

For our study of the bill of lading, it will be appropriate to record the four functions of this document. Broadly it is a receipt for the goods shipped, a transferable document of title to the goods thereby enabling the holder to demand the cargo, evidence of the terms of the contract of affreightment but not the actual contract, and a quasi-negotiable instrument.

Once the shipper or his agent becomes aware of the sailing schedules of a particular trade, through the medium of sailing cards, computer database or some form of advertisement, he communicates with the shipowner with a view to booking cargo space on the vessel or container. Provided satisfactory arrangements have been concluded, the shipper forwards the cargo. At this stage, it is important to note that the shipper always makes the offer by forwarding the consignment to the CFS/ICD/seaport, whilst the shipowner either accepts or refuses it. Furthermore, it is the shipper's duty, or that of his agent, to supply details of the consignment; normally this is done by completing the shipping company's form of bill of lading, and the shipping company then signs the number of copies requested.

The goods are signed for by the vessel's chief officer or ship's agent, and in some trades this receipt is exchanged for the bill of lading. If the cargo is in good condition and everything is in order, no endorsement will be made on the document, and it can be termed a clean bill of lading. Conversely, if the goods are damaged or a portion of the consignment is missing, the document will be suitably endorsed by the Master or his agent, and the bill of lading will be considered 'claused' or 'unclean'.

Bills of lading are made out in sets, and the number varies according to the trade. Generally it is three or four – one of which will probably be forwarded immediately, and another by a later mail in case the first is lost or delayed. In some trades, coloured bills of lading are used, to distinguish the original (signed) bills from the copies which are purely for record purposes.

Where the shipper had sold the goods on letter of credit terms established through a bank, or when he wishes to obtain payment of his invoice before the consignee obtains the goods, he will pass the full set of original bills to his bank, who will in due course arrange presentation to the consignee against payment.

The shipowner or his agent at the port of destination will require one original bill of lading to be presented to him before the goods are handed over. Furthermore, he will normally require payment of any freight due, should this not have been paid at the port of shipment. When one of a set of bills of lading has been presented to the shipping company, the other bills in the set lose their value.

In the event of the bill of lading being lost or delayed in transit, the shipping company will allow delivery of the goods to the person claiming to be the consignee, if he gives a letter of indemnity; this is normally countersigned by a bank, and relieves the shipping company of any liability should another person eventually come along with the actual bill of lading.

With the advent of combined transport and the enactment of new legislation (see pp. 223–9), radical changes have emerged regarding the bill of lading document. Basically, because different carriers' bill of lading terms and conditions vary so much (and are able to do so on account of the absence of mandatory law regarding combined transport in ports), shippers are urged to familiarize themselves with the terms of the contracts of carriage into which they enter.

Hence, although the bill of lading bears the legend 'combined transport', it is no guarantee that the carrier accepts liability for the transit throughout and it may be a through or transhipment bill in disguise.

The following items are common discrepancies found in bills of lading when being processed and should be avoided:

(a) Document not presented in full sets when requested.

(b) Alterations not authenticated by an official of the shipping company or their agents.

(c) The bill of lading is not clean when presented in that it is endorsed regarding damaged condition of the specified cargo or inadequate packing thereby making it unacceptable to a bank for financial settlement purposes.

(d) The document is not endorsed 'on board' when so required.

(e) The 'on-board' endorsement is not signed or initialled by the carrier or agent and likewise not dated.

(f) The bill of lading is not 'blank' endorsed if drawn to order.

(g) The document fails to indicate whether 'freight prepaid' as stipulated in the credit arrangements, i.e. CFR or CIF contracts.

(h) The bill of lading is not marked 'freight prepaid' when freight charges are included in the invoice.

(i) The bill of lading is made out 'to order' when the letter of credit stipulates 'direct to consignee' or vice versa.

(j) The document is dated later than the latest shipping date specified in the credit.

(k) It is not presented within 21 days after date of shipment or such lesser time as prescribed in the letter of credit.

(l) The bill of lading details merchandise other than that prescribed.

(m) The rate at which freight is calculated and the total amount are not shown when credit requires such data to be given.

(m) Cargo has been shipped 'on deck' and not placed in the ship's hold. Basically 'on-deck' claused bills of lading are not acceptable when clean on-board bills of lading are required.

(o) Shipment made from a port or to a destination contrary to that stipulated.

(p) Other types of bills of lading presented although not specifically authorized. For example, charter party to forwarding agents bills of lading are not accepted unless expressly allowed in the letter of credit.

Additionally, having regard to UCP 500, 511 and 515 (see pp. 247–8), shippers are urged to give attention to the following items:

(a) Use the correct Incoterm 1990.

(b) Do not prohibit transhipment for combined transport shipments.

(c) Avoid shipped on board requirements if the exporter wants earlier payment.

(d) Do not ask for detailed bill of lading descriptions.

(e) Control the letter of credit details through carefully worded sales contracts.

(f) If a door-to-door service is required obtain a combined transport document and not a marine bill of lading.

(g) Avoid calling for clauses or certificates that are not available from the carriers.

It is appropriate to record that buyers (importers) who normally call for a shipped on board bill of lading may consider it more advantageous to consider whether they need to include in their instructions the usual 'shipped on board bill of lading' wording, or whether it might be more appropriate to call for a combined transport bill of lading and omit all reference to 'on board'. This would in no way prejudice their interest, and would enable the necessary documents to be issued more quickly as there would be no delay awaiting confirmation of shipment on board.

An example of a bill of lading for combined transport shipment or port to port shipment is given in Fig. 12.1.

12.5 INTERNATIONAL CONVENTION CONCERNING THE CARRIAGE OF GOODS BY RAIL

Our study of bills of lading would not be complete without examining the CIM and CMR documentation – the latter being dealt with in the next section.

Bill of Lading for Combined Transport shipment or Port to Port shipment

Shipper

B/L No.

Booking Ref.:

Shipper's Ref.:

Consigned to the order of

P&O
Containers

Notify Party/Address (It is agreed that no responsibility shall attach to the Carrier or his Agents for failure to notify of the arrival of the goods (see clause 20 on reverse))

Place of Receipt (Applicable only when this document is used as a Combined Transport Bill of Lading)

Vessel and Voy. No.

Place of Delivery (Applicable only when this document is used as a Combined Transport Bill of Lading)

Port of Loading

Port of Discharge

Any Shipped on Board endorsement is invalid unless on the official P&O Containers endorsement label placed at the bottom of this document, bearing a design matching that in the signature box.

Marks and Nos; Container Nos;	Number and kind of Packages; description of Goods	Gross Weight (kg)	Measurement (cbm)

Above particulars as declared by Shipper, but not acknowledged by the Carrier (see clause 11)

* Total No. of Containers/Packages received by the Carrier

Movement

Freight and Charges (indicate whether prepaid or collect):

Origin Inland Haulage Charge... ... ...

Origin Terminal Handling/LCL Service Charge... ...

Ocean Freight ... ...

Destination Terminal Handling/LCL Service Charge...

Destination Inland Haulage Charge... ... ...

Received by the Carrier from the Shipper in apparent good order and condition (unless otherwise noted herein) the total number or quantity of Containers or other packages or units indicated in the box opposite entitled "*Total No. of Containers/Packages received by the Carrier" for Carriage subject to all the terms and conditions hereof (INCLUDING THE TERMS AND CONDITIONS OF THE REVERSE HEREOF AND THE TERMS AND CONDITIONS OF THE CARRIER'S APPLICABLE TARIFF) from the Place of Receipt or the Port of Loading, whichever is applicable to the Port of Discharge or the Place of Delivery, whichever is applicable. Before the Carrier arranges delivery of the Goods one original Bill of Lading, duly endorsed, must be surrendered by the Merchant to the Carrier at the Port of Discharge or at some other location acceptable to the Carrier. In accepting this Bill of Lading the Merchant expressly accepts and agrees to all its terms and conditions whether printed, stamped or written, or otherwise incorporated, notwithstanding the non-signing of this Bill of Lading by the Merchant.

ICS
CT B/L
April 78

Number of Original Bills of Lading

Place and Date of Issue

IN WITNESS of the contract herein contained the number of original stated opposite has been issued one of which being accomplished the other(s) to be void.

For P&O Containers Limited as Carrier:

CANCELLED SPECIMEN COPY

This is a RECEIVED FOR SHIPMENT Bill of Lading. Any Shipped on Board endorsement is invalid unless placed in this field by means of the official P&O Containers endorsement label.

As Agent for the Carrier

000199

P&OCL B/L3 4/94 (S)

Fig. 12.1 Bill of lading for combined transport or port-to-port shipment. (Reproduced by kind permission of P&O Containers Ltd.)

TERMS AND CONDITIONS

1. DEFINITIONS

2. CARRIER'S TARIFF

3. WARRANTY

4. SUB-CONTRACTING AND INDEMNITY

5. CARRIER'S RESPONSIBILITY – PORT-TO-PORT SHIPMENT

6. CARRIER'S RESPONSIBILITY – COMBINED TRANSPORT

7. SUNDRY LIABILITY PROVISIONS

8. SHIPPER-PACKED CONTAINERS

9. INSPECTION OF GOODS

10. CARRIAGE AFFECTED BY CONDITION OF GOODS

11. DESCRIPTION OF GOODS

12. SHIPPER'S–MERCHANT'S RESPONSIBILITY

13. FREIGHT

14. LIEN

15. OPTIONAL STOWAGE AND DECK CARGO

16. LIVE ANIMALS

17. METHODS AND ROUTES OF CARRIAGE

18. MATTERS AFFECTING PERFORMANCE

19. DANGEROUS GOODS

20. NOTIFICATION AND DELIVERY

21. FCL MULTIPLE BILLS OF LADING

22. GENERAL AVERAGE & SALVAGE

23. VARIATION OF THE CONTRACT

24. LAW AND JURISDICTION

25. VALIDITY

26. BOTH-TO-BLAME COLLISION

27. USA CLAUSE PARAMOUNT

P&O CONTAINERS LIMITED, BEAGLE HOUSE, BRAHAM STREET, LONDON E1 8EP

Fig. 12.1 continued

The International Convention concerning the Carriage of Goods by Rail (CIM) has existed in some form since 1893. It permits the carriage of goods by rail under one document – the consignment note (not negotiable) – under a common code of conditions applicable to 34 countries mainly situated in Europe and Mediterranean areas. It embraces the maritime portion of the transit subject to it being conveyed on shipping lines as listed under the Convention. The limitation of liability for loss or damage is SDR 17 per kilo. Advantages of the system embrace through-rates under common code of conditions; simplified documentation/accountancy; flexibility of freight payment; no intermediate handling usually or customs examination in transit countries; through transits; and minimum documentation.

The Convention is revised from time to time to reflect modern needs and the current one is the COTIF/CIM Convention of 10 May 1985, which contains a revised version of the CIM uniform rules of the international carriage of goods by rail.

On 1 January 1993 the CIM Note and the TIEx Note used for cargo-wagon containerized movement and swap-bodies passing through the Channel Tunnel or on international rail transits were replaced by a single form known as the 'Consignment Note CIM'.

12.6 CONVENTION ON THE CONTRACT FOR THE INTERNATIONAL CARRIAGE OF GOODS BY ROAD

The International Convention concerning the Carriage of Goods by Road (CMR) came into force in the UK in October 1967. It permits the carriage of goods by road under one consignment note under a common code of conditions applicable to 26 countries. These include Austria, Belgium, Bosnia-Herzegovina, Bulgaria, Croatia, the Czech Republic, Denmark, Finland, France, Germany, Greece, Hungary, Italy, Luxembourg, Macedonia the Netherlands, Norway, Poland, Portugal, Romania, Serbia and Montenegro, Slovakia, Slovenia, Spain, Sweden, Switzerland and the United Kingdom. Additionally, by order in Council, the convention has been extended to cover the Isle of Man, the Isle of Guernsey and Gibraltar. It applies to all international carriage of goods by road for reward to or from a contracting party. It does not apply to traffic between the UK and the Republic of Ireland.

This convention which has established the carrier's liability to SDR 8.33 per kg and the documentation to be used in respect of goods to be carried by road vehicles between two countries has facilitated the development of Ro/Ro UK/Europe traffic. The statutory provisions are embodied in the Carriage of Goods by Road Act 1965 as amended by the Carriage by Air and Road Act 1979.

12.7 COMBINED TRANSPORT

In the 1970s an attempt was made to draft a convention to cover loss or damage to goods carried under a combined transport document. It was known variously at different stages as the Tokyo-Rome rules, the Tokyo rules and the TCM convention. Regrettably it failed to gain adequate support and subsequently the International Chamber of Commerce revised particular elements of it, with the result the final draft was published as the 'ICC rules for a Combined Transport Document'.

However, UNCTAD was unhappy with this situation and decided to intervene with an international convention to govern combined transport. It was finally adopted at an international conference in Geneva in May 1980 as the 'United Nations Convention on International Multi-modal Transport of Goods' or as more commonly known the 'UNCTAD MMO Convention'.

Like the Hamburg Rules, if introduced, it is likely to increase the carrier insurance costs which will probably result in increased freight rates without any corresponding reduction in cargo insurance premiums. Some thirty countries need to ratify it before acceptance and by 1994 it had the support of only seven countries.

The UNCTAD MMO owes much in its drafting to the Hamburg Rules and its approach to limitation of liability may be described as 'a plateau with peaks showing through'. That is to say, the Rules set a limit (about 10% above the Hamburg limit and expressed in SDRs) with a dual weight/package alternative criterion, but where any unimodal conventions apply a higher limit of liability, and loss or damage occurs in their period of applicability, their limits apply in preference to the UNCTAD MMO limit.

12.8 COMMON SHORT FORM BILL OF LADING AND COMMON SHORT FORM SEA WAYBILL

The use of a negotiable bill of lading which has to be surrendered to the carrier at the destination in order to obtain delivery of the goods is traditional – but not without disadvantages. The document has to follow the goods, and often for commercial or financial reasons passes through a variety of hands, resulting in the goods being held up at the destination pending arrival of the document, and thereby expenses and additional risks are incurred and customer goodwill is possibly lost.

In 1979 the common short form bill of lading was introduced and replaced the traditional shipping company 'long form' bills. It is identical in legal and practical terms to the traditional bills, but is more simple and can be used with any shipping line.

The document covers the shipper/forwarder and provides bills from port to port and through-transport including container bills of lading. It does not cover combined transport bills of lading which are almost always completed by computer by the combined transport operator.

The common short form bill of lading is fully negotiable and the normal bill of lading lodgement and presentation procedures remain unchanged. However, instead of the mass of small print on the reverse, there is an approved 'short form' clause on the face which incorporates carriers' standard conditions with full legal effect.

An example of a non-negotiable waybill for combined transport or port to port shipment is given in Fig. 12.2. This is not a common short form waybill but is one used by P & O Containers featuring the incorporation clause and is broadly of the same format.

The common short form bill of lading has the following salient features:

(a) It has wide approval and may be used by shippers and freight forwarders and presented for signature to the carrier or his authorized agents, after a perusal and acceptance of the carriers' standard terms and conditions to which the incorporation clause in the short form bill of lading refers.

(b) It is suitable for outward shipments from the UK involving 'through' transit, or 'port-to-port' carriage of cargo for both 'break

Non-Negotiable Waybill for Combined Transport shipment or Port to Port shipment

Shipper

Waybill No.

Booking Ref.:

Shipper's Ref.:

Consignee

P&O Containers

Notify Party/Address (It is agreed that no responsibility shall attach to the Carrier or his Agents for failure to notify of the arrival of the goods)

Place of Receipt (Applicable only when this document is used as a Combined Transport Waybill)

Vessel and Voy. No.

Place of Delivery (Applicable only when this document is used as a Combined Transport Waybill)

Port of Loading

Port of Discharge

Marks and Nos; Container Nos;	Number and kind of Packages; description of Goods	Gross Weight (kg)	Measurement (cbm)

Above particulars as declared by Shipper, but not acknowledged by the Carrier

* Total No. of Containers/Packages received by the Carrier

Received by the Carrier from the Shipper in apparent good order and condition (unless otherwise noted herein) the total number or quantity of Containers or other packages or units indicated in the box opposite entitled "Total No. of Containers/Packages received by the Carrier" for Carriage from the Place of Receipt or the Port of Loading, whichever applicable, to the Port of Discharge or the Place of Delivery, whichever applicable, SUBJECT TO THE TERMS OF THE CARRIER'S STANDARD BILL OF LADING TERMS AND CONDITIONS AND TARIFF FOR THE RELEVANT TRADE, WHICH ARE MUTATIS MUTANDIS APPLICABLE TO THIS WAYBILL (copies of which may be obtained from the Carrier or his agents). Except for live animals and Goods which are stated herein to be carried on deck and are so carried, these terms and conditions are warranted by the Carrier in respect of the sea portion of the Carriage to apply the Hague Rules or Hague Visby Rules, whichever would have been applicable if this Waybill were a Bill of Lading. In either case the provisions of Article III Rule 4 of the Hague Rules or Hague Visby Rules are deemed to be incorporated herein.

The contract evidenced by this Waybill is deemed to be a contract of carriage as defined in Article 1 (b) of the Hague Rules and Hague Visby Rules. However this Waybill is not a document of title to the Goods.

Movement

Delivery will be made to the Consignee named, or his authorised agent, on production of proof of identity at the Port of Discharge or the Place of Delivery, whichever applicable. Should the Consignee require delivery to a party and/or premises other than as shown above in the 'Consignee' box, then written instructions must be given by the Consignee to the Carrier or his agent. Unless the Shipper expressly waives his right to control the Goods until delivery by means of a clause on the face hereof, such instructions from the Consignee will be subject to any instruction to the contrary by the Shipper.

Freight and Charges (indicate whether prepaid or collect):

Unless instructed to the contrary by the Shipper prior to the commencement of Carriage and noted accordingly on the face hereof, the Carrier will, subject to the aforesaid terms and conditions, process cargo claims with the Consignee. Claims settlement, if any, shall be a complete discharge of the Carrier's liability to the Shipper. The Shipper accepts the said standard terms and conditions on his own behalf, on behalf of the Consignee and the Owner of the Goods, and authorises the Consignee to bring suit against the Carrier in his own name but as agent of the Shipper, and warrants that he has authority so to accept and authorise. The Shipper further undertakes that no claim or allegation in respect of the Goods shall be made against the Carrier by any person other than in accordance with the terms and conditions of this Waybill.

Origin Inland Haulage Charge ... ...

Origin Terminal Handling/LCL Service Charge ... ...

Ocean Freight ... ...

Destination Terminal Handling/LCL Service Charge ...

Destination Inland Haulage Charge ... ...

Place and Date of Issue

ICS
C/T W/B
April 78

This Waybill is issued subject to the CMI Uniform Rules for Sea Waybills.

IN WITNESS whereof this Waybill is signed.
For P&O Containers Limited as Carrier:

065018   P&O CONTAINERS LIMITED, Beagle House, Braham Street, London E1 8EP   P&OCL WB10 6/94

As Agent for the Carrier

Fig. 12.2 Non-negotiable waybill for combined transport or port-to-port shipment. (Reproduced by kind permission of P&O Containers Ltd.)

bulk' and 'unit loads' of all types traditionally covered by 'long form' bills of lading.

(c)   It is based upon an internationally accepted layout adopted by the United Nations. (See p. 454.)

(d)   As confirmed by the ICC it is acceptable within the Uniform Customs and Practice for Documentary Credits.

(e)   It is a document recommended by the Chamber of Shipping for use on all outward shipments from the UK and particularly by all UK shipper/carriers and their conference associates.

(f)   It is a document of title under which the contracting carrier undertakes to deliver the subject goods against surrender of an original document.

(g)   It is a 'received-for-carriage' bill with provision for endorsement evidencing goods shipped on board when so required.

(h)   It is suitable for conventional and through-liner services irrespective of whether the vessel is chartered or owned by the contracting carrier. (Use of the form is not currently available for goods carried by combined transport operators.)

(i)   It is described as a 'short form' document because of the use of an abridged standard clause on the face of the document which incorporates the conditions of carriage of the contracting carrier. The change eliminates the mass of small print on the reverse side of bills of lading without affecting the status of the document or rights and obligations of any interested party (see Fig. 12.2).

(j)   It is a document fully aligned to the SITPRO 'master' (see p. 459).

(k)   It is an aid to achieving lower stationery costs through a reduced need to hold a variety of stocks of long form bills of lading with the individual carrier's name and conditions and eliminates the risk of using obsolescent forms together with attendant complications.

The Chamber of Shipping with the co-operation of SITPRO has also developed the concept of a non-negotiable type of transport document – termed a common short form sea waybill – in place of the negotiable traditional bill of lading. Its basic feature is that it provides for delivery to the consignee named in it without surrender of the transport document.

The common short form sea waybill has the following salient features which are similar in many ways to the common short form bill of lading:

(a) It is a common document upon which the shipper adds the name of the contracting carrier to be used.

(b) It is a non-negotiable document consigned to a named consignee and not requiring production to obtain possession of the goods at destination – a salient advantage thereby obviating delays in the release of goods at destination.

(c) It is a received-for-shipment document, with an option for use as a shipped document.

(d) It is an aid to achieving lower stationery costs through a reduced need to hold stocks of individual carriers' bills with their individual names and conditions.

(e) It is a document fully aligned to the SITPRO 'master' (see p. 453).

(f) It is described as a 'short form' document because of the use of an abridged standard clause on the face of the document which incorporates the conditions of carriage of the contracting carrier. The change eliminates the need to reprint documents to accommodate changes and conditions.

(g) It facilitates earlier release of the goods – if received for shipment – and thereby reduces delays associated with negotiability. Moreover, it helps the speedier flow of goods to the consignee. One must bear in mind the named consignee is not required to produce the sea waybill to obtain possession of the goods at destination.

(h) It is widely approved and may be used by shippers and freight forwarders and presented for signature to the carrier or his authorized agents, after a perusal and acceptance of the carrier's standard terms and conditions to which the incorporation clause in the sea waybill refers.

(i) It is suitable for outward shipments from the UK involving 'through' transit or 'port-to-port' carriage of cargo for both 'break bulk' and 'unit loads' of all types. Moreover, it is suitable for conventional and through-liner services, irrespective of whether the vessel is chartered or owned by the carrier.

(j) It is based upon an internationally accepted layout adopted by the United Nations. (See p. 454.)

(k) It is not a document of title. Hence the shipper retains his waybill as a receipt for the goods and delivery is made to the nominated consignee at destination upon proof of identity.

(l) It is evidence of the contract with the shipper only so that he remains in control and can vary instructions to the carrier all the time that the goods are in transit, unless he waives this control with a 'NODISP' (no disposal) clause on the face of the waybill.

(m) There is no requirement to send a document of title to the destination to secure delivery as is necessary with a bill of lading.

(n) There is no possibility of a requirement for a letter of indemnity for delivery of cargo without a bill of lading.

(o) In many trades carriers charge for producing bills of lading but not waybills so there is an opportunity to reduce the cost to the shipper as well as modernize systems.

(p) A waybill can be a paper document or electronic message. It is therefore the ideal medium to bridge the gap between paper and EDI trading in the most cost-effective way.

Finally, the implementation of the Carriage of Goods by Sea Act 1992 and UCP 500 1994 new uniform customs and practice for documentary credits will enhance the use of the sea waybill in preference to the bill of lading.

The commercial and financial feasibility of using the waybill clearly rests with the shipper/consignee and is dependent upon the type of trade transaction involved. The waybill is ideal for use in the following circumstances:

(a) House-to-house shipments such as shipments between associated companies or branches of multinational companies where no documentary credit transaction is involved.

(b) Open account sales which arise where goods are shipped to an agent for sale at destination on an account sale basis.

(c) Transactions between companies where the security of a documentary credit transaction is not required perhaps because of trust stemming from a long trading relationship or an alternative basis of payment being arranged.

The point at which sea waybills are released will depend upon whether the document is 'received for shipment' or 'shipped on board'. In signing waybills, the carrier or his agent is required to insert the carrier's cable address within the signature or date stamp.

If a received-for-shipment document was issued and cargo was subsequently short-shipped or a carrier's clause required (for example, to indicate that damage was sustained whilst the goods were on the quay) then a qualification report should be issued to the shipper, consignee and those concerned within the carrier's organization; information concerning such reports should also be made available to insurers on request. Use of the 'shipped' option would, however, obviate the need for a qualification report, and, in such circumstances, the normal bill of lading procedures would apply.

In examining the bill of lading and sea waybill it is important to mention that the new Uniform Customs and Practice for Documentary Credits UCP 500 was introduced on 1 January 1994 by the International Chamber of Commerce and replaced UCP 400. The major change is that provision is made for the use of waybills in documentary credits.

The types of documents recognized by UCP 500 are as follows:

Article 23   Marine/Ocean Bill of Lading;
Article 24   Non-negotiable Sea Waybill;
Article 25   Charter Party Bill of Lading;
Article 26   Multi-modal Transport Document;
Article 27   Air Transport Document;
Article 28   Road, Rail or Inland Waterways Transport Document;
Article 29   Courier and Post Receipts;
Article 30   Transport Documents Issued by Freight Forwarders.

Areas which may give rise to problems and thereby result in payments delay include the following:

(a)   certificate of cover in a 'P & I Club';
(b)   certificate of vessel's age;
(c)   temperature clausing – associated with food shipments and related regulations.
(d)   values in bills of lading;
(e)   supplementary documents and clauses.

Finally other relevant ICC publications recently issued are given below and must be reconciled with the foregoing analysis:

UCP 511 Documentary Credits (replacing UCP 400).
UCP 515 ICC Guide to Documentary Credit Operations Recommendations (new publication).

12.9 STANDARD SHIPPING NOTE

In 1975 a standard shipping note (SSN) was introduced and is available for use for the delivery of FCL and LCL goods to the CFS or CB or for uncontainerable items direct to the terminals. It is a six-part document and fully aligned to the SITPRO master. It is also used by the CFS operator to record details of the container and number of the seal used after completion of packing.

It is used when delivering cargo to any British port, container base or other freight terminal. It must accompany the goods to the receiving berth/dock or container base etc., or be lodged at the receiving authority's designated office before arrival of the goods for shipment according to local port practice. Only goods for shipment to one port of discharge on one sailing and sometimes relating to only one bill of lading may be grouped on one shipping note.

The SSN contains the following information:

(a) name and address of the exporter/shipper;
(b) vehicle booking reference, when relevant, as issued by the receiving authority;
(c) (i) customs' reference;
    (ii) exporter's reference;
    (iii) forwarding agent's reference;

(d) shipping company's booking reference where issued;
(e) details of company responsible for FOB/receiving authority's export charges;
(f) name of shipping line or combined transport operator;
(g) name and address of forwarding agent or merchant;
(h) (i) ship's receiving date(s);
    (ii) berth and dock/container base etc.;
(i) ship's name and port of loading;
(j) port of discharge and, for less than container loads, final destination depot;
(k) name of receiving authority, e.g. port authority, shipping company, container base, to whom the shipping note is addressed;

(l)   port scale of charges;
(m)   (i) marks and numbers of packages in full. With regard to container shipments details of container owner's marks, serial numbers and seal number to be given;
(ii) number and kind of packages;
(iii) description of goods;
(iv) package dimensions in centimetres;
(n)   (i) gross weight in metric units for each item;
(ii) total gross weight;
(o)   (i) cubic measurement of packages in cubic metres;
(ii) total cubic measurement;
(p)   indication of cargo status, i.e.
(i) HM Customs free status;
(ii) pre-entry (bonding or drawback formalities etc.);
(iii) hazardous or other special stowage cargo;
(q)   (i) name of company/telephone/fax number;
(ii) name and status of person preparing the note;
(iii) place and date of issue.

Overall the use of the SSN may vary according to individual port practices.

12.10 EXPORT CARGO SHIPPING INSTRUCTION

Most major shipowners now require their shippers or agents to complete an export cargo shipping instruction (ECSI). This is completed and despatched at the time of booking the consignment and most major shippers transmit this data via on-line computer access to the shipowner. It provides all the relevant data which the carrier needs to complete the bill of lading and specifies who is responsible for freight charges. This includes packing specifications. Additionally the ECSI makes provision for supplementary services such as customs entries. It applies to both general cargo, LCL and FCL cargo.

CHAPTER 13

Cargoes

13.1 CARGO STOWAGE/PACKING OVERVIEW

Cargo stowage is the process of accommodating an item of merchandise in a transport unit with a view to its arrival in a mercantile condition and has regard to the nature of the transit, any likely hazards and the most economic conveyance of the cargo.

As we progress through the 1990s the significance of cargo stowage and packing will grow in international trade. It is an area where cost-effective cargo stowage can aid overseas market development through lower distribution costs. Factors influencing such developments are given below and reflect the changing pattern of international trade distribution.

(a) The development of the LCL and NVOCC transport mode requires more skill in stowage of compatible cargo.

(b) New technology involving computers and packing techniques will add a new dimension to cargo stowage.

(c) More pressure is being placed on shippers to reduce their distribution unit cost. This can be realized through more productive stowage techniques and more sophisticated skills in formulating the stowage plan.

(d) The transport unit, especially in the area of combined transport operation, is tending to become of greater capacity as found in the trailer and high-capacity cube container. This will require more skills for effective stowage.

(e) As world trade develops especially in the growth market of consumer goods, it will intensify the competition in the market place to have/receive quality goods in an undamaged condition. This requires more advanced stowage/packing techniques.

(f) Technology is developing rapidly in international destinations. New equipment is constantly being introduced and existing equipment improved. Moreover, new regulations are being adopted continuously. Furthermore the range of equipment is being designed so as to reduce packing specifications/cost and thereby lower distribution costs. For example, the range of container types introduced in the past ten years have all striven towards improved quality international distribution. For example, the purpose-built ISO container has encouraged bulk shipment thereby eliminating packing needs as found in cement, fertilizers, and so on.

(g) The development of combined transport operation multi-modalism has encouraged door-to-door transit with no tranship-ment. Again, packing costs/needs are much reduced.

(h) The producer should ideally design the product with regard to making transportation relatively easy and so capable of being lifted and secured safely, clearing factory doors and entrances, and not exceeding the weight or size restriction of transit.

The foregoing must be reconciled when examining cargo stow-age and packing in the late 1990s. Future needs will involve better co-operation/consultation by all interested parties in the transit with the principal carrier and buyer taking the lead. The exporter must ensure the production process/packing specification is so designed to make the best use possible of the transport unit capacity available both in cubic and weight terms. Full use must be made of computer technology to maximize utilization of cargo space effectively.

13.2 STOWAGE OF CARGO

The ultimate responsibility for the stowage of cargo rests with the Master. In practice, whilst the Master retains overall respons-ibility, the supervision of stowage of cargo normally is delegated to the chief officer. His task is to see that neither the ship nor her cargo is damaged. Furthermore, he is responsible for safe hand-ling, loading, stowage and carriage, including custody of the cargo throughout the voyage. Above all, he must ensure that the safety of the ship is not imperilled by the carriage of goods. His aim must be to have the cargo evenly distributed throughout the ship, to ensure her general stability. In regard to container ships shore-based computers are used to formulate the stowage plan. In practice, it is usual for the ship to be loaded a little deeper aft, to improve the vessel's movement through the water. This is called 'trimmed by the stern', the term 'trim' referring to the difference in draught between the stem and stern. A vessel trimmed by the bow refers to the difference in draught between the stern and bow. It is regarded as an unseaworthy vessel. A ship with a centre of gravity too low will be stiff and consequently apt to strain heavily in rough weather. Conversely, a ship with a centre of gravity too high will be tender and inclined to roll, thereby creating an unstable vessel.

Basically, there are two types of cargo: bulk and general cargo. Bulk cargoes present little difficulty in stowage, as they tend to be conveyed in specialized vessels between two ports, and are often loaded and discharged by modern technology. Cargoes such as grain, coal, copra and similar cargoes are usually carried in bulk, and must be adequately ventilated during the voyage, as they are liable to spontaneous combustion.

With general cargo, the problem is more difficult, and calls for much greater skill when shipped in a loose condition and conveyed in cargo liners provided with numerous decks, including 'tween decks, which act as pigeon holds to facilitate stowage. Today, most liner cargoes are conveyed in containers, often in consolidated consignments, whilst in the UK/European trade, a substantial volume of traffic is conveyed by international road haulage – again usually under consolidated arrangements involving road trailer movement throughout.

In regard to container tonnage it involves a mammoth task of extensive pre-planning to ensure up to 3500 TEUs are unloaded and loaded from the vessel operating on a quick port turn-round time. Some containers would be locally customs cleared through the port whilst an increasing number would travel by rail or road to an ICD or CFS outside the port or in an industrial centre under multi-modal arrangements (see p. 424). It involves co-ordination with customs, port authorities, rail/road/lighterage operators, stevedoring personnel, agents and so on. Computers play a major role in the planning, stowage and operation of such a task in a modern port and shipping company. A similar criterion applies to the consolidated consignment conveyed under international road haulage arrangements.

There are four main factors to consider in the stowage of cargo:

1. The best possible use should be made of the ship's dead-weight and cubic capacity. Hence, broken stowage, which is space

wasted in the ship by cargo of irregular-shaped packages, or irregularity of cargo spaces, should be kept to a minimum consistent with the general stability of the ship. Generally 10 to 15% of the total cubic capacity is allowed for broken stowage. Thus, as far as practicable, full use should be made of the cubic capacity of the vessel, with a view to ensuring that the ship is down to her marks when she sails. If there is not an even distribution of cargo when the ship sails, with no compensating ballast, hogging or sagging may arise. Hogging arises when most of the cargo's weight has been stowed in the forward and after holds of the vessel, causing the two ends of the ship to drop lower than the amidship portion. Conversely, if most of the cargo is stowed amidships, the two ends of the vessel tend to be higher than the amidship portion. This is called sagging. Both hogging and sagging have an adverse effect on the hull, and impair the general stability of the vessel. It can largely be overcome by ballasting the portion of the ship empty of cargo.

2. Associated (to some extent) with the previous factor, is the need to prevent damage to the ship. Not only must there be a proper distribution of cargo to ensure adequate stability and trim, but also it must be properly secured to prevent shifting. If there is a movement of the cargo during the voyage it will tend to cause the ship to list. Furthermore, the position can be seriously aggravated if the cargoes involved are dangerous, where spontaneous combustion for example could cause a fire or explosion. Shifting of cargo applies primarily to bulk cargoes such as grain, small coal, flint stone or iron ores, and is not usually associated with liner cargo shipments. To reduce movement of cargo, dunnage is provided. This is in the form of foam rubber, polystyrene, inflatable bags, timber boards or mats which are placed between the cargo to prevent movement during the voyage.

3. Similarly, cargo which is fragile, taints very easily, is liable to leakage, scratches easily, has strong odours or is liable to sweat requires proper segregation; otherwise the shipowner will be faced with heavy claims and possible loss of much goodwill amongst shippers.

4. Finally, a proper segregation of stowage of different consignments for various ports must be made, to prevent delay in discharging and avoid double handling, which is not only costly and increases the risk of cargo damage and pilferage, but also

increases turn-round time. The computerized stowage plan plays a vital role in realizing this objective. This applies equally to container vessels which call at fewer ports compared to the 'tween deck tonnage they displaced.

Our study of cargo stowage would not be complete without an examination of the principles of ISO container stowage, which is an increasingly popular method of international distribution. The container specifications are found on pp. 381–4 (and see Fig. 16.1). Moreover, an increasing number of exporters are using the full container load consignment and undertaking their own stowage. The principles of container stowage are as follows. Again it cannot be stressed too strongly that safe container transport depends primarily on a correct and immovable cargo stow and an even weight distribution.

1. The container must be stowed tightly so that lateral and longitudinal movement of the cargo within is impossible. Tight stowage can be achieved by making the shape and the dimensions of the package an optimum module of the container. Alternatively, if a unit load is being used such as a pallet, the base of it must form a module of the container.

2. As an alternative to item 1, the cargo must be effectively restrained within the container. This is necessary for a variety of reasons including: (a) to prevent collapse of the stow while packing, unpacking or during transit, for example rolls of felt on end; (b) to prevent any movement during transit of part-loads or single heavy items, for example large pieces of machinery (the heavier the item the more damage it will do if allowed to move); and finally, (c) to prevent the 'face' of the stow collapsing and leaning against the container doors, that is to prevent it from falling out when the doors are opened at final destination or for customs inspection.

3. The consignment must be adequately secured. Details of the various techniques are given below:

(i) shoring – bars, struts and spars located in cargo voids to keep the cargo pressed against the walls or other cargo;

(ii) lashing – rope, wire, chains, strapping or net secured to proper anchoring points within the container and tensioned against the cargo;

(iii) wedging – wooden distance pieces, pads of synthetic material, inflatable dunnage to fill voids in the cargo and keep it immobile against the container walls;

(iv) locking – cargo built up to give a three-dimensional brick wall effect.

Basically, there is no simple formula to apply when securing cargo in a container and only experience can aid perfection and solution. Each cargo must be treated on its merits with regard to the type of cargo, the way in which it is stowed, the cargo handling equipment available and the permanent fittings in the container. The built-in securing points, dunnage brackets, etc., should be used extensively. Any timber dunnage used must be dry and comply with any quarantine regulations. Any shoring which presses against the container wall should have extra timber laid longitudinally between the wall and point of support to spread the weight over two or more side posts. Useful filler pieces for wedging or preventing chafe include old tyres, polyurethane slabs, macerated paper pads and, for light packages, rolled-up cardboard. Unless an identical stow is anticipated on the return container journey, it is best if the lashing equipment be chosen and considered as expendable. Where synthetic strapping material is used terylene is preferable to nylon for heavy loads as it is less liable to stretch.

To restrain cargo various techniques exist. Again it depends on the commodity involved. Top-heavy articles should be wedged, shored and lashed to prevent toppling. Heavy weights should be secured to stout ring-bolts (sited in the container floor and side walls) and/or be shored with timber. Chain or wire with bottle screws may be used. Wheeled vehicles should be chocked and lashed with Spanish windlasses, with the chocks chamfered or padded to protect the tyres. If the floor is of extruded aluminium, portable securing devices must be used. Resilient loads can cause lashings to slacken. This may be overcome by introducing elasticity, for example rubber rope, into the lashing pattern. No securing of pallets is necessary, provided the load is properly secured to the pallet, if the distance between pallets and container walls is 100 mm (4 in) or less. Pallets must not be allowed any longitudinal movement. If securing is necessary, stow pallets against container walls and wedge wooden blocks between the pallets. It may be necessary to insert sheets of board between pallet loads to protect against chafe and prevent bags, cartons, etc., interweaving and jamming the stow.

In many instances there is a space 25.4–152.4 mm (1–24 in) remaining between the face of the cargo and container doors. Cargo must be prevented from collapsing into this space. This can be achieved in a variety of ways as follows:

1. Use of suitably positioned lashing points with wire, rope, strapping etc. woven across.

2. A simple wooden gate for the wider gaps and heavier cargo.

3. Use of filler pieces, that is macerated paper pads, polystyrene, wood, wool pads, etc., for the narrower gaps and lighter cargoes, for example cartons of biscuits.

Care must be taken to ensure that there is no 'fall out' when the container doors are opened. This is particularly relevant to a container which has been completely packed with cartons or sacks. Although this can sometimes be achieved by interlocking tiers of packages, it is better to make sure by using any fixing points located in the door posts of the container. Nylon strapping, polypropylene or wire threaded through such points forms an effective barrier.

To ensure there is adequate and correct overall distribution of cargo within the covered container, the goods must be secure within their packages. Moreover, the pack itself must be as full as possible so as to resist pressures external to it. Packages must be sufficiently rigid to withstand the weight imposed upon them when stacked, usually to a minimum height of 2.10 m (6.88 ft). If more than one type of cargo is stowed in the container, it is essential they are all compatible and cannot contaminate or be contaminated. Heavy items and liquids should be placed at the bottom with light and dry ones on the top. Within practical physical limitations of handling, the unit package should be as large as possible since this can reduce costs by up to 20% and increase volumetric efficiency by up to 10%. Consult when practicable the consignee about the proposed method of loading and sequence. This will facilitate discharge at the destination. Where relevant, stowing should be carried out in sequence which will permit rapid checking and stowage operations during and subsequent to unloading. In the event of the consignment being subject to customs pre-entry procedures, it would facilitate customs examination should this occur and obviate unloading if such cargo was stowed at the door end of the container. Shippers should avoid having a gap in the stow along the centre line of the container or at the sides as this will generate cargo movement in the transit and possibly result in cargo damage.

13.3 TYPES AND CHARACTERISTICS OF CARGO

The following is a broad selection of the main cargoes carried, together with their characteristics, including stowage factors where appropriate. The stowage factor is the space occupied in cubic metres in the ship's hold by one metric tonne of cargo (1000 kg). Heavy cargoes shipped in bulk, such as those with a low stowage factor, occupy the smallest space, and are most suitable for single deck type of ships. Those cargoes of a higher stowage factor, such as garments and machinery, are lighter, occupy more space, and are best suited usually to container vessels. Accordingly, most of the following cargoes are now containerized and the shipper must reconcile the type required and the main areas of shipment as explained on pp. 378–93).

Apples are packed in cases, boxes, cartons or pallet boxes and stowed at a temperature of about 1°C. If the temperature is too high, the fruit becomes sticky and soft. Apples breathe after being picked, and are individually wrapped in chemically treated paper to help absorb carbon dioxide. Their stowage factor is about 2.266, and they are mainly shipped in fruit carriers; cargo liners with suitable accommodation; or containers. The latter involves the Scoresby tray pack carton of either pulp or polystyrene trays which are accommodated in cartons. Each 20 ft (6.1 m) covered container has a 518-carton capacity. The fruit is packed diagonally allowing more and larger fruit to be packed per layer in the non-pressure tray pack design.

Butter is packed in cases, cartons, boxes or kegs, with a stowage factor varying from 1.558 to 1.699. It is normally conveyed in cargo liners with refrigerated space; in specialized refrigerated vessels; or in containers.

Cement A very large volume of the world's cement is now distributed in purpose-built cement bulk carriers and on liner containerized services in specialized containers. It has a stowage factor of 1.0 to 1.133.

Coal constitutes a dangerous cargo. It is liable to spontaneous combustion, especially on long voyages, and therefore, it is undesirable for it to be shipped with acids or chemicals. The stowage factor varies from 1.0 to 1.416, according to the grade of cargo. Coal (especially small coal) is liable to shift on a long voyage. It therefore must be well trimmed into the sides and ends of the holds if a full cargo is to be loaded, to maintain the ship's stability. The cargo loses its value if broken into small pieces or dust during loading and discharge. Main shipments originate in the UK, Poland, Germany, Holland, Belgium, Australia, South Africa, Canada and the USA. Coal is generally conveyed in vessels with a single deck, large hatches and self-trimming holds.

Coffee is packed in hessian bags. It must be kept dry and taints very easily. With a stowage factor of 1.699, it is normally shipped in ventilated containers.

Confectionery is shipped in many forms of packing, the most common of which are cartons. Shipments originate in many parts of the world and are carried on most liner services much of it being containerized. It has a somewhat high stowage factor, and must be given cool stowage. The cargo must be kept dry. It is particularly suitable for FCL container shipments.

Copra is usually shipped in bulk, but small shipments may be carried in second-hand (S/H) bags in containers. It has a stowage factor varying from 2.125 to 2.266. This commodity gives off oily odours and should therefore never be shipped with such commodities as tea or sugar. It is liable to heat, and good ventilation is essential. Copra is liable to spontaneous combustion.

Cotton is shipped in pressed bales in containers, and has a stowage factor varying, according to the quality of the cargo, from 1.416 to 2.833. It is highly inflammable, and liable to spontaneous combustion if shipped damp or greasy. Cotton should be kept dry and conveyed in Combi carriers or liner tonnage (containers).

Eggs are conveyed in crates or cases. Raw eggs taint very easily, and can be refrigerated down to about 2°C, but must not be frozen. The stowage factor is somewhat high and varies according to the type of packing. Vessels with refrigerated accommodation are most suitable. The bulk of the shipments are containerized.

Esparto grass is shipped in bales in containers. It is liable to spontaneous combustion, and must be well ventilated. It has a low stowage factor varying from 2.833 to 4.249.

Fertilizers are shipped in bulk in single deck vessels or containers. It should be kept dry. Their stowage factor varies according to the variety.

Flour is generally shipped in bulk in containers, and must be kept dry. It taints very easily, and is subject to weevil damage. It has a stowage factor of 1.416.

Grain is usually conveyed in bulk, although a small proportion of it may be shipped in bags to improve the general stability of the vessel. The IMO convention on Safety of Life at Sea includes grain regulations. This emerged in the SOLAS International Convention amendment 1973, Chapter VI. Provision is made for ships constructed specially for the transport of grain and a method for calculating the adverse heeling movement due to a shift of cargo surface in ships carrying bulk grain is specified. It also provides for documents of authorization, grain loading, stability data and associated plans of loading. Copies of all relevant documents must be available on board to enable the master to meet the IMO requirements.

Grain must be kept dry and requires good ventilation, as it is liable to heat and ferment. Its stowage factor varies according to the type of grain and whether it is shipped in bulk or bags. The heavy grains such as wheat, maize and rye have a stowage factor of approximately 1.416, whilst with the lighter grains, which include barley, oats and linseed, it is about 1.558 to 2.408. If the cargo is

260 *Cargoes*

shipped in bags, these figures need to be increased by 10%. Grain is most suitably conveyed in single deck vessels with self-trimming holds, and it forms one of the major tramp cargoes. Main shipments originate in Australia, Canada, the USA, Russia, Romania, Bulgaria and the Argentine.

Jute is usually shipped in bales in containers, and is liable to spontaneous combustion. It has a stowage factor of 1.699.

Meat is shipped frozen in refrigerated holds, at a temperature of − 10°C or is chilled at − 3°C. It is a worldwide market and shipped in reefer containers or refrigerated carriers.

Motor vehicles are generally shipped unpacked to reduce freight. Each vehicle must be individually secured and stowed on a firm level floor. Space must be left round each vehicle to avoid damage by scratching or rubbing. Cars cannot be over-stowed, and space is lost if other cargo cannot be built-up under vehicle stowage. More recently, an increasing number of ships have been adapted by incorporating skeleton decks built into the holds to which the vehicles are secured thus in effect increasing the number of 'tween decks. This has permitted bulk shipments of motor vehicles in vessels called multi-purpose containers ships (see p. 45). The decks can be removed either wholly or partly for the return voyage, thus allowing cargoes of a different nature to be carried. The vehicles are transhipped by means of a ramp. Nowadays, the distribution of motor vehicles – frequently termed as trade cars – is very much a growth sector of international trade development. To meet this expansion, purpose-built pure car and truck carriers with up to 13 decks and capable of conveying 5800 cars are now operational, with 'drive on/drive off' facilities at the ports. Main shipments originate in the UK, Sweden, Japan, USA, France, Italy, Malaysia, Korea and Germany (see p. 66). It is a very large global market.

Oil cakes are conveyed in bulk or bags in containers. They are liable to sweat damage and spontaneous combustion. Their stowage factor is 1.558.

Oil and petroleum are conveyed in specialized vessels, called tankers, and are dangerous cargoes. Oil, being a liquid, will follow all movement of the ship, and thus have a large free surface, unless some method is employed in breaking up this surface. This is done by the use of longitudinal bulk heads, which divide the vessel into either three or four longitudinal sections. Other bulk heads athwartships divide the longitudinal sections into tanks. The number of tanks depends on the design of the tanker. During the voyage the tanks are never filled to capacity, i.e. there is always a free surface in the tanks of a tanker. Cofferdams are found fore and aft of the tank space as a protection against the serious fire risk inherent with this cargo. Oil is classified as clean or dirty, according to type, and it is usual for vessels to carry the same type on consecutive voyages, as the cost of tank-cleaning is high. Dirty oils include fuel oil and crude oil, whereas clean oil covers refined petroleum, lubricating oil, diesel oil and so on. Shipments of oil are mainly from the Persian Gulf, the West Indies, the USA, the Black Sea, Nigeria, Libya, Venezuela and the East Indies.

Oranges are shipped in cartons. They should not be stowed anywhere near cargo liable to taint. They are usually shipped in containers and have a stowage factor of about 1.841 to 2.125.

Ores There is a great variety of ores, including chrome, manganese, copper, bauxite, iron, zinc and barytes. Ores are essentially bulk cargoes, conveyed in specialized single-deck ore carriers and, depending on the type of cargo, have a stowage factor varying from 0.340 to 0.850. They are therefore very heavy cargoes, and, although the vessel may be fully loaded down to her marks, very little of the actual space in the vessel is utilized. Consequently, the whole weight of the cargo is concentrated in the bottom of the vessel, which tends to make the vessel 'stiff' and causes her to roll heavily in bad weather, with consequent stress and strain. There is very little risk of most types of ores shifting, and in order to raise the height of the cargo so that the ship will ride more easily, the cargo is heaped up in the middle of the holds, and not trimmed into the wings (the sides of the holds). Some ores are, however, shipped wet, and set in stowage to reduce the possibility of the cargo shifting. Ores form one of the major tramp cargoes, and specialized ore carriers are used. Main shipments of iron ore originate in Newfoundland, Brazil, Spain, Australia and North Africa; copper ore from Chile, Spain and East Africa; chrome ore from Turkey and South Africa; bauxite from Malaysia and British Guiana; zinc ore from Chile, Newfoundland and Spain; barytes from Nova Scotia; and manganese ore from Ghana, Sierra Leone and India.

Rice is shipped in bags, and is liable to heat and sweat. Rice bran is generally shipped as a tramp or liner filler cargo. Rice generally is stowed by itself although there can be consignments of polished and brown rice in the same stow. Good ventilation is essential. The stowage factor is 1.416, and main shipments originate in Burma, Italy, Thailand, Egypt and Brazil.

Rubber is conveyed in bags, bales or cases. Its stowage factor varies from 1.481 to 2.125. Latex is shipped in containers.

Salt is shipped in bulk or bags in containers, and must be kept dry as it absorbs moisture very rapidly. Excessive ventilation results in loss of weight in very dry weather. It has a stowage factor of 1.000, and is best shipped in single-deck vessels.

Sugar is usually shipped in bulk (raw), or bags (raw or refined). If it is overheated it sets hard, and if too cold the sugar content diminishes. Sugar must be kept dry, and is liable to taint. When shipped in bulk, it is conveyed in single-deck sugar carriers. Its stowage factor varies from 1.133 to 1.416, and main shipments originate in Australia, Brazil, Cuba, Jamaica, the Philippines, Java and San Domingo. Sugar is shipped in bulk, in containers or on Combi carriers.

Tea is shipped in lined cases, and loses its aroma and value if not kept dry. It taints very easily, and has a low stowage factor of about 1.481. Tea is shipped in liner tonnage in containers or Combi carriers.

Timber is carried both under deck and on deck. The stowage of timber varies considerably, according to the type of timber carried. Hardwoods, such as teak and mahogany, have a stowage factor of about 0.708 to 0.850, pitprops about 1.699 and DBB (deals, battens and boards) about 2.550. Hardwoods are carried on a metric tonne basis, whilst props and DBB are conveyed on a fathom and standard basis respectively. A large quantity of timber is moved under the Nubaltwood charter party terms which provides the following definitions in regard to the method of shipment (see p. 352).

(a)   Battens to be considered 44 mm × 100 mm and up to 75 mm × 175 mm.

(b)   Slattings to be considered 25 mm and under in thickness, and 75 mm and under in width.

(c)   Packaged goods will have a single length and size in each package except that where the residue is insufficient for complete package lengths they may be combined provided that one end of each package is squared off.

(d)   Truck bundled goods involves goods bundled in mixed lengths of one size provided that one end of each bundle is squared off.

(e)   Pre-slung goods involves the owner providing slings to place around the cargo before loading onto vessel and for these to remain during the voyage until the cargo has been discharged.

The most suitable vessel for bulk shipments is the single-deck three-island type with well decks and a broad beam, which make for easier stowage and a good deck cargo. Considerable quantities of softwoods are also conveyed in tramps, whilst hardwoods are usually shipped in liner tonnage, either in logs or cut. Shipments of softwoods originate in the Baltic and the White Sea, and North and South America, whilst hardwoods emanate from Southern Europe, Japan and numerous tropical countries. Today, to facilitate speedy transhipment, much of the timber is shipped as packaged unit loads.

Tobacco is packed in hogsheads, bales or cases. Moisture causes mildew, and excessive ventilation reduces the flavour. It is a cargo that taints very easily. This cargo is conveyed in liner cargo tonnage in containers or Combi carriers.

Wines are shipped in bulk in containerized glass-lined tanks, but in the European trades small tank vessels are employed. Main shipments originate in South Africa, the USA, Australia, France and Spain.

Wool is shipped in pressed bales or large bags. It is an inflammable cargo, and needs to be kept dry. Its stowage factor varies from 5.099 to 7.932, according to the quality. Wool is shipped in containers in cargo liner tonnage.

13.4 CARGO AND CONTAINER HANDLING EQUIPMENT

The form of cargo-handling equipment employed is basically determined by the nature of the actual cargo, the type of packing used and the environment in which it operates such as a modern computer-controlled warehouse.

The subject of handling facilities raises the important question of mechanization and computerization. Bulk cargoes such as grain, sugar, coal, ore and oil lend themselves to high-tech computerized handling, and, provided the equipment is well utilized to cover capital charges and interest, it cheapens and speeds output. Such equipment is normally situated at a special berth.

So far as bulk cargoes are concerned, handling facilities may be in the form of power-propelled conveyor belts, usually fed at the landward end by a hopper (a very large container on legs) or grabs, which may be magnetic for handling ores, fixed to a high capacity travelling crane or travelling gantries. These gantries move not only parallel to the quay, but also run back for considerable distances, thus covering a large stacking area, as well as being able to plumb the ship's hold. These two types of equipment are suitable for handling coal and ores. In the case of bulk sugar, for which the grab is also used, the sugar would be discharged into a hopper, feeding by gravity a railway wagon or road vehicle below.

Elevators are normally associated with grain. They may be bucket elevators, or operated by pneumatic suction which sucks the grain out of the ship's hold. The Port of London (Tilbury) grain terminal uses both bucket and pneumatic suction. Faster operation is with the plastic buckets although the other type is preferred once the hold is near empty. This latter type is now very popular and is designed to weigh the grain at the same time. Elevators may be situated on the quayside or be of a floating type, involving the provision of special pipes. The elevators are connected to the granaries (bulk grain storage warehouse) by power-operated conveyor belts.

The movement of bulk petrol and oils from the tanker is undertaken by means of pipelines connected to the shore-based storage tanks. Pumping equipment is provided in the tanker storage plant or refinery ashore, but not on the quayside. In view of the dangerous nature of such cargo, it is the practice to build the special berths some distance from the main dock system on the seaward side.

With regard to general merchandise virtually all liner cargo trades are containerized. Meanwhile the system of dockers handling cargo does continue, particularly in Third World countries where dock labour costs are more moderate, but doubtless every effort will be made to expand the already extensive use of mechanized cargo-handling equipment. Nevertheless, it must be recognized that containerization has now been very firmly established in the distribution of international trade under liner cargo arrangements, and that very few maritime countries will not be served by a container service. Moreover, it should be noted that not every liner cargo trade will be containerized, completely but partially, as circumstances will dictate otherwise.

When the cargo consists of a heterogeneous collection of packages of different sizes, weight and shapes, its loading and unloading, compared with the handling of bulk shipments, presents a very different problem, particularly in regard to the use of mechanized equipment.

General loose non-containerized cargo is handled by cranes on the quay, floating cranes or by the ship's own derricks. Attached to such lifting gear is a U-shaped shackle which links the crane or derricks with the form of cargo-handling equipment being used. The shackle is joined at its open end by means of a loose pin to form a link. For most lifts a hook is used. It will be appreciated that the volume of loose cargo using 'tween-deck tonnage is very much diminished following the emergence of containerization, the Combi carrier, Ro/Ro, and the change in the general pattern of world trade. Hence much of the equipment described in the following paragraph is primarily used in less developed countries and have been displaced elsewhere by the fork-lift truck and other modern methods of cargo-handling equipment/techniques.

There are numerous types of cargo-handling equipment that can be attached to the lifting gear. They include the sling or strop, which is probably the most common form of cargo-handling gear. Such equipment, generally made of rope, is ideal for hoisting strong packages, such as wooden cases or bagged cargo, which is not likely to sag or damage when raised. Similarly, snotters or canvas slings are suitable for bagged cargo. Chain slings, however, are used for heavy slender cargoes, such as timber or steel rails. Can or barrel hooks are suitable for hoisting barrels or drums. Cargo nets are suitable for mail bags and similar cargoes that are not liable to be crushed when hoisted. Heavy lifting beams are suitable for heavy and long articles such as locomotives, boilers or railway passenger coaches. Vehicle-lifting gear, consisting of four steel wire legs (with spreaders) attached to one lifting ring, are suitable for hoisting motor vehicles. Cargo trays and pallets, the latter being wooden or of steel construction, are ideal for cargo of moderate dimensions, which can be conveniently stacked, such as cartons, bags, or small wooden crates or cases. Additionally, dog or case hooks, and case and plate clamps are suitable for transhipping cargo to railway wagons or road vehicles, but not to or from the ship, except to facilitate transhipping the cargo in the hold to enable suitable cargo-handling gear to be attached. Dog hooks are not suitable for frail cases and should only be used to enable slings to be placed. Plate clamps are used for lifting metal plates.

Dockers working in the ship's hold also use pinch- or crowbars for heavy packages, and hand hooks for manoeuvring packages into position.

Much equipment is provided to facilitate movement of the cargo to and from the ship's side and the transit shed, warehouse, barge, railway wagon or road vehicle. These include two-wheeled hand barrows and four-wheeled trucks either manually or mechanically propelled, and mechanically or electrically propelled tractors for hauling four-wheeled trailers. There are also conveyor belts mechanically or electrically operated, or rollers, all perhaps extending from the quayside to the transit shed, warehouse, railway wagon or road vehicle. Mechanically powered straddle carriers are designed to straddle their load or set, pick it up and convey it to a convenient point on the quayside, transit shed, or elsewhere in the dock area. In appearance they are similar to a farm tractor with a raised chassis, below which are clamps to raise and carry the cargo underneath the 'belly' of the tractor. They are suitable for timber, pipes and long cases. The larger straddle carriers distribute the ISO containers on the quay and stand over 12 m high giving an appearance of an inverted 'U'-shaped structure.

A wide range of cargo-handling equipment exists. The handling method used should be the one which gives the greatest efficiency with economy and which makes full use of any existing facilities and equipment.

Fork-lift trucks are battery, electric or gas operated and fitted in front with a platform in the shape of two prongs of a fork or other device. The prongs lift and carry the pallet either by penetrating through specially made apertures, or passing under it. The platform, affixed to a form of mast, can be raised and tilted, and the truck can travel with its load at any height up to its maximum. It is very manoeuvrable, and can stack cargo up to a height of 5 m. The lifting capacity varies from 1000 to 3000 kg, when the trucks are called freight lifters. The majority of trucks in use are limited to 1000 kg lifting capacity.

Details are given below of the types of fork-lift trucks available:

(a) *Side shift mechanism.* It enables the fork to move laterally either side of centre and thus considerably reduces the necessity to manoeuvre the fork-lift truck in the container or confined space.

(b) *Extension forks.* Ideal for handling awkward loads and to obtain extra reach. Subject to the fork truck being of sufficient capacity for clearing a space equivalent to the depth of two pallets on each side of a trailer-mounted container thus providing easy operation of the pallet. Numerous other examples of its use exist.

(c) *Boom.* Ideal for carpets, pipes, etc.

(d) *Crane jib.* Converts the fork-lift truck into a mobile crane.

(e) *Squeeze clamps.* Suitable for handling unit loads and individual items without the aid of pallets.

(f) *Drum handler.* Handles one or two drums at a time.

(g) *Barrel handler.* Not only does it clamp the barrel with two sets of upper and lower arms, but it also revolves so that the barrel can be picked up and handled on the roll or in the upright position.

(h) *Push-pull attachment*. It is specifically designed for use with slip sheets on containers.

(i) *Lift truck satellite*. A form of powered pallet truck which can be attached to a fork-lift truck carriage and used both to load/ unload and also to transport pallet loads down the length of containers under remote control from the fork-lift truck which remains on the ground outside the container.

A selection of fork-lift trucks is found in Fig. 13.1.

An increasing number of fork-lift trucks are now computer operated which aids efficiency in the warehouse. Moreover, the bar code system is widely used for identifying, routeing and recording stowage location in the warehouse. Ned Lloyd Distri-centres are all individually computerized which enables the shipper to have on-line access and provides a data integration system between the producer and distributor. Each commodity is coded on arrival into the Districentre using the bar code system. This enables orders to be processed automatically and uses a tracking system to check the total flow of goods thereby maintaining accurate stock control.

The pallet transporter/truck may be battery, electric or manually operated. It is very manoeuvrable and efficient in transporting and positioning loads into and within the container, railway wagon or trailer. The manually operated pallet truck has a capacity of 1 tonne and the powered type 1½ tonnes.

The portable hydraulic roller has a capacity of 2 tonnes. It is capable of loading/unloading any size or weight up to the maximum dimensions and weight capacity of the container. Parallel lines of channel track connected together are laid on the container floor and the requisite number of roller sections placed into them. The load, suitably fitted with a flat base or cross bearers, is positioned on the roller sections by crane, large capacity fork truck or other equipment.

The roller sections are then raised by the hydraulic units which are always exposed beyond the load and pushed into the container with the load which is now lowered into prefixed bearers by operating the hydraulic units. The channels and rollers are then withdrawn.

The portable pneumatic roller unit, unlike the hydraulic unit which has separate channels, is integral and consists of a channel, an air hose and roller conveyor. Units to give any desired length

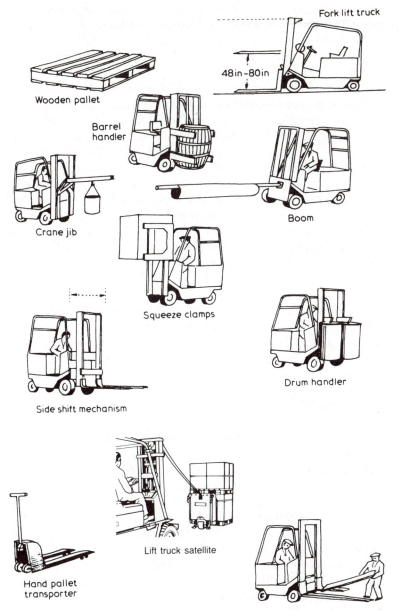

Fig. 13.1 Fork-lift trucks.

run are connected up in parallel lines and the load placed upon them. The air bags are inflated from an air supply thus raising the roller conveyor and enabling the load to be moved into the container. By releasing the air the load is lowered onto prefixed bearers and the units withdrawn.

For handling small packages the conveyor belt is ideal. A wide variety of powered mobile or static conveyors exist. The conveyor can be of a flexible type which can be extended and retracted, and which has a boom controlled by the operator, adjustable in the lateral and vertical planes. It may operate from a loading bank or ground level involving final stowage in a trailer, container, warehouse, or simply discharging the cargo from such situations.

Cargo-handling equipment is also available in the form of dock levellers, mobile ramps, bridge plates and elevating platforms.

The dock leveller is designed to bridge both the vertical and horizontal gap, for example between a loading bank and a trailer-mounted container. There are two types primarily: those positioned exterior to the loading bank and those made integral with the bank.

The mobile ramp obviates the need for a loading bank. It is ideal for stuffing/unloading a trailer or container affixed to a trailer. The ramp is attached securely to the rear of the container or trailer unit. The height of the operation from ground to the trailer/container is adjustable.

Bridge plates simply bridge the gap either from a loading bank or at ground level. They are portable and can be moved to different positions as required.

The elevating platform can be either static or mobile and thereby obviate the need for a loading bank. The mobile type can easily be positioned at the doors of a trailer-mounted container adjacent to any vehicle, or any other situation. The platform raises the mechanical handling equipment, load and operator from the ground, for example to the level of the container floor, onto which it is driven by means of an integral bridge plate. They are powered usually by electro/mechanical or electro/hydraulic packs.

The fork-lift truck, and such equipment as the pallet and pallet truck, operate on the basis that goods at first handling are placed on boards, skids or pallets. The fork-lift truck inserts its forks through or under the pallet, situated in the railway wagon, transit shed or on the quayside, raises the load and carries it to the ship's side. The pallet is then used as a sling and hoisted direct into the ship's hold where the contents are stowed. The fork-lift truck can also be used to tier cargo in a shed or on the quay. This system is called palletization, and is well established. It is used in less developed countries and especially in transhipment ports involving lighterage serving the warehouse which distributes/receives the maritime cargo from the deep-sea liner cargo services. It has to some extent changed methods of cargo handling in many liner ports. Both the fork-lift truck and to a lesser extent the pallet truck are used in stuffing and discharging containers on a very wide scale.

With the containerized shipment, particularly the full load, despatched by one shipper as distinct from the consolidated break bulk consignment, the total consignment is sometimes fully palletized. In such circumstances it facilitates container-contents stowage and permits quicker loading/discharging of the contents. The pallet forms an integral part of the packaging and remains with the cargo until it reaches its final destination which may be a lengthy rail or road journey to the importer distribution depot.

More recently the high cube dry container has been introduced of 8 feet (2.44 m) width, 9 ft 6 in (2.9 m) high and either 40 feet (12.20 m) or 45 feet (13.72 m) long. Such containers are ideal for low weight high cube products such as garments from the Far East markets. Other types of containers and equipment exist – see Chapter 16, pp. 378–93.

Other containerized handling equipment include the following:

(a) *Power jacks.* Four jacks which fit into the bottom corner castings of the container and controlled from a console. They lift and lower individually or in unison by selection and are either electro/hydraulic or electro/mechanical. Manually operated versions are also available.

(b) *Mobile gantries.* Electro/hydraulic operated with self-adjusting rams to ensure even lifting. Swivel lock castors permit the gantries when unladen to be manually manoeuvred and towed to different positions but off-balance loads need to be compensated by chain sling adjusters.

Containerization is fully examined in Chapter 16 and a selection of container-handling equipment is found in Fig. 13.2.

Container spreader

Bridge plate

Dock leveller

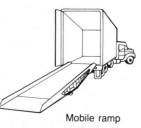

Mobile ramp

Elevating platform (static type)

Fig. 13.2 Container handling equipment. (Courtesy of P&O Containers.)

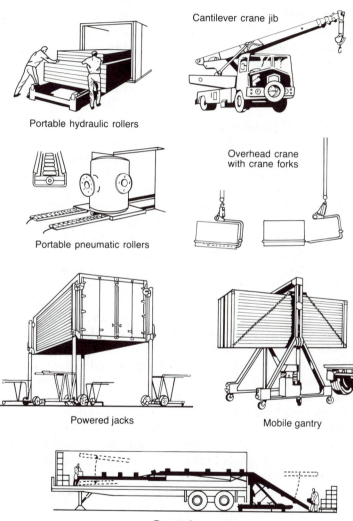

Portable hydraulic rollers

Cantilever crane jib

Portable pneumatic rollers

Overhead crane with crane forks

Powered jacks

Mobile gantry

Powered conveyors

Fig. 13.2 continued

Container terminals are purpose-built and fully described on p. 368–78.

With the development of the multi-purpose vessel conveying road haulage vehicles and trailers – some of the latter being unaccompanied – the tug master has emerged as an essential part of port equipment. The tug master is a motorized unit which can be attached to the unaccompanied trailer enabling it to be driven on or off the vessel.

13.5 TYPES OF PACKING

The method of packing depends primarily on the nature of the goods themselves and the method of transit for the anticipated voyage. Further subsidiary factors include the use to which the packing may be put when the goods reach their destination; the value of the goods (low value goods have less packing than those of high value); any customs or statutory requirements that must be complied with; ease of handling (awkward-shaped cargo suitably packed in cartons or cases can facilitate handling); marketing requirements; general fragility; variation in temperature during the voyage; the size of the cargo and its weight, and, in particular, whether elaborate packing is likely to increase the freight to the extent that it might price the goods out of the market; facilities available at the ports (in some ports they may not have highly mechanized cargo-handling equipment or elaborate storage accommodation); type and size of container; and lastly, the desirability of affixing to the packing any suitable advertisement. Overall the export product price will include packing cost which will have particular regard to transit, packaging design and its cost.

A recent development concerns the packing needs for a consignment found in a distribution warehouse such as a districentre. The goods arrive in an FCL consignment and require distribution in small lots to clients situated in different countries: overall this is a break-bulk consignment, though the goods can also be consolidated with products from other sources. The packing requires consideration of the transport mode to be used for the on-carriage, the culture/language needs as regards labelling/instructions such as translation into French/Italian/German/Spanish, and the value added concept – if the goods are for a retail outlet, the packing has a role to play in the method of selling to be used at the point of sale. Other examples are where goods are received into a warehouse and processed. Such goods may be foodstuffs or require assembly from unit components to form the final finished product for the market. The goods are then sold to neighbouring countries with differing cultures and languages, which affects the labelling and instructions on the packing. This type of operation is found in many trading ports such as Singapore, and overall is a growth market.

Packing, therefore, is not only designed as a form of protection to reduce the risk of the goods being damaged in transit, but also to prevent pilferage. It is, of course, essential to see not only that the right type of packing is provided, but also that the correct quality and form of container is used. There are numerous types of packing and a description of the more important ones follows.

Many goods have little or no form of packing whatsoever, and are carried loose. These include iron and steel plates, iron rods, railway sleepers and steel rails. Such cargoes are generally weight cargoes, with a low stowage factor. Heavy vehicles, locomotives and buses are also carried loose, because of the impracticability and high cost of packing.

Bailing is a form of packing consisting of a canvas cover often cross-looped by metal or rope binding. It is most suitable for paper, wool, cotton, carpets and rope.

Bags made of jute, cotton, plastic or paper are a cheap form of container. They are suitable for cement, coffee, fertilizers, flour and oil cakes. Their prime disadvantage is that they are subject to damage by water, sweat, hooks or, in the case of paper bags, breakage.

A recent development in packaging technique has emerged with the liquid rubber containers. It is called a bulk liquid bag or container, and can store various kinds of liquid cargo. When not in use the bag can be folded to 2% of its volume. Other cargoes can then be conveyed in the unit on the return trip. The fold-up facility eliminates wasted space in the rigid tank containers and steel drums which otherwise could not carry dry goods on the return journeys. Moreover, in cost terms the bulk liquid bag is one sixth of the price of a steel drum and one fourth of a tank container. Each bulk liquid bag can carry a volume of liquid cargo equivalent to 210 large capacity steel drums.

Cartons are a very common form of packing, and may be constructed of cardboard, strawboard or fibreboard. This form of packing is very much on the increase, as it lends itself to ease of handling, particularly by palletization. The principal disadvantage is its susceptibility to crushing and pilfering. It is a very flexible form of packing and therefore prevents the breakages which may occur if rigid containers are used. A wide range of consumer goods use this inexpensive form of packing, and it is ideal for container cargo. Polystyrene now features more and more as a packing aid in cartons. The triwall in common with the carton may be palletized with provision for fork-lift handling.

Crates, or skeleton cases, are a form of container, half-way between a bale and a case. They are of wooden construction. Lightweight goods of larger cubic capacity, such as light machinery, domestic appliances like refrigerators, cycles and certain foodstuffs, for instance oranges, are suitable for this form of packing.

Carboys, or glass containers, enclosed in metal baskets have a limited use, and are primarily employed for the carriage of acids and other dangerous liquids transported in small quantities.

Boxes, cases and metal-lined cases are also used extensively. Wooden in construction, they vary in size and capacity, and may be strengthened by the provision of battens and metal binding. Many of them, such as tea chests, are lined to create airtight packing so as to overcome the difficulties that arise when passing through zones of variable temperature. Much machinery and other items of expensive equipment, including cars and parts, are packed in this form.

Barrels, hogsheads and drums are used for the conveyance of liquid or greasy cargoes. The main problem associated with this form of packing is the likelihood of leakage if the unit is not properly sealed, and the possibility of the drums becoming rusty during transit. Acids can also be carried in plastic drums and bottles. The drum is usually of 45 gallons or 205 litres capacity and may also convey liquid (oil, chemicals) or powder shipments. They are usually stowed in a cradle to facilitate mechanical handling stowage and stacking.

Shrink wrapping has arisen through the need to reduce packaging costs particularly with regard to wooden cases and similar relatively high-cost materials. It is undertaken by placing the goods to be covered on a base – usually a pallet for ease of handling – and covering it with a film of plastic which is shrunk to enclose the items by the use of hot-air blowers (thermo-guns). It is a relatively cheap form of packing particularly in comparison with timber and fibreboard cartons. Moreover, it gives a rigid protection and security to the cargo and its configuration follows the outline of the goods. Packing in shock-absorbent polyurethane foam with a plastic foil in the pallet is also widely used.

Shrink wrapping is also used extensively with palletized consignments to secure the goods to the pallet unit. This ensures a more rigid unit and improves the security of the goods throughout the transit. It can facilitate handling of the palletized unit and stacking of the goods in the warehouse. The palletized goods maybe in a trailer movement, container (LCL or FCL) or break bulk shipment as for example in lighterage and so on. Colour films are available to protect light-sensitive cargo, and to provide a degree of protection against pilferage.

A more recent packaging development is the cov pak which is a pal box. Overall it is a jumbo fibreboard box placed on an independent pallet. Seven sizes are available including the ½ Europa (800 mm × 600 mm × 830 mm), the ½ container (1100 mm × 900 mm × 710 mm), the ISO No. 2 (1200 mm × 1000 mm × 685 mm) and ISO No. 1 (1200 mm × 1000 mm × 1040 mm). The container body is made from twin-wall heavy duty board and internal fittings can be provided to suit individual needs. A four-way pallet base is provided and the self-locking integral construction of the container ensures the pack is unitized throughout the transit. The cov pak is supplied flat with its own patented self-locking timber pallet. It offers multi-stacking subject to weight constraints and the container body can be delivered flat with the pallets inter-nested. The goods are placed into the container body and sealed by means of polypropylene strapping with metal seals for greater protection, or it can be sealed with tape. It is also termed the mac pak and some have polystyrene legs. Many shippers have smaller boxes inside the container body. Mixed loads are permitted and the cov pak is reusable for several transits.

Another form of packaging is the jiffy bag of which there are 67 different types. The bags are an envelope with bubble-wrap

J.B. LTD. No. 2
2.5 m x 1.8 m x 1.3 m
Rotterdam

Fig. 13.3 Example of the marking of cargo.

padding inside and are ideal for small consignments such as medical samples, promotional items and computer discs.

A further packaging resource is the metal envelope which is used in the movement of steel shipments and encapsulates the consignment thereby making it more secure.

It is apparent that, as containerization develops, packing needs for shipped cargo will change, as containerization requires less packing. Undoubtedly, packing will become less robust.

Associated with the types of packing is the marking of cargo. When goods are packed, they are marked on the outside in a manner which will remain legible for the whole of the voyage. First of all, there is some mark of identification, and then immediately underneath this, the port mark is shown. For example, the merchant may be J. Brown Ltd, and the goods are being shipped in the S.S. *Amsterdam* to Rotterdam, in which case the marks will be as in Fig. 13.3.

These simple markings are adequate for identification, and are entered on the bill of lading. In the event of there being several cases in one shipment, the number of the case is also entered, in this case No. 2. It is essential all goods are marked on at least two sides clearly with a shipping mark, which includes the name of the destination port/depot, and that the marks on the shipping documents correspond exactly with those on the goods. The figures below the number are the dimensions of the case in metres, and may be used in assessing the freight. An internationally recognized code sign may also be stencilled on the case to facilitate handling, and indicate the nature of the cargo. Such code signs would indicate 'sling here', 'fragile goods', 'keep dry' (as illustrated in Fig. 13.3), 'do not drop', etc. A selection of the labels used in the international cargo-handling code is found in Fig. 13.4.

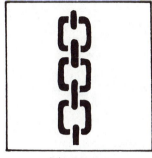

Sling here

Fragile—handle with care

Use no hooks

This way up

Keep away from heat

Centre of gravity

Fig. 13.4 Recognized international marking symbols.

13.6 DANGEROUS CARGO

Dangerous goods have been defined as those substances so classified in any Acts, rules or bye-laws or having any similar properties or hazards. The legislation applicable to all British-registered tonnage or other vessels loading in British ports are contained in the Merchant Shipping (Dangerous Goods and Marine Pollutants) Regulations 1990. These require that all packaged goods are:

(a) classified and declared by the shipper to the Master;

(b) packaged in a manner to withstand the ordinary risk of handling and transport by sea, having regard to their properties;

(c) marked with proper shipping name and indication of the danger;

(d) properly stowed and effectively segregated from others which may dangerously interact;

(e) listed in a manifest or stowage plan giving stowage details. This must be aboard the ship.

The requirements of the Merchant Shipping (Dangerous Goods and Marine Pollutants) Regulations reflect the International Maritime Dangerous Goods (IMDG) Code, produced by the International Maritime Organization (IMO). The Code has been adopted by 50 countries, representing 85% of world tonnage. A consolidated four-volume 1990 edition produced by the IMO incorporates extensive revisions adopted by the IMO Maritime Safety Committee at its 1989 session and effective from 1 January 1991. The latest IMDG Code is the 27th amendment effective from 1 July 1995. A supplement to the Code contains emergency procedures, Medical First Aid Guide, Code of Safe Practice for Solid Bulk Cargoes, Reporting Procedures for Incidents, IMO/ILO Guidelines for Packing Cargo in Freight Containers and recommendations for the safe use of pesticides in ships.

It is estimated that more than 50% of the cargoes transported by sea today can be regarded as dangerous, hazardous and/or harmful (marine pollutants) under the IMO classification, designation or identification criteria. Some of them are dangerous or hazardous from a safety point of view, but are also harmful to the marine environment; others are harmful to the marine environment alone. The cargoes concerned include products which are transported in bulk such as solid or liquid chemicals and other materials, gases and products for and of the oil refinery industry. Between 10% and 15% of the cargoes transported in packaged form, including shipborne barges on barge-carrying ships, freight containers, bulk packagings, portable tanks, tank-containers, vehicles, intermediate bulk containers (IBCs), unit loads and other cargo transport units, fall under these criteria.

As the world becomes increasingly industrialized and as industry itself becomes even more complex, so the transport by sea of these cargoes will continue to rise and the lists of products will grow. It is essential, if shipping is to maintain and improve its safety record, that these cargoes are stored, handled and transported with the greatest possible care.

Volume I also contains the alphabetical General Index of dangerous substances, materials and articles, and the marine pollutants. This index is followed by the Numerical Index (the table of UN numbers with corresponding IMDG Code page numbers, EmS numbers and MFAG table numbers) and a list of definitions, including commonly used abbreviations.

Revised Annex I to the IMDG Code, containing the packing recommendations
Revised Annex I to the IMDG Code contains recommendations on the packing of dangerous goods, and on the construction and testing of packagings. Annex I was adopted by the Maritime Safety Committee in 1984 and is included in Volume I of the IMDG Code. From 1 January 1991, only tested and marked packagings should be used for the transport of dangerous goods.

The recommendations take into account the mandatory requirements on packing set forth in Regulation 3 of Chapter VII of the 1974 SOLAS Convention, as amended. Regulation 3 requires packages containing dangerous goods to be capable or withstanding the ordinary risks of handling and carriage by sea and lays down other specifications.

Annex I closely follows the United Nations Recommendations in respect of the packing of dangerous goods, as contained in Chapter 9 of the Orange Book. This is published every two years by UN in Transport of Dangerous Goods and takes the form of recommendations but has no legal status.

The principle of dividing dangerous goods, other than those covered by classes 1, 2, 6.2 and 7, into three packaging groups according to the degree of danger they present, i.e.

packaging group I: goods presenting great danger;
packaging group II: goods presenting medium danger; and
packaging group III: goods presenting minor danger

is reflected in the recommendations of Annex I and has an impact on the detailed provisions for the construction and performance testing of types of standard receptacles, packagings and packages ready for shipment.

The recommendations of Annex I are intended for manufacturers of dangerous goods and of packagings for these goods, the shippers and carriers as well as competent authorities, and are to be used in conjunction with the IMDG Code.

General Index of the IMDG Code
All substances, materials and articles which appear in the IMDG Code are listed in alphabetical order of the proper shipping name (correct technical name) in the General Index of the IMDG Code, which also gives the product's UN number, its Emergency Schedule number (EmS No.), Medical First Aid Guide Table Number (MFAG Table No.), the IMDG Code page number of the individual schedule, class, packaging group and subsidiary risk label(s).

A number of dangerous goods are not listed by name in the Code and, therefore, will have to be shipped under a generic name/entry or a Not Otherwise Specified (NOS) entry. These entries have also been included in the General Index. For some goods, secondary names and synonyms also appear.

Following the General Introduction, Annex I and the indices, the IMDG Code then details the nine classes of dangerous goods, divided as follows:

Volume II   Class 1 – Explosives
                  Class 2 – Gases: compressed, liquefied or dissolved under pressure;For stowage and segregation purposes, class 2 is divided further according to the hazards presented by gases during transport, namely:

Class 2.1 – Flammable* gases
Class 2.2 – Non-flammable gases
Class 2.3 – Poisonous gases**
Class 3 – Flammable* liquids
Class 3.1 – Low flashpoint group
Class 3.2 – Intermediate flashpoint
group
Class 3.3 – High flashpoint group
Volume III Class 4 – Flammable* solids or substances
Class 4.1 – Flammable solids
Class 4.2 – Substances liable to
spontaneous combustion
Class 4.3 – Substances which, in
contact with water, emit
flammable gases
Class 5 – Oxidizing substances (agents) and
organic peroxides
Class 5.1 – Oxidizing substances
(agents)
Class 5.2 – Organic peroxides
Volume IV Class 6 – Poisonous (toxic***) and infectious
substances
Class 6.1 – Poisonous (toxic)
substances
Class 6.2 – Infectious substances

*   'Flammable' has the same meaning as 'inflammable'; see also
Annex 2, Regulation 2.
**   Poisonous gases which are flammable should, for segregation
purposes, be treated as class 2.1 flammable gases.
*** 'Toxic' has the same meaning as 'poisonous'.

Class 7 – Radioactive materials
Class 8 – Corrosives
Class 9 – Miscellaneous dangerous substances and
articles

In the Code, class 9 comprises:

(a) substances and articles not covered by other classes which
experience has shown, or may show, to be of such a dangerous
character that the provisions of Part A of Chapter VII of the

International Convention for the Safety of Life at Sea 1974, as amended, should apply; and

(b) substances not subject to the provisions of Part A of Chapter VII of the aforementioned Convention, but to which the regulations of Annex III of the International Convention for the Prevention of Pollution from Ships 1973, as modified by the Protocol of 1978 relating thereto (MARPOL 73/78), apply.

Non-classified materials

A list of materials hazardous only in bulk (MHB) is included in section 24 of the General Introduction to the Code. Each class or category of goods is identified by a distinctive mark, label or placard. The marks, labels and placards are shown in Annex 4 (see Fig. 13.5). Where appropriate, each individual schedule (page) in the Code shows the label or labels (100 mm × 100 mm) and, if applicable, the marine pollutant mark to be affixed to a receptacle, package, article, unit load or IBC, or as placards (enlarged labels of 250 mm × 250 mm) to be affixed to portable tanks, freight containers, vehicles or other cargo transport units, as provided for in the IMDG Code. Some consignments of dangerous goods should have the UN number of the goods displayed in the lower half of the placard or on a rectangular orange panel (120 mm × 300 mm) to be placed immediately adjacent to the placard.

All placards, orange panels and marine pollutant marks should be removed from cargo transport units or masked as soon as both the dangerous goods or their residues, which led to the application of those placards, orange panels and marine pollutant marks, are discharged.

The individual schedules of the Code follow a similar pattern. The substance's, material's or article's proper shipping name (correct technical name), and any known and commonly used alternative names (synonyms) appear at the top left of the schedule. To the right of this, other relevant information or observations are given, such as the UN identification number (UN No.) assigned to a substance or article by the United Nations Committee of Experts on the Transport of Dangerous Goods, its chemical formula, explosive limits, flashpoint and so on. As an example, the schedule for 1,1,1-Trichloroethane (Methylchloroform) (UN No. 2831), which is given with Trichlorobutene (UN

No. 2322) on IMDG Code page 6272, is reproduced in Annex 5. 1,1,1-Trichloroethane is widely used as the typewriter cleaning fluid and thinner,' Tipp-Ex'.

The other headings used in the individual schedules include properties or descriptions (such as the substance's, material's or article's state and appearance), special observations, packing, stowage and segregation. The schedule also shows the label or labels or placards and, if applicable, the marine pollutant mark, as appropriate to the substance, material or article. This is basically one of the marks, labels or placards shown in Annex 4, but a label or placard may also contain additional information. Those used for explosives, for example, also give the substance's or article's division number and compatibility group. Class 3 labels or placards sometimes contain a reference to the flashpoint or flash-point group. For class 7 labels or placards additional information on the contents, activity and transport index is required.

Details of the salient points emerging from the IMO regulations are as follows:

(a) dangerous goods to be declared by their correct technical name and their principal hazard to be shown by reference to their dangerous-goods class;

(b) persons responsible for loading vehicles/containers to complete a container/vehicle packing certificate;

(c) packagings, vehicles, containers, etc., to be marked to indicate the hazard or hazards presented by the contents;

(d) the goods to be packed in an adequate manner;

(e) the goods to be stowed so that they do not give rise to a hazard;

(f) the employer/employee to ensure health and safety as far as possible of those involved in transport of dangerous goods;

(g) the ship's Master to have a record of dangerous goods on board and where they are stowed;

(h) regulations apply to all UK ships and other vessels while they are loading or discharging cargo within the UK;

(i) prohibition for certain dangerous goods on passenger ships;

(j) on deck only stowage and away from accommodation when specified in IMDG Code must be strictly applied;

(k) powers described for prosecution for non-compliance with statutory requirements.

According to regulation 4 (marking, labelling and placarding) of part A of chapter VII of the 1974 SOLAS Convention, as amended, packages containing dangerous goods shall be durably marked with the correct technical name and be provided with distinctive labels or stencils of the labels, or placards, as appropriate. The method of marking the correct technical name and of affixing labels or applying stencils of labels, or of affixing placards on packages, shall be such that this information will still be identifiable on packages surviving at least three months' immersion in the sea.

Labels and placards are assigned to each class of dangerous goods in the IMDG Code, and denote the hazards involved by means of colours and symbols. Colours and symbols should be as illustrated except that symbols, texts and numbers on green, red and blue labels and placards may be white.

The class number should appear in the bottom corner of the label or placard. The use of the texts shown on the illustrations and of further descriptive texts is optional. However, for class 7 the text should always appear on the labels and the special placard. If texts are used for the other classes, the texts shown on the illustrations are recommended for the purpose of uniformity.

Dangerous goods which possess subsidiary dangerous properties must also bear subsidiary risk labels or placards denoting these hazards. Subsidiary risk labels and placards should not bear the class number in the bottom corner.

Labels for packages should not be less than 100 mm × 100 mm except in the case of packages which, because of their size, can only bear smaller labels. Placards for cargo transport units should not be less than 250 mm × 250 mm, should correspond with respect to colour and symbols to the labels and should display the number of the class in digits not less than 25 mm high.

Some consignments of dangerous goods should have the UN number of the goods displayed in black digits not less than 65 mm high either against a white background in the lower half of the placard or on a rectangular orange panel not less than 120 mm high and 300 mm wide, with a 10 mm black border, to be placed immediately adjacent to the placard.

All labels, placards, orange panels and marine pollutant marks should be removed from cargo transport units or masked as soon as the dangerous goods are unpacked and any residue removed. The detailed requirements regarding marking, labelling and placarding are contained in the IMDG Code.

Fig. 13.5 IMO dangerous goods labels and placards. (Reproduced by kind permission of the IMO.)

LABELS

ACTUAL SIZE:
100 × 100 mm.

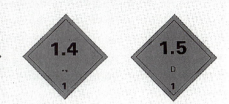

* The appropriate division number and compatibility group are to be placed in this location, e.g. 1.1.D.

** The appropriate compatibility group is to be placed in this location, e.g. G.

For goods of class 1 in division 1.4 compatibility group S, no label is required. Each package should be marked **1.4 S.**

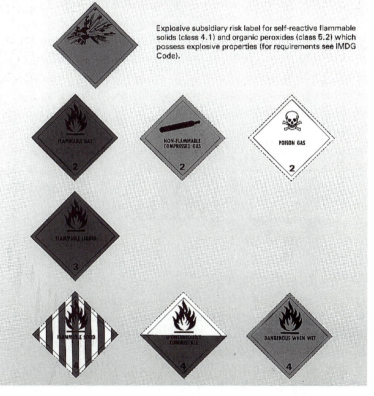

Explosive subsidiary risk label for self-reactive flammable solids (class 4.1) and organic peroxides (class 5.2) which possess explosive properties (for requirements see IMDG Code).

Fig. 13.5 continued

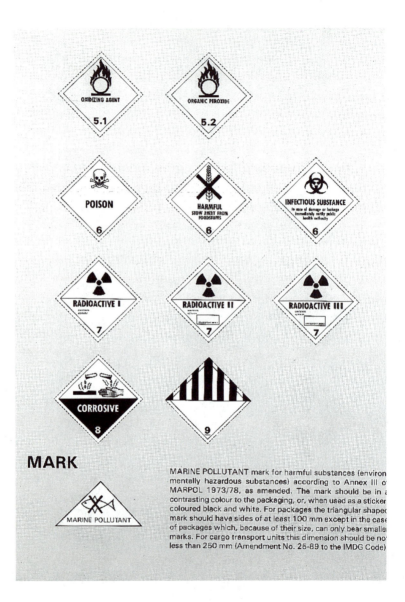

MARINE POLLUTANT mark for harmful substances (environmentally hazardous substances) according to Annex III o' MARPOL 1973/78, as amended. The mark should be in a contrasting colour to the packaging, or, when used as a sticker coloured black and white. For packages the triangular shaped mark should have sides of at least 100 mm except in the case of packages which, because of their size, can only bear smalle' marks. For cargo transport units this dimension should be no' less than 250 mm (Amendment No. 25-89 to the IMDG Code)

Fig. 13.5 continued

PLACARDS

SCALE: 4:1
ACTUAL SIZE: 250 × 250 mm.

Samples of display of the UN number on placards or the orange panel for cargo transport units.

* Location of UN number.

ALTERNATIVE 1

ALTERNATIVE 2

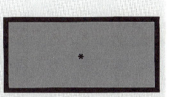

FOR CLASS 7

Fig. 13.5 continued

The International Maritime Dangerous Goods Code are recommendations. For them to become mandatory, a particular national government must ratify them.

In fact the regulations state in a number of places that in the event of an incident, if it can be shown that the recommendations of the IMDG Code have been met, then the requirements of the regulations have been complied with.

The shipowner will only handle such dangerous cargo by prior written arrangement and with the express condition that the shipper provides a very full and adequate description of the cargo. If accepted a special stowage order – often referred to as a dangerous goods form – will be issued which will indicate to the Master that the cargo conforms to the prescribed code of acceptance laid down by the shipowner. It cannot be stressed too strongly that shipment will not take place until a special stowage order has been issued by the shipowner, which is the authority to ship. Moreover, the shipper must fully describe the cargo and ensure it is correctly packed, marked and labelled. This he can do through a freight forwarder, which is often the practice.

Before dangerous goods can be authorized for shipment the following information is required:

(a)   name of sender;
(b)   correct technical name of the dangerous goods (the trade name may not be sufficient to identify the hazard) followed by the words 'Marine Pollutant' (if applicable), trade names alone are not sufficient;
(c)   class of dangerous goods;
(d)   flashpoint (where applicable);
(e)   UN No. to identify substance;
(f)   details of outer packing;
(g)   details of inner packing;
(h)   quantity to be shipped in individual packages and in total;
(i)   additional information for radioactive materials, explosive and consignments in bulk (e.g. tank containers, road tankers, etc.).

The dangerous goods authority form will bear a reference number and will show the sailing details including port of departure and destination on which consignment is authorized, the hazard class, UN No., labels, key number (for emergency in event of any incident, spillage, etc.), and any special instructions (i.e. special Department of Transport (DTp) approval or restrictions on stowage, i.e. on deck only (passenger ship), freight vessel only, etc.).

On arrival of the goods at the departure port the goods and authority to ship are submitted to the Master of the ship for ultimate approval prior to loading and customs clearance.

The Master of the ship carrying packaged goods shall cause a special list, manifest or stowage plan to be carried in the ship. It will identify where in the ship the goods are stowed. Also it will provide details obtained from the shipping documents submitted by the shipper of the packaged goods on board, including the correct technical name of the goods, their classification in accord with the Regulation 7(2) of the Merchant Shipping (Dangerous Goods and Marine Pollutants) Regulations 1990, and their mass or volume.

Packaged goods shall be stowed, segregated and secured on board the vessel in accordance with the IMDG Code. In regard to container shipments, it is the responsibility of the person loading the vehicle or freight container to ensure the packaged goods are correctly stowed, segregated and secured in accordance with the IMDG Code. In regard to the shipment of explosives none may be carried unless the Master fully complies with the provisions of the Merchant Shipping (Dangerous Goods and Marine Pollutants) Regulations 1990, Part II, Section 13, and the relevant parts of the IMDG Code.

Deep-sea container shipment is ideal for the transport of dangerous cargo particularly as it avoids multiple handling, protects the goods from interference by unauthorized persons and eliminates the risk of damage from the use of inappropriate methods of slinging. The following information is required at the time of booking the container:

(a) name of vessel;
(b) port of loading;
(c) port of discharge;
(d) number, kind and size of individual packages (including inner packages if valid) and total quantity, i.e. gross and net weight in kilos;

(e) correct technical name of substance, as defined in IMDG Code;

(f) hazard classification of substance (IMO);

(g) UN number of substance;

(h) marine pollutant – if applicable;

(i) packaging group;

(j) flashpoint – if any;

(k) EmS Number if NOS – Emergency Schedule for Dangerous Goods – not otherwise specified; (as listed in IMDG Code);

(l) MFAG Table Number (as listed in IMDG Code).

With 'tween deck or bulk cargo shipments the loading of the ship is undertaken by stevedores, but with containerization this is done by container packers which are usually container operators or freight forwarders. Accordingly, with regard to the latter, a 'packing certificate' must be completed and signed which certifies the following:

(a) The container was clean, dry and fit to receive the cargo.

(b) No cargo known to be incompatible has been stowed therein.

(c) All packages have been inspected for damage, and only dry and sound packages loaded.

(d) All packages have been properly stowed and secured and suitable materials used.

(e) The container and goods have been properly labelled and placarded.

(f) A dangerous goods declaration has been received/completed for each dangerous consignment packed in the container.

It is paramount the packing certificate is duly completed and signed by the shipper as it confirms to the shipping line and the Master that the task of packing the container has been properly carried out. The document accompanies the goods throughout the voyage. In regard to FCL containers, the Dangerous Goods Packing Certificate may be incorporated in the IMO Dangerous Goods Note.

To comply with Classification, Packaging and Labelling of Dangerous Substances Regulations 1984, and the Road Traffic (Carriage of Dangerous Substances in Packages etc.) Regulations

1986, a Transport Emergency Card (Tremcard) or equivalent must be supplied for substances within the following groups:

(a) any quantity of an organic peroxide or self-reactive flammable solid which has a self-accelerating decomposition temperature of 50°C or below, or where it is required to be conveyed below a specified temperature;

(b) in receptacles with a capacity of 51 or more where the substance is an organic peroxide (not subject to above paragraph), a flammable or toxic gas, asbestos or asbestos waste, certain other hazardous wastes and any other substance allocated to Packing Group I of CPL/IMO regulations;

(c) in receptacles with a capacity of 2001 or more where the substance is allocated to Packing Group II of CPL/IMO regulations;

(d) in receptacles of 2001 or more where substance is allocated to Packing Group III of CPL/IMO regulations.

A Tremcard is only required under road regulations not by sea, although it is useful in order to supply information to the driver. It is also required for bulk packages such as tank containers and road tankers. Basically the code of 'one class-one container' must be observed unless the container operator has expressly agreed to a relaxation. Substances which fall into the same class but are incompatible must also be stowed in different containers, for example peroxides and permanganates (both oxidizing substances).

Dangerous goods may be incompatible with certain non-dangerous substances. Examples are poisons and foodstuffs, or those which react in contact with harmless organic materials, such as nitrates, chlorates, etc. Does the substance have any subsidiary risk? An example arises with normal-propyl chloroformate, a Class 6.1 chemical with two subsidiary risks: it is both a corrosive and flammable liquid. Its schedule states: segregation as for Class 3 (flammable liquid) and not Class 6.1, which is the prime hazard. The principle segregates according to the hazard which requires the most stringent segregation.

A container in transit is subjected to acceleration and deceleration factors in a longitudinal and to some degree, a lateral direction when travelling overland, and in a vertical and lateral direction at sea. At all times it is subjected to some degree of vibration. Hence, the contents must be firmly stowed and secured against movement and chafing. Particular care with dangerous cargoes must be taken to ensure that the contents will not fall outwards when the doors are opened. Dangerous cargoes forming only part of the load must be stowed in the door area of the container for ease of access and inspection. In the case of non-dangerous goods, damage arising from poor stowage is usually confined to the container concerned, but in the case of dangerous goods the effects could be widespread.

It is relevant to note that obnoxious/irritant substances are classified as non-hazardous, but must be stowed and treated as dangerous cargo. Hence, any cargo having such substances must be clearly labelled prior to shipment and the carrier notified.

Labels and placards (Fig. 13.5) are assigned to each class of dangerous goods in the IMDG Code, and denote the hazards involved by means of colours and symbols. Colours and symbols should be as illustrated, except that symbols, texts and numbers on green, red and blue labels and placards may be white.

The class number should appear in the bottom corner of the label or placard. The use of the texts shown on the illustrations and of further descriptive texts is optional. However, for Class VII the text should always appear on the labels and the special placard. If texts are used for the other classes, the texts shown on the illustrations are recommended for the purpose of uniformity.

Dangerous goods which possess subsidiary dangerous properties must also bear subsidiary risk labels or placards denoting these hazards. Subsidiary risk labels and placards should not bear the class number in the bottom corner.

Labels for packages should not be less than 100 mm × 100 mm, except in the case of packages which, because of their size, can only bear smaller labels. Placards for cargo transport units should not be less than 250 mm × 250 mm; correspond with respect to colour and symbols to the labels; and display the number of the class in digits not less than 25 mm high.

Some consignments of dangerous goods should have the UN number of the goods displayed in black digits not less than 65 mm high, either against a white background in the lower half of the placard or on a rectangular orange panel not less than 120 mm high and 300 mm wide, with a 10 mm black border, to be placed immediately adjacent to the placard.

All labels, placards, orange panels and marine pollutant marks should be removed from cargo transport units or masked as soon as the dangerous goods are unpacked and any residue removed. The detailed requirements regarding marking, labelling and placarding are contained in the IMDG Code.

The universal adoption of the International Maritime Dangerous Goods Code (IMO) has greatly facilitated the movement of dangerous goods between countries. Accordingly, a dangerous goods labelling code for maritime consignments exists and some codes are given on pp. 287–8.

Finally, with regard to all UK ships carrying hazardous cargo and noxious liquid chemicals in bulk, such tonnage is subject to the Merchant Shipping (Control of Pollution by Noxious Liquid Substances in Bulk) Regulations 1987, as amended, and by the Merchant Shipping (Dangerous Goods and Marine Pollutants) Regulations 1990.

CHAPTER 14

The shipping company

14.1 SIZE AND SCOPE OF THE UNDERTAKING

As we enter the next millennium the size and scope of the shipping company will continue to change. Its structure will focus primarily on market conditions and in so doing will be geared to the most advantageous organization to realize company objectives. Hence it will be market driven.

A further factor is the impact of information technology (see Chapter 20) which continues to become more sophisticated and quickens the pace of the decision-making process. It extends to all parts of the shipping company organization and in many companies has resulted in layers of management structure – especially in the middle management range – being eliminated. This has shortened the decision management chain and resulted in quicker decisions thereby making the company more competitive.

At the same time the headquarters structure tends to be much smaller with authority devolved to encourage more accountability of personnel at all management levels. The profit centre concept has been developed through strong budgeting management techniques. The devolution of executive authority has involved cross-border structures and in so doing yielded tax benefits and lower wage scales. The development of computerized technology has greatly facilitated this devolution and change.

A further factor is the diversification of the business. Whilst shipping may remain the core of the business many entrepreneurs have other interests which include real estate and construction, including ancillary activities of the core business such as road haulage, seaports, warehouse, shipbroking and so on.

The outcome of these developments is the emergence of a new breed of shipping executive who must be thoroughly professional in the shipping business to which he or she is assigned, professionally qualified, market driven in attitude, very assiduous, culture orientated, multilingual, profit motivated and computer literate. Moreover, such personnel must be subject to continuous training to keep ahead of technology, market environment/opportunity, and business techniques/strategy.

The size of the shipping undertaking, its organization and cost structure, and the pricing of sea transport services are influenced largely by the type of service which is operated, and particularly by the difference between liner and tramp operation.

Hence there is a great variation in size among shipping undertakings, which range from the single ship company, to the giant groups. From an economic standpoint, the entrepreneur will try to maximize his profits and therefore expand his output, so long as the increase in his total costs is less than the increase in his total revenue. He will therefore continue to expand to the point where his marginal additional cost is equal to his marginal additional revenue.

The tendency in recent years, both with liner and tramp shipping companies, is to merge. The reasons are numerous and include economies realized on administration cost; improved prospects of raising more capital for new tonnage; rationalization of facilities, for example port agents, departments, overseas offices, berths, ports of call, etc.; the long-term consideration of likely improvement on tonnage utilization and productivity, with possible limited rationalization of a fleet and centralization of marine department activities covering manning, management, survey programme and new building; a larger customer portfolio; a larger trading company with improved competitive ability and the long-term possibility of a more economical service at lower cost with consequently improved tariffs; and finally the larger the company, generally speaking, the better it will be able to combat the challenges of the next century, in particular with regard to new investment, which will be vast, and competition, which will intensify.

The alternative is to outsource many of the marine activities for the smaller shipping company. One example is Manx Ship Management Ltd, based in the Isle of Man. They offer a wide range of services including ship manning, competitive purchasing of ship stores, sale and purchase of tonnage, new building supervision, repair and dry docking, competitive insurance, day-to-day worldwide ship management, crew travel and finances including taxation, factoring, budgetary control, sales ledger administration and so on.

14.2 LINER ORGANIZATION

The production unit in the liner trade is the fleet, and the operator must plan and think in terms of a service rather than a number of self-contained voyages. The liner service implies the operation of a fleet of vessels which provides a fixed service at regular advertised intervals between named ports; the owners offer space to cargo destined for the named ports and delivered to the ship by the advertised date. The liner company, unlike the tramp operator, must seek its own cargo, which originates mainly in relatively small consignments from a multitude of shippers. This involves an expensive organization ashore at all ports and agents/regional offices are required inland to market the services and process shipments both for import and export. Such offices are located near an ICD/CFS and are usually linked by computer to the shipping company database.

The liner company – which may contain an element of tonnage on charter or available for charter – tends to have a diverse organization reflecting the complex nature of its business and extent of its trades involving numerous countries/ports.

The shipping company is managed by a general manager, who is responsible to a board of directors, and normally sits on the board. He is responsible for carrying out the board's directions dealing with all major issues of policy, including finance, senior executive appointments, the introduction of new services, and major items of capital expenditure including new tonnage, etc. In some companies, to facilitate a more prompt decision-making process and streamline administration, the general manager post has been abolished and the day-to-day control and management of the company vested in the managing director. Each board director is usually responsible for certain aspects of the business, such as finance, marketing, passengers, cargo, staff and adminis-tration, etc.

The organization may be functional or departmental. The functional system involves direct responsibility for a particular activity of the company business, such as the post of trade or service manager for a particular route, the holder of which would be responsible for its ultimate performance and control embracing all operating/commercial/marketing/financial aspects, etc. The advantage of such a system is that it produces better financial discipline. The departmental system involves the splitting up of all the company activities into various departments, i.e. commercial/operating/technical etc. Both types of organization have merit and one must decide which suits the situation best. Generally the larger the company, the greater the advantages of a functional organization which encourages better financial control through a budget – driven strategy.

It will be appreciated that the organizational structure of a shipping company engaged in the liner business will vary according to a number of factors which may be detailed as follows:

(a) Fleet size and overall financial turnover.

(b) The trade(s) in which the company is engaged.

(c) The scale of the business involved. For example, the company may rely on agents to develop the business in terms of canvassing for traffic and thereby have only a few salesmen in the field. Additionally, all new tonnage design may be entrusted to a consultant naval architect, and thereby avoid the need to have a full-time naval architect employed in the company with an intermittent workload. Another example is that the company may have a shipbroker's department to diversify the company business.

(d) It may be a subsidiary company reporting to a parent company which may have common services such as a legal department, planning organization, etc.

(e) The company may have offices abroad, rely on agencies, or be part of a consortium.

(f) The company may outsource many of the ship management activities such as those mentioned on p. 315 and available from Denholm Ship Management Ltd.

A possible shipping company organizational structure is found in Fig. 14.1 and a commentary on each of the departments follows. Again it cannot be stressed too strongly the need to ensure each company devises its organizational structure to suit best its business needs etc. and this should be reviewed from time to time to reflect changed situations. It is essential each employee has a job specification.

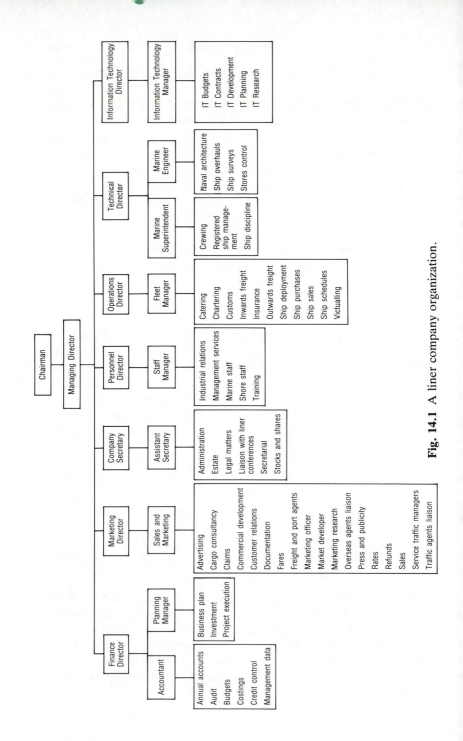

Fig. 14.1 A liner company organization.

In the company structure found in Fig. 14.1 the policy and control of the company is vested in the chairman with some seven directors including a managing director. This overall constitutes the company board which in turn is responsible to shareholders if it is a public company or a government minister if it is state owned.

It is assumed the company has some twenty-five ships engaged in six deep-sea liner cargo services with an element of passenger business in two short sea trade routes.

(a) Chairman and directors
The chairman's role is one of ultimate control and management of the company. He is responsible for company policy and development of the business in collaboration with his board of directors who overall form the most senior management team. He works very closely with the managing director. In the American style shipping company structure (see p. 310) the chairman is designated chief executive officer (CEO). At the next level is the position of president who is a deputy to the chairman. Executive vice-presidents are the equivalent broadly to the directors found in Fig. 14.1.

The managing director's role tends to be the liaison link in general management terms between the board of directors and senior managers. He is essentially concerned with the day-to-day running of the business, particularly its development, and formulating policy in consultation with his directors. It is a key post in the company and a good managing director can greatly influence the company's financial results in its favour.

(b) Finance director
The finance director would have an accountant responsible to him. The accountant's department is responsible for the annual accounts; budgets covering revenue, expenditure, investment and cash flow forecasts; credit control involving the billing of customers/shippers and payment of accounts; preparation of management data which may cover every month's traffic carryings, revenue and expenditure results against budget; and costing data such as voyage costs and economics of individual traffic flows. It is likely that the accountant's department would be so organized to have an individual officer responsible for each function such as audit officer, budgets officer, costing officer, credit controller, etc.

All would have supporting staff and be responsible to the accountant and liaise with other departments.

The planning manager features only in a large shipping company. He is under the finance director's control in this particular
company. This department is particularly concerned with developing company policy and strategy over a wide range of activities. It
embraces the development and implementation of capital
projects, formulation of a 5- to 10-year business plan, and liaison
with government and other national and international organizations relative to general matters appertaining to shipping. The
planning department works in very close liaison with other
departments and officers within the company.

(c) Operations director

The operations director has the responsibility of producing the
optimum performance from the fleet. In so doing it requires a
reconciliation of traffic needs with ship capacity availability and
other aspects to ensure the most viable service is devised taking
into account both short- and long-term needs. It may also involve
reconciling the sailing schedules with obligations of a joint service
or liner conference whereby each operator may be allocated a
certain percentage of the sailings. The operations director's policy
must be to ensure as far as practicable that such sailings are
profitable. Basically the success of a shipping line depends on the
efficient operation of its ships under a budgetary control system.

The operations department is under the control of the fleet
manager who is responsible to the operations director. The fleet
manager covers ship schedules, ship deployment, customs formalities (including the entering and clearance of ships), chartering,
insurance, victualling, ship sale and purchase, inwards freight and
outwards freight departments.

Ship schedules may be entrusted to the operations officer, which
includes customs formalities (including the entering in and clearance of ships), and port operation. The operations officer would
work closely with the marine superintendent on ship manning/
crew costs having regard to the required schedules. He would
liaise and appoint port agents/loading brokers, etc. Additionally
he is likely to become involved in negotiating with port authorities,
the provision of berthing/quay facilities and related equipment/
handling equipment, etc. A qualified shipbroker would look after

chartering, insurance and ship sale and purchase. In such circumstances the chartering department would fix additional tonnage, and secure fixtures for the company's own vessels when offered on the market. In some cases he may act in his own capacity of a shipbroker.

The inwards freight department deals with the customs clearance of imports and their delivery to consignees. It also deals with the transhipment of such cargo, if necessary. Likewise the outwards freight department processes export cargo and related documentation, and supervises the provision of shipping space for cargo bookings. The processing of the international consignment is an important function and is usually fully computerized (see pp. 471–8). It involves close liaison with the ports. Pre-booking of cargo shipping space – with the development of containerization – is now computerized and this extends to the billing of customers, preparation of bills of lading, etc.

(d) Personnel director

The personnel director's responsibilities cover all aspects of staff and include those both ashore and afloat. The staff manager is responsible to the personnel director. This post covers: training, education, recruitment, career development, appointments, redundancy, shore discipline, wages and salaries negotiation, industrial relations, service conditions, etc. Management services provide a consultancy service within the company. The staff manager's department would work in close liaison with other departments and the extent of the management services role will much depend on the company policy of employing such a specialist or engaging outside consultants for specified projects such as reorganization, recruitment of senior managers, etc.

(e) Technical director

The marine engineer and marine superintendent are under the technical director. The marine engineer's department embraces marine engineering, electrical engineering, naval architecture, ship contracts for new building and surveys. It provides technical advice and service etc. on new construction design, negotiation and monitoring of shipbuilding contracts and fleet maintenance/surveys to required statutory/classification society obligations. The annual survey programme of the fleet would be undertaken in this department in consultation with the fleet manager's organization to reflect ship availability and traffic needs. The naval architect is responsible for ship design and providing data on ship stability etc. In smaller companies a consultant is engaged on ship design when new tonnage is required. The marine workshop and stores control is part of the marine engineer's department together with bunkering arrangements. All these three activities may be co-ordinated under a marine services officer, responsible to the marine engineer.

Also responsible to the technical director is the marine superintendent who is the registered manager. This latter task devolves on the marine superintendent who is legally responsible for the maintenance and operation of the registered fleet in accordance with the relevant merchant shipping legislation. It could be equally undertaken by the fleet manager but it is usual to entrust the responsibility to someone who is of wide nautical experience and of high professional calibre. The marine superintendent within the organizational structure of this particular company is also responsible for crewing involving the level of manning and appointments of ship officers. Additionally the marine superintendent is very closely involved in ship safety, relevant navigational matters and ship discipline. The marine superintendent is very closely concerned in the acceptance and conveyance of dangerous cargo and the related procedures/conditions.

(f) Marketing director

The marketing director's responsibilities are extensive and primarily involve the development of the company's business within the freight and passenger markets. In this particular organization the sales and marketing manager is the departmental head but, depending on the size of the business, the job could be split between the marketing, passenger and freight managers. The marketing function in the liner shipping company today is an important one.

The marketing and sales manager would have a number of officers under him to facilitate the smooth running of the department to aid quick decision-making and maximize market impact within the commercial policy of the board as processed through the marketing director.

The marketing manager would be responsible for the sales and marketing plan devised annually. His job includes selling responsibilities including a field salesforce, advertising – particularly promotions – and publicity material including public relations.

(g) Public relations
The public relations/press officer role could include development of the market/business in both the passenger and freight sectors in liaison with the passenger and freight managers. This would include market research. The marketing manager would also be responsible for the appointment of the advertising agency.

The freight manager's task includes dealing with freight rates; freight and customs documentation; liaison with trade associations, chambers of commerce and shippers' councils; liner conferences and cargo claims. Some companies have a cargo consultancy organization to advise on the most ideal methods of transit involving the technique of transport distribution analysis. The freight manager would be responsible for the appointment and liaison with port agents and freight forwarders.

The passenger manager would cover fares, refunds, baggage, appointment and liaison with travel agents, passenger complaints and liaison with passenger associations and liner conferences.

It cannot be stressed too strongly the need for the passenger, freight and marketing managers to liaise closely to realize the best results.

Some companies have a service, sector or route manager who is responsible for the traffic management of the route(s), covering fares, rates, service pattern and so on. Overall, it is a profit centre and subject to strict budgetary control techniques. Such a company structure ensures the optimization of resources on the route(s) compatible with market demand. It comes under the control of the marketing manager but requires close liaison with the freight and passenger managers and other departments including the fleet manager.

(h) Company secretary
The company secretary is responsible for convening board meetings, preparation and circulation of board minutes, and looking after the shipping company's statutory affairs. In this particular

company, the assistant secretary takes charge of the department and reports to the company secretary. The department is likely to be small compared with the marketing manager's organization. It will include maintaining records of stocks and shares; processing estate matters such as land and property sales and purchases; general administration of the company's affairs; and dealing with legal matters. The larger company would employ a solicitor whilst the smaller company would merely engage a solicitor as required.

The department is the organization responsible for liaising with liner conferences but this could be equally undertaken by the marketing manager. The assistant secretary's department would be responsible for the retention of any company agreements such as a revenue pooling agreement with four other operators on a particular service. Negotiations for the renewal of any such agreements or the development of other similar agreements would involve this department in consultation with other parts of the organization, particularly the fleet and marketing managers.

(i) Information technology director

The information technology director is a specialist in this field of activity and has a high profile in many shipping companies today which are computer driven and involve extensive use of EDI (see Chapter 20). The director would have various managers under him or her to cover budgetary control of all computer activities concerning both hardware and software; a contracts manager to negotiate new and existing contracts; a development manager liaising with the computer industry and departments within the shipping company to develop/expand the role/activities of information technology and EDI within the company; a planning manager to ensure the effective use of computer technology within the company and formulate the ongoing investment budget; and finally a research manager to improve the end-user and customer satisfaction aspects of the company's computer network. Such a post would liaise with the market research manager in the marketing department and also with appointed market research agencies. The computer research manager would be responsible for monitoring and interpreting the research data and would work closely with the development manager to implement the research findings. The area of training could come under the research manager.

To conclude our examination of the organization structure, one must stress that each shipping company must devise its organization to suit best its needs and thereby maximize its profitability and long-term future.

The size of each department, and in fact its actual existence, does depend on the size of the company and the trades in which it operates. The larger the company the greater is the tendency to have a larger number of departments. Overall there is much merit in reviewing the adequacy of an organization in the light of market considerations every two years.

The shipping companies conduct their business abroad by means of branch offices or agents; these act as the owners' local representatives in the clearance and discharge of the owners' vessels, and they secure cargo for shipment. At head office, the departmental managers specialize in the particular duties performed by their departments; but the manager of a branch or agency has a much wider range of duties, and is usually responsible for all aspects of the shipping work of his office.

Two examples of the structure of major shipping companies are detailed below. Hanjin Shipping based in Seoul, Korea, and the Peninsula and Oriental Steam Navigation Company (P&O) located in London.

The Hanjin Group, established in 1937, is a land, sea and air transport conglomerate which in addition includes heavy construction industries, financing and information communications, and marine insurance, education, travel, medical and banking services. Overall it embraces 24 companies and in 1994 had 40 000 employees. Its total assets were 11 trillion won and gross revenue was 7.5 trillion won. By the year 2000 transportation and heavy industries will contribute to the development of such global logistics companies. It is expected the Hanjin Group will grow into a major technological conglomerate embracing 50 companies with a workforce of over 100 000, assets totalling 50 trillion won and gross revenue 40 trillion won.

Hanjin operates a global shipping line with a turnover of 10 billion dollars and maritime fleet of 300 ships covering the markets of North America, Europe, Africa and Asia. The company provides a total logistics operation embracing shipping, inland transportation, dedicated terminals and warehouse resources. By the end of 1996 the company will have seven 4000 TEU class container ships in addition to the six already in service. The company also has ten Cape sized specialized carriers, four Panamax size trampers and two Handy size liners, plus 60 vessels on charter. Currently the company operates a total of 14 liner routes including three routes on the growth market of the Far East–North America; the Far East–Europe route; the Australian route; the Intra–Asia route; the Korea–China route. Future expansion includes new routes across the Atlantic, to Africa and to South America. The company has local incorporated logistics companies in Japan, China and Singapore with others planned for the European, American and Asian markets. The Hanjin organization is illustrated in Fig. 14.2.

P&O is a conglomerate global shipping company embracing a total logistics system, property, corporate business and investment portfolios. Overall the group has some 95 separate subsidiaries and associate companies. The shipping sector is all operated and managed separately within the Group and includes Cruises, Ferries, Containers, Bulk Shipping, European Transport Services and P&O Australia. Total turnover of the shipping activities in 1993 was £5746.0 m with net operating assets of £4150.9 m. P&O Containers is the world's sixth largest operator in terms of capacity and conveyed 971 000 TEUs in 1993.

As we progress through the 1990s numerous shipping companies will develop diversified business interests as demonstrated by P&O and Hanjin Shipping discussed above. Such policies are largely determined by the need to lessen the impact of trade recessions and low profitability levels and to provide an adequate profitable cash flow.

14.3 TRAMP ORGANIZATION

Tramp companies do not have the many specialized departments found in liner companies. The function of the tramp operator is to provide ships for hire or charter. Therefore he must keep in close touch with the market for tramp ships. The other main departments will be those dealing with operation, maintenance and victualling.

The board of management concerned with tramp ships is similar to that of the liner organizations.

The tendency for specialized functions to be outsourced is even greater in the case of tramp companies.

An increasing number of family-owned tramp shipping companies are experiencing extreme difficulty in raising funds to embark on new tonnage provision. With profitability being at a low ebb for many years and high inflation in shipbuilding costs the tramp shipping company is resorting more to the sale and lease concept (see p. 319) of new tonnage provision. Alternatively they are merging with other shipping companies.

An example of a high-profile tramp tanker operator is the Maersk Line which is a corporation of world renown. It has a very modern fleet totalling 40 ships with a total dwt of 4 million. This embraces crude carriers, gas tankers (LPG/C) and product carriers. Such tonnage conveys crude oil, oil products, lpg, chemical gases and liquid chemicals. The fleet includes ULCC, VLCC, Suezmax, Aframax and semi- and fully- refrigerated gas carriers. Details of the Maersk Line tanker department structure is given in Fig. 14.3.

This type of chartered tonnage operation with a very high profile and high level of professionalism in all aspects of the chartering business is on the increase and has substantial resources for further development to meet the increasing level of competitiveness. Maersk Line tramp operation also features bulk/car carrier tonnage.

14.4 HOLDING COMPANIES AND SUBSIDIARIES INCLUDING ANCILLARY ACTIVITIES OF SHIPPING UNDERTAKINGS

In the liner trade, with its greater financial requirements, there has been considerable growth, and several large groups of associated and subsidiary companies have been formed. Frequently two companies competing on the same route have found it advantageous to arrange a merger or amalgamation.

In other cases, the companies have arranged to retain their individual identities, but have made provision for exchange of shares and common directorships. Sometimes successful companies

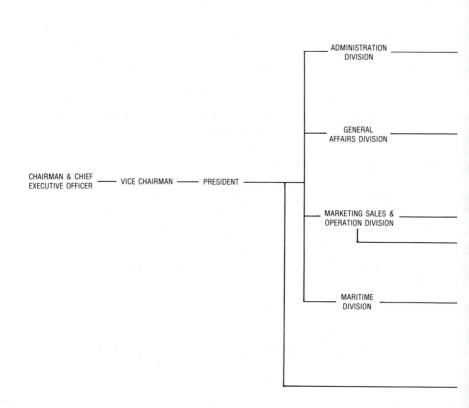

Fig. 14.2 Organization chart of the Hanjin Shipping Co.

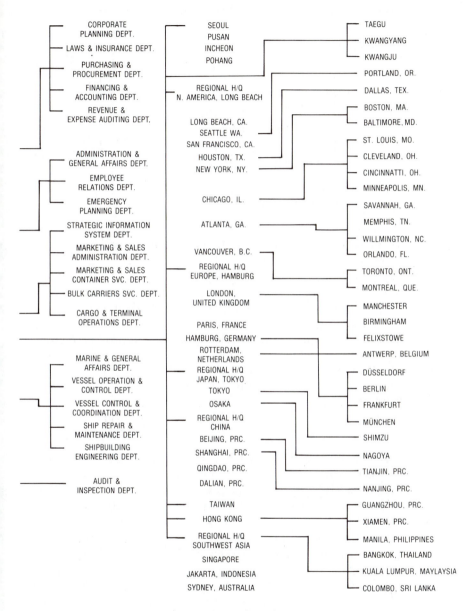

Fig. 14.2 continued

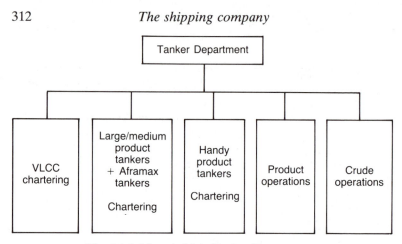

Fig. 14.3 Maersk Line Tanker Department.

have bought out unsuccessful companies, often with a view to securing their goodwill and loading rights in a particular trade.

Many of these groups are controlled by means of holding companies. The term 'holding company' was originally used to describe a company formed with the object of taking shares in two or more operating concerns. But more recently the term has come to include companies which, besides having a controlling interest in others, carry on business themselves. Generally, the associated and subsidiary companies in these groups are run as individual concerns with separate identities, organizations and ships.

With the expansion of containerization in recent years it has stimulated the development of the consortium concept. The merits of the consortium concept are given below (see also pp. 205–6):

(a) It is impracticable for a sole shipowner to raise capital and bear the risk involved of such an assignment.

(b) It facilitates good development/relationships with governments/countries involved through the shipping company resident in the country.

(c) A consortium is best able to counter state-subsidized fleets through concerted action through their governments. A sole operator would not be so effective in dealing with such a situation.

(d) A consortium which is broadly based strengthens the economic ties amongst the countries involved which in turn helps to influence trade to such a service and counter trade depression.

(e)   It reflects the shipping corporation formally associated with the trades/markets which in turn reflects much experience. A sole operator could not achieve such expertise/commercial intelligence.

(f)   A consortium produces economies of scale particularly in terms of agents and encourages the use of common services.

(g)   It involves individual shipping companies of varying nationalities which permit the maritime countries involved to make, if available, any contribution to subsidize new building terms.

(h)   A consortium can yield substantial tax benefits, reduced manning costs and new tonnage investment grants/subsidies.

14.5 SHIP MANAGEMENT COMPANIES

Ship management companies are now becoming more common and their expansion in recent years can be attributed to the gradual change from the traditional shipping company to two new shipping groups: the developing nation bloc and the large bulk shippers who are seeking greater involvement in shipping operation. Additionally, for many years a number of multinational companies have tended to rely on ship management companies.

Ship management companies primarily become involved in the efficient manning, chartering and maintenance of a vessel for an owner. Other areas of ship management include the recruitment, training and appointment of both ship- and shore-based personnel; advice on the most suitable type of vessel, method of financing and source of ship supply; advice on the options available of ship registration, manning, trading and maintenance – this situation tends to emerge with companies in developing nations which are required by law to have their ships manned by nationals, whilst the management company has the flexibility to register the vessel elsewhere yet use her as a training ship for national crews for subsequent additions to the fleet. A further area is the ability of the management company to obtain cheaper insurance by inclusion of the vessel(s) on the main owner-fleet cover to take the advantages of sharing in bulk buying of spares, stores, etc., overall. To be really effective the shipowner must seek a manager who relects this philosophy.

The ship management company has long been recognized by the major oil companies who operate on an owner/time chartered/spot chartered mix of vessels. Accordingly the management company provides the ideal method for ensuring that the daily operation and maintenance of the vessels are correctly superintended rather than indulging in the expense of setting up their own operations department. There is also the advantage of being able to terminate the agreement when the market can no longer support the chartered tonnage.

The basic aim of the ship management service is to provide the owner, for a management fee, with vessels attaining quality service standards at a reasonable competitive cost.

During the past decade some multinational companies have built up their own fleets to carry their raw materials or manufactured products to overseas markets. This offers many benefits to the multinational company, including complete control of the transport distribution system which can be fully integrated into the manufacturer's distribution programme; it aids competitiveness of the product as the goods are conveyed at relatively low cost and not at the normal market tariffs found on liner cargo services; it permits flexibility of operation inasmuch as when trade is buoyant additional tonnage can be chartered; and finally it enables the multinational company to exploit the economics of scale by permitting various countries to specialize in particular products thereby avoiding duplication of investment plant. This latter arrangement can be very advantageous in free trade areas. More recently the tendency of multinational companies is to charter tonnage or rely on existing liner cargo services, rather than develop their own fleets. This trend will continue as the pattern of world trade changes.

The ship management company may be a subsidiary of an established liner company and thus is able to draw on the expertise available within the parent shipowning group. In so doing a package deal can be concluded of a most comprehensive nature.

An example of a leading ship management company is Denholm Ship Management Ltd based in Glasgow. Its clients include international shipowning companies, investment groups, oil companies, major banks, commodity traders, national shipping companies, entrepreneurial shipowners, off-shore constructional and diving companies and traditional shipowners.

Denholm's services may be summarized as follows:

(a) *Operational ship management*. The owner remains responsible for the commercial trading of the ship; Denholm looks after day-to-day functions, e.g. manning, storing, technical supervision, insurance management, general administration and accounting.

(b) *Commercial ship management*. Denholm takes responsibility for maximum voyage efficiency: liaison with brokers, charterers, shippers and receivers; all voyage instructions and arrangements; monitoring performance of the ship on behalf of the owner.

(c) *'Turnkey' ship operation*. The most complete ship management service, combining operational and commercial management. Denholm takes responsibility for the ship as a business venture and provides the owner with a complete accounting package.

(d) *Offshore vessels management services*. Denholm has considerable experience in the worldwide operation of offshore units, including dynamically positioned multi-support vessels.

(e) *Shipping portfolio analyses*. A comprehensive service to banks and other lending institutions who are involved in ship financing in order to help in evaluation of their loan portfolios. A financial analysis would include an assessment of the liabilities outstanding on the ship with appropriate cash flow projections; a commercial analysis would assess the employment potential for the type of ship with due regard to its configuration, age and economy; and a technical analysis would review the current condition of the ship, anticipated operating costs and forward projection of major expenditure.

Another ship management company, Manx Ship Management Ltd. To cater for the growing market of ship management BIMCO in 1988 formulated a standard ship management agreement, a copy of which is reproduced as Fig. 14.4.

14.6 OWNERSHIP OF VESSELS

The Merchant Shipping Act 1988 incorporates the following relative to the registration of British ships:

(a) the exclusion of Commonwealth citizens and companies from those persons qualified to be owners of British ships;

1. Date of Agreement	THE BALTIC AND INTERNATIONAL MARITIME COUNCIL (BIMCO)
	STANDARD SHIP MANAGEMENT AGREEMENT
	CODE NAME: "SHIPMAN"
	PART I

2. Owners (name, place of registered office and law of registry)	3. Managers (name, place of registered office and law of registry)
Name	Name
Place of registered office	Place of registered office
Law of registry	Law of registry

4. Day and year of commencement of Agreement (Cl. 2.1.)

5. Crewing (state "yes" or "no" as agreed) (Cl. 2.3 (i) and Cl. 3)	6. Technical Management (state "yes" or "no" as agreed) (Cl. 2.3.(ii) and Cl. 4)
7. Insurance (state "yes" or "no" as agreed) (Cl. 2.3.(iii) and Cl. 5)	8. Freight Management (state "yes" or "no" as agreed) (Cl. 2.3 (iv) and Cl. 6)
9. Accounting (state "yes" or "no" as agreed) (Cl. 2.3.(v) and Cl. 7)	10. Chartering (state "yes" or "no" as agreed; if "yes", also state period of employment) (Cl. 2.3 (vi) and Cl. 8) period of employment in excess of which owners' prior consent shall first be obtained
11. Sale or purchase of vessel (state "yes" or "no" as agreed) (Cl. 2.3 (vii) and Cl. 9)	12. Provisions (state "yes" or "no" as agreed) (Cl. 2.3 (viii) and Cl. 10)
13. Bunkering (state "yes" or "no" as agreed) (Cl. 2.3 (ix) and Cl. 11)	14. Operation (state "yes" or "no" as agreed) (Cl. 2.3 (x) and Cl. 12)
15. Annual management fee (state lump sum amount) (Cl. 15.1.)	16. Redundancy costs (state maximum amount) (Cl. 15.3 (b))

17. Day and year of termination of Agreement (Cl. 23.1.)

18. Law and arbitration (state 24.1., 24.2. or 24.3. of Cl. 24. as agreed; if 24.3. agreed also state place of arbitration) (If Box 18 not filled in 24.1. shall apply) (Cl. 24)

19. Notices (state postal and cable address, telex and telefax number for service of notice and communication to the Owners) (Cl. 25)	20. Notices (state postal and cable address, telex and telefax number for service of notice and communication to the Managers) (Cl. 25)

It is mutually agreed between the party mentioned in Box 2 (hereinafter called "the Owners") and the party mentioned in Box 3 (hereinafter called "the Managers") that this Agreement consisting of PART I and PART II as well as ANNEX "A" or ANNEX "B" (as applicable) and ANNEX "C" attached hereto, shall be performed subject to the conditions contained herein. In the event of a conflict of conditions, the provisions of PART I shall prevail over those of PART II and ANNEX "A" or ANNEX "B" (as applicable) and ANNEX "C" to the extent of such conflict but no further

Signature(s) (Owners)	Signature(s) (Managers)

Fig. 14.4 The 'Shipman' standard ship management agreement. (Reproduced by kind permission of BIMCO.)

(b) the replacement of the present obligation to register a British ship by an entitlement to register;

(c) the introduction of a requirement to appoint a representative person when a company qualified to own a British ship wishes to register it in the UK, but has its principal place of business outside the UK;

(d) the Secretary of State for Transport to have the power to refuse or terminate the registration of a ship; and

(e) powers to restrict the size and types of ships registered in the British Dependent Territories (with the exception of Hong Kong).

The above represent Part I of the Merchant Shipping Act 1988: Part II deals with the registration of British fishing vessels.

British vessels have to be registered (through the customs at their local port) with the 'General Register and Record Office of Shipping and Seamen', a section of the Department of Transport.

14.7 CAPITALIZATION AND FINANCE OF SHIPPING UNDERTAKINGS

Most British shipping companies grew up during the nineteenth century on the retention of profits earned, short-term finance for expansion being obtained by security on the fleet. The shares of the larger companies were normally quoted on the stock exchanges, but large-scale public subscriptions to form new undertakings were rare, as shipping has always been considered a risky undertaking.

Since 1945 the only public subscriptions have been in the form of loan capital, but with the increase in the number of long-term charters for 12 or even 15 years (practically the whole of the life of a tanker), mortgages can be obtained from many international finance houses, insurance companies and similar organizations. Thus, anyone with some knowledge of ship management can get a long-term charter from an oil company or iron and steel organization, and borrow money to have the vessel built. The charter hire is pledged against interest and repayments of the mortgage.

Resulting from the vulnerability of freight rates, profits and depreciation funds have been barely sufficient to allow shipowners to renew their fleets at current shipbuilding prices. To stimulate shipbuilding and ship operation, many governments have adopted a policy of cheap loans for the shipping industry, and give operating subsidies, particularly for new independent countries with maritime fleets. The USA practises both building and operating subsidies extensively.

Ship finance is a specialist sector of banking and has four salient features:

(a) *Capital intensity*. Shipping is one of the world's most capital intensive industries. In 1995 a 250 000 dwt tanker cost $85 m, a 65 000 dwt bulk carrier $28 m and a 3500 TEU container ship $70 m. Each would have a crew of about 30. The ship is likely to have an operational life of up to 15 years but many owners – especially liner cargo operators – renew their fleet every 10–12 years depending on market conditions and ship management efficiency factors.

(b) *Mobility of assets*. The vessel has a global operating potential and its registration may change to put it under the legal jurisdiction of a 'flag of convenience'.

(c) *Volatility of market*. Overall the market is very volatile, especially with regard to chartered bulk tonnage, both in the area of ship purchase and the daily earnings of the vessel. The same applies in the deep-sea container market earnings as demonstrated in the trans-Atlantic trade whereby earnings per TEU fell from $1500 in 1985 to $950 in 1992. Likewise the consolidated cargo rate UK/North Atlantic declined from $2900 in November 1989 to $950 in November 1991 for a 40-ft container.

(d) *Limitation of information*. Many substantial shipping companies are owned by individuals who prefer not to publish organization structures or audited accounts. This makes it very difficult to carry out the conventional 'credit analysis' on which most bank lending relies.

Today many shipowners finance their new tonnage from three sources: loan capital obtained on the open market including a bank mortgage or provided by government on very favourable low interest terms; money provided by the shipping company through liquidation of reserve capital; and finally government grants, which are usually conditional. Very few shipping companies today are able to finance their new tonnage from within their own financial resources. This is due to the low level of profitability and return on capital, often between 2% and 3%; depressed trading conditions; and the failure in many trades for rates to keep pace with rising costs.

A further method of financing new tonnage is through a leasing arrangement with a finance company. This enables the maximum benefit to be taken of any available tax advantage, and the quarterly or half-yearly leasing payments will reflect this. With these sort of agreements, however, it is not normal for legal ownership of the vessel to pass to the shipping company even after the leasing period expires. Usually there is provision for a peppercorn rental to be paid until it is desired to dispose of the vessel, when the shipping company would take all but a tiny percentage of the sale value realized. With the development of the oil resources of the Arab countries with their consequential industrial expansion, the situation has emerged whereby such oil producers have taken over the distribution of the product. Such countries have now their own oil tanker fleets.

There are four main types of financial structures used in ship finance today:

(a) *Equity finance* entitles the investor to share in the risks and rewards of the business, usually without any time span; to liquidate his investment the investor has to sell the shares.

(b) *Debt finance* is a legally enforceable loan agreement in which the lender receives interest at predetermined intervals with the repayment of the principal after a specified period.

(c) *Mezzanine finance* involves an intermediary form of financial structure which contains elements of both debt and equity. This is the least popular finance method.

(d) *Leasing* is a hire-purchase arrangement in which the borrower 'bareboat' charters the vessel from its nominal owner (see p. 332). This is occasionally used as an alternative to debt financing.

A further factor to bear in mind is that an increasing number of countries are now subsidizing in one way or other their fleets. This may be a building or operating subsidy. Alternatively some other financial contribution may be provided such as subsidized bunker fuel, state aid for social contributions by crew personnel, etc. Overall such practices tend to be found in former Eastern bloc fleets and those fleets emerging from developing countries.

This subject is more fully dealt with in *Economics of Shipping Practice and Management*, Chapter 4.

14.8 INCOME AND EXPENDITURE

This will vary according to the type of operations conducted by the shipping organization.

With a liner company conveying passengers and cargo, there are many items of income and expenditure. Items of income would include revenue from passengers, cargo, catering, postal parcels, letter mails and perhaps chartering. This last item would arise if a liner company releases a vessel on charter to another undertaking. Expenditure items would include crew costs, maintenance of ships, fuel, lubricants, port disbursements (including dues and cargo-handling cost), depreciation, publicity expenses, administration costs, insurance, commission to agents, passenger and cargo claims, interest on capital, compensation for accidents in collisions, and any chartering expenses involving the hire of additional vessels to augment the fleet.

In the case of the tramp undertaking, there is of course only one main source of income and this accrues from chartering. The items of expenditure, however, do vary according to the type of charter party. With a 'demise' charter, there are very few items of expenditure, and these broadly include ship depreciation, interest on capital and administration costs. The number of expenditure items is, however, increased with non-demise 'time' and 'voyage' charters, and include crew costs, ship maintenance, depreciation, insurance, interest on capital, compensation for accidents in collisions and administration costs. The administration costs form a very small portion of the expenditure of a tramp undertaking compared with the liner company.

In view of the large payments incurred when new vessels are purchased, shipping companies as far as possible maintain reserves in easily redeemable securities.

14.9 STATISTICS

Statistics play an important role in the successful management of shipping and the shipowner must keep under constant review the performance of his ships, items of earnings and costs. A careful and detailed analysis must thus be made of the revenue and expenditure accounts of each voyage.

Important operational statistics include, for example, voyage distances, fuel consumption, load factors and fleet utilization. The shipowner will particularly require to know the voyage distances in relation to the fuel consumed per nautical mile. This will give an indication of engine performance. Passengers and/or cargo conveyed have to be recorded and related on a voyage basis to the available capacity. This will give the ship's load factor on a percentage basis, indicating how much of the available revenue earning capacity on a particular voyage has been filled. For example, if a ship with a passenger certificate of 1000 conveyed 750 passengers, it would have a load factor of 75%. It will also be necessary to record the number of days a vessel is at sea and the time spent in port loading and/or discharging or alternatively undergoing survey and overhaul. Turn-round time in port will be influenced by the cargo handled and port resources, and will necessitate the compilation of statistics showing average tons loaded or discharged per day in various ports which the ship visits and their related costs. The aim should be, of course, to keep turn-round time to an absolute minimum, as it represents idle time to the shipowner, and earns no revenue. Similarly, time spent on surveys and overhauls should be kept to a minimum, and if possible undertaken outside times of peak traffic. How successful the shipowner is in achieving these objectives can only be established if proper statistics are maintained. These will enable him to relate the days a vessel spends at sea with the time spent either in port or in a shipyard.

The victualling department of passenger-carrying lines will require such statistics as meals served and cost per meal and profitability per day or per head. Such data, when related to the number of passengers carried, will help to establish the general popularity and profitability of the meals, and enable the victualling results on one ship to be compared with another.

Traffic analysis is also important, and statistics must be kept of various commodity movements and average freight earnings. Bills of lading, sea waybills and charter parties must be carefully analysed and data abstracted regarding commodities, ports of loading and discharge, weight and stowage factors, and other features of interest, such as damage or pilferage to cargo. When properly analysed, this data will enable the shipowner to estimate in advance his future tonnage requirements throughout the year, and provide valuable information which will influence the design of future ships.

In the shipping industry, statistics have become more important, particularly in recent years, because greater emphasis has been placed on improved efficiency, and there is an ever-increasing cost consciousness involving the development of profit centres in a trade or on a particular area basis. Statistics are one of the most reliable means of measuring the performance and efficiency of the individual ship and the fleet. The provision of statistics can be very costly, however, and the volume of data should be kept under constant review. Most major shipping companies today use computers to provide essential management information to run their businesses. This includes traffic analysis, voyage costs, load factors, etc. Such data are produced maybe weekly or monthly and related to budget predictions.

14.10 FREIGHT FORWARDERS

Basically, a freight forwarder is a person or company which is involved in the processing and/or movement of goods on behalf of another company or person which crosses international boundaries. The freight forwarder provides services in two main fields: the movement of goods out of a country on behalf of exporters or shippers, in which case the forwarder would be termed an export freight agent; and the bringing of goods into the country on behalf of importers, in which situation the forwarder is called an import freight agent, customs clearance agent or customs broker.

The freight forwarder has four prime activities: to provide a range of independent services such as packing, warehousing, port agency and customs clearance; to provide a range of advice on all the areas relative to international consignment distribution as found in transport distribution analysis (pp. 432–4); to act as shipper agent processing transport/shipping space on behalf of his principal/shipper and executing his instructions; and finally, to act as a principal, usually as a multi-modal transport operator conveying goods from A to B across international frontiers and involving usually several carriers, often as an NVOCC (See pp. 417–20).

The freight forwarder provides some or all of the following services depending on the trade in which the company operates and the resources available.

(a) Export

(a) *Transport distribution analysis* – an examination of the options available to the shipper to distribute the goods (pp. 432–4).

(b) *Transportation arrangements* – a major function involving the booking and despatch of the goods between the consignor's and consignee's premises or other specified points.

(c) *Documentation* – provision of all the prescribed documentation for the goods having regard to all the statutory requirements and terms of the export sales contract.

(d) *Customs* – all the customs clearance arrangements including documentation and entry requirements at the time of exportation and importation.

(e) *Payment of freight and other charges* – payment of freight to the prescribed carrier including any handling charges raised by the airport, seaport or elsewhere during the transit.

(f) *Packing and warehousing* – packing of goods for transit and warehousing provision.

(g) *Cargo insurance* – the process of insuring goods during the transit.

(h) *Consolidation, groupage and special services* – many forwarders specialize in consolidation offering major benefits to the shipper (p. 231).

(b) Import

(a) *Notification of arrival* – the process of informing the importer of the date and location of the goods' arrival and the requisite documents required for customs clearance. It is likely the exporter and importer will have different agents and the two agents will liaise to ensure the smooth flow of the goods through customs, keeping their principals fully informed. Full use will be made of the EDI system.

(b) *Customs clearance* – presentation and clearance of the cargo through customs. This closely involves all the requisite documents. Many major seaports and airports now operate a computerized customs clearance system thereby speeding up the process and eliminating the risk of errors (pp. 471–9).

(c) *Payment of VAT, duty, freight and other charges* – the forwarder will co-ordinate and effect payment of all such payments on behalf of his principal at the time of importation. This avoids delay in the despatch of the goods to the importer.

(d) *Delivery to the importer* – the process of delivering the goods to the importer's premises following customs clearance.

(e) *Breaking bulk and distribution* – the agent may be an umbrella agent whereby he consolidates not only his own client's merchandise, but also those of other agents with whom he has a contractual arrangement. On arrival of the goods in the destination country, the cargo is handed over to the respective agents to process through customs and distribute.

The freight forwarder will despatch cargo by air or surface transport modes. By air it will involve scheduled passenger aircraft; combi, the modern generation of jets permitting a flexible use of space combining freight and passengers according to market demands; chartered aircraft; and scheduled freighters. For surface distribution it will involve conventional or break-bulk vessels involving the 'tween deck specification; containers usually involving multi-modalism; international road transport/trucking embracing the Ro/Ro ferry; international rail movement involving the through train or wagon, from 1994, the Channel Tunnel; and finally the specialized movement involving project forwarding, consolidators, bloodstock, 'out of gauge' loads, household effects, refrigerated goods or bulk liquids. An increasing number of freight forwarders provide services as a NVOCC or NVOC (pp. 417–20).

The freight fowarder is very closely involved in the customs clearance/processing arrangements, at the time of both exportation and importation. Today an increasing number of the major forwarders have now the facility to undertake on their own premises the clearance of cargo at the time of exportation and/or their importation. This speeds up the operation and avoids delays at the sea or airports. It is a feature of multi-modalism. It is called forwarders' local export control (FLEC), and for importation, forwarders' local import control (FLIC). Under FLIC the examination of cargo takes place at the forwarders' premises, whilst the actual entry can be lodged at the seaport or other entry processing unit (EPU) convenient to the forwarder.

The British International Freight Association (BIFA) represents the freight forwarding industry and incorporates the Institute of Freight Forwarders. Both organizations are committed to developing the industry and the attainment of quality control as through the application of the British Standards in Quality Systems, BS 5750 (see pp. 328–31). BIFA has established a Quality Assurance Manual, and also lays down trading conditions and companies which have been engaged in the business of moving freight for a period of not less than three years can apply for registered trading membership, provided they meet the criteria laid down by the Association. Affiliated trading membership is also available to other firms not directly involved in the freight moving industry yet having a working relationship with the forwarder.

Circumstances giving rise to the employment of a freight forwarder by an exporter/importer include dealing with an unfamiliar overseas market; endeavouring to sell under DDP terms; complex shipping or customs arrangements; the workload of the exporter subject to significant peaks and troughs; the exporter is a small firm and needs to concentrate on the careful marketing of the product overseas; the freight forwarder can obtain more favourable freight rates especially for groupage shipments; the freight forwarder has access to priority of booking cargo space on transport modes, and the provision of specialist services/resources including groupage/antiques/perishable cargo/livestock/'out of gauge' consignments, etc. The exporter examining the merits of having an 'in house' shipping department in preference to employing a freight forwarder must consider the capital and revenue expenditure in office space and equipment; the volume of overseas business; the number of markets and their degree of similarity; the availability of suitable qualified staff; the pattern of the business and the degree of seasonal variation; and the nature of the business including the degree of specialism. Overall, a financial appraisal is required.

Monitoring the performance of a freight forwarder enables the exporter to ensure the situation remains competitive. It involves monitoring the budget against actual results in terms of price, transit time, etc.; seeking the buyer/consignee's opinion; undertaking test transits; and the overall quality/reliability of the service and competence/calibre of the management. Shippers in their evaluation of possible freight forwarders, should check out the viability of the company; any legal disputes; the trading conditions; the calibre of the management and their qualifications; experiences of other customers; the degree of technology; quality of overall service; the competitiveness of the tariffs; nature of the business and suitability of the equipment/resources; the company position in the marketplace; the liability insurance maintained by the firm; and so on.

Project forwarding is a growth area of freight forwarding. It is often allied to turnkey projects. Project forwarding involves the despatch/conveyance arrangements which stem from a contract award. For example, a company in country A has a contract with a consortium in country B to build a factory which involves the importation of substantial quantities of merchandise, especially technical equipment. Thus much co-ordination, involving the buyer/seller in terms of despatch arrangements and the site construction programme, is required.

To conclude, shippers wishing to use a freight forwarder must consider in selection and economic criteria the following:

(a) Membership of BIFA very desirable and BS 5750 registration (see pp. 328–31).
(b) Profile of freight forwarder and nature of business.
(c) Value added benefit emerging from employing the freight forwarder's operations.
(d) Alternative cost of the shipper doing the work and the requisite organization structure.
(e) Volume of business and any seasonal variation.
(f) Terms of export sales contract.

An increasing number of shippers entrust part of their business to the freight forwarder, especially spasmodic shipments to new markets, whilst the core of the business is undertaken 'in house' through their own shipping department direct with a carrier. Smaller companies with limited experience and resources use the freight forwarder. Finally, the role and image of the freight forwarder is changing. An increasing number operate as a NVOCC and thereby form part of the multi-modal network, especially through the European trucking system and global container network. BIFA trading conditions are dated 1989.

14.11 CHARTERED SHIPBROKERS

The basic function of the shipbroker is to bring together the two parties concerned involving the ship and cargo owners. In so doing, following negotiations between them, a charter party is ultimately concluded. The broker's income is derived from the commission payable by the shipowner on completion and fulfilment of the contract.

A further role of the shipbroker – other than fixing vessels – is acting as agent for the shipowner. As such he is responsible for everything which may concern the vessel whilst she is in port. This embraces customs formalities; matters concerning the crew; loading/discharge of vessels; bunkering/victualling and so on.

Duties of the shipbroker can be summarized as follows:

(a) Chartering agent whereby he acts for the cargo merchant seeking a suitable vessel in which to carry the merchandise.

(b) Sale and purchase broker acting on behalf of the buyer or seller of ships and bringing the two parties together.

(c) Owner's broker whereby he acts for the actual shipowner in finding cargo for the vessel.

(d) Tanker broker dealing with oil tanker tonnage.

(e) Coasting broker involving vessels operating around the British coast and/or in the short sea trade, e.g. UK/Continent. Additionally he can at the same time act for the cargo merchant in this trade should circumstances so dictate. The deep-sea broker, however, will act for the shipowner or cargo merchant – not both at the same time.

(f) Cabling agent involving the broker communicating with other international markets.

The Institute of Chartered Shipbrokers is the professional body for the shipbrokering industry. It was founded in 1911 and conducts examinations on which membership grade is issued. Membership is open to any citizen of any country in the world, and is regarded as the professional body for those engaged in all aspects of the shipping business.

There is no doubt the shipbroker is a man or woman of many roles. In reality he or she is the middle person between the two principals concerned in a charter party.

14.12 SHIP'S AGENTS

An agent is a person who acts for, or on behalf of, another (the principal) in such a manner that the principal is legally responsible for all acts carried out under such agency.

Basically, the ship's agent represents the shipowner/Master at a particular seaport, either on a permanent or temporary basis. This includes notification of arrival and departure of vessel; acceptance of vessel for loading, discharge, repairs, storing and victualling; arranging berths, tugs, harbour pilots, launches; ordering stevedores, cranes, equipment, etc., and so on. 'In port' requirements include the requirements of the Master, covering bunkers, stores, provisions, crew mail and wages, cash, laundry, engine and deck repairs, and crew repatriation; completion of customs, immigration and port health formalities; hatch and cargo surveys; collection of freight; collection and issuing of bills of lading; completion of manifests; notorial and consular protests and so on. The agent also has a marketing and sales role in accord with the guidelines laid down by the principal.

The Federation of National Associations of Shipbrokers and Agents (FONASBA) introduced in 1993 the fourth edition of their Standard Liner Agency Agreement which BIMCO recommends for global use. A specimen is reproduced in Fig. 14.5.

14.13 MANAGEMENT OF QUALITY: BS 5750

As we progress through the 1990s the dominance of 'management of quality' will become paramount and companies which do not have the appropriate achievement of registration, as found in BS 5750, are unlikely to survive in a competitive environment. Moreover, such companies are unlikely to be successful in competitive tendering as a prerequisite will be that the successful tender has BS 5750 registration.

Basically, BS 5750 is a set of guidelines for the professional management of any commercial venture. It is particularly geared towards manufacturing industries, but it does encompass service

The Federation of National Associations of Ship Brokers and Agents

STANDARD LINER AGENCY AGREEMENT

Fourth Edition
Revised and adopted JULY 1993
Recommended by The Baltic and International Maritime Council (BIMCO)

It is hereby agreed between:

.... of .... *(hereinafter referred to as the Principal)*

and

.... of.. *(hereinafter referred to as the Agent*

dated the .... day of .... 19............

that:

1.00   The Principal hereby appoints the Agent as its Liner Agent for all its owned and/or chartered vessels including any space or slot charter agreement serving the trade between .... and ....

1.01   This Agreement shall come into effect on .... and shall continue until .... Thereafter it shall continue until terminated by either party giving to the other notice in writing, in which event the Agreement shall terminate upon the expiration of a period of .... months from the date upon which such notice was given.

1.02   The territory in which the Agent shall perform its duties under the Agreement shall be............................ hereinafter referred to as the "Territory".

2.00   General Conditions

2.01   This Agreement covers the Port and/or Inland Agency work within the Territory. It includes the duties of marketing the Principal's services and of handling of all types of cargo entering or leaving the Territory whether direct or by transshipment. It also includes the handling of vessels owned, chartered (including any slot or space charter agreement) or otherwise operated by the Principals within the port(s) of the Territory. Work performed as Liner Agent under this Agreement will be strictly separated from any work performed as General Agent for which a separate Standard General Agency Agreement and separate remuneration will be applicable.
In case of any ambiguity as to which agreement governs the work in question, the terms of the Standard Liner Agency Agreement will prevail.

2.02   The Agent undertakes not to accept the representation of other shipping companies nor to engage in NVOCC or such freight forwarding activities in the Territory, which are in direct competition to any of the Principal's transportation activities, without prior written consent, which shall not unreasonably be withheld.

2.03   The Principal undertakes not to appoint any other party in the Agent's Territory for the services defined in this Agreement.

2.04   Where any of the activities of the Agent in the Territory are not covered by this Agreement, then the local General Conditions in the latest version or established custom of the trade and/or port shall apply and form part of this Agreement, unless otherwise agreed. The Agent undertakes to acquaint the Principal with any relevant local custom or practice and to furnish the Principal with a copy of the local General Conditions if any.

2.05   In countries where the position of the agent is in any way legally protected or regulated, the Agent shall have the benefit of such protection or regulation, unless otherwise agreed.

2.06   All aspects of the Principal's business are to be treated confidentially and all files and records pertaining to this business are the property of the Principal.

Fig. 14.5 FONASBA Standard Liner Agency Agreement recommended by BIMCO.

industries including transport and freight forwarding. BIFA fully endorses BS 5750. Overall, it focuses attention on aspects of the organization, and its management systems and procedures, rather than the specific technicalities of the product or service. The strategy is simple, reliable and consistent assurance of quality emerging from a well-structured, professionally run company.

BS 5750 involves three parts, and the requirements of Part II are outlined below because of their relevance to the freight forwarding industry.

(a)   Clear polices and strategies for quality with well-defined operational and service standards.

(b)   Structured and effective management organization with specific allocation of responsibility for all aspects of quality management.

(c)   A documented quality system and operational procedures.

(d)   Specified methods of understanding and recording customers' service requirements and verification that the needs have been met.

(e)   Timely and precise control of all documentation including procedures, standard forms, paperwork systems and software. This to include the relevant communication of all revisions and amendments.

(f)   Knowledge of the quality abilities of suppliers and evidence that this is taken into account in purchasing decisions.

(g)   Establishing routines for work planning and the execution of the basic administrative and legislative systems of the business.

(h)   Management controls and performance measurement and corrective action.

(i)   Clear plans and procedures for identification and rectification of mistakes, deficiencies and causes of customer complaints.

(j)   A code of conduct to cover product handling, packaging, transportation and storage whenever these activities are performed within the company.

(k)   Preplanned and structured senior management reviews of the major aspects of the quality system supported by formal routine auditing of all operational practices and procedures.

(l)   Appropriately experienced and trained personnel.

(m)   Records to demonstrate consistent compliance with all the foregoing issues.

Organizations in the UK which conduct assessment and registration include the British Standards Institution (BSI), Lloyd's Register Quality Assurance Ltd (LRQA) and Bureau Veritas Quality International (BVQI). Companies on achievement of registration will be subject to routine annual surveillance and periodic reassessment to confirm the continued effective operation of the quality system. BS 5750 also complies with International Standard ISO 9000 and European Standard EN 29000. (See also ISM, pp. 27–30.)

CHAPTER 15

Charter parties

A very large proportion of the world's trade is carried in tramp vessels. It is quite common to find that one cargo will fill the whole ship, and, in these circumstances, one cargo owner or one charterer will enter into a special contract with the shipowner for the hire of his ship – such a contract is known as a charter party. It is not always a full ship-load, although this is usually the case.

A charter party is a contract whereby a shipowner agrees to place his ship, or part of it, at the disposal of a merchant or other person (known as the charterer), for the carriage of goods from one port to another port on being paid freight, or to let his ship for a specified period, his remuneration being known as hire money. The terms, conditions and exceptions under which the goods are carried are set out in the charter party.

15.1 DEMISE AND NON-DEMISE CHARTER PARTIES

There are basically two types of charter parties: demise and non-demise.

A demise or 'bareboat' charter party arises when the charterer is responsible for providing the cargo and crew, whilst the shipowner merely provides the vessel. In consequence, the charterer appoints the crew, thus taking over full responsibility for the operation of the vessel, and pays all expenses incurred. However, in some situations it is the practice for the chief engineer to be the shipowner's representative and thereby provide experience of the shipboard maintenance needs of the vessel's machinery. A demise charter party is for a period of time which may vary from a few weeks to several years.

A non-demise charter arises when the shipowner provides the vessel and her crew, whilst the charterer merely supplies the cargo. It may be a voyage charter for a particular voyage, in which the shipowner agrees to carry cargo between specified ports for a pre-arranged freight. The majority of tramp cargo shipments are made on a voyage charter basis. Alternatively, it may be a time charter for a stated period or voyage for a remuneration known as hire money. The shipowner continues to manage his own vessel, both under non-demise voyage or time charter parties under the charterer's instructions. With a time charter, it is usual for the charterer to pay port dues and fuel costs, and overtime payments incurred in an endeavour to obtain faster turn-rounds. It is quite common for liner companies to supplement their services by taking tramp ships on time charter, but this practice may lessen as containerization develops.

There are several types of non-demise voyage charters and these are given below. It will be seen that they all deal with the carriage of goods from a certain port or ports to another port or ports, and the differences between them arise mainly out of payment for the cost of loading and discharging, and port expenses.

1. *Gross terms form of charter*. This is probably the most common form of charter used by tramp ships today. In this form, the shipowner pays all the expenses incurred in loading and discharging and also all port charges plus of course voyage costs. It can be varied by having gross terms at the loading port and nett terms at the discharging port in which case it is called gross load, free discharge.

2. *FIO charter*. Under this charter, the charterer pays for the cost of loading and discharging the cargo, hence the expression of FIO (meaning 'free in and out'). The shipowner is still responsible for the payment of all port charges. It can be described as net terms.

3. *Lump sum charter*. In this case, the charterer pays a lump sum of money for the use of the ship and the shipowner guarantees that a certain amount of space (i.e. bale cubic metres) will be available for cargo, along with the maximum weight of cargo that the vessel will be able to carry. A lump sum charter may be on either a gross basis or an FIO basis. Such a charter is very useful when the charterer wishes to load a mixed cargo – the shipowner guarantees that a certain amount of space and weight will be

available and it is up to the charterer to use that space to his best advantage.

The above forms of charter are all quite common today, and in each case the shipowner pays the port charges.

4. *Liner terms*. This is an inclusive freight rate more usually found on cargo liner services and covers not only the sea freight, but also loading and discharging costs for a particular consignment. Under a voyage charter the shipowner is paid freight which includes the costs of loading, stowing and discharging the cargo. It is particularly evident in the short sea area of tramp shipping. It is desirable the shipowner agrees with the shipper or receiver on the appointment of the stevedores.

5. *Berth terms*. Under this term the shipowner agrees to his vessel's loading or discharging operation begin subject to the custom of the port where the cargo handling is taking place, or he may be agreeing that the vessel will load or discharge as fast as possible or under customary despatch or any or all of this type of term. Hence the shipowner is responsible to pay for loading and discharging costs and only indefinite laytime exists.

There are, of course, numerous variations that may be made to the above broad divisions and this is a matter for negotiation when the vessel is being 'worked' for future business. For example, the gross and FIO charters may be modified to an FOB charter (free on board) meaning that the charterer pays for the cost of loading and the shipowner pays for the cost of discharge, or alternatively the charter may be arranged on the basis of free discharge, i.e. the charterer pays for the cost of discharging.

The same general terms of contract are found in all the above types of charter.

A significant proportion of the charters are negotiated through a shipbroker on the Baltic Exchange situated in London (see pp. 156–60).

The following items would be included when formulating a remit to a shipbroker to obtain a general cargo vessel on charter.

(a) vessel capacity;
(b) vessel speed;
(c) actual trade/ports of call including cargo specification and volume;

(d) duration of charter;

(e) type of charter, i.e. demise or non-demise, voyage or time;

(f) date of charter commencement and duration – the latter with any options for extensions;

(g) overall dimensions of vessel, draught, length and beam;

(h) any constraints likely to be imposed, e.g. carriage of dangerous cargo;

(i) classification of vessel and any trading limits;

(j) possible band of fixture rate likely to be viable;

(k) any shipboard cargo-handling equipment needs.

The extent to which the foregoing items would need to be included would depend on circumstances. Moreover, the urgency of the need of the tonnage would be significant and whether the market fixture rates were falling or rising. Given time, the charterer could examine the market in greater depth and have the benefit of securing a more suitable vessel which may not be immediately available.

The negotiations are carried out by word of mouth in the Exchange, not by letter, and when the contract has been concluded the vessel is said to be 'fixed'. Factors influencing the ultimate fixture rate are described on pp. 182–4. The charter party is then prepared and signed by the two parties or their agents. In addition to the trade to and from this country, a large number of cross voyages, i.e. from one foreign country to another, are fixed on the London market, quite often to a vessel owned in yet another foreign country. There is no compulsion to conduct negotiations through a shipbroker on the Baltic Exchange. Many negotiations are conducted direct between charterer and shipowner. It is a matter for the shipowner's judgement whether he engages a shipbroker to conduct his negotiations direct with the charterer. Obviously, when the shipbroker is negotiating a series of voyage charters for his principal, the shipowner will endeavour to reduce to an absolute minimum the number of ballast voyages. These arise between termination of one voyage charter, for example at Rotterdam, and commencement of the next voyage charter, for example at Southampton, involving a ballast voyage Rotterdam-Southampton. The use of the BIMCO approved documentation on chartering (see pp. 350–56) is of paramount importance to minimize risk of any misinterpretation of the terms.

The report of a vessel's fixture is recorded in the shipping press. Extracts of two fixtures in grain and two time-charter fixtures are given below:

Interpretation of two fixtures in grain and two time-charter fixtures

(i) Chicago-Belfast: *Sugar Crystal*, 14 000 HSS $27.50, option Glasgow/Leith $28.00, 3 days/3000, 2–14 May (Peabody).

Loading Chicago, discharging Belfast: MV *Sugar Crystal*; cargo 14 000 tonnes heavy grains, sorghums or soyabeans at a freight rate of US $27.50 per tonne, with the charterer's option to discharge instead at Glasgow or Leith at the freight rate of US $28.00; 3 days allowed for loading; 3000 tonnes rate per day allowed for discharging. Vessel to present ready to load between laydays 2 May and the cancelling date of 14 May, charterers being Messrs Peabody.

(ii) US Gulf-Constanza: *Myron*, 19 000/19 800 min/max SBM, $31.50, FIO, 3000/1000, option 4000 load at $31.25, 26 May – 15 June (Coprasol).

Loading at a port in the US Gulf, discharging Constanza: MV *Myron*; cargo minimum 19 000 tonnes/maximum 19 800 tonnes soyabean meal, at a freight rate of US $31.50 per tonne; cargo to be loaded and discharged free of expense to the owner (FIO). 3000 tonne rate per day for loading, 1000 tonnes rate per day for discharging, with charterer's option to increase the speed of loading to 4000 tonnes per day, in turn paying a reduced freight rate of US $31.25 per tonne. Vessel to present ready to load between laydays 26 May and the cancelling date of 15 June, charterers being Messrs Coprasol.

(iii) *Acropolis* (Fortune type): Greek, built 1988, $5350 daily. Delivery Casablanca trip, redelivery Le Havre. 20–25 April (Dreyfus).

MV *Acropolis* (a Japanese Fortune type of vessel), Greek flag. Built 1988, $5350 daily hire. Delivery to charterers at Casablanca for a time charter trip, redelivery to owners at Le Havre. Delivery not earlier than 20 April, not later than 25 April, charterers being Messrs Dreyfus.

(iv) *Camara*, 25 689 dwt, 1.2 m ft^3, Danish, built 1989, 15 knots on 37 tonnes, 1500 s. 5 × 15 tonne cranes. $6250 daily. Delivery

Antwerp, trip via North France and Bulgaria, redelivery Gibraltar. Spot (Philipp Bros.).

MV *Camara*, 25 689 summer deadweight 1 200 000 ft³ capacity, Danish flag, built 1989. 15 knots on 37 tonnes (CS 180) F/O, 5 × 15 tonne cranes, US $6250 daily hire. Delivery on time charter at Antwerp for a time charter trip via North France and Bulgaria with redelivery to owners upon vessel passing Gibraltar. Vessel available immediately at Antwerp (spot), charterers being Messrs Philipp Bros.

15.2 VOYAGE AND TIME CHARTER PARTIES

Basically, there are no statutory clauses required to be incorporated in a charter party. The terms and conditions found in a charter party represent the wishes of the two parties to the contract. In extreme cases it has been known for a charter party contract to be completed on the back of a stamp. Nevertheless, there are certain essential clauses necessary to some charter parties, whilst other clauses are of an optional nature. For example, an ice clause would be essential if the vessel were trading in the White or Baltic Seas but would not be necessary if the ship was operating in the Tropics. Given below are the desirable essential clauses found in a voyage charter party together with possible problem areas but it is stressed they are not always found in all charters.

1. *The preamble.* The contracting parties; description of the vessel; position of vessel and expected readiness date to load.

2. *Description of the cargo.* The quantity of cargo is usually stated as a full and complete cargo, with a minimum and a maximum quantity. This means that the ship guarantees to load at least the minimum and the ship may call for any quantity up to the maximum, which the charterer must supply; in other words, the quantity of cargo loaded is any quantity between the minimum and the maximum in the shipowner's option. The normal margin is 5 to 10% more or less than a stated quantity. The cargo must be clearly described both in negotiations and in the charter party. If the cargo is liable to occupy a lot of space (or cubic) it is advisable to

have the stowage factor stated in the charter. The word 'stemmed' means that the cargo (or bunkers) for the ship have been booked, or reserved.

3. *Loading date and cancelling date.* This is the period of time (anything from a few days to a few weeks) given in the charter during which the vessel may present herself for loading, and is sometimes rather loosely referred to as her laydays, although this is not the correct meaning of laydays. The charterer is not bound to load the vessel before her loading date, even though the vessel may be ready. If the vessel is not ready to load on or before the cancelling date, the charterer shall have the option of cancelling the charter with a right of damages against the shipowners. Even if it is quite obvious that the vessel will miss her cancelling date, she is still legally bound to present for loading, even if it means a long ballast voyage, and it is only then that the charterers need declare whether they will cancel or maintain the vessel. In practice, if the vessel looks like being late the shipowner will approach the charterer to get an extension of the cancelling date or else a definite cancellation before the vessel proceeds to the loading port.

Finally, when stating the layday/cancelling dates two salient points must be borne in mind, namely the contractual position if the vessel presents herself for loading too early, and the position if the vessel cannot meet the cancelling date. (See also item 8.)

4. *Loading port or place.* The loading port or place is always stated in a voyage charter. Sometimes it is just a single named port, or one out of a range of picked ports (i.e. several good named ports) or a port to be nominated along a certain stretch of coastline (e.g. 'A/H Range' which means a port between Antwerp and Hamburg inclusive). If the loading port is named, the vessel is under an obligation to get to that port, and if a particular berth or dock in that port is named in the charter, then the vessel is under an obligation to get to that dock or berth. In other words, when fixing his vessel to load at a named port it is up to the owner to make sure that the vessel can both enter and leave the port safely. These remarks also apply if the vessel is to load at one or more named ports out of a selection. If they are named in the charter then the shipowner undertakes to get there, and is excused only if he is frustrated from so doing. Quite often a vessel is fixed to load

at any port in the charterer's option out of a range (i.e. a particular stretch of coastline) in which case the charterer could order the vessel to any port in that range. The shipowner, to protect his interest, should stipulate, when fixing, for a *safe port*. The charterer can then order the vessel only to one which the owner and the Master consider safe for the vessel. A safe port means a port which a vessel may go to and leave safely, without danger from physical or political causes. The port must not only be safe when the vessel is ordered to it, but also safe when the vessel arrives at the port. If, in the meantime, the port has become unsafe the shipowner may refuse to send his ship there, and request the charterer to nominate another port.

5. *Discharging port or place.* The above remarks apply to the discharging port. As soon as a discharging port is ordered (out of, say, a range of ports) then that port becomes the contract terminus of the voyage.

6. *Alternative ports of discharge; seaworthy trim between ports; geographical rotation.* When there is more than one port of discharge, the shipowner should stipulate that the ports are in geographical rotation, i.e. in regular order along the coast, either north to south, east to west, or vice versa, and not jumping about from one to another, backwards and forwards in a haphazard manner.

7. *Payment of freight.* Unless there is a condition to the contrary (e.g. special terms of contract as to 'advance freight' etc.) freight is construed in the ordinary commercial meaning, i.e. the reward payable to the carrier on arrival of the goods, ready to be delivered to the consignee. The true test of the right of freight is whether the service in respect of which freight was contracted has been substantially performed. The following circumstances are relevant.

(a) Ships to deliver cargo on being paid freight. This establishes that freight is payable as the cargo is discharged, i.e. concurrent with discharge. Literally it means that as each ton is discharged freight is payable. In practice, freight is paid so much on account at various stages of the discharge, e.g. day by day on out-turn.

(b)   On right and true delivery of the cargo. In this case freight is earned only after delivery of the cargo, but is paid for day by day on out-turn and adjusted on final delivery.

(c)   On signing bills of lading. Freight is payable when the ship is loaded and the bills of lading have been signed. This is usually followed by the words 'dis-countless and non-returnable, ship and/ or cargo lost or not lost', i.e. once the shipowner receives his freight he retains it. Payment in this manner is known as advance freight and the bill of lading is endorsed 'freight paid'. (The above is not to be confused with advance of freight which may be issued to the shipowner to cover his disbursements at the loading port. This advance of freight should really be considered as a loan, and the charterer who gives the shipowner this facility usually makes a small charge of, say, 10%).

(d)   The insurance of freight. Irrespective of how the freight is paid, both parties to the contract incur certain expenses in preparation for the voyage, and in the event of the ship being lost do not wish to lose the freight as well, and it is therefore insured. If freight is payable on delivery the shipowner will insure the freight in case the vessel is lost. If freight is paid in advance, then the charterer will insure the freight, because if the ship is lost he will not receive any refund from the shipowner.

Finally it is important that the currency of payment is closely evaluated, with particular consideration of exchange rate fluctuations and measures available to counter them; if the freight rate payment and the currency in the country of the recipient are different; and/or if freight is not directly payable to his bank at the place of domicile but is collected by an agent.

8. *Laydays*. This is the rate of discharge per weather working day. Laydays are the number of days permitted in a charter party for loading and discharging the vessel. Alternatively, it may be either applied for loading or discharging a vessel in calculating the implications when the layday period prescribed has been exceeded. In such a situation demurrage arises the terms of which arise in the following clause. Conversely, despatch arises when the loading and/or discharge is completed sooner than prescribed. Various types of laydays exist, as detailed below:

(a)   Running or consecutive days concern consecutive calendar days (midnight to midnight) including Sundays and holidays when laydays count. Hence once laydays commence this runs continuously unless any holidays arise which specifically exclude laydays.

(b) Reversible laydays confirming all time saved or lost on loading vessel may be added or deducted from the time allowed for discharge.

(c) Weather working days indicate that laydays do not count when adverse weather conditions prevail thereby preventing loading or discharging to take place.

(d) Surf days arise when a heavy swell or surf prevents loading or discharging at ports which are usually roadsteads. Surf days do not count as laydays.

(e) Working days are days when work is normally performed. These exclude Sundays (when recognized) and holidays officially recognized. The number of working daily hours depends on the custom of the port. To lessen such risks brokers are urged to check the BIMCO holiday calendar (see p. 357).

9. *Demurrage and despatch.* If a ship loads and/or discharges in less than the prescribed time, the owners pay a despatch money as a reward for time saved; if, on the other hand, the prescribed time is exceeded, then demurrage is payable at an agreed rate to the owner as compensation for delay of the ship. The term 'all time saved' within the context of despatch money should be used with caution as it can result in a situation in which the number of days on which despatch has to be paid exceeds the number of days agreed as laytime allowed.

10. *Cessor or limitation of liability clause.*

11. *Lien clause.* This gives the shipowners the right to hold cargo against payment of freight or hire.

12. *Loading and discharging expenses.*

13. *Appointment of agents and stevedores.*

14. *Lighterage.*

15. *Deviation and salvage clause.*

16. *Bills of lading clause.*

17. *Exemptions from liability clause.*

18. *General average*

19. *Arbitration*

20. *Ice clause.*

21. *Strikes and stoppages.*

22. *Overtime*

23. *Sailing telegram.*

24. *Sub-letting.* This gives or refuses to allow permission of the ship to be sub-let, or sub-chartered under the charter party.

25. *Address commission.* A percentage of commission sometimes specified due to charterers based on the amount of freight.

26. *Brokerage.* Indicates the rate of brokerage that shall be paid.

27. *Penalty for non-performance.*

28. *War clause.*

29. *New Jason clause.*

30. *Both to blame clause.*

31. *Clause paramount.*

Finally it is important to stress that it is the shipowner's right to decide who should represent his interests and attend to his vessel at any particular port. In the event shipowner may have to employ a port agent named or appointed by the charterers. The port agent so appointed should be fully aware that no matter what his connections with the charterers may be, he is the agent of the vessel and his duty is to represent/defend the interests of the shipowner.

An example of a voyage charter codenamed 'GENCON' used for general cargo is given in Fig. 15.1. and contains 17 clauses. This charter party is widely used.

A time charter, as earlier indicated, is defined as a contract of affreightment under which a charterer agrees to hire, and the shipowner agrees to let, his vessel for a mutually agreed period of time or a specified voyage, the remuneration being known as hire. There are certain advantages and disadvantages both to the shipowner and the charterer in placing a vessel on time charter as compared with ordinary voyage charter trading.

From the shipowner's standpoint, the ship is employed for a definite period of time, with a regular income to the shipowner and the minimum of risk. Time charter provides the shipowner with a 'good cover' against a decline in freight rates. The shipowner does not have to worry about the day-to-day trading of the vessel so far as bunkers, port charges and cargo expenses are concerned; moreover the vessel will remain on hire even if delayed through port labour troubles. The disadvantages to the shipowner are that to a certain extent he loses control of his vessel, although he still appoints the Master and crew, but subject to the charter limitations he does not control the cargo loaded in the vessel or the voyage. If the freight market should rise the shipowner is unable to take advantage of it, and the charterer gets the benefit instead. The vessel may not be in a convenient position for the owner to perform maintenance work on his vessel, although the disadvantage would apply only in the case of a long-term charter.

In contrast, from the charterer's viewpoint there is the advantage of being able to trade the vessel almost as if it were his own, subject only to the charter party limitations. He can hire the vessel on a long – or short-term basis (generally the longer the period the cheaper the rate at which he can secure tonnage), and it provides him with a good cover if the freight markets show any signs of rising. The liner companies can take tonnage on time charter and so supplement their own sailing if the volume of trade is such as to warrant additional tonnage. The disadvantages to the charterer are that he is committed to the payment of hire over a period of time and, should trade diminish, he may have to face a loss. The charterer, by the terms of the charter, may be limited in his range of trading, but this is a point he should take into consideration when negotiating the charter. The charterer is responsible for the ship's bunker supply, port charges and cargo-handling expenses.

There is an increasing tendency for modern bulk purpose-built carriers, including tankers, to be on time charters of seven years duration or longer. Special provision can be made in the charter party for the fixture rate to be reviewed, which at the time of the initial fixture negotiation broadly reflects a modest return to the shipowner on his capital investment throughtout the duration of the charter.

1. Shipbroker	RECOMMENDED **THE BALTIC AND INTERNATIONAL MARITIME CONFERENCE** **UNIFORM GENERAL CHARTER (AS REVISED 1922 and 1976)** **INCLUDING "F.I.O." ALTERNATIVE, ETC.** (To be used for trades for which no approved form is in force) CODE NAME: "**GENCON**" Part I
	2. Place and date
3. Owners/Place of business (Cl. 1)	4. Charterers/Place of business (Cl. 1)
5. Vessel's name (Cl. 1)	6. GRT/NRT (Cl. 1)
7. Deadweight cargo carrying capacity in tons (abt.) (Cl. 1)	8. Present position (Cl. 1)
9. Expected ready to load (abt.) (Cl. 1)	
10. Loading port or place (Cl. 1)	11. Discharging port or place (Cl. 1)
12. Cargo (also state quantity and margin in Owners' option, if agreed, if full and complete cargo not agreed state "part cargo") (Cl. 1)	
13. Freight rate (also state if payable on delivered or intaken quantity) (Cl. 1)	14. Freight payment (state currency and method of payment; also beneficiary and bank account) (Cl. 4)
15. Loading and discharging costs (state alternative (a) or (b) of Cl. 5; also indicate if vessel is gearless)	16. Laytime (if separate laytime for load. and disch. is agreed, fill in a) and b). If total laytime for load. and disch., fill in c) only) (Cl. 6)
	a) Laytime for loading
17. Shippers (state name and address) (Cl. 6)	b) Laytime for discharging
	c) Total laytime for loading and discharging
18. Demurrage rate (loading and discharging) (Cl. 7)	19. Cancelling date (Cl. 10)
20. Brokerage commission and to whom payable (Cl. 14)	
21. Additional clauses covering special provisions, if agreed.	

It is mutually agreed that this Contract shall be performed subject to the conditions contained in this Charter which shall include Part I as well as Part II. In the event of a conflict of conditions, the provisions of Part I shall prevail over those of Part II to the extent of such conflict.

Signature (Owners)	Signature (Charterers)

Printed and sold by Fr. G. Knudtzon Ltd., 55 Toldbodgade, DK-1253 Copenhagen K, Telefax +45 33 93 11 84 by authority of The Baltic and International Maritime Conference (BIMCO), Copenhagen.

Fig. 15.1 The 'GENCON' BIMCO Uniform General Charter Party. (Reproduced by kind permission of BIMCO.)

PART II

"Gencon" Charter (As Revised 1922 and 1976)

Including "F.I.O." Alternative, etc.

1. It is agreed between the party mentioned in Box 3 as Owners of the steamer or motor-vessel named in Box 5, of the gross/nett Register tons indicated in Box 6 and carrying about the number of tons of deadweight cargo stated in Box 7, now in position as stated in Box 8 and expected ready to load under this Charter about the date indicated in Box 9, and the party mentioned as Charterers in Box 4 that:
The said vessel shall proceed to the loading port or place stated in Box 10 or so near thereto as she may safely get and lie always afloat, and there load a full and complete cargo (if shipment of deck cargo agreed same to be at Charterers' risk) as stated in Box 12 (Charterers to provide all mats and/or wood for dunnage and any separations required, the Owners allowing the use of any dunnage wood on board if required) which the Charterers bind themselves to ship, and being so loaded the vessel shall proceed to the discharging port or place stated in Box 11 as ordered on signing Bills of Lading or so near thereto as she may safely get and lie always afloat and there deliver the cargo on being paid freight on delivered or intaken quantity as indicated in Box 13 at the rate stated in Box 13.

2. Owners' Responsibility Clause
Owners are to be responsible for loss of or damage to the goods or for delay in delivery of the goods only in case the loss, damage or delay has been caused by the improper or negligent stowage of the goods (unless stowage performed by shippers/Charterers or their stevedores or servants) or by personal want of due diligence on the part of the Owners or their Manager to make the vessel in all respects seaworthy and to secure that she is properly manned, equipped and supplied or by the personal act or default of the Owners or their Manager.
And the Owners are responsible for no loss or damage or delay arising from any other cause whatsoever, even from the neglect or default of the Captain or crew or some other person employed by the Owners on board or ashore for whose acts they would, but for this clause, be responsible, or from unseaworthiness of the vessel on loading or commencement of the voyage or at any time whatsoever. Damage caused by contact with or leakage, smell or evaporation from other goods or by the inflammable or explosive nature or insufficient package of other goods not to be considered as caused by improper or negligent stowage, even if in fact so caused.

3. Deviation Clause
The vessel has liberty to call at any port or ports in any order, for any purpose, to sail without pilots, to tow and/or assist vessels in all situations, and also to deviate for the purpose of saving life and/or property.

4. Payment of Freight
The freight to be paid in the manner prescribed in Box 14 in cash without discount on delivery of the cargo at mean rate of exchange ruling on day or days of payment, the receivers of the cargo being bound to pay freight on account during delivery, if required by Captain or Owners.
Cash for vessel's ordinary disbursements at port of loading to be advanced by Charterers if required at highest current rate of exchange, subject to two per cent. to cover insurance and other expenses.

5. Loading/Discharging Costs
* *(a) Gross Terms*
The cargo to be brought alongside in such a manner as to enable vessel to take the goods with her own tackle. Charterers to procure and pay the necessary men on shore or on board the lighters to do the work there, vessel only heaving the cargo on board.
If the loading takes place by elevator, cargo to be put free in vessel's holds. Owners only paying trimming expenses.
Any pieces and/or packages of cargo over two tons weight, shall be loaded, stowed and discharged by Charterers at their risk and expense.
The cargo to be received by Merchants at their risk and expense alongside the vessel not beyond the reach of her tackle.
* *(b) F.i.o. and free stowed/trimmed*
The cargo shall be brought into the holds, loaded, stowed and/or trimmed and taken from the holds and discharged by the Charterers or their Agents, free of any risk, liability and expense whatsoever to the Owners.
The Owners shall provide winches, motive power and winchmen from the Crew if requested and permitted; if not, the Charterers shall provide and pay for winchmen from shore and/or cranes, if any. (This provision shall not apply if vessel is gearless and stated as such in Box 15).
* *indicate alternative (a) or (b), as agreed, in Box 15.*

6. Laytime
* *(a) Separate laytime for loading and discharging*
The cargo shall be loaded within the number of running hours as indicated in Box 16, weather permitting, Sundays and holidays excepted, unless used, in which event time actually used shall count.
The cargo shall be discharged within the number of running hours as indicated in Box 16, weather permitting, Sundays and holidays excepted, unless used, in which event time actually used shall count.
* *(b) Total laytime for loading and discharging*
The cargo shall be loaded and discharged within the number of total running hours as indicated in Box 16, weather permitting, Sundays and holidays excepted, unless used, in which event time actually used shall count.
(c) Commencement of laytime (loading and discharging)
Laytime for loading and discharging shall commence at 1 p.m. if notice of readiness is given before noon, and at 6 a.m. next working day if notice given during office hours after noon. Notice at loading port to be given to the Shippers named in Box 17.
Time actually used before commencement of laytime shall count.
Time lost in waiting for berth to count as loading or discharging time, as the case may be.
* *indicate alternative (a) or (b) as agreed, in Box 16.*

7. Demurrage
Ten running days on demurrage at the rate stated in Box 18 per day or pro rata for any part of a day, payable day by day, to be allowed Merchants altogether at ports of loading and discharging.

8. Lien Clause
Owners shall have a lien on the cargo for freight, dead-freight, demurrage and damages for detention. Charterers shall remain responsible for dead-freight and demurrage (including damages for detention), incurred at port of loading. Charterers shall also remain responsible for freight and demurrage (including damages for detention) incurred at port of discharge, but only to such extent as the Owners have been unable to obtain payment thereof by exercising the lien on the cargo.

9. Bills of Lading
The Captain to sign Bills of Lading at such rate of freight as presented without prejudice to this Charterparty, but should the freight by Bills of Lading amount to less than the total chartered freight the difference to be paid to the Captain in cash on signing Bills of Lading.

10. Cancelling Clause
Should the vessel not be ready to load (whether in berth or not) on or before the date indicated in Box 19, Charterers have the option of cancelling this contract, such option to be declared, if demanded, at least 48 hours before vessel's expected arrival at port of loading. Should the vessel be delayed on account of average or otherwise, Charterers to be informed as soon as possible, and if the vessel is delayed for more than 10 days after the day she is stated to be expected ready to load, Charterers have the option of cancelling this contract, unless a cancelling date has been agreed upon.

11. General Average
General average to be settled according to York-Antwerp Rules, 1974. Proprietors of cargo to pay the cargo's share in the general expenses even if same have been necessitated through neglect or default of the Owners' servants (see clause 2).

12. Indemnity
Indemnity for non-performance of this Charterparty, proved damages, not exceeding estimated amount of freight.

13. Agency
In every case the Owners shall appoint his own Broker or Agent both at the port of loading and the port of discharge.

14. Brokerage
A brokerage commission at the rate stated in Box 20 on the freight earned is due to the party mentioned in Box 20.
In case of non-execution at least 1/3 of the brokerage on the estimated amount of freight and dead-freight to be paid by the Owners to the Brokers as indemnity for the latter's expenses and work. In case of more voyages the amount of indemnity to be mutually agreed.

15. GENERAL STRIKE CLAUSE
Neither Charterers nor Owners shall be responsible for the consequences of any strikes or lock-outs preventing or delaying the fulfilment of any obligations under this contract.
If there is a strike or lock-out affecting the loading of the cargo, or any part of it, when vessel is ready to proceed from her last port or at any time during the voyage to the port or ports of loading or after her arrival there, Captain or Owners may ask Charterers to declare, that they agree to reckon the laydays as if there were no strike or lock-out. Unless Charterers have given such declaration in writing (by telegram, if necessary) within 24 hours, Owners shall have the option of cancelling this contract. If part cargo has already been loaded, Owners must proceed with same, (freight payable on loaded quantity only) having liberty to complete with other cargo on the way for their own account.
If there is a strike or lock-out affecting the discharge of the cargo on or after vessel's arrival at or off port of discharge and same has not been settled within 48 hours, Receivers shall have the option of keeping vessel waiting until such strike or lock-out is at an end against paying half demurrage after expiration of the time provided for discharging, or of ordering the vessel to a safe port where she can safely discharge without risk of being detained by strike or lock-out. Such orders to be given within 48 hours after Captain or Owners have given notice to Charterers of the strike or lock-out affecting the discharge. On delivery of the cargo at such port, all conditions of this Charterparty and of the Bill of Lading shall apply and vessel shall receive the same freight as if she had discharged at the original port of destination, except that if the distance of the substituted port exceeds 100 nautical miles, the freight on the cargo delivered at the substituted port to be increased in proportion.

16. War Risks ("Voywar 1950")
(1) In these clauses "War Risks" shall include any blockade or any action which is announced as a blockade by any Government or by any belligerent or by any organized body, sabotage, piracy, and any actual or threatened war, hostilities, warlike operations, civil war, civil commotion, or revolution.
(2) If at any time before the Vessel commences loading, it appears that performance of the contract will subject the Vessel or her Master and crew or her cargo to war risks at any stage of the adventure, the Owners shall be entitled by letter or telegram despatched to the Charterers, to cancel this Charter.
(3) The Master shall not be required to load cargo or to continue loading or to proceed on or to sign Bill(s) of Lading for any adventure on which or any port at which it appears that the Vessel, her Master and crew or her cargo will be subjected to war risks. In the event of the exercise by the Master of his right under this Clause after part or full cargo has been loaded, the Master shall be at liberty either to discharge such cargo at the loading port or to proceed therewith. In the latter case the Vessel shall have liberty to carry other cargo for Owners' benefit and accordingly to proceed to and load or discharge such other cargo at any other port or ports whatsoever, backwards or forwards, although in a contrary direction to or out of or beyond the ordinary route. In the event of the Master electing to proceed with part cargo under this Clause freight shall in any case be payable on the quantity delivered.
(4) If at the time the Master elects to proceed with part or full cargo under Clause 3, or after the Vessel has left the loading port, or the

Fig. 15.1 continued

PART II
"Gencon" Charter (As Revised 1922 and 1976)
Including "F.I.O." Alternative, etc.

last of the loading ports, if more than one, it appears that further 205
performance of the contract will subject the Vessel, her Master and 206
crew or her cargo, to war risks, the cargo shall be discharged, or if 207
the discharge has been commenced shall be completed, at any safe 208
port in vicinity of the port of discharge as may be ordered by the 209
Charterers. If no such orders shall be received from the Charterers 210
within 48 hours after the Owners have despatched a request by 211
telegram to the Charterers for the nomination of a substitute discharg- 212
ing port, the Owners shall be at liberty to discharge the cargo at 213
any safe port which they may, in their discretion, decide on and such 214
discharge shall be deemed to be due fulfilment of the contract of 215
affreightment. In the event of cargo being discharged at any such 216
other port, the Owners shall be entitled to freight as if the discharge 217
had been effected at the port or ports named in the Bill(s) of Lading 218
or to which the Vessel may have been ordered pursuant thereto. 219

(5) (a) The Vessel shall have liberty to comply with any directions 220
or recommendations as to loading, departure, arrival, routes, ports 221
of call, stoppages, destination, zones, waters, discharge, delivery or 222
in any other wise whatsoever (including any direction or recom- 223
mendation not to go to the port of destination or to delay proceeding 224
thereto or to proceed to some other port) given by any Government or 225
by any belligerent or by any organized body engaged in civil war, 226
hostilities or warlike operations or by any person or body acting or 227
purporting to act as or with the authority of any Government or 228
belligerent or of any such organized body or by any committee or 229
person having under the terms of the war risks insurance on the 230
Vessel, the right to give any such directions or recommendations. If, 231
by reason of or in compliance with any such direction or recom- 232
mendation, anything is done or is not done, such shall not be deemed 233
a deviation. 234

(b) If, by reason of or in compliance with any such directions or re- 235
commendations, the Vessel does not proceed to the port or ports 236
named in the Bill(s) of Lading or to which she may have been 237
ordered pursuant thereto, the Vessel may proceed to any port as 238
directed or recommended or to any safe port which the Owners in 239
their discretion may decide on and there discharge the cargo. Such 240
discharge shall be deemed to be due fulfilment of the contract of 241
affreightment and the Owners shall be entitled to freight as if 242
discharge had been effected at the port or ports named in the Bill(s) 243
of Lading at which the Vessel may have been ordered pursuant 244
thereto. 245

(6) All extra expenses (including insurance costs) involved in discharg- 246
ing cargo at the loading port or in reaching or discharging the cargo 247
at any port as provided in Clauses 4 and 5 (b) hereof shall be paid 248
by the Charterers and/or cargo owners, and the Owners shall have 249
a lien on the cargo for all moneys due under these Clauses. 250

17. GENERAL ICE CLAUSE 251
Port of loading 252

(a) In the event of the loading port being inaccessible by reason of 253
ice when vessel is ready to proceed from her last port or at any 254
time during the voyage or on vessel's arrival or in case frost sets in 255
after vessel's arrival, the Captain for fear of being frozen in is at 256
liberty to leave without cargo, and this Charter shall be null and 257
void. 258

(b) If during loading the Captain, for fear of vessel being frozen in, 259
deems it advisable to leave, he has liberty to do so with what cargo 260
he has on board and to proceed to any other port or ports with 261
option of completing cargo for Owners' benefit for any port or ports 262
including port of discharge. Any part cargo thus loaded under this 263
Charter to be forwarded to destination at vessel's expense but 264
against payment of freight, provided that no extra expenses be 265
thereby caused to the Receivers, freight being paid on quantity 266
delivered (in proportion if lumpsum), all other conditions as per 267
Charter. 268

(c) In case of more than one loading port, and if one or more of 269
the ports are closed by ice, the Captain or Owners to be at liberty 270
either to load the part cargo at the open port and fillup elsewhere 271
for their own account as under section (b) or to declare the Charter 272
null and void unless Charterers agree to load full cargo at the open 273
port. 274

(d) This Ice Clause not to apply in the Spring. 275

Port of discharge 276

(a) Should ice (except in the Spring) prevent vessel from reaching 277
port of discharge Receivers shall have the option of keeping vessel 278
waiting until the re-opening of navigation and paying demurrage, or 279
of ordering the vessel to a safe and immediately accessible port 280
where she can safely discharge without risk of detention by ice. 281
Such orders to be given within 48 hours after Captain or Owners 282
have given notice to Charterers of the impossibility of reaching port 283
of destination. 284

(b) If during discharging the Captain for fear of vessel being frozen 285
in deems it advisable to leave, he has liberty to do so with what 286
cargo he has on board and to proceed to the nearest accessible 287
port where she can safely discharge. 288

(c) On delivery of the cargo at such port, all conditions of the Bill 289
of Lading shall apply and vessel shall receive the same freight as 290
if she had discharged at the original port of destination, except that if 291
the distance of the substituted port exceeds 100 nautical miles, the 292
freight on the cargo delivered at the substituted port to be increased 293
in proportion. 294

Fig. 15.1 continued

When fixing a vessel on time charter, the shipowner should consider the trading limits, or the areas where the vessel will be trading, and also the type of trade in which the vessel will engage.

Many charters stipulate that the vessel shall trade within Institute Warranty Limits (i.e. the districts considered safe by the insurance authorities). (See p. 12.) If the vessel is to break these warranty limits the question of who is to pay the extra insurance must be decided. The owner must also consider what trade his vessel is to be employed in. For example, regular employment in the ore trade is likely to cause heavy wear and tear on the vessel; moreover, loading and discharging of ore is usually very quick and the vessel has little time in port in which to carry out maintenance on the engine.

The clauses that go to make up a time charter are rather different from those found in voyage charters by reason of the different nature of the trade. A number of clauses are common to both types of charter and in these cases nothing more need be added to what has already been said.

Further BIMCO approved charter, party, codename 'BOX-TIME', is illustrated in Fig. 15.2. It is used in the container trade for time charters and has 22 clauses with 844 lines, incorporating Part II featuring the terms of the charter party, and Part III the vessel specification.

15.3 APPROVED FORMS OF CHARTER PARTIES AND RELATED BILLS OF LADING

It will be appreciated that the terms and conditions of a charter party will vary according to the wishes of the parties to the contract. Nevertheless the Chamber of Shipping of the UK and/or the Baltic and International Maritime Conference (BIMCO) have approved or recommended a number of charter parties – about sixty – for certain commodities in specified trades. Most of these charter parties have been negotiated with organizations representative of charterers. Owners and charterers are recommended to use the printed texts but there is no power of sanction and amendments are made to suit the requirements of individual fixtures. A selection of the more popular forms is found in Table 15.1. Associated with the charter parties listed in Table 15.1 there exist a number of bills of lading with specific code names for use

1. Shipbroker	THE BALTIC AND INTERNATIONAL MARITIME COUNCIL (BIMCO) UNIFORM TIME CHARTER PARTY FOR CONTAINER VESSELS CODE NAME: "BOXTIME"
	PART I

		2. Place and Date	
3. Owners/Disponent Owners & Place of Business, Telephone, Telex and Telefax Number		4. Charterers & Place of Business, Telephone, Telex and Telefax Number	
5. Vessel's Name		6. Call Sign/Telex Number	
7. GRT/NRT	8. DWT on Summer Freeboard	9. TEU Capacity (Maximum)	
10. Class (Cl. 5)	11. Flag	12. Service Speed (See Part III)	13. Fuel Consumption (See Part III)
14. Type(s) of Fuel(s) (Cl. 12 (d))		15. Maximum Bunker Capacity	
16. Bunkers/Price on Delivery (Min.-Max.) (Cl. 12 (a) and (c))		17. Bunkers/Price on Redelivery (Min.-Max.) (Cl. 12 (a) and (c))	
18. Place of Delivery (Cl. 1 (b))		19. Earliest Date of Delivery (local time) (Cl. 1 (b))	
20. Latest Date of Delivery (local time) (Cl. 1 (b))		21. Place of Redelivery (Cl. 6 (m))	
22. Trading Limits (Cl. 3 and Cl. 5 (c))			
23. Period of Charter and Options if any (Cl. 1 (a), Cl. 6 (m) and Cl. 7 (f))		24. State number of Days Options have to be declared after commencement of Charter Period (Cl. 1 (a))	
25. Rate of Hire per Day and to whom payable (Cl. 1 (a), Cl. 7 (a) and (b))		26. Quantity of Hazardous Goods allowed (Cl. 4 (b))	
27. Insured Value of Vessel (Cl. 18 (a))		28. Daily Rate for Supercargo (Cl. 13 (h))	
		29. Victualling Rate per Meal for other Charterers' Servants etc. (Cl. 13 (j))	
30. Name of Owners' P & I Club (Cl. 18 (b))		31. Name of Charterers' P & I Club (Cl. 18 (b))	
32. Charterers' maximum Claim settlement authority (Cl. 16 (h))		33. General Average to be adjusted at (Cl. 14 (c))	
34. Law and Arbitration (state a, b, or c of Cl. 20, as agreed; if c agreed also state Place of Arbitration) (Cl. 20)		35. Brokerage Commission and to whom payable (Cl. 21)	
36. Number of Additional Clauses covering special Provisions			

It is mutually agreed between the party mentioned in Box 3 (hereinafter referred to as "the Owners") and the Party mentioned in Box 4 (hereinafter referred to as "the Charterers") that this Contract shall be performed in accordance with the conditions contained in Part I including additional clauses, if any agreed and stated in Box 36, and Part II as well as Part III. In the event of a conflict of conditions, the provisions of Part I and Part III shall prevail over those of Part II to the extent of such conflict but no further.

Signature (Owners)	Signature (Charterers)

Fig. 15.2 The 'BOXTIME' BIMCO Uniform Time Charter Party for Container Vessels. (Reproduced by kind permission of BIMCO.)

with such charter parties. Their use is purely optional and details of the bills of lading and sundry other forms are also given in Table 15.1 (pp. 350–56).

15.4 BALTIC AND INTERNATIONAL MARITIME COUNCIL

The Baltic and International Maritime Council (BIMCO) was formed in 1905 in Copenhagen and is a non-political, private and non-profit-making organization. In 1905 it had 102 owner members from ten countries with 1056 vessels. Ninety years later it has a membership of 2600 companies in 108 countries involving 950 shipowner members embracing a fleet of 360 million dwt. Some 1575 shipbrokers display the BIMCO crest. There are 60 club members including most leading P&I Clubs and 30 associate members including leading classification societies, specialized maritime lawyers, and other operators involved in shipping. It is based in Bagsvaerd, Denmark.

BIMCO is a global organization whose influence and diversity of maritime related activities continues to grow annually within its defined objectives. These include to unite shipowners and other companies and individuals involved in shipping; to take action on matters affecting shipping and to act as spokesperson for the industry; to inform members of instances of unfair charges and other restrictive practices; to provide advice in matters affecting the industry; and to develop charter parties and other shipping documents by means of friendly negotiations with the interested parties. BIMCO works closely with the IMO, UNCTAD and IACS. It is very active to promote the development throughout the industry – especially through the vehicle of IMO and BIMCO membership – of ship safety and prevention of pollution. Overall BIMCO is a market leader in the shipping industry with regard to the development of standard shipping documentation such as charter parties, bills of lading, waybills and various other commercial forms for worldwide use (see Table 15.1). Recent examples include the development of documentation for the offshore, chemical and ship management industries (see p. 356), the international wreck removal marine contract and the standard slot and boxtime charter party designed for the container trade (see Fig. 15.2).

Table 15.1 Examples of standard charter parties, associated bills of lading and other forms approved by Chamber of Shipping and/or BIMCO

Commodity	Description	Code name
Voyage charter parties		
Cement	Standard Voyage Charter Party for the Transportation of Bulk Cement Clinker in Bulk 'Cementvoy' Japanese Terms	CEMENTVOY —
Coal (including coke and patent fuel)	The Baltic and White Sea Conference Coal Charter 1921	BALTCON
	The Baltic and International Maritime Conference Coal Voyage Charter 1971 (Rev. 1976)	POLCOALVOY
	'Polcoalvoy' Slip-1990 Loading and Demurrage Scales	—
	'Polcoalvoy-ATC' Terms for Shipments of Coal to France (Rev. 1976) (Applicable as from 1 November 1988)	—
	'Polcoalvoy' Rider-1990 for use with the 'Polcoalvoy' Charter	
	The Baltic and International Maritime Conference German Coal Charter 1957 (Amended 1975)	GERMANCON-NORTH
	Soviet Coal Charter 1962 (Amended 1971, 1981 and 1987). For Coal, Coke and Coaltarpitch from the USSR (Layout 1971)	SOVCOAL
	'Sovcoal-ATIC' Terms for Shipments of Coal to France (Applicable as from 1 November 1988)	—
	The Japan Shipping Exchange, Inc., Coal Charter Party	NIPPONCOAL
	Americanized Welsh Coal Charter	AMWELSH 93
Fertilizers	Chamber of Shipping Fertilizers Charter 1942	FERTICON
	North American Fertilizer Charter Party 1978 (Amended 1988)	FERTIVOY 88
	Hydrocharter Voyage Charter Party (Amended 1975)	HYDROCHARTER
	Soviet Fertilizer Charter Party	FERTISOV
	Fertilizer Voyage Charter Party	QAFCOCHARTER

Gas	Gas Voyage Charter Party to be used for Liquid Gas except LNG	GASVOY
General	The Baltic and International Maritime Conference Uniform General Charter (As revised 1922, 1974 and 1976)	GENCON
	The Baltic and International Maritime Conference Uniform General Charter (Spanish Edition) (As revised 1922, 1974 and 1976)	GENCON
	The Baltic and International Maritime Conference Scandinavian Voyage Charter 1956 (Amended 1962 and 1993)	SCANCON
	Universal Voyage Charter Party 1984 (Revised Voyage Charter Party 1964) published by Polish Chamber of Foreign Trade, Gdynia	NUVOY 84
	The World Food Programme Voyage Charter Party	WORLDFOOD
Grain	Australian Wheat Charter 1990 (Amended 1991)	AUSTWHEAT 1990
	Continent Grain Charter Party	SYNACOMEX 90
	North American Grain Charterparty 1973, issued by the Association of Ship Brokers and Agents (USA) Inc.	NORGRAIN 89
	Grain Voyage Charter Party 1966 (Revised and Recommended 1974)	GRAINVOY
Ore	Soviet Ore Charter Party for Ores and Ore Concentrates from USSR Ports (Amended 1987)	SOVORECON
	Apatite Charter Party for Shipments of Apatite Ore and Apatite Concentrate from Murmansk (Amended 1987)	MURMAPATIT
	The Japan Shipping Exchange, Inc., Iron Ore Charter Party	NIPPONORE
	The Baltic and International Maritime Conference Standard Ore Charter Party	OREVOY
Stone	Chamber of Shipping Stone Charter Party, 1920	PANSTONE

Table 15.1 continued

Description	Code name
Bills of lading	
Combined Transport Bill of Lading 1971	COMBICONBILL
Uniform Bill of Lading Clauses 1946 (To be used when no Charter Party is signed)	CONBILL
Bill of Lading to be used with Charter-Parties (Edition 1978)	CONGENBILL
Liner Bill of Lading (Liner Terms approved by The Baltic and International Maritime Conference) (Edition 1978)	CONLINEBILL
Liner Bill of Lading (French Edition) (Edition 1978)	CONLINEBILL
Liner Bill of Lading (German Edition) (Edition 1978)	CONLINEBILL
Liner Bill of Lading (Spanish Edition) (Edition 1978)	CONLINEBILL
Liner Bill of Lading (Liner Terms approved by The Baltic and International Maritime Conference) to be used in Trades where Hague-Visby Rules are compulsory	VISCONBILL
Liner Bill of Lading (German Edition)	VISCONBILL
Liner Bill of Lading (Spanish Edition)	VISCONBILL
BIMCO Blank Back Form of Liner Bill of Lading	—
For Shipments on the 'Cementvoy' Charter	CEMENTVOYBILL
For Shipments on the 'Polcoalvoy' Charter (Edition 1985)	POLCOALBILL
For Shipments on the 'Germancon-North' Charter	GERMANCON-NORTH
For Shipments on the 'Sovcoal' Charter	SOVCOALBILL
For Shipments on the 'Hydrocharter': Norsk Hydro a.s. Bill of Lading	—
For Shipments on the 'Fertisov' Charter	FERTISOVBILL
For Shipments on the 'Qafcocharter'	QAFCOBILL
For Shipments on the 'Scancon' Charter (Edition 1993)	SCANCONBILL
For Shipments on the 'Novoy-84' Charter	NUVOYBILL-84
For Shipments on the 'Austwheat' Charter	AUSTWHEATBILL
For Shipments on the 'Norgrain' Charter Party: the North American Grain Bill of Lading Form	—

For Shipments on the 'Grainvoy' Charter	GRAINVOYBILL
For Shipments on the 'Sovrecon' Charter	SOVRECONBILL
For Shipments on the 'Murmapatit' Charter	MURMAPATITBILL
For Shipments on the 'Orevoy' Charter	OREVOYBILL
For Shipments on the Tanker Voyage Charter Party: the 'Intankbill 78' Bill of Lading	INTANKBILL 78
For Shipments on the 'Biscoilvoy' Charter	BISCOILVOYBILL
For Shipments on the 'Chemtankvoy' Charter	CHEMTANKVOYBILL
For Shipments on the 'Blackseawood' Charter	BLACKSEAWOODBILL
For Shipments on the 'Nubaltwood' Charter	NUBALTWOOD
For Shipments on the 'Sovconround' Charter	SOVCONROUNDBILL
For Shipments on the 'Heavycon' Contract	HEAVYCONBILL

Non-negotiable waybills/cargo receipts

BIMCO Blank Back Form of Non-Negotiable Liner Waybill	—
Non-negotiable General Sea Waybill for Use in Short-Sea Dry Cargo Trade	GENWAYBILL
International Association of Independent Tanker Owners Non-Negotiable Tanker Waybill	TANKWAYBILL 81
Non-negotiable Chemical Tank Waybill	CHEMTANKWAYBILL 85
Non-negotiable Gas Tank Waybill for Use in the LPG Trade	GASTANKWAYBILL
The World Food Programme Non-Negotiable Liner Waybill	WORLDFOODWAYBILL
Non-negotiable Cargo Receipt to be used with 'Worldfood' Charter	WORLDFOODRECEIPT
Non-negotiable Cargo Receipt to be used with 'Heavycon' Contract	HEAVYCONRECEIPT

Sundry other forms

Standard Statement of Facts (Short Form)	—
Standard Statement of Facts (Long Form)	—
Standard Time Sheet (Short Form)	—
Standard Time Sheet (Long Form)	—
Standard Statement of Facts (Oil and Chemical Tank Vessels) (Short Form)	—
Standard Statement of Facts (Oil and Chemical Tank Vessels) (Long Form)	—
Standard Disbursements Account	—

Table 15.1 continued

Commodity	Description	Code name
Tank	International Association of Independent Tanker Owners Tanker Voyage Charter Party	TANKERVOY 87
	International Association of Independent Tanker Owners Tanker Consecutive Voyage Clauses	INTERCONSEC 76
	The Baltic and International Maritime Council Standard Voyage Charter Party for Vegetable/Animal Oils and Fats	BISCOILVOY 86
	Standard Voyage Charter Party for the Transportation of Chemicals in Tank Vessels	CHEMTANKVOY
	International Association of Independent Tanker Owners Tanker Contract of Affreightment	INTERCOA 80
Wood (including pitwood, props, pulpwood, roundwood and logs)	Black Sea Timber Charter Party for Timber from USSR and Romanian Black Sea and Danube Ports	BLACKSEAWOOD
	Chamber of Shipping Baltic Wood Charter Party 1973	NUBALTWOOD
	Soviet Wood Charter Party 1961	SOVIETWOOD
	'Sovietwood' Temporary Metrication Clause, 1970	—
	The Baltic and International Maritime Conference Soviet Roundwood Charter Party for Pulpwood, Pitwood, Roundwood and Logs from Baltic and White Sea Ports of the USSR	SOVCONROUND
	The Japan Shipping Exchange, Inc., Charter Party for Logs 1967	NANYOZAI 1967

Description	Code name
Time Charter Parties	
The Baltic and International Maritime Conference Uniform Time-Charter (Box Layout 1974)	BALTIME 1939
The Baltic and International Maritime Conference Uniform Time-Charter (Traditional Layout)	BALTIME 1939
The Baltic and International Maritime Conference Uniform Time-Charter (French Edition)	BALTIME 1939
The Baltic and International Maritime Conference Uniform Time-Charter (Italian Edition)	BALTIME 1939
The Baltic and International Maritime Conference Uniform Time-Charter (Spanish Edition)	BALTIME 1939
The Baltic and International Maritime Conference Deep Sea Time Charter (Box Layout 1974)	LINERTIME
Uniform Time Charter Party for Offshore Service Vessels	SUPPLYTIME 89
Uniform Time Charter Party for Container Vessels	BOXTIME
The Baltic and International Maritime Conference Uniform Time Charter Party for Vessels Carrying Liquified Gas	GASTIME
International Association of Independent Tanker Owners Tanker Time Charter Party	INTERTANKTIME 80
The Baltic and International Maritime Conference Uniform Time Charter Party for Vessels Carrying Chemicals in Bulk	BIMCHEMTIME
New York Produce Exchange Time Charter	NYPE 93
Bareboat charters	
The Baltic and International Maritime Council Standard Bareboat Charter	BARECON 89
'Barecon 89' Japanese Terms	—

Table 15.1 continued

Description	Code name
Liner Booking Note to be used with 'Conlinebill' Liner Bill of Lading	CONLINEBOOKING
Liner Booking Note to be used with 'Visconbill' Liner Bill of Lading	VISCONBOOKING
BIMCO Blank Form of Liner Booking Note	
Voyage Charterparty Laytime Interpretation Rules 1993	VOYLAYRULES 93
The Baltic and International Maritime Conference Dangerous Goods Declaration	—
The Baltic and International Maritime Conference Dangerous Container/Trailer Packing Certificate	—
Memorandum of Agreement (Revised 1983 and 1986)	SALEFORM 1987
Recommended Standard Bil of Sale	BIMCOSALE
Standard Contract for the Sale of Vessels for Demolition 'Salescrap 87' Japanese Terms	SALESCRAP 87
International Association of Independent Tanker Owners Tanker Contract of Affreightment, Code Name: 'INTERCOA 80' see 35-0	—
Standard Volume Contract of Affreightment for the Transportation of Bulk Dry Cargoes 'Volcoa' Japanese Terms	VOLCOA
Combined Transport Document (Edition July 1st, 1977) Issued Subject to ICC Rules	COMBIDOC
Combined Transport Document (Edition July 1st, 1977) (French Edition)	COMBIDOC
International Ocean Towage Agreement (Daily Hire)	TOWHIRE
International Ocean Towage Agreement (Lump Sum)	TOWCON
The Baltic and International Maritime Council Standard Transportation Contract for Heavy and Voluminous Cargoes	HEAVYCON
Standard Ship Management Agreement	SHIPMAN
Standard Slot Charter Party	SLOTHIRE
International Wreck Removal and Marine Services Agreement (Daily Hire)	WRECKHIRE
International Wreck Removal and Marine Services Agreement (Lump Sum)	WRECKCON
FONASBA General Agency Agreement (for Liner Services)	—
FONASBA Standard Liner Agency Agreement	—

Finally, BIMCO has a comprehensive computer database covering port costs, information on the labour situation in ports, working hours at seaports, draft limitations in ports, freight taxes, and the interpretation of charter party clauses.

Overall BIMCO's port database and information service is widely used together with guidance on the interpretation and use of BIMCO chartering and related documentation. BIMCO produces news bulletins, shipping news and reports on port conditions, bunkers, markets, ice conditions and third-party databases.

15.5 VOYAGE ESTIMATES

The aim of a voyage estimate is simply to provide the shipowner (or charterer) with an estimate of the probable financial return that can be expected from a prospective voyage. Provided with this information, the owner will be able to compare several possible alternatives and decide upon the most profitable and suitable venture. Although every estimator should aim to be as accurate as is reasonably possible, in modern shipbroking it will inevitably be found that time often does not permit a series of detailed estimates to be undertaken for each and every 'open' vessel. In practice, a 'rough' estimate is usually performed for each alternative, and only when two or three desirable voyages are thus identified does the more 'exact' estimating become necessary, along with the results of which must be borne in mind the owner's preferred direction of voyage, etc.

Needless to say, the final objective is for the estimate to compare favourably with the eventual voyage result, and normally reasonable comparisons can be made with experience of both the vessel and her trade, despite the vagaries of wind and tide, and, of course, the usual quota of man-made difficulties.

Voyage estimating is, however, an art, and an estimator – in order to succeed at his task – should aim to understand all the many complexities of ship operating and trading, together with the various methods of chartering and analysing voyage returns, in order to perform his duties efficiently. An example is given below.

MV *Trader*
Open Seville
26 500 tonnes summer deadweight
15 knots (about) on 32 tonnes per day if IF C/S fuel oil and 11½
tonnes marine diesel oil at sea. 1½ tonnes MDO in port.
Running costs: US $4000 per day.

Cargo estimate: Sailing Philadelphia

Summer deadweight		26 500 tonnes
less		
1. Bunkers ROB	1000	
2. Constant weights	500	1 500
	Estimated cargo:	25 000 tonnes

MV Trader
Full cargo grain – Philadelphia/Bremen – US $16.50 per tonne –
Fiot – 4 days L/5000 MT D – per WWDAY – Shex Bends – 2.5%
A/C Chartcon – vessel open Seville

Freight (less commissions)
25 000 metric tonnes at $16.50 = $412 500
less 2.5% commission = $402 187 net freight

Days		Ports	Disbursements		
					Agency fees Despatch
			Port		
Steaming	Lay		charges	Cargo	Sundries
9		Seville/Philadelphia			
	6	Philadelphia	$20 000	$–	$1500
11		Philadelphia/Bremen	$15 000	$–	$1500
—	7	Bremen			
20	13				

Fuel consumption:

At sea: 20 days at 32 tonnes p d	=	640 tonnes	F/O
In port: 13 days at – tonnes p d		– tonnes	F/O
		640 tonnes	

At sea: 20 days at 1.5 tonnes p d   =   30 tonnes D/O
In port: 13 days at 1.5 tonnes p d   =   20 tonnes D/O

                                50 tonnes

Bunker oil:
On board: 640 tonnes F/O at \$135 = \$86 400
              50 tonnes D/O at \$215 = \$10 750

Total bunker cost:	\$ 97 150
plus voyage expenses:	\$ 38 000
Total voyage expenses:	\$135 150

Net freight	\$402 187
less	
Total voyage expenses	\$135 150
Gross profit	\$267 037

Gross profit: \$267 037 ÷ 33 days voyage duration = gross daily profit \$8092
Gross daily profit: \$8092 less daily running cost \$4000 per day = \$4092 net daily profit

An example of a time sheet and a statement of facts are given in Figs 15.3 and 15.4, based on the following charter party terms.

1. Discharge rate, 5000 metre tonnes per weather working day of 24 consecutive hours.
2. Sundays and holidays excepted, unless used, when half time actually used in excepted period to count as laytime.
3. Notice of readiness to be tendered in office hours Monday/Friday 0900/1700 h.
4. Time to count from first working period on first working day following acceptance of notice of readiness to discharge.
5. Time not to count between midnight Friday (or day preceding a holiday) until commencement of first working period Monday (or day following a holiday).
6. Despatch on working time saved.

The time sheet and laytime calculations are based on the MV *Trader* voyage estimate for discharge at Bremen.

1. Agents	STANDARD TIME SHEET (SHORT FORM)
Johan Smitzen Bremen	RECOMMENDED BY THE BALTIC AND INTERNATIONAL MARITIME CONFERENCE (BIMCO) AND THE FEDERATION OF NATIONAL ASSOCIATIONS OF SHIP BROKERS AND AGENTS (FONASBA)

2. Vessel's name	3. Port
m.v. Trader	Bremen

4. Owners Disponent Owners	5. Vessel berthed
Trader Shipping Enterprises Monrovia	Thursday 14th June 0600 hrs

8. Cargo	6. Loading commenced	7. Loading completed
	–	–

	9. Discharging commenced	10. Discharging completed
25000 Mtons Grain	14 June 1300	22 June 1000

	11. Cargo documents on board	12. Vessel sailed
	–	22 June 1210

13. Charter Party *	14. Working hours meal hours of the port *
Norgrain 1st May 19	0800/1200 ⎫

15. Bill of Lading weight/quantity	16. Outturn weight/quantity	1300/1700 ⎬ Monday/Friday
25000 MT	24995 MT	1800/2200 ⎭

17. Vessel arrived on roads	18. Time to count from 1st Working Period next
13 June 17.00 (Weser Pilot)	working day following acceptance Nor

19. Notice of readiness tendered	20. Rate of demurrage	21. Rate of despatch money
14 June 0900	£ 5000 pd.	£ 2500 pd.

22. Next tide available	23.
13 June 2330	

24. Laytime allowed for loading	25. Laytime allowed for discharging	26.
	5 WW Days	

LAYTIME COMPUTATION *

Date	Day	Time worked		Laytime used			Time saved on demurrage			Remarks *
		From	to	days	hours	minutes	days	hours	minutes	
14 June	Thursday	–	–	–	–	–				(NOR tendered and (accepted 0900 hrs
15	Friday				16					Laytime commenced 0800 hrs
16	Saturday	0800	1200		2					Overtime
17	Sunday									Holiday
18	Monday				16					Laytime recommenced 0800 hrs
19	Tuesday	1300	1500	–	2					(Rain 0300/1300
				–	1	30				(" 1500/2230
20	Wednesday			1	0	0				
21	Thursday			1	0	0				
22	Friday				10					Completed discharge
							1	0	30	1000 hrs
				3	23	30	1	0	30	

General remarks *

Place and date	Signature *
Bremen 23/6/-	

Signature *	Signature *

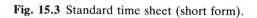

* See Explanatory Notes overleaf for filling in the boxes

Fig. 15.3 Standard time sheet (short form).

1. Agents		
Johan Smitzen		

2. Vessel's name	3. Port	
m.v. Trader	Bremen	

4. Owners Disponent Owners	5. Vessel berthed	
Trader Shipping Enterprises Monrovia	Thursday 14th June 0600 hrs	
	6. Loading commenced —	7. Loading completed —

8. Cargo	9. Discharging commenced 14/6/- 1300	10. Discharging completed 22/6/- 1000
25000 Mtons grain	11. Cargo documents on board —	12. Vessel sailed 22/6/- 1210

13. Charter Party*	14. Working hours meal hours of the port*
Norgrain 1st May 19	0800/1200)

15. Bill of Lading weight quantity	16. Outturn weight quantity	1300/1700) Monday/Friday
25000 MT	24995 MT	1800/2200)

17. Vessel arrived on roads	18.
13 June 1700 (Weser Pilot)	

19. Notice of readiness tendered	20.
14 June 0900	

21. Next tide available	22.
13 June 2330	

DETAILS OF DAILY WORKING*

Date	Day	Hours worked From	to	Hours stopped From	to	No. of gangs	Quantity load disch	Remarks*
14 June	Thursday	1300	1700	1700	1800	Two	1800 MT	Commenced
		1800	2200	2200	2400	Two	1698	discharge
15 June	Friday			0001	0800			
		0800	1200	1300	1300	Two	1727	
		1300	1700	1700	1800	Two	1715	
		1800	2200	2200	2400	Two	1720	
16 June	Saturday			0001	0800			
		0800	1200	1200	2400	Two	1637	Overtime
17 June	Sunday			0001	2400			
18 June	Monday			0001	0800			
		0800	1200	1200	1300	Two	1401	
		1300	1700	1700	1800	Two	1224	
		1800	2200	2200	2400	Two	1330	
19 June	Tuesday			0001	1300		)	Rain
		1300	1500	1500	2400	Two	601)	
20 June	Wednesday			0001	0800			
		0800	1200	1200	1300	Two	1426	
		1300	1700	1700	1800	Two	1630	
		1800	2200	2200	2400	Two	1558	
21 June	Thursday			0001	0800			
		0800	1200	1200	1300	Two	1550	
		1300	1700	1700		Two	1597	
		1800	2200	2200	2400	Two	1525	
22 June	Friday			0001	0800			
		0800	1000			Two	856	Completed discharge

General remarks*

24995 MT

Place and date	Name and signature (Master)*
Bremen 23/6/-	
Name and signature Agents.*	Name and signature (for the Charterers Shippers Receivers)*

Fig. 15.4 Standard statement of facts (short form).

Laytime calculation:

Laytime allowed	5 days	0 h	0 min
Laytime used	3 days	23 h	30 min
Laytime saved	1 day	0 h	30 min

1 day 0 h 30 min = 1.02 days
1.02 days at $2500 per day = $2550 despatch money

15.6 SALE AND PURCHASE OF SHIPS

The sale and purchase of vessels is a very specialized activity and is undertaken by a sale and purchase broker. He normally acts either for the buyer or seller of a ship, and occasionally acts between buyer's broker and seller's broker, each of which may be situated in different countries dealing with a foreign ship. The market is international and the ship may be sold for scrap or operational purposes. In the latter case the new owner must change the ship's name and usually is forbidden to operate in trades competitive to her former owner.

Details are given below of the information circulated of a possible ship sale:

(a) Classification society.

(b) Ship's deadweight, dimensions and draught; year of build, place, shipbuilder; cubic capacities, deck arrangements, water ballast capacities, number of holds and hatches; machinery details and builders, horse power, speed and consumption; bunker capacity, special and classification survey position.

(c) The purpose-built tonnage details of special facilities, i.e. refrigeration plant, tanker capacity, container capacity, passenger accommodation, derricks, car decks, etc.

(d) Light displacement including propeller details, i.e. bronze or iron, and if spare tail shaft on board. Such data only given in event of ship being sold as scrap.

(e) Ship price and position for inspection and delivery.

The brokers' function is not to express an opinion of the vessel's condition, unless there exists a serious defect, but to leave this assessment to the buyer's superintendent or consulting surveyor. On this aspect the ship classification records are critical. The ship inspection may take place prior to sale negotiations commencing, or be a condition of the sale offer. A dry dock inspection is usually not necessary. However, if conducted, it is the seller's responsibility and cost to bring the vessel to the dry dock and subsequently from the dry dock to the berth or place of delivery. The buyer bears the expense of putting in and taking out of dry dock the vessel plus the dry dock dues. The seller, however, would meet this expense if the rudder, propeller, bottom, or other underwater part(s) or tailend shaft were defective.

The buyer will make his offer for delivery at a specified port or time, with the option to cancel if the vessel is not delivered by the latest specified date. Moreover, the vessel's classification must not lapse. Additional payment to the seller is involved on delivery for on-board ship stores and bunkers. The vessel's trading certificates must be valid at the time of delivery.

On conclusion of the haggling over the price and conditions of sale, the seller's broker draws up a memorandum of agreement, which operates under the code name 'Saleform 1993'. A specimen is given in Fig. 15.5 which contains 16 clauses ranging from the price to arbitration and involving 283 lines, as well as provision for an appendix.

The occasion of a ship sale for scrap is a simpler procedure carried out by the execution and delivery of a bill of sale under seal, a specimen of which is given in Fig. 15.6. The bill of sale is handed over against a letter releasing the deposit and a banker's draft for the balance of the price. Payment, if any, for bunkers and stores is dealt with at the same time.

The broker arranges to have provided for the vessel sold for operational purposes the following documents which must be attached to any insurance cover and handed over at the time of delivery:

   (i) Certificate of registry.
  (ii) Load line certificate.
 (iii) Factories Act book.
 (iv) Deratting certificate.
  (v) Safety construction certificate.
 (vi) Safety radio certificate.
(vii) Safety equipment certificate.
(viii) Classification certificates.

MEMORANDUM OF AGREEMENT

Norwegian Shipbrokers' Association's Memo-
randum of Agreement for sale and purchase of
ships. Adopted by The Baltic and International
Maritime Council (BIMCO) in 1956.
Code-name
SALEFORM 1993
Revised 1966, 1983 and 1986/87.

Dated:

hereinafter called the Sellers, have agreed to sell, and	1
hereinafter called the Buyers, have agreed to buy	2
Name:	3
Classification Society/Class:	4
Built: By:	5
Flag: Place of Registration:	6
Call Sign: Grt/Nrt:	7
Register Number:	8
hereinafter called the Vessel, on the following terms and conditions:	9

Definitions   10

"Banking days" are days on which banks are open both in the country of the currency   11
stipulated for the Purchase Price in Clause 1 and in the place of closing stipulated in Clause 8.   12

"In writing" or "written" means a letter handed over from the Sellers to the Buyers or vice versa,   13
a registered letter, telex, telefax or other modern form of written communication.   14

"Classification Society" or "Class" means the Society referred to in line 4.   15

1.   Purchase Price   16

2.   Deposit   17

As security for the correct fulfilment of this Agreement the Buyers shall pay a deposit of 10 %   18
(ten per cent) of the Purchase Price within   banking days from the date of this   19
Agreement. This deposit shall be placed with   20

and held by them in a joint account for the Sellers and the Buyers, to be released in accordance   21
with joint written instructions of the Sellers and the Buyers. Interest, if any, to be credited to the   22
Buyers. Any fee charged for holding the said deposit shall be borne equally by the Sellers and the   23
Buyers.   24

3.   Payment   25

The said Purchase Price shall be paid in full free of bank charges to   26

on delivery of the Vessel, but not later than 3 banking days after the Vessel is in every respect   27
physically ready for delivery in accordance with the terms and conditions of this Agreement and   28
Notice of Readiness has been given in accordance with Clause 5.   29

Fig. 15.5 'Saleform 1993' memorandum of agreement of sale (first page only). (Reproduced by kind permission of the Norwegian Shipbrokers' Association.)

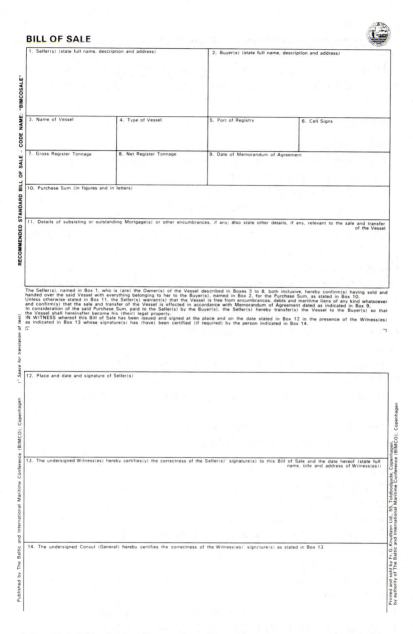

Fig. 15.6 Bill of sale. (Reproduced by kind permission of BIMCO.)

(ix) Plans.
(x) Passenger certificate – if applicable.

In the event of the broker requiring to register the vessel in the new owner's name, he presents the following documents to the registrar:

(a) Bill of sale.
(b) Declaration of ownership.
(c) Appointment of managing owner or ship's husband.
(d) Articles of association.
(e) Certificates of incorporation.
(f) Appointment of public officer.

The latter three items are only presented if the buyer has not previously owned a ship. With regard to foreign buyers, usually the bill of sale must be signed before a notary public and bear the visa of the buyer's consul. The Certificate of British Registry is returned to the registrar at the port of registry. The foreign buyer for his own registration purposes will require a transcript of the cancelled British registry available from the registrar after the ship sale.

Frequently vessels are sold under extended terms of payment in which case a security for the unpaid portion of the purchase price is through a banker's guarantee, otherwise a mortgage has to be given.

Details of vessels available for sale are recorded in the shipping press and examples are given below.

EWL Suriname – container
8020 MTDW on 6.581 m
Built 1982 Rickmers
Classed GL ice strengthened
127.67 m LOA 117.23 m LBP 20.1 m beam
2 decks 2 holds 2 hatches
10060 grain 10010 bale
582 TEU 50 reefer
CR: 2 × 35T
1 × Deutz Koeln RSBV12M540 6000 BHP 1 thruster
15.5K on 23.5 DO (80.5 CAP.) HV (599.5 CAP.)
DM 15 million

Port au Prince – tanker
38549 MTDW on 9.722 m
Built 1979 Imabari Marugame
Classed LR SSH + CSM due 5/99 last DD 5/94
184.16 m LOA 172.02 m LBP 30.05 m beam
12 tanks 43200 oil
Pumps 2/3000 M3 HR centrifugal 2 × stripping
MHI/Sulzer 6RND76 12000 BHP
13.75K on 30 TS FO + 1.2 DO
Zinc silicate coating/uncoiled
NO IGS/NOW COW
Owners have no official price ideas but are asking for outright offers in line with the market

Evangelia T – bulkcarrier
66289 MTDW on 13.691 m
Built 1974 Hakodate Hakodate
Classed NV SS 3/97 DD passed 8/94
219.08 m LOA 208.01 m LBP 32.29 m beam
1 deck 7 holds 7 hatches McGregor covers
63004 grain
CR: 4 × 15T
IHI/Sulzer 6RND90 17400 BHP
13 K ON 38 TS 180
Try USD 6 million
(Details without guarantee)

CHAPTER 16

Containerization

Containerization is a method of distributing merchandise in a unitized form thereby permitting an intermodal transport system to be developed providing a possible combination of rail, road, canal and maritime transport. The system is long established and was in being at the turn of the century in a somewhat less sophisticated form. It came more into use in the North American coastal trade in the 1930s when the vessels were called Van ships. Today we have seen the evolution of the fourth generation of container ships as the benefits of containerization become more attractive on a worldwide scale thereby aiding rising living standards and facilitating trade expansion.

16.1 CONTAINER SHIPS – TERMINALS – TRADES

Examples of modern container ships are found in Figs 3.3 (p. 41) and 4.1 (p. 51). Both such vessels have been designed with flexibility of operation as paramount. There does exist, especially with the larger tonnage, the cellular vessel. Each hold is fitted with a series of vertical angle guides adequately cross braced to accept the container. Such holds are completely dedicated to either the 20- or 40-ft container and ensures that each succeeding container in a stack rests securely on the weight-bearing corner castings of the one below. The guides also facilitate discharging and loading by guiding spreader frames of container cranes onto the corner castings of containers without any need for the crane driver to make any fine adjustments to line up the lifting frame. Many of the non-cellular type ships are conversions and operate as feeder services. The modern cellular vessel found in the deep-sea trades is free of open deck obstructions – including derricks – to facilitate unimpeded container handling.

Third generation cellular tonnage which emerged in the late 1970s has 3000 TEUs capacity with a draught of 18.30 m. The fourth generation of container vessels encourages greater rationalization in ports of call and relies on smaller container tonnage or surface (rail) transport to act as distributors/feeders. An example is the fleet of nine Maersk vessels of 4700 TEUs capacity and speed of 27 knots which operate a round-the-world container service. It has resulted in high capacity berths to cater for such tonnage, more pre-planning of port operation, rationalization of ports of call and greater reliance of feeder service by sea and overland. Such tonnage reduces the unit cost of container shipment.

The P & O container fleet consist of 46 vessels of which 18 ships are 'chartered in'. The speed range is 18–23 knots and capacity range 445–4038 TEUs. The Maersk Line container ships total 45 and have a deadweight tonnage ranging from 20 350 to 60 340. The Maersk Line operates services Europe–Middle East/Far East, Europe–South America and Caribbean, Europe–West/East Africa, and Inter-European.

The Taiwan-based shipping company Evergreen has a fleet of 51 container ships with a service speed range 14–21 knots and a capacity range 510–3428 TEUs. The company trades in West Mediterranean/US East Coast and Canada, the Far East/ Mediterranean, Japan/Pacific North West Coast, Taiwan/Hong Kong/US West Coast and east- and westbound round-the-world services which are both routed through the Panama Canal.

The eastbound round-the-world service conveys cargoes on the following routes: Japan and Korea to California; the Far East to the Caribbean, Central America and US East Coast, Central America, the Caribbean and the US East Coast to North Europe and North Europe to the Far East. Overall it is a very comprehensive shipping system with four service routes linking exporters and importers in Asia, Europe and America. The vessels are of the 'G type' with a 2728 TEU capacity and service speed of 20 knots. The round-the-world eastbound services rely on a feeder network of container ships based in the major ports and the nearby regional markets thereby exploiting the hub and spoke system. Overall there are 21 major ports served and each has a seven-day sailing frequency.

The westbound round-the-world Evergreen container service consists of four separate route sectors: the Far East to North Europe, North Europe to the US East Coast, the Caribbean,

Central America and California; the US East Coast, the Caribbean and Central America to the Far East, and California to Japan and Korea. The westbound round-the-world service has the same features as the eastbound route involving major ports relying on feeder services. Overall 19 ports are served with a six-day sailing service. The 'GX type' vessels have a service speed of 20 knots and TEU capacity of 3428.

The organization necessary to feed/distribute vessels of 2000/3000 TEUs at a specialized berth requires much pre-planning. Computers are provided to assist in the container control/distribution task. Rail has become more prominent in many countries in the feeder/distribution arrangements serving the container berth, especially in western Europe, the USA and the trans-Siberian rail link.

Container berths are either purpose-built for exclusive container use, or multi-purpose in which container and other types of cargo vessels are handled. The purpose-built container berth is usually the more efficient and produces the most productive container throughput. The most modern would be computer-operated and handle double stack container trains. Basically there are three methods of container handling detailed as follows:

(a) Quay portainer crane working in association with van carriers.
(b) Quay portainer crane working in association with tractor/trailer operation.
(c) Quay portainer crane working in conjunction with tractor/trailer operation and container stacking cranes – the latter situated often some distance from the actual berth area.

The actual quay portainer crane may be of the type with long outreach over the water and a short landward reach behind or with long outreach over both water and quay. The latter is the more favoured type as it permits a stowage for containers under the crane structure. All the foregoing three methods involve the import landed container being moved away from the crane by van carrier/tractor and trailer to a container stacking area.

With increasing emphasis being given to quicker port turn-round times, the most modern system uses a 336-ft long gantry crane which moves containers overhead to and from the berthed vessel instead of using the traditional straddle carrier. A notable saving is in the straddle carriers. The 500-tonne capacity gantry crane can handle five containers at a time. It functions like a huge cartridge and is fed continuously by rubber-tyred yard cranes. This transfer device enables both the shipside crane and the yard gantry to operate simultaneously but independently with an obvious saving in work time. Computerization plays an important part in the operation, controlling the delivery and pick-up of containers from the truckers as well as the movement and positioning of all containers in the terminal.

The container is then processed through customs clearance unless it is destined for an inland clearance depot in which case the container under bond is transferred to a rail or road vehicle for despatch. In the case of the locally cleared containers it may be despatched by road or rail to importers' premises/inland situated container base/or simply discharged locally through the port/berth container base. The process is reversed with exported containers. Straddle carriers are used extensively to move containers within the berth area.

Examples of modern container berths are found in the Port of Singapore. The container berth at Pasir Panjang is designed to handle mother container ships of 4000/5000 TEUs and feeder tonnage of 1000/1500 TEUS. At the Brani terminal in Singapore the equipment is linked to the Computer Integrated Terminal Operations System (CITOS). The quay cranes have full digital drive systems to achieve consistent performance and have container number recognition systems (CNRS). Up to five quay cranes are available to be assigned to a vessel. The chassis positioning system speeds up the loading of containers in the prime mover's chassis. The container number recognition system automatically tracks and verifies all containers handled at the berth. The rubber-tyred container yard cranes can stack containers up to eight across and up to six high. Hence, the container stacking capacity per slot is substantially increased. To complement the high-tech service-oriented operations at Brani, the yard cranes are equipped with the Automatic Travel Control System (ATCS) and the Automatic Positioning Indication System (APIS) to allow auto-tracking of all container movements. The terminal is also equipped with double-stack trailers for terminal operations. Each trailer can handle four 20-ft or two 40-ft loaded containers which is double the ordinary trailer capacity. A number of multi double-stack trailers are also available which have twice the capacity of the double-stack trailers.

The container berth varies greatly in size. Much depends on the anticipated annual throughput and vessel capacity. It can vary from 5 ha to 8 ha for the second generation cellular ship, to one of up to 30 hectares with the fourth generation vessel. Stacking of containers in excess of three high is rarely exceeded as it creates many problems. Two high is usually the most common.

A typical terminal would be 8.5 ha designed to handle 3000 containers on and off ship within 72 hours. Stacking area would be of 1800 general cargo and 400 insulated containers – the latter being housed in a specially cladded stack connected to a refrigerated plant. This area is much increased where double stack container trains serve the container berth as found in most major ports of the east and west coast of North America.

The loading of containers on board the vessel can create many problems particularly when a number of different container lengths and port destinations are involved. The vessel has to be properly trimmed by the stern and the loading plan must take into account dangerous cargo and those containers requiring special attention, e.g. an open container with a commercial vehicle in excess of the accepted container height and so requiring to be stowed on the upper or open deck. The formulation of the stowage plan is usually done on the computer.

Container ships usually carry substantial quantities of such cargo on the open deck where special equipment/fittings are provided. Stacking up to five high on open deck is quite common. Such a practice of open-deck container shipments enhances the productivity of such ships and is particularly ideal for distributing empty containers caused through imbalanced working.

The third generation of container ships are stowed nine high and ten rows across below decks. The fourth generation has produced a new design philosophy. The Econ class formerly intended for US lines has a maximum capacity of 4258 TEUs within the Panamax dimensions involving 32.2 m beam and overall length of nearly 300 m which reflected the earlier design. The new Nedlloyd container tonnage termed the Ultimate Container Carrier (UCC) of 266 m length and beam of 32.3 m has a capacity of 3100 TEUs. Emphasis in ship design has been placed on optimizing the voyage performance. Accordingly the holds have a capacity of 149 containers compared with the earlier tonnage of 124 containers. This involves the containers being stowed on deck in 13 rather than ten rows across. The containers are stowed four high and the holds are 100 feet to accommodate the high cube containers of 45 or 49 feet in length. A feature of the UCC is a quicker and easier system for the stowing, loading and unloading of containers which is critical to the need to minimize layover time in port. Welded into the ship's hull, the cell guides rise in vertical columns from the bottom of the hold to a height above deck equal to four standard containers stacked one on top of the other. This means that once slotted into the cell guide the container becomes securely locked into position with no risk of it shifting or falling overboard.

The time spent in loading and discharging containers varies by port and circumstances. In very broad terms, one can attain 25/30 containers per hour for discharging cargo, whilst for cargo exports the figure falls to 20/25 per hour per crane of single container capacity. Many ports now have cranes of two-container capacity with much improved loading/discharging rates.

A modern container berth handling third generation container ships with 7/8 vessels per month is likely to handle 22 000–26 000 containers. This is more than seven times a conventional berth handling capacity.

Container trades have emerged significantly during the late 1960s/early 1970s in all parts of the world.

Details of some container routes are given below:

(a) The Australia/New Zealand – Europe Container Service (ANZECS) is a consortium of British, continental and New Zealand conference lines operating integrated services between Europe and Australia/New Zealand maintained by a fleet of 16 container ships.

(b) BEACON (British and European Shipping Lines Joint Container Service) provides regular services between Europe and the Red Sea and East Africa and Mauritius.

(c) COBRA is a group of British and continental lines operating container ships serving ports in India, Pakistan and Sri Lanka.

(d) Trans Freight Lines is a leading Atlantic carrier operating a modern fleet of vessels between Europe and North America.

(e) SAECS Southern Africa Europe Container Services offers container and Ro/Ro services between UK/North Continent and South Africa.

(f) The Far Eastern Freight conference contains the TRIO Group which is a consortium of British, German and Japanese lines operating a fleet of 21 container ships on the Europe/Far East route.

Examples of transit times from Felixstowe/Southampton/Tilbury involving P&O Containers vessels are given below:

Far East and Jeddah	Jeddah 8 days; Busan 27 days; Yokohama 31 days; Singapore 19 days; Kaohsiung 25 days; Kobe 29 days.
Australia and New Zealand	Adelaide 34 days; Sydney 39 days; Melbourne 36 days; Auckland 44 days; Wellington 47 days.
North America and Carribbean	Long Beach 23 days; Houston 13 days; Port Everglades 10 days; Charleston 9 days; New York 11 days; Boston 9 days.
Middle East, Gulf, South Asia, Bay of Bengal	Bombay 21 days; Madras 20 days; Cochin 27 days; Colombo 25 days; Dubai 14 days.

A significant feature of containerization involving the 'through-transport system concept' is the growing use of computers. With the use of data transmission systems often backed up by satellites, it is now possible to provide an instantaneous communications link between a number of container terminals and the ships on the high seas. Complete bills of lading, stowage plans and container terminal layouts may be quickly processed and transmitted, transforming a slow and laborious job into a moment's work on a computer keyboard.

A number of companies, such as Sea Containers, lease containers to shippers. It is a computer-operated/managed system and when on hire features details of the client, the date unit will be off hire, container 'depot out' and container 'depot in' dates, the billing and interchange arrangements. The computer also logs whether containers are available for immediate leasing, any damaged containers, if damaged to what extent and who is responsible, and billing for repair. Basically, when the container leaves the depot, control of the container is transferred to the lessee. All new Sea Container units are fitted with a recess so that a tag can be fitted for automatic container control.

A major development in the 1990s, is the rapid growth of the double-stack container train. This is especially significant in North

America and Australia. It has resulted in a rationalization of ports of call by container tonnage. A modern double-stack container train of nearly one mile length is capable of conveying 820 TEUs. The double-stack container trains which are completely integrated with specific container shipping line sailings are called mini land bridges and journey overland in North America distances of between 2000 and 3000 miles. The trains convey 6.10 m or 12.20 m containers of 2.4 m width and 2.6 m height. The wagons are 60 or 80 ft long.

In the early 1990s modernization plans were completed to provide ten new waterfront rail transfer facilities for double-stack operations at the West Coast ports of Long Beach and Los Angeles. This is resulting in a recession of some US East Coast ports, particularly those in the Mexican Gulf. Shipping lines hitherto calling at these ports are now discharging containers in the US West Coast and sending the consignments on to the US South and Gulf destinations by rail.

An example is the Japan Line which has discontinued calling at all US East Coast ports and has inaugurated a pure inter-modal rail connection into US East Coast port destinations from the US West Coast. Four main West Coast ports – Los Angeles, San Francisco, Seattle and Vancouver – serve as gateways for import entries while US exports move through the same ports plus Portland. This has enabled a rationalization of the Japanese flag container fleet resulting in more productive use of container tonnage and further development of the next generation of container ships exploiting the economies of scale and further crew reductions attained through new technology. Other maritime lines serving the USA and European seaboards are in the process of doing likewise as the economic benefits of the double-stack container movement offering lower overland distribution cost, and rationalization of ports of call by container operators are realized. By 1995 over 200 double-stack container trains per week were operating from the West Coast ports. A further example of an innovative shipping strategy is that adopted by the Maersk Line is for its distribution operation in North America. Double-stack container trains operate between the East, Gulf and West Coast seaports of Seattle, San Francisco, Halifax, Boston, New York, Charleston and New Orleans.

As we progress through the 1990s the multi-purpose container-Ro/Ro vessel will become more common primarily in the deep-sea trades. Such vessels will be capable of conveying a combination of both ISO containers and Ro/Ro units. The Ro/Ro units are usually unaccompanied trailers plus trade cars, lorries, etc. Advantages of this type of tonnage include flexibility of ship capacity involving a varying capacity of Ro/Ro units and containers. This facilitates the most productive use of ship capacity in a varying international market situation. Moreover, the vehicle traffic which is driven on and off the ship aids quick port turn-round of the vessel. It also facilitates the shipment of the indivisible load which is very much on the increase. Usually, such vessels do not require a portal ramp facility, but have their own ramp facility accommodated on the ship hydraulically operated.

16.2 CONTAINER DISTRIBUTION

Modern-day container operations require many skills, one of which is to ensure the right container is at the right place at the right time to meet the shipper's ever more demanding needs. This involves a massive logistics operation (see pp. 428–31) aided by computers. Overall, for the container operator it means the constant repositioning of containers. This arises from the imbalance of trade, and perhaps more significantly from a lack of harmonization between those goods imported into a country and those exported. For example, commodities imported may consist of heavy capital goods requiring flat-rack containers whilst those exported may consist of foodstuffs needing high cube reefer containers.

The Far East is an interesting market in which to examine the rationale behind the movement of containers. It is the fastest growing region in the world and seven of the top ten container ports are located there. Asia has become a major supplier of departmental store goods from countries such as China, Japan, Malaysia, Indonesia, Burma, Hong Kong, Taiwan, Korea, Thailand, the Philippines and the subcontinent of India and Pakistan. The container trades involved are Europe/Asia and Asia/America.

Asia receives raw materials and semi-finished goods from Europe. These are generally bulky cargoes which are often heavy. Exactly the opposite applies with regard to exports. The consumer goods produced in Asia are relatively light. For a container ship this means that imports into Asia are carried in 20-ft containers whilst exports are shipped in 40-ft containers. This results in an imbalance of containers that more or less compels shipping operators to carry empty containers back to their area of origin.

In addition to these substantial logistics problems, the value of the cargo in the containers must also be taken into consideration. There is no doubt that basic products have a considerably lower value per unit weight than the finished exports. These problems and the characteristics of the goods are also reflected in the tariffs of the shipping operators and the freight rates for Asian exports. So far as the sea freight for containers is concerned, these have to compensate for the low rates for imports.

The round-the-world service concept allows a very extensive re-use of containers in other imbalanced world trades thus considerably helping to reduce cost. The bigger and more diversified the cargo areas, the more successful these measures become. The Far East with its multi-country structure offers ideal conditions in this respect.

In the trade between the Far East and the USA the flow of containers is much the same as in the Europe/Asia trade: heavy incoming cargo and light outgoing cargo. The big difference is that in contrast to the trade with Europe, the heavy cargo is also carried in 40-ft containers. In this respect there is a balance between the container types. However, the American market constitutes a special challenge to shipping operators in the Far East.

Because of the geographical situation, all ships coming from the Far East call at American West Coast ports. The big shipping companies on the Pacific have established land bridge services involving rail connections between ports such as San Francisco and New York in order to bring the cargo to the East Coast. Hence we have the round-the-world carrier having to compete with the relatively cheap east-west rail links in the USA.

Vietnam, Burma, Thailand, Taiwan, Indonesia and Korea are relatively new sources of supply for department stores in Europe and the USA. The port installation infrastructure of most of these countries is not yet adequately developed to handle relatively large container ships of 3500/4000 TEUs. Hence feeder services have been developed with shipboard craneage facilities. Hence the region is covered by an extensive network of feeder services which will remain so until the port infrastructure is developed probably by the year 2000.

The European Single Market, the former Eastern bloc countries and those with Mediterranean seaboards will have a profound impact on the Far East within the next decade. The countries of the Far East will increase their demand for capital goods and basic products, whilst at the same time export more consumer goods. To conclude, the Far East container trades will be subject to continuous change in the next few years.

16.3 CONTAINER TYPES

The range of container types tends to expand annually to meet the increasing market demands on this fast-growing international method of distributing merchandise. Basically the majority of containers used are built to ISO (International Standards Organization) specification thereby permitting their ease of ubiquitous use on an international scale.

Given below are details of some of the types of containers available and their salient features (see also Fig. 16.1). Details of the dimensions of specific containers, pallet-wide intermodal containers and swapbody types are given in Table 16.1.

(a) *General purpose containers.* These are closed and are suitable for the carriage of all types of general cargo and with suitable temporary modification for the carriage of bulk cargoes, both solid and liquid. The containers are basically a steel framework with steel, glass reinforced plastic or aluminium alloy used for cladding; the floors are either hardwood timber planked or plywood sheeted. Access for loading and unloading is through full width doors. Aluminium cladded containers have plywood lined interior walls. Cargo securing/lashing points are located at floor level at the base of the side walls.

With suitable temporary modifications solid bulk commodities, granular or powder, may be loaded into general purpose containers. These modifications, depending on the nature of the cargo to be loaded, usually involve the location of a bulkhead at the door end of the container and in most but not all instances the fitting of a polythene liner.

This method of transport has proved successful in reducing costs to both shipper and consignee due to the reduction of manpower involved in both loading sacks or bags and the stuffing and/or stripping of same into and out of the container, and much of the cost of packaging, e.g. poly bags, is of course eliminated.

The commodity payload may also be increased thus allowing an increased cargo to freight margin.

Before implementing a bulk movement system it is necessary to consider the following points:

(i) Ensure that loading point is capable of loading bulk, e.g. that throwers, blowers, etc. capable of end loading are available.

(ii) Ensure suitable receiving facilities are available, e.g. bulk silos, receiving hoppers, etc., and that premises are high enough to accept (if under cover) a container when in the tipping position.

(iii) Ensure that tipping trailers are available at the final destination.

It is also possible to transport certain non-hazardous bulk liquids in general purpose containers which have been fitted with special flexible tanks. These tanks are laid out in the container and a securing harness attached. A bulkhead is then positioned at the door end of the container and the left-hand door closed. The tank is then ready for fitting. Overall these are popular containers for both the FCL and LCL markets.

(b) *Fantainer*. The fantainer is identical to the general purpose container and similar to the dual-purpose Sea Vent (see (l) below). It has similar internal dimensions to the general purpose container, but located high in the left-hand container door is a special hatch which when closed and TIR sealed allows the use of the container as a general purpose unit. However, the hatch can also be fitted with an electric extraction fan which must have an electric supply when operated as a fantainer. In this mode the cargo is stowed upon pallets which form a false floor and creates an air duct under the cargo. Air at ambient temperature is then drawn into the floor by the extraction fan via a specially designed perforated lower front sill. The aim is to remove any respiratory heat developed by the cargo and balance the internal temperature of the container plus the cargo with that outside in order to prevent the formation of condensation. This is ideal for a wide variety of cargoes carried in a general purpose unit.

(c) *Insulated containers*. These protect against heat loss or gain and are used in conjunction with a blown-air refrigeration system to convey perishable or other cargo which needs to be carried under temperature control. Internally the containers are equipped

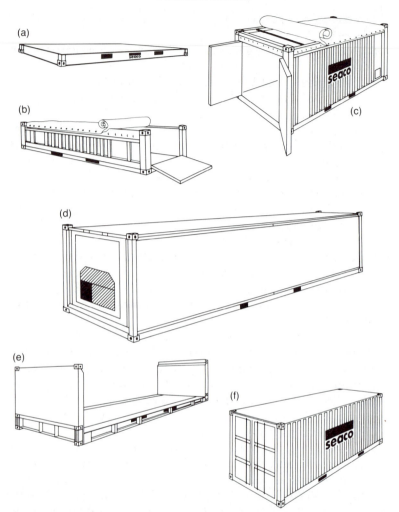

Fig. 16.1 Container types: (a) 20 ft platform flat (bolster) – 40 ft size available – for building materials, vehicles, indivisible loads, lumber, etc. (b) 20 ft half height with ramp end door – tarpaulin roof – for heavy loads, building materials. (c) 20 ft open top – 40 ft size available – for large awkward items such as machinery – tarpaulin roof for water tight integrity – door header swings to assist loading of high items. (d) 40 ft refrigerated container with integral refrigeration machinery for chilled and frozen cargoes. (e) 20 ft spring assisted folding end flat rack – 40 ft size available – can be provided with built in interlocking mechanism for multiple empty transportation. (f) 20 ft covered container – 8 ft 6 in high – 40 ft available.

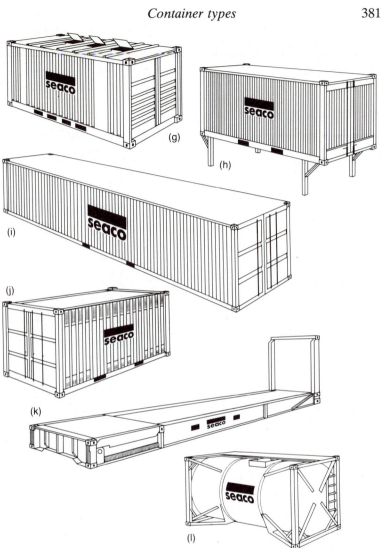

(g) 20 ft bulk container for grain, powders, etc. (h) 7.15 m swap body with demountable legs – 2.5 m width for two pallet wide European operation. (i) 40 ft high cube 9 ft 6 in high – 45 ft also available – for cargoes that cube out. (j) 20 ft ventilated container for cargoes such as coffee and cocoa that experience condensation damage. (k) 40 ft sea deck style combined flat rack and platform flat – 20 ft size available for large items of machinery, construction equipment, etc. (l) 20 ft tank container for bulk hazardous and non-hazardous liquids. (Reproduced by kind permission of Sea Containers.)

Table 16.1 ISO container dimensions by type

Container type	Overall dimensions (ft/m)	Interior dimensions (minimum)			Door dimensions		Cubic capacity (minimum) (m^3)	Tare weight (maximum) (kg)	Gross weight (maximum) (kg)
		Length (mm)	Breadth (mm)	Height (mm)	Breadth (mm)	Height (mm)			
General purpose	20×8×8½ (6.1×2.4×2.6)	5 890	2 345	2 400	2 335	2 290	32.7	2 450	24 000
General purpose	40×8×8½ (12.2×2.4×2.6)	12 015	2 345	2 362	2 335	2 260	66.3	3 700–4 380	30 480
Insulated	20×8×8½ (6.1×2.4×2.6)	5 760	2 260	2 235	2 260	2 215	29.0	2 413	24 000
Fruit	20×8×8½ (6.1×2.4×2.6)	5 770	2 300	2 275	2 300	2 215	30.19	2 362–2 732	24 000
Refrigerated	20×8×8½ (6.1×2.4×2.6)	5 450	2 260	2 247	2 260	2 247	27.7	3 460	24 000
Refrigerated	40×8×8½ (12.2×2.4×2.6)	11 550	2 270	2 200	2 270	2 170	57.8	4 670–4 940	30 480
Bulk	20×8×8½ (6.1×2.4×2.6)	5 892	2 347	2 379	2 335	2 285	33.1	2 730	24 000
Ventilated	20×8×8½ (6.1×2.4×2.6)	5 892	2 303	2 380	2 305	2 273	32.3	2 720	24 000

Container type	Overall dimensions (ft/m)	Interior dimensions (minimum)			Side openings		Cubic capacity (min) (m^3)	Tare weight (max) (kg)	Gross weight (max) (kg)
		Length (mm)	Breadth (mm)	Height (mm)	Length (mm)	Height (mm)			
Flat rack	20×8×8½ (6.1×2.4×2.6)	5 940	2 400	2 310	5 576	2 310	31.9	2 610–2 810	30 480
Flat rack	40×8×8½ (12.2×2.4×2.6)	12 066	2 263	2 134	11 662	2 134	58.6	5 960–6 100	40 640

Container type	Overall dimensions (ft/m)	Overall interior dimensions			Door dimensions		Roof aperture		Cubic capacity (min) (m^3)	Tare weight (max) (kg)	Gross weight (max) (kg)
		Length (mm)	Breadth (mm)	Height (mm)	Breadth (mm)	Height (mm)	Length (mm)	Breadth (mm)			
Open top	20×8×8½ (6.1×2.4×2.6)	5 890	2 345	2 340	2 335	2 260	5 712	2 175	32.4	2 093–2 513	24 000–30 480
Open top tarpaulin	40×8×8½ (12.2×2.4×2.6)	12 025	2 247	2 305	2 235	2 200	11 832	2 150	63.47	3 949–4 650	30 480
Top sliding roof bows half height	20×8×4¼ (6.1×2.4×1.3)	5 906	2 313	1 075	2 280	1 003	5 775	2 224	14.3	1 724	24 000
Half height	40×8×4¼ (12.2×2.4×1.3)	12 010	2 235	940	2 284	980	11 900	2 073	25.2	3 656	30 480

Tank

Container type	Overall dimensions (ft/mm)	Total water capacity (litres)	Tare weight (maximum) (kg)	Tank material	Gross weight (maximum) (kg)
Tank	20×8×8½ (6.1×2.4×2.6)	24 000	3 150	Stainless steel	30 480

Open sided

Container type	Overall dimensions (ft/m)	Minimum interior dimensions gates in position			Minimum door dimensions		Minimum side dimensions		Cubic capacity (min) (m³)	Tare weight (max) (kg)	Gross weight (max) (kg)
		Length (mm)	Breadth (mm)	Height (mm)	Breadth (mm)	Height (mm)	Length (mm)	Height (mm)			
Open sided	20×8×8½ (6.1×2.4×2.6)	5 892	2 310	2 300	2 335	2 180	5 602	2 235	31.1	3 365	24 000–30 480

Bulk

Container type	Overall dimensions (ft/m)	Minimum interior dimensions gates in position			Door dimensions		Cubic capacity (min) (m³)	Tare weight (max) (kg)
		Length (mm)	Breadth (mm)	Height (mm)	Breadth (mm)	Height (mm)		
Bulk	20×8×8½ (6.1×2.4×2.6)	5 892	2 347	2 379	2 335	2 285	–	33.1	2 730	–

Container type	Overall dimensions (ft/m)	Interior dimensions			Door opening		Cu. cap. (min) (m³)	Tare weight (max) (kg)	Payload (max) (kg)	Gross wt (max) (kg)	Top opening		Side opening	
		Length (mm)	Breadth (mm)	Height (mm)	Breadth (mm)	Height (mm)					Length (mm)	Breadth (mm)	Length (mm)	Breadth (mm)
40 high cube dry container (aluminium container)	40×8×9½ (12.2×2.4×3.0)	12 056	2 347	2 684	2 340	2 585	76.0	2 900	29 600	32 500	–	–	–	–
45 high cube dry container (aluminium container)	45×8×9½ (13.7×2.4×3.0)	13 582	2 347	2 690	2 340	2 585	85.7	3 900	28 600	32 500	–	–	–	–
Open-side open-top containers	20×8×8½ (6.1×2.4×2.6)	5 928	2 318	2 259	2 236	2 278	31.0	2 775	21 225	24 000	5 352	2 118	5 352	2 161

Table 16.1 continued

Sea containers	Overall dimensions (ft/m)	Number that interlock into 8 ft 6 in	Door openings				Tare weight (maximum) (kg)	Payload (maximum) (kg)	Cubic capacity (minimum) (m³)	Gross weight (maximum) (kg)
			End door		Side door					
			Width (m)	Length (m)	Width (m)	Length (m)				
Platform flat	20×8×8½ (6.1×2.4×2.6)	7	—	—	—	—	1 500	25 400	—	—
Platform flat	40×8×8½ (12.2×2.4×2.6)	4	—	—	—	—	4 200	35 780	—	—
Fixed end flat rack	20×8×8½ (6.1×2.4×2.6)	—	—	—	—	—	2 900	20 320	—	—
Collapsible flat rack	20×8×8½ (6.1×2.4×2.6)	4	—	—	—	—	2 900	22 100	—	—
Spring-assisted flat rack	20×8×8½ (6.1×2.4×2.6)	5	—	—	—	—	2 600	27 400	—	—
Fixed-end flat rack	40×8×8½ (12.2×2.4×2.6)	—	—	—	—	—	5 098	25 383	—	—
Spring-assisted flat rack	40×8×8½ (12.2×2.4×2.6)	3	—	—	—	—	4 995	30 567	—	—
Sea deck flush deck	20×8×8½ (6.1×2.4×2.6)	7	—	—	—	—	2 560	27 920	—	—
Sea deck flush deck folding end	40×8×8½ (12.2×2.4×2.6)	4	—	—	—	—	5 300	39 700	—	—
40' Palletwide 8'6" high unit inter-modal container	(12.19×2.5×2.59)	—	2.4	2.2	—	—	3 860	26 620	70.1	30 480
40' Palletwide 8'6" side door unit inter-modal container	(12.19×2.5×2.6)	—	2.4	2.2	2.3	2.2	4 100	26 280	70.8	30 480
40' Palletwide 9' high unit – inter-modal container	(12.19×2.5×2.74)	—	2.4	2.3	—	—	3 950	26 530	74.6	30 480
40' Palletwide 9'6" cube unit – inter-modal container	(12.19×2.5×2.89)	—	2.4	2.5	—	—	4 000	26 480	79.1	30 480
7.15 m stackable box swapbody	—	—	—	—	—	—	—	—	—	—

with an aluminium T-section floor and the inside face of the doors is fitted with moulded vertical battens to permit air flow around the cargo. It is important that when cargo requiring temperature control is loaded in this type of container, an air space of approximately 7.5 mm is left over the top of the cargo to allow free air circulation. Securing points are positioned along each side of the floor, while lashing points to prevent cargo falling out are sited at the door end of the container by the corner posts. This is an ideal container for the movement of foodstuffs.

(d) *The fruit container*. This has been developed to carry fresh, deciduous and citrus fruit, the internal dimensions being slightly larger than the standard insulated container to accommodate the packing of standard fruit pallets and cases. The internal structure of the fruit container is basically the same as the insulated container.

(e) *Refrigerated containers*. These are usually termed reefer containers and are designed to operate independently of a blown-air refrigerated system and are fitted with their own refrigeration units which require an electrical power supply for operation. Each container is capable of being set at its own individual carriage temperature. The internal structure of these containers is similar to that of the 'port hole' insulated container with alloy T-section floor and securing points each side at the base of the side walls and fall-out lashing points at corner posts. The container is of steel construction with the cladding of stainless steel lined or aluminium alloy. The electrical supply will usually operate on either 200 to 220 volts, single phase or 380 to 440 volts three phase at 32 amps both at 50/60 Hz. A modern reefer container would also feature microprocessor-controlled refrigeration machinery which provides instant error detection, reporting of malfunction area and temperature deviation alarm which permits on-board reefer electricians to act immediately. The remote monitoring system ensures central registration of all vital data. Reefer containers are available with humidity control to ensure correct relative humidity inside the container, data loggers for monitoring cold treatment, and controlled/modified atmosphere to prolong the shelf-life of chilled products (see Fig. 16.1, p. 380).

(f) *High cube reefer container*. The latest generation of reefer containers are high cube with a module of 40 feet (12.20 m) long, 8 feet (2.44 m) wide, and 9 feet 6 inches (2.90 m) high or 49 feet

(14.94 m) long, 8 feet (2.44 m) wide and 9 feet 6 inches (2.90 m) high. Such containers are of aluminium construction, and are especially popular in the Far East and North American markets.

(g) *Bulk containers.* These are designed for the carriage of dry powders and granular substances in bulk. To facilitate top loading three circular hatches (500 mm diameter) are fitted in some containers in the roof structure. For discharge a hatch is fitted in the right-hand door of the container. Full width doors are fitted to allow loading of conventional cargo. Constructed of steel frame-work with steel cladding, the containers are usually equipped with mild steel floors to enable ease of cleaning. Lashing points are fitted at the base of the sidewall and at the top of the container along the top side rails to enable the securing of polythene liners (if required) (see Fig. 16.1, p. 381).

(h) *Ventilated containers.* These are of steel construction, and are broadly similar to the general purpose container specification, except for the inclusion of full length ventilation galleries sited along the top and bottom side rails, allowing the passive ventilation of the cargo. The ventilation arrangement is such that the ingress of water is prevented. This type is called gallery style and is suitable for products such as coffee (see Fig. 16.1, p. 381).

(i) *Flat rack containers.* These are designed to facilitate the carriage of cargo in excess of the dimensions available in either general purpose or open top containers. They consist of a flat bed with fixed or collapsible ends, the external dimensions conforming in all respects to the ISO requirements. Suitable lashing points are fitted to the floor and/or side rails of the container with in some cases four corner rings (see Fig. 16.1, p. 380).

There are four types. Fixed-end flat racks are designed for balanced trades where cargoes travel in both directions. The flat racks have end walls which can be folded down when empty, thereby taking less storage space in a depot, or fewer slots when on board ship. The simplest model is found in the collapsible flat rack. The end wall is not spring-assisted but can be easily raised and lowered by two men. Finally, the spring-assisted flat racks permit each end wall to be raised or lowered. The end wall is locked into place in both raised and folded positions. Many units have reinforced load areas (over the centre two metres) to accommodate the carriage of heavy loads. These four types have been developed by Sea Containers and a feature of the folding flat racks is the 'built-in' interlocking mechanism which allows mixed stacks of the same length of unit to be transported as they can be stacked and lifted together.

A combination of two or more flat rack containers can be used to form a temporary 'tween-deck space for uncontainerable cargo moved on a 'port to port' basis provided the total weight and point of loading of the cargo does not exceed the static capabilities of the flat racks. It is ideal for oversized, awkward and heavy cargoes.

(j) *The Sea Deck.* This is a new container developed by Sea Containers and combines the benefits of the flat rack and platform flat. The unit has folding ends which, in a folded position, fit flush with the floor. It allows three possibilities: with the ends up it is a flat rack (see (g) above); with both ends down it is a platform, and with one end up and the other down it creates a 'headache board' to comply with the forward bulkhead requirements of some road and railway authorities. Sea Decks are built with empty handling pockets and interlocking mechanisms enabling them to be stacked with other Sea Decks, Sea Containers' 40-ft spring-assisted flat racks and 40-ft platform flats (see Fig. 16.1, p. 381).

(k) *Platform flats.* These are simple platforms for carrying loads such as machinery, steel, boats and other indivisible cargoes that will not fit regular ISO container modules. They can be used to create temporary 'tween decks in containerships, allowing large items to be transported. These items are usually loaded separately and spread over a number of pre-positioned platform flats located in the hold or the weather deck of a containership. The use of platform flats helps to speed up intermodal operations as well as reducing costs, by allowing the transfer of the platform and cargo from road to rail to barge (or any other combination) without the need to handle or unlash the cargo. Loaded platforms flats are top lifted by wire ropes attached to the corner castings and in Ro/Ro operations the platform and cargo are loaded either by fork-lift truck or by trailer. Similar benefits are achieved when platforms are used to accelerate the loading of general cargo ships. The platform with cargo is delivered intermodally direct to the ship and only unloaded once inside the ship's hold. The platform is then returned empty for reloading. Empty units of the same length can be interlocked to maximize the number of units positioned in one ISO slat.

(l) *The Sea Vent.* A dual-purpose container termed the Sea Vent has been devised by Sea Containers. It is capable of conveying moisture-sensitive cargo in one transit and general cargoes on the next transit. It may be 20 or 40 feet in length with ventilator chambers fitted into corrugations at the top and bottom along the length of each side of the container. The upper chambers are fitted at the extreme top so that warm, moist air which rises naturally to the top of the container can exit without resistance. In the vent chambers a Venturi pressure drop draws this air out of the container and causes cool dry air to be drawn through the lower row of ventilators creating natural air circulation. Cross air is equally important and is created by hold ventilation or natural breeze entering ventilators on one side and departing via the chambers on the other taking with it any warm moist air. The self-draining ventilators are designed to deflect rain or spray and prevent water ingress. To ensure water integrity, each unit undergoes a full pressure ISO water test after manufacture. The riveted ventilator panels are easily removed for repair and are economical to replace if damage occurs. Sea Vents have identical payloads, internal capacities and door configurations as standard dry freight containers, and have been specially designed to allow use for general cargo when not required for goods needing ventilation. The Sea Vent container is ideal for coffee shipments from Columbia, Brazil, West Africa, East Africa, India, Indonesia and Central America; cocoa from Brazil, Indonesia and West Africa; vegetables from the Canaries, Holland and France; tobacco from Indonesia and the Dominican Republic; spices from Sri Lanka and Indonesia; onions from South Africa and Australasia; pulses from Burma; and garlic from Argentina.

(m) *Open top containers*. With their top loading facility these are designed for the carriage of heavy and awkward-shaped cargoes, and those cargoes whose height is in excess of that which can be stowed in a standard general purpose container. The floor of the containers are of hardwood timber plank or plywood, and there are a number of cargo securing points in the floor or along the bottom side rail at the base of the sidewalls. The containers have a swinging or removable door header and either removable or sliding roof bows to allow loading either directly through the roof aperture or through the door using overhead lifting equipment. In operation the header is usually swung out of the way leaving one pin engaged. Tarpaulin tilts are available to protect the cargo. Also there exists the overheight tilt for use with overheight cargo. It can also be described as an open sided/open top container, and is ideal for sheet glass, timber and machinery.

(n) *Half-height open top containers*. The half-height version of the open top container is designed for the carriage of heavy, dense cargoes such as steel, pipes and tubes, etc. It is ideal for shippers whose premises have a restricted height for loading or discharge. The steel containers have a tarpaulin top, a removable door header bar and securing points set into the floor (see Fig. 16.1, p. 380).

(o) *Tank containers*. These are generally constructed with the carriage of a specific product or range of products in mind. It is usual for shippers to provide their own tanks. Such containers are owned or leased by the shipper. They are usually constructed of stainless steel and for liquid cargoes may be used for either dangerous goods or non-hazardous cargo. A wide variety of products are shipped in tank containers ranging from the wet to dry bulk cargoes. Many are dedicated to one product. Examples of dangerous cargoes include toxic, corrosive, oxidising and highly flammable products as well as cyanides, acids, phosphorus and mercaptans (see Fig. 16.1, p. 381).

(p) *Open sided containers*. These are designed to accommodate the carriage of specific commodities such as plywood, perishable commodities and livestock. These steel containers have a fixed roof, open sides and end opening doors, the sides being closed by full height gates in 1.37 m wide sections, and nylon reinforced PVC curtains (the curtains may be rolled up to the top side rail when not in use) which meet TIR requirements. There are eight lashing points each side affixed to the bottom side rail (outside) below floor level, nine rings located in the floor and five rings vertically up each corner post.

(q) *Open side/open top containers*. This type of container is designed for transporting 'live' products such as potatoes and onions. An open side/open top container is equipped with tarpaulin covers and removable side grating, top rails, roof bows and door header. This permits easy access for stuffing and stripping as well as extensive possibilities for cargo ventilation.

(r) *Artifical 'tween-deck containers*. These are without end walls, side walls or a roof and also known as platform carriers. They are 6.10 m long and 2.4 m wide or 12.20 m long and 2.4 m wide. These units are used for oversize and overweight cargo which cannot otherwise be containerized. By combining several artificial 'tween decks on board a vessel it is possible to obtain a very high payload. See also (i) above.

(s) *Hanger containers*. These are used for dry cargo and are equipped with removable beams in the upper part. They are used for the shipment of garments on hangers. They are 12.20 m long, 2.4 m wide, and 3.0 m high, or 6.10 m long, 2.4 m wide and 3.0 m high.

The high cube dry container of 45 ft (13.72 m) or 49 ft (14.94 m) long or 8 feet (2.44 m) width and 9 ft 6 in (2.90 m) high has been developed by many major container operators including the Maersk Line. The 45-ft container has some 27% larger cubic capacity than the general purpose container which is 12.20 m long, 2.4 m wide and 2.4 m high. It is ideal for a wide variety of consumer products which have a high cube but low weight ratio. This includes garments carried on removable beams in the upper part of the container provided by the Maersk Line, low tech products usually made up of components to be assembled and a wide variety of other dry cargoes. It is very popular in the Far East and North American markets and features in multi-modal operation involving the double-stack container trains operating from the East and West Coast ports of North America (see Fig. 16.1).

(t) *Bin containers*. These have a cargo capacity of 21 600 kg, a tare weight of 2400 kg and a length of 6.06 m, a width of 2.44 m and a height of 1.30 m. They are ideal for heavy dense cargoes such as steel, pipes, etc. They have no doors.

(u) *Bolster flat containers*. These have a cargo capacity of 23 000 kg, a tare weight of 1940 kg and a length overall of 6.06 m, a width of 2.44 m and a height of 0.23 m. They are ideal for a variety of heavy cargoes (see Fig. 16.1, p. 380).

(v) *Palletwide inter-modal containers*. The expansion of inter-modalism has resulted in the development more specialized container-handling equipment and major operators like Sea Containers have introduced the 40-ft Palletwide inter-modal container. These units are designed for both domestic use and short sea operation giving users major advantages over the standard 8-ft wide marine containers. The major benefit is that the extra width allows additional standard pallets to be carried as they can be stowed side by side. This is not possible in a standard 8 ft unit.

These inter-modal containers are fitted with a slim profile door, which gives extra internal length and allows the full 2440 mm internal width in the side-door version, even across the side-door location. Other features of the 40-ft inter-modal container include: units built as inter-modal containers, not converted ISO 8-ft containers, steel construction for strength and ease of repair; four-high laden stacking; corner castings top and bottom inset at 8 ft positions to allow standard top lift spreaders and chassis lock-downs to be used; two palletwide full strength 800×1000 mm = 36 pallets, 1000×1200 mm = 24 pallets, and 1170×1170 mm = 20 pallets; twistlock protection recess in front and rear cills to reduce incorrect location damage; lashing 15 top and bottom rail each side; bottom lift by lifting shoe; top lift spreader; side doors available to operators who wish to load/discharge through side rather than end doors; and two customs-approved ventilators each side.

(w) *Stackable box swapbody*. The 7.15m stackable box swap-body is another example of the equipment used in the development of multi-modalism by Sea Containers. The benefits and applications of a demountable swapbody have been greatly extended by the use of inter-modal container technology. These include three-high laden stacking for container yards and use in lift-on/lift-off, short sea or barge operations. Other features include adjustable leg heights, top lift by spreader, bottom lift by grapple, laden lift fork pockets, base frame strengthened for body lift, steel construction for strength and ease of repair, castings at 20 ft for lockdown to road vehicles and rail wagons, full width rear doors, extended side rail which acts as a rubbing strip for pallet loading, lashing bar full length mid-point between floor and roof plus four lashing points on bottom and top rail each side, rear stowable access ladder and external document box and two customs-approved ventilators each side (see Fig. 16.1, p. 381).

The swapbody was pioneered largely in Germany to meet domestic transport requirements from the starting point of the road vehicle. Today it is a fast growing industry and a wide variety of swapbody types exist including tank, reefer, box side door, tautliner curtain side, tilt, speciality units, i.e. storage modules, and flat bases onto which ISO containers can be locked.

The average operational life of a container is 12 years.

As we progress through the latter part of the 1990s, the growth of containerization will continue and with it the use of the high cube and swapbodies. This growth is market driven in response to the needs of the shipper to develop multi-modalism and achieve lower unit cost through the use of larger high cube containers. These offer an increase of more than 38% in cubic capacity compared with the 40-ft unit. Some of these containers and swapbodies are oversized but are here to stay and can be successfully operated on a regional basis without upsetting the overall infrastructure of the commercial world. At 2.5/2.6 m width they fall outside the ISO standard width of 8 ft. but represent some 5% of the container/swapbody fleet. Such oversize units are found especially in the European, Australian and North American regions.

The super cube containers at 9 ft 6 in high and 45 feet or 49 feet long are becoming very popular. They pose problems for both ship operators and port authorities who are having to modify their equipment/resources to handle this new breed of container which is outside the ISO module of 20/40 feet long with a width of 8 feet and a height of 8 ft 6 in. The fourth-generation container vessels as operated by Nedlloyd have 100 foot holds replacing the 80 foot holds in the earlier container tonnage.

The development of multi-modalism (see pp. 417–31) embraces all container types and swapbodies. It features strongly the railway as part of an integrated service and frequently involves the land bridge concept. In North America the East and West Coast ports are now firmly integrated into the double-stack container train distribution network. The network will include the use of the high cube at 9 ft 6 in. Similar networks are in evidence in Australia from Adelaide to Alice Springs and Perth, It is very unlikely the high cube will find use in Europe as the railway gauge is too small. The US double-stack container train network is dominated by 9 ft 6 in high containers and even domestic units are invariably longer than 40 feet at 45, 48 and 53 feet.

The argument that you cannot put everything into boxes will always be valid but as most trades and ships are geared up to containerization so the box manufacturers are producing more specialized designs to increase the range of commodities which can be boxed. This has accelerated since the early 1990s.

To date the 'specials market' has been responsible for the development of container types such as the platform flat, the flat rack, the folding-end flat rack, the half-height container, the tank, special tanks for hazardous liquids, the Sea Vent container for two-way operation, the Palletwide intermodal container, the stackable box container, the swapbody, the reefer and the bulk-tainer, amongst others. More variations on these themes are likely to be seen as container builders respond to shipping demands in the latter part of the 1990s.

The flat rack, folding-end flat rack and cargo platform market forms a considerable part of the whole 'specials' picture. Already used by 'combi'-vessel and Ro/Ro shipping operators, they are increasingly being utilized by pure container operators. They are now considered essential tools in international shipping since there is still a great deal of cargo unsuited for transportation in standard containers, particularly high weight/density industrial products. For awkward cargo, the shipper or consolidator needs the alternative of either top or side loading.

Overwidth or overheight cargo can also be accommodated easily in units of this nature, permitting a high percentage of so-called 'non-containerizable' cargo to be shipped within a pure container transport system. Since a loaded flat rack can be top lifted – often even when loaded with overheight cargo – and can be incorporated within a container stack, it is almost invariably preferred over the cargo platform by lift-on/lift-off container operators.

In cellular container ships, it is becoming increasingly popular to provide a 'tween-deck within a hold by positioning two or more flat racks side by side in the container cells. Large items can then be lowered into the hold to straddle the units.

16.4 NON-CONTAINERIZABLE CARGO

Non-containerizable cargo can be divided into four categories (see also Table 16.2) as follows:

(a) Rollable cargo with its own wheels or trailers that can be driven aboard or towed. Road vehicles and agricultural machinery are examples.

(b) Cargo that is carried on trailers. This involves MAFI and heavy-duty trailers for pier-to-pier movements, flatbed trailers for door-to-door transportation, and trailers for the movement of exceptionally large or heavy loads door-to-door.

(c) Special project cargo that requires experience and expertise to find a cost-effective solution. This includes, for example, the conveyance of trains in the Ro-Ro decks by laying rail lines into the ship; purpose-built road bogies to carry subway carriages door-to-door and special extendable flatbed trailers for the carriage of 22 m (72 ft) long aircraft wings.

(d) Neo-bulk cargo, a term given to a wide range of staple products that can be efficiently carried in the Ro/Ro decks as unitized break-bulk (e.g. wood-pulp, board, paper, logs and steel). Details of the range of equipment used for non-containerizable cargo are given below and in Table 16.3.

Capacity (tonne)	Length (mm)	Width (mm)	No. of axles	Commentary
Roll trailers				
20	6 096	2438	1	Units with capacities of up
30	12 190	2438	2 bogie	to 180 tonnes are available
40	12 190	2438	2 bogie	for pier-to-pier movements.
55	12 190	2438	2 bogie	Operational advantages
60	12 190	2438	2 bogie	include low timber surfaced
100	12 190	3048	4 bogie	cargo platforms, multi-
180	12 954	3454	8	wheel bogies for extreme
				manoeuvrability, separate
				lashing points for cargo and
				trailer, and high degree of
				stability, even when
				carrying oversize units.
Flatbed trailers				
20	12 190	2438	2	Special house-to-house
				trailers for through
				transport of machinery and
				other outsize and/or high
				cargo units. These are
				either owned by the shipper
				or available on lease.
				Special heavy-lift trailers for
				house-to-house movement
				of extra heavy loads
				available from shipowner.

Table 16.2 Categories of non-containerizable cargo

Rollable	Trailer/MAFI	Special projects	Neo-bulk
Tractors	Boats	Subway carriages and rolling stock	Woodpulp
Backhoes	Yachts	Fixed-wing aircraft	Linerboard
Trucks	Machinery	Aircraft wings	Plywood
Cars	Linerboard	Helicopters	Newsprint
Earthmovers	Cotton liner pulp	Forging machines and presses	Lumber
Mobile cranes	Flowerbulbs	Crankshafts	Waferboard
Combine harvesters	Mining shields	Transformers	Particle board
Buses	Hay balers	Boilers	Press board
Bulldozers	Specialized steel products	Pipe mills	Iron and steel products
Excavators	Crane parts	Dryers	Logs
Wheel-loaders	Injection moulds	Press rolls	
Trackloaders	Compressors	Steel rolls	
Motorgraders	Cranes	Convertors	
Air compressors	Alternators	Military vehicles	
	Rotors	Street cars	
	Turbines	Oilrigs	
	Constructionals	Earthmovers over 55 tonnes	
		Railway locomotives	
		Ballast cleaners	
		Metal working machinery	
		Large boats and yachts	
		Long and wide loads	

Table 16.3 Equipment for non-containerizable cargo

Rollable	Trailer/MAFI	Special projects	Neo-bulk
Maximum weight varies according to machine. Items over 132 275 lb (60 tonne) are considered special projects. Refer to the vessel's cargo specification on weight and dimension. Items may be towed or driven under their own power into the ship. Cargo is normally delivered to the port of loading by the shipper or his agent and collected at the port of discharge by the consignee or his agent. The normal ship's securing system using chains etc. is employed on board the vessel. Shipowner does not usually supply tarpaulins.	*Road trailers for door-to-door transportation* Consignments may be considered 'in gauge' where dimensions do not exceed L40 ft (12.19 m) × W 8 ft (2.43 m) × H 8 ft 6 in (2.59 m). Maximum payload without additional charges for 'in gauge' cargo is 39 682 lb (18 tonne). Heavier, indivisible loads can be carried, but prior arrangements and clearance must be obtained. Normal available equipment is the 40-ft (12.19-m) flatbed trailer with side-pockets for stanchions. Equipment may be loaded or discharged at the shipper's or consignee's	The shipowner defines special projects as cargo where any one of the following dimensions is exceeded: L 40 ft (12.19 m) × W 10 ft (3.05 m) × H 10 ft (3.05 m), or where the weight exceeds 121 252 lb (55 tonne). Rollable cargo is classed as a special project when the weight exceeds 132 275 lb (60 tonne). Note that any cargo, regardless of weight, which is exceptionally dense will require prior clearance before carriage by shipowner. Roll trailers are available for payloads up to 55 tonne and 60 tonne; heavy duty trailers for up to 100 tonne and 180 tonne. Leased trailers,	Maximum dimensions for a consignment loaded on a 20-ft bolster are: L 20 ft (6.10 m) × W 8 ft (2.43 m) × H 8 ft 6 in (2.59 m). Payload maximum is 44 000 lb (20 tonne). Cargo may be loaded on a 20-ft (6.10 m) bolster or on a 40-ft (12.19 m) flatbed trailer. In some cases, the cargo may be blockstowed on the Ro/Ro decks of the ship. Equipment may be loaded or discharged at the shipper's or consignee's factory, or at the ocean terminal. For inland transportation of door-to-door cargo on a 20-ft (6.10 m) bolster or a 40-ft (12.19 m) flatbed trailer, container rules apply.

factory, or at the ocean terminal.

For inland transportation of 'in gauge' cargo normal container rules apply, but 'out of gauge' cargo requires prior clearance.

Chains, nylon web lashing and signode banding may be used to secure the cargo.

If required, tarpaulins must be supplied by the shipper or trucker.

MAFI trailers for pier-to-pier transportation

The maximum dimensions of cargo should normally not exceed

L 40 ft (12.19 m) ×
W 10 ft (3.05 m) ×
H 10 ft (3.05 m).

Normal maximum weight is 121 252 lb (55 tonne). Cargo in excess of this is considered a special project.

Roll trailers are available to carry up to 20 tonne, 30 tonne, 40 tonne, 55 tonne and 60 tonne.

including drop frames, well trailers and extendables, are available on a one-trip basis from the shipowner.

Roll and heavy duty trailers are for pier-to-pier cargo only but leased trailers may move over the road with permits if required.

Securing is achieved by chains, steel banding, wire and bottlescrews (turnbuckles) as necessary.

Shipowner does not supply tarpaulins.

Web lashing, signode steel banding, tarpaulins and shrink-wrapping are used to secure the cargo. Tarpaulins are normally supplied by the trucker or shipper.

Capacity (tonne)	Length (mm)	Width (mm)	No. of axles	Commentary

Bolsters – flats without hardboards

20	6 000	2438		This is a unit constructed with a strengthened floor which can be stowed from either the top, sides or ends.

The Ro/Ro container vessels are large and very flexible, with the ability to carry a variety of cargo mixes. The Ro/Ro decks incorporate hoistable car decks which can be raised or lowered according to market demand at the time. Even in the lowered position, the space underneath these car decks allows the block-stowing of a wide range of neo-bulk commodities and the stowage of normal Ro/Ro cargo. With the car decks raised, the height permits the carriage of out-of-gauge Ro/Ro cargo, which can be on trailers or wheeled or tracked. Examples include heavy machinery, locomotives, yachts, aircraft, earthmovers, automobiles and caravans. Alternatively, blockstowing in several layers is possible and therefore a high utilization can be achieved in such tonnage.

The vessel is fitted with a 'jumbo angled stern ramp' which permits the simultaneous two-way movement of roll trailers and other Ro/Ro cargo. Loading and discharging of Ro/Ro or blockstowed cargo at the same time as cars is achieved by providing separate ramp systems within the vessel.

16.5 ADVANTAGES/DISADVANTAGES OF CONTAINERIZATION

The advantages/disadvantages of containerization can be summarized as follows:

(a) Advantages of containerization

(i) It permits a door-to-door service being given which may be from the factory production site to the retail distributor's store – an overall distance of maybe 10 000 km.

(ii) No intermediate handling at terminal (port) transhipment points.

(iii) The absence of intermediate handling plus quicker transits permits less risk of cargo damage and pilferage.

(iv) Low risk of cargo damage and pilferage enables more favourable cargo premiums to be obtained compared with conventional cargo shipments, i.e. 'tween-deck tonnage.

(v) Elimination of intermediate handling at terminal transfer points, i.e. ports, enables substantial labour savings to be realized, which in industrialized countries with high incomes per capita can realize considerable attractive financial savings.

(vi) Less packing needs for containerized shipments. In some cases, particularly with specialized containers, e.g. refrigerated tanks (liquid or powder), no packing is required. This produces substantial cost savings in international transport.

(vii) The elimination of intermediate handling coupled with the other advantages of containerized shipments, permits the cargo to arrive in a better condition when compared with conventional cargo shipments.

(viii) Emerging from the inherent advantages of containerization, rates are likely to remain more competitive when compared with the former conventional tonnage ('tween-deck) shipments. A significant reason is that containerization is in the main a capital-intensive transport system compared with conventional liner systems, and has rationalized ports of call coupled with more intensive ship use.

(ix) Transits are much quicker compared with conventional cargo shipments. This is achieved through a combination of faster vessels, the rationalization of ports of call and substantially quicker cargo handling. An example is the UK/Australia service where the round voyage time has been reduced from the twenty weeks taken by conventional services 15 years ago to the five weeks (approximately) taken by container vessels nowadays.

(x) Emerging from faster transits and the advantages under items (vii) and (viii) it encourages trade development and permits quicker payment of export invoices.

(xi) Containerization has permitted fleet rationalization. On average one container vessel – usually of much increased capacity and faster speed – has displaced up to eight 'tween-deck vessels on deep-sea services. This development has been facilitated by the rationalization of ports of call and the development of the 'hub and spoke' container ship feeder system.

(xii) Container vessels attain much improved utilization and generally are very much more productive than the 'tween-deck tonnage.

(xiii) Faster transits usually coupled with more reliable schedules and ultimately increased service frequency, are tending to encourage many importers to hold reduced stocks/spares. This produces savings in warehouse accommodation needs, lessens risk of obsolescent stock, and reduces importers' working capital.

(xiv) Containerization produces quicker transits and encourages rationalization of ports of call. This in many trades is tending to stimulate trade expansion through much improved service standards. Accordingly it will result in increased service frequency which will aid trade development.

(xv) Provision of through documentation (consignment note) – bill of lading.

(xvi) Provision of a through rate. This covers both maritime and surface transport cost. This factor and (xv) very much aids the marketing of the container concept.

(xvii) More reliable transits – particularly disciplined controlled transit arrangements.

(xviii) New markets have emerged through container development and its inherent advantages.

(xix) Overall a total quality service which in turn adds value to the ports/countries served.

(b) Disadvantages of containerization

(i) Containerization is a capital-intensive project and as such is beyond the financial ability of many shipowners. In many cases container services are now operated by members of the old conference groupings funding a new consortium. Even so, the finance required is very great for not only has a specialized ship(s) to be built but at least three sets of containers for each ship. With regard to the latter, ownership has tended to be held by container hire operators, by industrial companies and by the ship owning consortia. In all three sectors, however, there has been a good deal of leasing of containers with the operational control resting with the lessors. The expense does not end here for at the chosen terminals the authority has to bear the cost of providing specialized cranes, trailers, van carriers, etc., as well as strengthening quays and creating stacking space.

(ii) Not all merchandise can be conveniently containerized. The percentage of such traffic, however, is now very small as new types of containers are introduced. Nevertheless, it is a constraining factor and can involve the shipper in capital outlay to adapt his production processes/ premises/packaging, etc., to suit the restrictive dimensions/weights imposed by the container.

(iii) The container in itself is a high capacity carrying unit, and in consequence, exporters with limited trade are unable to fill the container to capacity, and thereby take full advantage of an economical through rate, for example from exporters' factory premises to importers' warehouses. This situation has been largely overcome by the provision of container bases situated in industrial areas or port environs, where less than container load traffic (LCL) is stowed (stuffed) into a container with other compatible traffic of similar destination/area.

(iv) In some trades a very, very small percentage of the traffic is incapable of being containerized due to its nature such as certain livestock. This does involve the shipowner in providing specialized – non-container – facilities on the vessel which inflates the capital cost of the project, and sometimes results in poor utilization of such facilities on the return passage.

(v) The stratification of some trades varies considerably by time of year and direction. For example, a trade may have a preponderance of perishable cargo in one direction eight months of the year, whilst in the reverse direction the cargo may be consumer goods. This situation has to be reconciled in an acceptable container type(s) for use in both directions. Additionally in some trades, as a result of imbalance, extensive repositioning of containers is required (see pp. 376–8). Another example is to have cargo in one direction with a low stowage factor, whilst in the reverse direction it is a high stowage factor. Such problems although *prima facie* difficult, have been overcome by the co-operation of all interested parties, particularly shippers/ shipowners. Technological development in recent years such as food storage/processing etc. have eased the shipowners' problems considerably and tended to level out the, hitherto, peak seasonal nature of the traffic in some trades.

(vi) The container-owning company, which may be a consortium of shipowners, or container operator has a complex task in ensuring full utilization of such equipment. Most shipowner consortia have computer equipment to monitor and control their inventory of containers. The task is an international one and involves many parties to ensure strict control of the container when it is in their hands. Some method of container control is essential to ensure good utilization of the equipment in the interest of maximizing revenue.

(vii) In some countries restrictions exist regarding the internal movement, particularly by road, of certain containers exceeding a certain dimension/weight. This has tended to restrict the full development of the larger container, particularly the 40-footer (12.20 m), the 45-footer (13.72 m) and the 49-footer (14.94 m), but long term the constraint is likely to disappear in many markets. Restrictions by canal/rail are virtually non-existent in many countries, although by rail there may be some constraints on the use of the high cube container of 9 ft 6 in (2.90 m).

To conclude our analysis of containerization, one cannot stress too strongly that its existence is responsible for the development of world industrial and consumer markets. It has brought enormous economic and social changes to many countries, especially less developed countries, newly industrialized countries and developing/emerging countries. Overall its efficiency, as manifest in multi-modalism of which the major leg is sea transport, is of paramount importance in the continuing development of world trade. Moreover, it has stimulated the growing development of logistics in the global market environment. In short, countries which are not on the global container network are seriously disadvantaged in their economic and social development.

16.6 CONTAINER BASES

The function of a container base is to consolidate break-bulk cargoes (i.e. less than full container load consignments) into full container loads. The container base may be under the management of a consortium of ship container operators, a container operator(s) engaged in the freight-forwarding business, a consortium comprising freight forwarders, road hauliers, etc., and others engaged in such business, or a local port authority. It can be situated in the port itself, the port environs, or an industrial area which can support the facility in generating adequate quantities of containerized import/export traffic through it. The container base is served by road and the larger bases often have rail facilities.

Overall the role of the container base can be summarized as a convenient point to assemble LCL cargo; to provide export packing and handling services for FCL and out-of-gauge cargo; to provide inland customs clearance local to customers' business premises; to provide totally secure storage and packing for empty and loaded containers together with cleaning and repair services; and to offer office accommodation on the spot for container operators, freight forwarders and other maritime service companies.

The object of the facility is to consolidate break-bulk cargoes destined for the same area/country into full container loads and thereby provide a service in that area, particularly for the smaller importer/exporter. Consequently the process of stuffing (loading) and unstuffing (unloading) containers is performed at the container base. Many of the larger container bases are inland clearance depots which have the added facility of customs clearance for both import and export cargoes.

The major advantage of the container base is to provide a service to the importer/exporter situated in the base's hinterland and relieve the port authority of local customs clearance of import/export cargoes. This latter advantage tends to reduce the problems of port congestion, i.e. containers awaiting clearance due to non-availability of documents, and enables the throughput of the container berth to be maximized. Ultimately it speeds up transit as no inordinate delay is usually experienced at the port and thereby encourages the development of international trade. Undoubtedly the number of container bases will increase as the container trades expand.

To conclude our examination of containerization, it is likely that, as we progress through the late 1990s, the pattern of cargo liner trade featuring predominantly containers will change. Substantial growth can continue to be expected in the Far East markets. Moreover, container capacity is likely to increase with the introduction of the 45 ft long and 9 ft 6 in high container, especially in the North American and Far East markets.

The development of the intermodal transportation network is likely to grow to include sea and air. The combination of these two transportation methods offers an economical alternative, and an average journey time is cut by approximately 75% when compared with sea freight. Transportation costs are reduced by up to 50% compared to pure air freight. Examples include the following:

Sea Transit		Air Transit	
Seaport	*Seaport*	*Airport*	*Airport*
Hong Kong	Sharjah	Sharjah	Frankfurt
Osaka	Vancouver	Vancouver	Frankfurt
Fukuoka	Vladivostok	Vladivostok	Leningrad
Valparaiso	Recife	Recife	Frankfurt
Caracas	Miami	Miami	Frankfurt

The air waybill and bill of lading documents are used. To aid faster development, compatible containers are being provided which go directly from the ship into the aircraft without the goods needing to be loaded. Boeing Jumbo air freighters with a payload of up to 103 tons, and capable of conveying pallets and containers are used. A number of other sea/air routes exist between the Middle East and North America, with the air transit commencing from the North American East Coast ports. High value, and perishable or urgent cargoes tend to use such services. In the container terminal area, the latest generation of equipment will speed up handling as demonstrated by the Port of Singapore (see pp. 371–2).

16.7 INTERNATIONAL AUTHORIZATION

Emerging from the International Convention for Safe Containers (CSC) sponsored by the International Maritime Organization and the UN in 1972, was the Health and Safety Executive. This was entrusted with the task of establishing an effective procedure for the testing, inspection and approval of containers. This was introduced in September 1977 whereby all international container constructions had to be tested or otherwise approved by one of the accredited organizations appointed by the Health and Safety Executive. After approval each container is appropriately plated. Ship classification societies featured strongly among the accredited organizations.

Lloyd's Register was one of the accredited organizations appointed. It operates a container certification scheme which provides for a system of quality control inspection during the manufacture of containers. The scheme ensures that all types of container are built to reliable and safe standards. It also ensures, through certification, compliance with the international conventions concerning container transport.

Details of the international authorization to issue certification for containers that comply with the appropriate requirements are given below:

(a) CSC operative from 1977.

(b) International Customs Convention.

(c) International Agreement for the Transportation of Perishable Foodstuffs (ATP).

Where the carriage of dangerous goods in tanks is involved, containers can be certified in accordance with the following:

(d) International Maritime Dangerous Goods Code for Sea Transport (IMDG).

(e) International Regulations concerning the Carriage of Dangerous Goods by Rail (RID).

(f) European Agreement concerning the Carriage of Dangerous Goods by Road (ADR).

(g) US DOT Regulations CFR49 for the Transportation of Intermodal Portable Tanks (IM101 & IM102).

(h) Canadian Regulations for the Transportation of Dangerous Commodities by Rail (CTC).

Tank containers, special containers or those manufactured in low volume production runs are inspected usually on an individual basis. When containers are manufactured in large production runs each container is inspected and certified. However, series production of general cargo containers can be monitored under a quality assured scheme. The scheme normally involves a review of the manufacturer's works by:

(a) assessing the quality manual and ensuring compliance with its requirements by a thorough audit of the works;

(b) advising, if necessary, how quality assurance programmes can be implemented;

(c) auditing incoming materials;

(d) verifying corner castings are obtained from approved suppliers;

(e) ascertaining that subcontracted fabricated components comply with specification;

(f) reviewing production arrangements for orders to be certified;

(g) inspecting the works systematically to monitor quality control procedures during production;

(h) carrying out sample inspection of containers during production and on completion.

Any new design for a container must be type approved. This involved the following:

(a) appraising in detail the manufacturer's structural drawings;

(b) surveying the prototype container during construction;

(c) approving the testing establishments by reviewing procedures, test equipment, calibration records and methods of reporting;

(d) witnessing tests of the prototype in accordance with the ISO procedures applicable to the design including:

    (i) lifting and stacking;

    (ii) roof, floor, side and end wall tests;

    (iii) base restraint;

    (iv) transverse and longitudinal racking;

    (v) weathertightness;

    (vi) air leakage, thermal characteristics and refrigerating machinery capacity tests;

    (vii) pressure vessel hydraulic tests, safety valve setting and leaktightness;

(e) issuing type approval certificates.

The CSC has been subjected to four amendments in 1981, 1983, 1991 and 1993. The amendments focus on the plating of containers, on the re-examination of containers every 30 months with the option to choose between the original periodic examination scheme or a new continuous examination programme, and finally on the information contained in the CSC Safety Approval plate and new test loads and testing procedures.

Finally one must stress that all containers require the Australian Quarantine Certification (AQIS) for the container floor when operating in the Australasian trade. Most containers today are built to HM Customs TIR, UIC, Australian Floor, CSC and Lloyd's or other classification society approval.

CHAPTER 17

Seaports

17.1 THE ROLE OF SEAPORTS

As we progress through the 1990s, the role of seaports will change and the areas detailed below demonstrate such developments. Shippers are looking for dedicated schedules door-to-door with customs examination being undertaken at the consignor/consignee premises or at the nearby container freight station/dry port/freight village. Hence an increasing volume of business passing through the port will be customs examined outside the port environs thereby reducing congestion and infrastructure needs in terms of warehousing and so speeding up the transit. Moreover, it will intensify berth utilization and its infrastructure thereby increasing the throughput of the port. The elimination of customs examination will reduce substantially the size of the dock labour force, a development further accentuated by the provision of high-tech computerized cargo handling equipment.

An increasing number of major ports are becoming trade distribution centres, with such developments being concentrated in the port environment. Examples include the ports of Singapore and Rotterdam. The trading areas are called 'distriparks' and provide industrial companies with a central distribution location together with the major benefits of the nearby port infrastructure and a prosperous hinterland. Goods are imported and exported through the port and processed through the distripark warehouses and distribution centres. Companies lease the site and/or warehouses and import the products for assembly, processing, packaging and labelling to serve the nearby markets. This provides enormous cost savings in terms of:

(a) reduced customs duties;
(b) often lower labour handling costs;
(c) lower distribution costs to the local markets;

(d) lower inventory costs as a result of better control and less inventory.

The central distribution location provided through the distripark also facilitates:

(a) the international distribution of cargo;
(b) the development of customized products to serve the local market;
(c) an integrated logistics approach to the flow of goods through 'just in time' deliveries;
(d) centralized distribution;
(e) the stuffing and stripping of containerized general cargo;
(f) continuous access to the port infrastructure.

The range of products processed through the distripark is large, including foodstuffs, garments, machinery, consumer goods, industrial products and so on. Goods leave the distripark by sea, road, air and canal. An increasing number of exporters are now adopting a policy of purchasing the component parts of their products in different parts of the world and undertaking all the assembly work at a distripark, with each distripark reflecting the needs of the hinterland it serves. It is very cost effective and will develop especially in regions which have free trade agreements such as the EU, ASEAN, NAFTA and so on. Three such distriparks exist in Rotterdam port – that at Botlek covers an area of 86 ha, the second is at Eemhaven with a third under construction at Maasvlakte.

However, Singapore's port is the market leader in the provision and development of the distripark concept. It stems from its being a trading centre, and over 500 multinationals and international trading companies use Singapore as their central physical distribution base and logistics centre for the Asia-Pacific region. Distriparks are provided at Alexandra and Pasir Panjang, and a distribelt covering a 3700-ha distribution zone runs alongside a 20-km stretch on the southern coast. This includes the Container Terminal, Deppel Terminal, Pasir Panjang Terminal, cargo consolidation, Alexandra Distripark and Pasir Panjang Distripark. With shipping infrastructure and support, multinational corporations and international freight forwarders operate from this base.

The Pasir Panjang Distripark has ten single-storey centres enclosing a 162 000 m^2 space with purpose-built ceilings. Additionally, at Pasir Panjang Districentre a three-storey building is provided with 45 000 m^2 including office space of 2 000 m^2. These are ultra-modern warehouses, with each unit able to offer a customized service in consolidation, repacking, labelling and sorting. Round-the-clock security, fire services, fork lift accessibility to every floor, high ceilings, specialized facilities, CCTV security and PR systems are provided. Overall, the Port of Singapore has 14 districentres within the distriparks; all have EDI and are fully computerized and automated.

A total of over 750 free trade zones (FTZs) now exist worldwide. The sites are usually situated in the port environs and are free of customs examination and duty until leaving the area. It enables companies to import products/components for assembly, processing, labelling and distribution to neighbouring markets or to despatch to more distant ones. Examples of FTZ are found in the ports of Liverpool, Southampton and Hamburg.

Dubai and Singapore are two major ports which have developed the fast-growing sea/air market to Europe and North America using the nearby airport. Singapore port is regarded as the major trading centre of the Far East and more recent facilities include a conference centre.

A new generation of container berths is emerging an example of which is the Brani terminal at the Port of Singapore. It has an area of 80 ha and a handling capacity of 3.8 million TEUs. It has 15 000 TEU ground slots and five main berths, together with four feeder berths. Total berth length is 2600 m; the minimum depth alongside the main berth is 15 m, the feeder berth 12 m. It has 1000 power points for reefer containers and 20 single-trolley and four double-trolley quay cranes; some 96 rubber-tyred yard cranes are provided. Overall, 100 prime movers are available, and likewise 100 double-stacked container trailers; it has 14 lanes. Brani terminal, situated on an island just across Tanjon Pagar terminal, is linked to Tanjong Pagar terminal and Keppel distripark by a four-lane causeway. It is equipped wtih the Computer Integrated Terminal Operations System (CITOS) which integrates and automates planning, control and documentation procedures at Brani.

The container freight station (CFS) is an inland depot handling containers. It is usually associated with one or more ports and has all the facilities to handle container imports/exports, stuffing/unstuffing, and servicing, cleaning, maintenance and repair. With customs facilities and served by road and rail, such stations are found in Australia and the Middle East and in other parts of the world where they are also known as container bases/container yards.

Finally, a major function of a seaport is to maintain high levels of cargo or passenger throughput. It involves extensive co-ordination and planning in the seaport operation. A number of seaports, particularly in less developed or developing countries, experience excessive delays in the acceptance of ships on the berth. This arises through cargo congestion and seasonal variation in cargo throughput. In order to help recover the additional costs involved – which may involve up to a week's waiting for a berth – shipowners/container operators raise a delay surcharge per container handled.

As multi-modalism (see Chapter 18) develops in the current decade, the role of ports will change further. Greater emphasis will be placed on trading centres and the provision of a focal point in terms of resources, infrastructure and professional services for the markets served. It will involve port authorities becoming more closely involved in the markets they serve, both local and international. Also an increasing number will become privatized as governments opt out of state ownership and investment of their ports.

17.2 FACTORS INFLUENCING THE SHIPOWNERS' CHOICE OF SEAPORT

As we progress through the next decade the strategy on which the shipowner determines the choice of seaport will become more complex. It will be viewed against an overall logistics plan which considers cost, transit time and the value added benefit which emerges from using a particular seaport. No longer do we live in an era when the international consignment is viewed simply on a port-to-port basis, but is now based on the whole journey from point of origin to destination of which the sea leg forms a part. We are also seeing more innovation in international distribution, especially through the development of the land bridge and sea/air bridge concepts (see pp. 422–6). Moreover, the shipper is constantly looking for rising standards and has a much greater influence over the shipowner than hitherto through demanding a

continuing improvement in service quality. Hence the international distribution infrastructure must be continuously improved
to meet this objective and thus bringing markets closer together
both in transit time and comparative cost. At the same time
empathy must be developed between the shippers' needs/
aspirations and the service provision available from the shipowner.

It is against this background that we examine below the factors
influencing the shipowner's choice of seaport.

(a) Ship specification will determine the range of ports a vessel
may call on her schedule. This includes draught, beam, length,
capacity and the facilities ashore required to handle the cargo or
passengers.

(b) Location of the port is a key factor. A seaport situated on a
shipping lane has distinct advantages in terms of being on a trade
route thereby requiring, no detour to gain access to/from the port
thus reducing voyage time.

(c) The level of traffic available from the port, including both
import and export cargoes. This covers existing and potential
levels of traffic and analysis of the traffic handled, which may be
from transhipment, free trade zone, rail, road, inland waterway
and so on. Rotterdam and Singapore are major trading and
transhipment ports.

(d) The profitability the shipowner will generate from the port.
This is a major factor to consider and the shipowner will usually
favour the port with the greatest potential. Shipowners are tending
to rationalize their ports of call and develop the 'hub and spoke'
system, the spoke being the the feeder service to the hub. A good
example is again the Port of Singapore (see p. 409).

(e) The operating costs are a major factor: port and cargo/
passenger dues, berth charges, victualling, hire of handling equipment, pilotage, towage and passenger and cargo handling costs.
Some ports adopt a policy of flag discrimination favouring national
registered tonnage with lower port tariffs compared with foreign
vessels. Additionally, they give priority to berth access.

(f) Numerous efficiency factors exist when undertaking a
comparison of ports. These not only include port tariffs and any
local taxes, but also operational efficiency factors such as tonnage
handled per gang hour and the cost; the number of TEUs handled
per hour, segregating the import and export cargoes; turn-round

time in port per type of ship; custom's clearance period and cost; breakdown periods and industrial dispute records; stacking area for containers and storage capacity for bulk cargoes and liquid cargoes such as tank farms; and finally whether the tariff is based on a local currency or a third currency such as the US dollar.

(g) Competition is a major factor and all the aspects discussed in this list require analysis and evaluation to seek out especially any trends and both short- and long-term prospects/developments.

(h) Peripheral resources within the port are significant and their pricing. This includes bunkering, victualling, ship repair facilities, container cleansing, servicing and repair facilities, medical facilities, maintenance of cargo handling equipment, security resources, tanker cleaning, and so on. On the commercial front one could also include the availability and cost of freight forwarders, hauliers, port agents, customs, shipbrokers, ship agents, liner cargo agents and so on.

(i) The quality of the port management is an important aspect, especially its calibre and the strategy and policies adopted. An important factor is the degree of understanding between port users and the management team. Continuous liaison between the trade and port management is essential in any well-run port to provide the flexibility to deal with emerging problems.

(j) Many ports still remain unionized and the discerning ship operater examines closely the industrial relations record and trends. Disruption to port operations has an adverse impact on planning schedules, places at risk the shipper's loyalty to the service and increases costs to the shipowner.

(k) The degree of technology employed in the port's operation. This includes all areas of the business, such as berth planning, operation and allocation; the processing of cargo documentation; billing; the cargo-handling operation; and communications. A good example of advanced technology is found in the Port of Singapore (see p. 409).

(l) Allied to (k) is the computerized port operation. Most ports of the world have this facility. Many are called traffic management schemes which enable ships to enter and leave the seaport under a computerized radar network. This substantially improves ship safety and enables continuous access to and from the port in all weathers including dense fog. A modern traffic scheme exists in the port of Rotterdam.

(m) The level of infrastructure serving the port is a major consideration, particularly in the new age of multi-modalism. This includes rail, road and inland waterway systems. Dunkerque and Rotterdam are connected to extensive inland waterway systems and dedicated services are provided to integrate these systems with the shipping schedules. In Port Klang and Southampton dedicated rail services are provided with customs clearance being undertaken at an inland rail depot. Such services are increasing globally. In other ports the land bridge has been developed. West and East Coast North American ports link the container rail services with the sea leg from the Far East to Europe (see pp. 376–8). In Dubai and Singapore a maritime/air service is provided from Japan/Far East to Frankfurt and the United States. This involves a sea leg to Singapore or Dubai from where the containerized cargo is air freighted to Frankfurt and/or the United States.

Another area is the trading port such as Singapore and Rotterdam. Goods are received and processed/assembled and subsequently sold and distributed. The area is usually a free trade zone and may be described as a distripark as in Rotterdam (see p. 407).

(n) The final factor is termed the value added benefit offered to the shipowner/shipper – in other words, what is the benefit to the shipper/shipowner from using a particular port? It may be potential for market growth, better infrastructure, greater profitability, less competition, or a combination of factors.

17.3 RELATIONSHIP BETWEEN SHIPS AND PORTS

The role of seaports is changing rapidly worldwide and more of the major ports are becoming trading centres incorporating free trade zones. Accordingly, their development is being driven by market research and port authorities and shipowners are changing rapidly to meet the changing market opportunities. Ports are thus fast becoming trading and distribution centres in order to exploit the economics of a well configured infrastructure of road/rail/inland waterway on which they rely. A good example is Rotterdam which is regarded by many shippers/shipowners as the gateway to Europe. It relies heavily on rail and inland waterway networks with some 70% of its business categorized as transhipment traffic.

An increasing volume of its business passes through the distri-parks.

As a result of their cost-effective global networks shipowners are bringing markets closer together through quicker voyage times and faster transhipment. Less and less cargo is being customs cleared at the port. The tendency is either to place it into a free trade zone for processing or assembly or convey it on a dedicated service such as rail to an inland depot (CFS – see p. 402) usually in an industrial area. It is against this background that progressive ports are developing by providing the infrastructure to meet such market opportunities. Overall it requires much planning and flexibility in operation. Computers play a major role in this operation as demonstrated in the Port of Singapore through CITOS (see p. 409).

Port authorities work closely with the shipowners they serve and trades in which they operate. Market trends are carefully analysed as are any changes in the international distribution of trade. More and more countries are no longer shipping their indigenous products but are adding value to them. This increases the product value and provides more local employment with fresh skills. Moreover, the distribution infrastructure changes to meet the higher valued cargo and often attracts more disciplined schedules and higher quality service than before. The emerging markets in the sub-continent and Far East fall into this category.

Seaport operations are no longer labour intensive relying on casual workers for many of its stevedoring activities. Today, it is highly professional at all levels and more marketing focused and flexible in its work practices and attitudes. All activities of the business are being constantly evaluated with a view to improving cargo throughput, raising efficiency and developing the business. Computers and technology are playing a major role.

The shipper today no longer views international transit on a seaport-to-seaport basis. The entrepreneur views the international distribution network in its entirety and not as individual transport modes each with their own characteristics. Hence the seaport authorities and shipowners are only two elements in the distribu-tion network. Both play an important role in co-ordinating the development of the overall network. The more integrated the overall transit becomes the more attractive to the market and cost-effective the operation becomes, whether by sea/rail/sea, or by sea/air/road. The role of electronic data interchange (EDI) enabling cargo to be tracked throughout the transit plays a decisive role.

Governments and international agencies also play an important role in framing port development. Governments regard ports as the gateway to trade and their efficiency and profile are both critical in attracting business and developing that trade. Continuous investment is essential to maintain standards and remain competitive. Continuous utilization of assets is also vital to ensure capital investments are funded. A modern container vessel today does the work of ten 'tween deck ships two decades ago. Likewise a modern container berth can handle some eight times the freight the first-generation berth could a decade ago.

The interface between the ship and seaport is dependent not only on the compatibility between vessels and the port infrastructure on a cost-effective basis, but also on like-minded management teams with the same ideals, levels of professionalism and objectives.

To conclude this brief evaluation one must bear in mind that the shipowner and port operator are market driven in their objectives, and training, continuous investment, high technology plus overall professionalism will remain paramount. The mechanism of co-ordination must always remain.

It is significant that both Dubai and Singapore are the primary trading centres of their regions. Such ports are regarded as 'one-stop ports' as shipowners rely on feeder services to generate cargo. Dubai is strategically placed at the crossroads of Asia, Europe and Africa. Singapore is regarded as the trading hub of the Far East market. Manufacturing and trading companies around the world increasingly recognize that efficient production and marketing must be matched by an equally efficient system for shipping goods from the factory to the customer. Hence, Singapore and Dubai are the distribution hubs of their regions (see Table 18.1, p. 425).

The development of sea/air transfers at Dubai and Singapore is a growth market in both ports. A range of established air freight consolidators serve the airports, offering daily services to a range of destinations. Cargo transfer from ship's deck to aircraft take-off takes less than five hours, involving the minimum of customs formalities, with only one customs document for the entire transhipment. Cargo handling facilities and services are provided continuously. The sea/air connection is fast, cost-saving and a reliable mode of transhipment. Repacking services are also provided for goods in transit. Substantial savings can also be made in many of the subsidiary costs of sea freight, warehouse fees, handling, wharfage, haulage costs and insurance. Overall, the transit time of transhipment cargo is guaranteed and insured against delay.

Singapore's port is served by 700 shipping lines and linked to 300 ports worldwide. The airport has 52 airlines serving 110 cities in 54 countries. Dubai's international airport is served by 53 airlines serving over 100 destinations. Its new cargo complex is one of the most modern in the world, handling both FCL and LCL TEUs, with the latest technology including computer-controlled temperature warehouses and handling 250 000 tonnes annually. The seaport is essentially a transhipment point served by over 100 shipping lines, with over 60% of import cargo destined for re-export; it handles over 750 000 TEUs annually.

Students are also urged to read my book: *Elements of Port Operation and Management*.

CHAPTER 18

Multi-modalism

Multi-modalism is the process of operating a door-to-door/ warehouse-to-warehouse service for the shipper involving two or more forms of transport with the merchandise being conveyed in the same unitized form for the entire transit. It may also be described as inter-modalism.

A variety of forms of multi-modalism exists which are listed below:

(a) containerization – FCL/LCL/road/sea/rail;
(b) land bridge via trailer/truck – road/sea/road;
(c) land bridge via pallet/IATA container – road/sea/air/road;
(d) trailer/truck – road/sea/road;
(e) swapbody – road/rail/sea/road.

18.1 FACTORS IN FAVOUR OF MULTI-MODALISM

As we progress through the latter part of the 1990s the international distribution network will become more integrated and multi-modalism will play a major role in the realization of this objective. The traditional seaport-to-seaport or airport-to-airport operation is no longer acceptable in the competitive global market environment in which we live today. The international entrepreneur will design the product in country A, assemble it in country B and source its component units from countries C, D and E. It is broadly an extensive logistics operation in which computers play a decisive part in its operation and control through electronic data interchange (EDI). Hence the overall operation is completely integrated, involving carriers, suppliers/manufacturers and the consignor and consignee. The efficiency of such an operation has a direct bearing on its scale and market penetration. Moreover, it is capital intensive and a high level of utilization is essential to fund the capital expenditure involved. Essentially, it is a global operation with no time barriers or trade barriers to impair its development. Moreover, the more extensive the global multi-modal network becomes, the greater the acceleration of world trade growth. Additionally the multi-modal infrastructure offers low-cost global distribution which, coupled with fast transit involving dedicated services, brings markets closer together and bridges the gap between the rich and the poor nations. It particularly aids the poorer nations who can compete in world markets with low-cost labour responsive to technical training and thereby provides added value to the indigenous commodities which they produce. Basically it results in the concept of the total product being applied to transportation on a global scale.

The key to the operation of multi-modalism is the non-vessel operating carrier (NVOC) or non-vessel operating common carrier (NVOCC). This may result in a container (FCL or LCL) movement or trailer transit. In such a situation, carriers issue bills of lading for the carriage of goods on ships which they neither own nor operate. The carrier is usually a freight forwarder issuing a 'house' bill of lading for a container or trailer movement or, if the trailer movement is in the UK/continental trade, a CMR consignment note.

As an example a freight forwarder offers a groupage service using a nominated shipping line and infrastructure. The freight forwarder offers his own tariff for the service but buys from the shipping line at a box rate. NVOCC allows shipping companies to concentrate on ship management and the freight forwarder to use his expertise in marketing and cargo consolidation. This type of operation is particularly evident in the Far East, US, African and European trades. Overall there must exist a good infrastructure to enable it to operate effectively.

All forms of multi-modalism involve a dedicated service usually under non-vessel operating common carrier (NVOCC) or non-vessel operating carrier (NVOC) arrangements.

The factors below outline why shippers are in favour of multi-modalism.

(a) The service is reliable, frequent and competitively priced. Goods arrive within a scheduled programme involving various transport modes and carriers operating in different countries.

(b) In many companies it features as a global network either as a supply or retail chain. The former may comprise an assembly/

process plant serving a local market whilst the latter involves the retailer buying the product in an overseas market. The retailer may be a shop, manufacturer, consumer, etc.

(c) Many companies operate their global schedules on the 'just in time' basis (see p. 428) requiring dedicated and integrated schedules within the shipper's warehouses and distribution arrangements. Multi-modalism is ideal for this system. Many companies regard it as a distribution arm of their business with on-line computer access. This frequently involves an EDI system (see p. 451) which strongly favours multi-modalism as a global distribution system.

(d) The service is tailor-made to the trade/commodities it serves involving high-tech purpose-built equipment. This provides adequate protection to the goods and arrival of the product in an excellent condition. The product may be refrigerated, fragile cargo or high-tech electrical goods.

(e) It has a high profile which is a good marketing ploy in the promotion of a company's business.

(f) Companies are looking for offshore manufacturing and sourcing outlets for their components and bulk cargo needs. Countries with an established multi-modal global network are especially well placed in such a selection process.

(g) The documentation requirements are minimal with the combined transport bill of lading involving one through rate and a common code of conditions (see p. 241).

(h) More and more companies are focusing on international distribution as an important element of their international business. Such companies identify two profit centres: the manufacture/ supply of the product and the channel of distribution from the supply point to the overseas destination.

(i) Companies using the multi-modal network as a supply chain are very conscious of transit times and the capital tied up in transit. Quicker transit times bring the sourcing and assembly plants situated in different countries closer together, thus reducing the amount of capital tied up in transport which in turn reduces the company's requirements for working capital, a critical factor with the multinational enterprise.

(j) A key factor is the level of facilities provided by the NVOCC at the terminal warehouse. Many are high tech utilizing a bar code sorting system and have purpose-built facilities for specialist cargoes as found in distriparks and districentres. Ned-lloyd are very much in this market as are the ports of Singapore and Rotterdam (see pp. 422–31).

18.2 RATIONALE FOR THE DEVELOPMENT OF MULTI-MODALISM

Multi-modalism is closely aligned to containerization. It is the development of the transit system beyond the sea leg on a port-to-port basis to the overland infrastructure. As described on p. 417, multi-modalism involves the complete integration of all transport modes through a professional co-ordination of all carriers thereby providing a through dedicated service. Maritime containers feature strongly in the multi-modal development and its ongoing progression to the next century. Today shippers are looking to the carrier to provide the optimum route for their buyers at a competitive tariff and acceptable through transit time. Hence in recent years more emphasis has been placed on technology, finance, market development, quality control, information systems, simplified documentation and common code of carrier's liability. These factors are driving the development of multi-modalism and are amplified below:

(a) Air/rail/sea/canal/ports operators are working more closely together to keep pace and facilitate trade development. Examples include the sea/air bridge from Singapore and Dubai and the sea/rail land bridge in North America (see p. 377).

(b) Governments are taking more interest in the development of their nations's economies by encouraging a global trade strategy and providing the infrastructure to facilitate this objective. China plans to build 17 seaports and develop contiguous economic zones.

(c) The development of distriparks, districentres and free trade zones continues to grow (see pp. 407–10).

(d) The documentation involving the carrier's liability and code of practice relative to multi-modalism is now in place through the auspices of the International Chamber of Commerce and other international bodies.

(e) World markets are rapidly changing and the Far East is the fastest growing market globally. Its infrastructure is continuously being improved and it is an established industrial zone. Many companies use it as a low-tech sourcing resource adopting multi-modalism as the global distribution system.

(f) Containerization technology continues to improve and the market in recent years has shifted from a product-driven to a consumer-led strategy whereby the shipper is the dominant factor in container design and development. An example is the high cube container 2.59 m high, 12.19 m long and 2.44 m wide which provides much increased capacity over the 40 footer. Such a container is ideal for the high cube and low weight ratio products emerging from the Far East markets (see p. 376).

(g) Operators such as Nedlloyd and Atlantic Container Line have customized logistics departments to advise their clients on providing the most cost-efficient method of distribution and the optimal route.

(h) The development of the Single Market among the 15 states in the European Union has resulted in a harmonized customs union which to the entrepreneur is a single market with no trade barriers. The same obtains in the North American Free Trade Area (NAFTA) covering Canada, Mexico and the USA. Such trading areas strongly favour multi-modalism and remove – especially in Europe – international boundaries as impediments to market-driven distribution centres operating the 'hub and spoke' system.

(i) Fast-moving consumer goods markets such as those for foodstuffs and consumer products require sophisticated distribution networks. These involve highly sophisticated logistics operations (see p. 411) as found in the 'hub and spoke' system. This speeds transit times, reduces inventory costs in terms of stock, provides a service to the consumer and overall means quicker movement through the supply chain to the consumer. The system is driven by its cost-effectiveness.

(j) EDI (see p. 448) has brought a new era in distribution logistics. It has no international boundaries or time zones and provides ultimate control over performance monitoring of the goods. Bar codes are now used in many distribution networks to route and segregate cargoes together with many other disciplines.

To conclude this analysis one must stress that technology will play a major role in the continuing expansion of the multi-modal network. It will be a major facilitator in the development of world trade.

18.3 FEATURES OF MULTI-MODALISM

The analysis of the salient features of multi-modalism reveals that the objectives of the discriminating shipowner involved in the movement of unitized cargo are to attain a high level of utilization of shipboard capacity coupled with a good return on capital employed to produce adequate levels of profitability thereby generating a rolling programme of tonnage replacement featuring the latest technology. This requires complete professionalism at all levels of management in the formulation and execution of the multi-modal service. The main features of multi-modalism are detailed below:

(a) It strongly favours EDI in a global network linking the shipper (exporter/importer) and carrier at all stages of the transit.

(b) It provides a dedicated service with each operator/carrier committed to the schedule.

(c) It operates under NVOCC or NVOC arrangements (see p. 418).

(d) It develops and co-ordinates the best features of the individual transport modes to the advantage of the shipper.

(e) There is good utilization of the multi-modal infrastructure which permits competitive door-to-door/warehouse-to-warehouse through rates to be offered. Thus it exploits economies of scale and yields a favourable return on the transport investment. Basically, it is a high-tech operation.

(f) It generates professionalism at all levels and encourages shippers to pre-book shipments cubic capacity months in advance. This facilitates good planning and the availability of the multi-modal resources. Moreover, on-line computer access to the carrier enables continuous dialogue between the shipper and carrier.

(g) An increasingly large number of operators are providing logistics departments which are customized to clients' needs. One example is Nedlloyd. This customization encourages closer harmony between the shipper and operator, and ensures an ongoing market-led commitment from both the user and provider of the multi-modal network.

(h) Good utilization of the overall infrastructure of the system encourages investment by the carrier and the shipper (exporter/importer). Overall it generates a spirit of partnership and understanding between the shipper and carrier.

(i) Multi-modalism is market led in its development. It brings the buyer and seller closer together and enables international business to flow unimpeded as the spirit of understanding, the common ideals and the high levels of professionalism develop. The multi-modal system is an extension of the factory supply chain and accordingly features very heavily as manufacturers plan their international business. Accordingly, continuous studies are undertaken to raise levels of efficiency and further exploit the levels of competitiveness to the advantage of both the exporter and importer. This includes packaging, transit times, documentation, stowage, EDI and transport capacity utilization.

(j) Multi-modal services are very competitive offering through rates door to door/warehouse to warehouse. This enables the shipper to continuously monitor the international distribution costs and compare alternative route options on a value added basis. Container ship operators like Nedlloyd operate through districentres and offer a complete package of services fully tailored to the individual needs of its customers. These include storage of goods in bonded and free warehouses, stock administration, order processing, assembly, modification, packing, national and international distribution and customs documents. It has 30 liner global services, 40 liner vessels and 140 000 containers.

(k) Under the auspices of the International Chamber of Commerce and other international bodies a common code of liability and processing of documents is now permitted. This has generated the immense confidence in which multi-modalism operates. Examples include the combined transport bill of lading (see p. 241), Incoterms 1990 – FCA, CPT, CIP, DDU, DDP – and ICC UCP No. 500 covering payment by documentary credits.

(l) Multi-modalism has generated a new climate in global international distribution. It is entirely driven by the market and a closer partnership obtains between the carrier and shipper. One area of especial concern is to maintain schedules and further improve them. This reduces the time the capital/goods are in transit and speeds up the distribution network thereby improving added value and providing greater profitability and better service to the importer, particularly for products such as foodstuff and those of high tech, low weight ratio. Hitherto the operator used to provide the service and its infrastructure. Today the shipper is looking continuously to improve and develop/penetrate new markets and the carrier is responding positively.

(m) Multi-modalism is giving new impetus to the role of seaports and airports. Port authorities worldwide are developing the port enclaves through districentres and free trade zones but are also initiating and encouraging the infrastructure operators on which they rely to develop and improve existing multi-modal networks. Examples of such developments may be found in the ports of Singapore, Dubai, Klang and Rotterdam. In general port authorities are tending to co-ordinate activities and develop strategies on an unprecedented scale, particularly with regard to transhipment cargo and the sea/air markets. Likewise shipowners are developing larger container vessels in response to the growth of the one-stop port operation and are operating the hub and spoke system to improve overall transit time and increase efficiency (see pp. 368–78). Table 18.1 provides examples of sea/air operations.

(n) Associated with (m) is the changing pattern of international distribution. It is less port to port and more multi-modalism. This relieves port congestion and enables the development of ICD/dry ports, free trade zones and local import and export control customs arrangements. It is the creation of a new vision and enthusiasm at all levels of the supply chain to develop and improve the value added benefits which has emerged both for the exporter and importer using the network system.

(o) Market research is essential to improve the system. This requires the continuous marketing of the network, involving commodity specification, variation in tonnage flow relative to origin and destination, transit time, and so on.

(p) The system favours both the large and small shipper and the full load or consolidated consignment.

(q) Multi-modalism develops new markets, improves product/commodity quality, raises loadability, lowers transit times, reduces packing and aids the growth of high-tech fast-moving consumer markets. Moreover, it brings cultures and the international business world closer together both in their objectives and ideology.

Table 18.1 Transit times (days)

Trade routes	Seaport	Markets	Sea	Transhipment	Air	Overall transit time
Japan–Europe	Singapore		8	2	1	11
South Korea–Europe	Singapore		9	2	1	12
Taiwan–Europe	Singapore	UK	5	2	1	8
Hong Kong–Europe	Singapore	France	4	2	1	7
Korea–Europe	Dubai	Belgium	17	2	1	20
Taiwan–Europe	Dubai	Italy	15	2	1	18
Hong Kong–Europe	Dubai	Germany	12	2	1	15
Singapore–Europe	Dubai	Switzerland	10	2	1	13
Bombay–Europe	Dubai	Spain	7	2	1	10
Madras–Europe	Dubai		9	2	1	12
Karachi–Europe	Dubai		7	2	1	10

To conclude our analysis, there is no doubt that multi-modalism will contribute to the changing pattern of international trade. It will open up countries with low labour costs to the industrialized Westernized markets with great buying power. Such industrialized high labour cost countries are increasingly reliant for the development of their global manufacturing business on producing within low-cost markets and then employing multi-modalism to distribute in a cost-effective manner their goods to high GDP markets. Moreover, the shipper/manufacturer/supplier/exporter/importer have developed a new attitude towards international distribution than hitherto by formulating high-profile logistics departments (see p. 428) responsible for their global distribution operations and strategy.

18.4 MULTI-MODALISM STRATEGY

The strategy to adopt with regard to multi-modalism is essentially market led and high tech. It is also an ongoing strategy with market growth providing the cash flow necessary to fund the continuing investment. Moreover, as the system develops, economies of scale will lower development costs, as has been experienced in computerization. It is an exciting time and full of opportunity but it is one requiring complete professionalism and high-quality training at all levels. Qualified experienced personnel are required with complete commitment and a clear vision of the market's needs.

Given below are matters which require special attention.

(a) Shippers and operators must study continuously trading patterns and trends to identify and develop new opportunities for multi-modalism. Existing systems must be continuously evaluated and improved as the trading patterns change. Markets must also be continuously studied to discern trends and opportunities. The lead time to introduce changes must be short and fully co-ordinated with all concerned.

(b) Trading blocs such as ASEAN, the EU and NAFTA need to review the structure of both their internal market and external market multi-modal systems. Countries with a good infrastructure are advantageously placed to develop their external markets and develop multi-modal systems. In general the more closely trading blocs work together, the greater will be the benefits to be reaped in terms of market growth and distribution arrangements. A spirit of understanding must prevail, involving all parties to the total distribution product.

(c) The markets of the Pacific Rim are a major growth sector and are very fast moving; it will require particular attention in terms of opportunities.

(d) The sub-continent, South Africa and China are also developing markets with good opportunities. The development of their global container networks will be greatly facilitated by multi-modalism.

(e) The role of swapbodies (see p. 391) is fast developing, especially in the European markets involving road/sea/rail. The implications of the value added benefit of the Channel Tunnel must also be considered.

(f) The airport and seaport – especially the latter – are key players in the development of multi-modalism. The need to develop inter-modal strategies and a strong interface with all concerned in the development of multi-modalism is paramount. Vision and pragmatism is required coupled with professionalism at all levels of the business.

(g) Multi-modalism strongly supports the 'just in time' strategy.

(h) Major shippers, particularly the multinationals, are companies with great investment resources and high-calibre personnel. They are leading the way in the development of multi-modalism in many markets. However, the smaller shipper, who may be a subcontractor, is also benefiting from such developments.

By the time the year 2000 arrives, the multi-modal network will have changed dramatically. Consumer markets especially will no longer rely on the seaport-to-seaport or airport-to-airport network, but rather the door-to-door or warehouse-to-warehouse system. Concepts such as 'just in time', the hub and spoke system and the one-stop port operation together with distriparks, distri-centres, FTZs, ICD/dry ports, air and land bridges, LEC/LIC and the industrial plant transplant will all become established on a global basis in conjunction with EDI. This transformation will contribute significantly to rising living standards worldwide.

18.5 LOGISTICS

Associated with multi-modalism is the subject of logistics. Shippers are today looking increasingly at the total production and value added chain: in consequence shippers are also looking more closely at the logistics part of their business. The shipper, then, is no longer interested in point-to-point operations such as airport to airport or seaport to seaport, but is concerned with the total product along the whole length of the value added chain. This is closely associated with the 'just in time' management technique.

Basically the art of logistics is the ability to get the right product at the right place at the right time. Overall it is the planning, organization, control and execution of the flow of goods from purchasing through production and distribution to the final customer in order to satisfy the requirements of the market. In international distribution terms this is the process of warehousing, transporting and distributing goods and cargo, and the positioning of containers and/or equipment. It is, then, an integrated and high-quality package of services in which emphasis is focused on care of the cargo and provision of the most efficient co-ordination and management of the transport process. It comprises transport, forwarding, storage and distribution, adapted to the specific requirements of the product, the supplier and his buyers: a total package which covers all the links in the logistic chain but where the different components can also be offered individually. It combines production, warehousing, distribution and transport for shippers on a global basis.

Nedlloyd are market leaders in logistic services and provide a total transportation service package geared to individual manufacturers and their customers' needs. It operates the complete logistics system termed Nedlloyd Flowmaster (Fig. 18.1) which manages both the flow of goods and information. It has seven elements as detailed below:

(a) Merchandise – in principle everything from computers to clothing and from wood products to chemicals.

(b) Equipment – embracing ships, aircraft, trucks and distri-centres.

(c) Loading units – ranging from the management, loading and repair of containers, trailers and swapbodies to the manufacture of boxes and crates for vulnerable cargo.

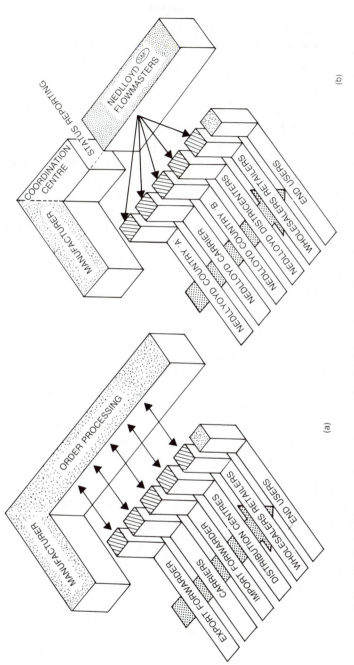

Fig. 18.1 The Nedlloyd Flowmaster logistics system: (a) how it usually is; (b) how it could be. (Reproduced by kind permission of Nedlloyd.)

(d)   Personnel – specialists who use their experience and professionalism to devise a solution to the logistics problem.

(e)   Payment – usually in electronic form.

(f)   Documents – all the paperwork and file space which is necessary to comply with all the necessary formalities.

(g)   Information – provided on paper, by telephone, telefax, telex or data network covering for example, where the goods are located at any one time, or the arrival time at a specific place.

Nedlloyd has a sophisticated information system which is essential to the build-up of networks and integrated transport. It has a computer program which determines the most suitable place for a distribution centre taking into account both internal and external factors such as road congestion, infrastructure and regional market developments.

The development of such logistics networks has emerged as a result of the following reasons:

(a)   Companies are increasingly concentrating on their 'core activities' of production and sales.

(b)   There is a growing tendency for companies to decentralize their production overseas.

(c)   The product life cycle is becoming shorter so that fast and flexible distribution is essential.

Hence companies tend to contract out areas of distribution such as physical transport and storage. Generally distribution can be carried out more efficiently and cheaply by means of a total transport company such as Nedlloyd, and the client also has the security of knowing that his cargo is in one pair of hands at all times from door to door.

The Nedlloyd Flowmaster system is a total transportation package geared to individual manufacturers and their customers' needs. The manufacturer despatches his products to a strategically located districentre which is virtually a warehouse. At this stage Nedlloyd takes over the management and control of the operation. The benefits include:

(a)   customer services are designed and delivered to each client's individual needs;

(b)   fully integrated services are provided, i.e. distribution logistics are co-ordinated with procurement and production logistics;

(c)   one-stop shopping is available for logistics services, most or all services being co-ordinated at one districentre;

(d)   improved reliability means the client is better able to keep promises made to customers;

(e)   broader market research is available for clients using an established distribution system;

(f)   there are shorter lead times for clients seeking to stream-line their reaction times in the marketplace;

(g)   increased flexibility means that a client's market opportun-ities are not limited by distribution constraints;

(h)   lower logistics costs are possible with economies of scale;

(i)   there is a higher satisfaction profile for both manufacturers and their clients;

(j)   there are value added benefits to be derived from such services.

The international consignment

Our study of shipping would not be complete without an examination of the international consignment in so far as suitability of transport modes, delivery trade terms of sale, and export documentation processing are concerned.

19.1 FACTORS TO CONSIDER IN EVALUATING SUITABILITY OF TRANSPORT MODE(S) FOR AN INTERNATIONAL CONSIGNMENT

The following factors must be considered when evaluating suitability of transport mode(s) for an international consignment:

(a) Nature of the commodity, its dimensions/weight and whether any special facilities are required during transit. For example, livestock require special facilities; gold requires special security/strong room; meat requires refrigerated accommodation.

(b) The degree of packaging and the costs thereof. Air freight, containerization and through international multi-modalism road/rail services require less packaging.

(c) The degree to which the consignment presented aids cargo handling. For example, palletized cargo facilitates handling by fork-lift truck, whilst lightweight cartons are ideal for containers. Conversely, awkwardly shaped packages may require special facilities and/or handling arrangements, and may be subject to a possible freight surcharge.

(d) Any statutory obligations imposed relative to the transit. Certain products need special facilities both in the transport mode and terminal. This in itself restricts route/service and transport mode choice. For example, the movement of meat/offal etc. requires special facilities both by the operator to ship it and inspection facilities at the import terminal. Statutory obligations also can influence type of packaging as found for example in the Australian trade in the use of straw and case wood.

(e) Dangerous cargo. Again, regulations are stringent regarding its packaging, stowage, and mixture with other cargoes during stowage. This can restrict service/routing schedules.

(f) Terms of export contract. For example it may stipulate that goods must be consigned to a national or specified shipping line/ airline operator to save currency. This policy in shipping is called flag discrimination.

(g) Suitability of available transport services. For example, air freighters have limited capacity/weight/dimensions; weight restrictions may apply at a particular berth/shipping service, etc.

(h) The transit time and related urgency of consignment.

(i) The overall transport cost and evaluation of alternatives. This is an important item and will include rate; evaluation of transit time; cost of packaging; and convenience/reliability of services. Additionally, one must consider that frequent service means less storage in warehouse; reduces risk of obsolescence of product; requires less working capital through less stockpiling etc; facilitates smoother production flow; and helps to produce better customer relations. Service, quality, risk of pilferage/damage and the condition of goods on arrival are also relevant.

(j) Quantity of cargo available and period over which shipment is to be made. It is desirable to undertake a transport distribution analysis of the options available, and thereby decide which is the most favourable in the light of the foregoing factors.

(k) Proximity and convenience, transport cost of the consignors/ consignees, promises relative to the seaport/airport, and the local facilities available.

(l) The range of shipping routes available, their cost, other costs, range of facilities, quality of resources, general availability, overall efficiency and convenience of operation.

(m) Distribution services used by the exporter's competitors, and their strengths and weaknesses.

(n) Likely changes in the foreseeable future, such as provision of modern tonnage.

(o) The value added benefit derived by the shipper resulting from the service used. This can be evaluated in financial and perceived benefit terms. In general this item is becoming increasingly important as companies focus more attention on their international distribution strategies, and especially on their logistics evaluation.

19.2 DELIVERY TRADE TERMS OF SALE AND THE EXPORT CONTRACT

The basis of the price quotation depends on correct interpretation of the delivery trade terms of sale. Hence they determine the following:

(a) The charges paid by the buyer and seller.

(b) Where delivery takes place in order to complete the export contract.

(c) When the property and risk pass from the seller to the buyer. The following examples are relevant:

(i) cash against documents – on payment;

(ii) documents against payment – on payment;

(iii) open account – payment by importer usually on receipt of merchandise;

(iv) documents against acceptance – on acceptance;

(v) letter of credit – on acceptance of documents by bank.

The financial aspects cannot be overstressed in the execution of the delivery trade terms of sale.

Details are given below of information found in a typical export contract in UK, but it must be stressed they can differ by individual country. This may be found in the export sales contract, or the commercial export invoice, and contains:

(a) Seller's name and address.

(b) Buyer's name and address.

(c) Confirmation that the document constitutes a contract of the goods sold to an addressee and that he has bought according to the terms and conditions laid down.

(d) Number and quantity of goods precisely and fully described to avoid later misunderstanding or dispute. In particular one must mention details of batches, etc. and reconcile goods description with custom tariff specification.

(e) Price – in UK often quoted in sterling unless otherwise required. This may be US dollars or the buyer's currency. To counter inflation, particularly with long-term contracts, it is usual to incorporate an escalation clause, and to reduce the risk of sterling fluctuations, the tendency is to invoice in foreign currencies.

(f) Terms of delivery, e.g. CIP Kuala Lumpur, CIF Lagos, FOB Felixstowe, EXW Luton.

(g) Terms of payment, e.g. letter of credit, sight draft.

(h) Delivery date/shipment date or period.

(i) Methods of shipment FCL or LCL, e.g. container routeing, Ro/Ro-trailer, air freight.

(j) Method of packing.

(k) Insurance – cover note terms.

(l) Import or export licence details or other instructions, such as certificate of origin, ATA carnet, etc.

(m) Shipping/freight/documentary requirements and/or details as found on the export cargo shipping instructions. Case marking instruction.

(n) Contract conditions, e.g. sale, delivery, performance (quality) of goods, arbitration, pre-shipment inspection (SGS), etc.

(o) Signature – copy for buyer to return signed to seller.

Details of the 13 Incoterms 1990 are given in Table 19.1. These are used by 90% of world trade.

Recommended usage of the Incoterms 1990 can be divided by modes of transport: all modes (i.e. combined transport/multi-modalism) – EXW, FCA, CPT, CIP, DAF, DDP, DDU; conventional port-to-port/sea transport only – FAS, FOB, CFR, CIF, DES and DEQ. A brief commentary on the more frequently used Incoterms is given below.

(a) *CFR – cost and freight (named port of destination)*. This term obligates the seller to pay all the costs necessary to bring the goods to the named port of destination. The risk of loss or damage to the goods is transferred from the seller to the buyer when the goods pass over the ship's rail. The buyer is responsible for funding and arranging the cargo insurance.

(b) *CIF – cost, insurance and freight (named port of destination)*. This term is identical to the CFR except the seller is responsible for funding and arranging the insurance. Both terms are long established and idea for sea transport in port-to-port operations.

(c) *CIP – carriage and insurance paid (named port of destination)*. This term is identical to CPT except the seller also arranges

Table 19.1 Incoterms 1990 (see pp. 435–7)

Group E		
Departure from factory – all carriage paid by buyer	EXW	Ex works
Group F		
Main carriage unpaid by seller	FCA	Free carrier
	FAS	Free alongside ship
	FOB	Free on board
Group C		
Main carriage paid by seller	CPT	Carriage paid to
	CIP	Carriage and insurance paid to
	CFR	Cost and freight
	CIF	Cost, insurance and freight
Group D		
Arrival – carriage to delivered paid by the seller	DAF	Delivered at frontier
	DES	Delivered ex ship
	DEQ	Delivered ex quay
	DDU	Delivered duty unpaid
	DDP	Delivered duty paid

and funds the cargo insurance. Both are ideal for multi-modal operation.

(d) *CPT – carriage paid (named port of destination)*. Under this term the seller pays the freight for the carriage of the goods to the named destination. The buyer's risk commences when the goods have been delivered into the custody of the first carrier who accordingly undertakes all the cargo insurance arrangements.

(e) *DAF – delivered at frontier (named point)*. This obligates the seller to deliver the goods to the named frontier point or customs examination border. This term is used primarily for rail- or road-borne traffic but can be used for other transport modes in varying circumstances. The buyer's obligations commence when the goods have been accepted at the named frontier point.

(f) *DDP – delivered duty paid (named point)*. This term places the maximum obligations on the seller regarding the cargo despatch arrangements. Under such terms the seller is responsible for the conveyance of the goods at his own risk and expense to the named destination in the buyer's country. This includes the task of processing the cargo through both exportation and importation including duties and taxes plus customs clearance, loading and unloading and related documentation.

(g) *DDU – delivered duty unpaid (named point)*. The seller fulfils his obligations when the goods have arrived at the named point or place in the country of importation. The seller bears the full cost and risk involved in bringing the goods thereto, excluding duties, taxes and other charges payable upon importation.

(h) *EXW – ex works*. This places maximum involvement on the buyer in the arrangements for the conveyance of the consignment to the specified destination. The exporter merely makes the goods available by an agreed date at his factory or warehouse. The seller minimizes his obligations whilst the buyer obtains the goods at the lowest possible price. It is usual for the buyer to appoint an agent in the seller's country to look after all the collection, transportation, insurance and documentation arrangements, possibly in consultation with the national shipping line or airline. Ideal for combined transport operation.

(i) *FCA – free carrier (named place)*. This term is primarily for the combined transport operation/multi-modalism such as a container or road trailer. The seller fulfils his obligations by delivering the goods into the custody of the carrier at the named placed detailed in the export sales contract. The risk of loss or damage to the goods is transferred from the seller to the buyer at the time the nominated carrier accepts the goods at the prescribed place. At this point onwards the cost of insurance, transportation and associated arrangements are the responsibility of the buyer.

(j) *FOB – free on board (sea transport)*. Under this long-established term the goods are placed in the ship by the seller at the specified port of shipment detailed in the sales contract and usually recorded in the export invoice. The risk of loss or damage to the goods is transferred from the seller to the buyer when the goods pass over the ship's rail. Under such terms the seller bears all the costs and the risk of conveyance up to the ship's rail and the buyer accepts the residue of the transit costs including sea freight and insurance. This is ideal for sea transport in port-to-port operations.

The practice today is that when the seller/exporter undertakes the main carriage arrangements the operation is treated as a profit centre in that the exporter is able to make a small profit. This refers to CIR, CFR, CPT, CIP, DAF, DDU and DDP. A further point is that there is now a tendency to deliver goods under a multi-modalism combined transport operation. This embraces EXW, FCA, CPT, CIP, DAF, DDU and DDP.

Other terms used in the trade include loco and turnkey which are examined below:

(a) *Loco*. This term includes in the price of goods the cost of packaging and conveyance to the place named.

(b) *Turnkey*. This term arises where the export sales contract provides for the seller (exporter) not only to supply the goods but also launch/introduce them in the area defined by the importer. It thus involves the exporter providing the facility and also setting it up on the site. This is particularly common with large-scale engineering projects where the seller is responsible for the entire operation through to construction to the point at which it is fully operational. It is particularly common in the Emirate States, the former states of the Eastern bloc and in a consortium situation.

19.3 RECEIPT OF EXPORT ORDER

Before dealing with the export order acceptance, it is appropriate to study the following check points which need careful scrutiny in any price list tendered. It emphasizes how important it is to ensure all the special costs which may enter into an export order are included together with the disciplined time scale to execute the order and ensure the goods arrive on time in a quality condition:

(a) Adequate clear – technical and not commercial – description of goods using the Harmonized Commodity Description and Coding System (H/S) (see p.000).

(b) Goods specification – use metric.

(c) Quantities offered/available with delivery details including address and required arrival date.

(d) Price:

    (i) amounts or per unit;
    (ii) currency;
    (iii) delivery terms which may involve part shipments over a scheduled period and/or transhipment – EXW, FCA, CPT, DAF – multi-modalism now more popular.

(e) Terms of payment including provision for currency rate variation.

(f) Terms of delivery, ex stock, forward, etc. – relevant estimate.

(g) Transportation mode(s), e.g. container, air freight, sea freight, road haulier.

(h) Cargo insurance and perhaps credit insurance.

(i) Packaging and packing together with marking of the goods.

(j) Offer by pro forma invoice.

(k) Identity of goods, country of origin and shipment.

(l) Specific documentation needs such as export licence, certificate of origin, preshipment certificate, etc.

(m) Tender bond to be followed by performance bond.

Prior to receipt of the indent/order a customer may need a pro forma invoice which is essential before a customer can open a bank credit in the supplier's favour. On receipt of the indent or order from the overseas client, the export marketing manager will check the specification and price in the order with the quotation together with its period of validity. Care must be taken to ensure the client is not trying to take advantage of an out-of-date quotation. For example where the quotation was FOB, the export marketing manager must note whether the customer wishes the supplier to arrange for freight and insurance on his behalf. The method of payment will be noted and checked with quotation terms. For example, where payment is to be made under a documentary credit, the documents the banks require must be carefully noted. The required delivery date will be particularly noted; if the delivery date is given and the client has been obliged to obtain an import licence for the particular consignment, the date of expiry must be noted.

Given below is a receipt of order checklist:

(a) *Goods*
   (i) quality; (ii) quantity; (iii) description.

(b) *Payment*
   (i) price; (ii) method, i.e. letter of credit, open account, or documents against payment or acceptance; (iii) time-scale; (iv) currency variation provision.

(c) *Shipment*
   (i) mode of transport/route/transhipment and whether buyer requests any specific carrier; (ii) any constraints, i.e. packing/weighing/dimensions/statutory and route restrictions; (iii) time-scale enforcing despatch and arrival date; (iv) any marks, i.e. special marking on cases/cartons to identify them.

(d) *Additional requirements*
   (i) insurance; (ii) preshipment inspection; (iii) documentation such as certificate of origin; (iv) specific packing – see item (c)(ii); (v) commissions or discount; (vi) details of agent handling buyer's order and likely specific request.

(e) *Comparison with quotation*
A pro forma invoice is a document similar to a sales invoice except that it is headed 'pro forma'. It is not a record of sales effected, but a representation of a sales invoice issued prior to the sale. The pro forma invoice contains all relevant details, e.g. full description of goods, packing specification, price of goods with period of validity, cost of cases, and where relevant cost of freight and insurance. It is particularly used for quotations to customers and for submission to various authorities. Terms of payment are also always shown but it may not be possible to give shipping marks until a firm order is received. When used as a quotation the pro forma invoice constitutes a binding offer of the goods covered by it, the price and conditions shown.

As soon as the exporter receives the letter of credit, he should check it against his pro forma invoice to ensure both documents agree with each other. Usually, the contract will be in a more detailed form than the letter of credit, but it is important the exporter should be able to prepare his documents complying with both the contract and the credit. The exporters must be fully aware of the terms and provisions of UCP 500, 511 and 515 (see pp. 247–8). For general guidance the following checklist should be adopted by the exporter.

1. The terms of the letter of credit which may be revocable or irrevocable.
2. The name and address of the exporter (beneficiary).
3. The amount of the credit which may be in sterling or a foreign currency.

4. The name and address of the importer (accreditor).

5. The name of the party on whom the bills of exchange arc to be drawn, and whether they are to be at sight or of a particular tenor.

6. The terms of the contract and shipment (i.e. whether EXW, FCA, CIF, DDU, CPT, CIP, and so on).

7. A brief description of the goods covered by the credit. Basically too much detail may give rise to errors which can cause delay.

8. Precise instructions as to the documents against which payment is to be made.

9. Details of shipment including whether any transhipment is allowed, data on the latest shipment date and details of port of departure and destination should be recorded.

10. Whether the credit is available for one or more shipments.

11. The expiry date.

It is important to check the reverse side of the letter of credit and any attachments thereto, the credit as further terms, and any conditions which form an integral part of the credit. Ideally both the seller (exporter) and the buyer (importer) should endeavour to make the credit terms as simple as practicable.

In situations where the seller (exporter) is uncertain of just how much of the credit he will draw, arrangements should be made with the buyer (importer) to have the value of the documentary letter of credit prefixed by the word 'about'. This will permit up to a 10% margin over or under the amount specified. The word 'about' preceding the quantity of goods also allows a 10% margin in the quantity to be shipped. Alternatively the documentary letter of credit may specify a 'tolerance' – such as 7½% to 5% more or less – by which the seller (exporter) should be guided.

Documentation will usually involve the clean on-board combined transport multi-modal bill of lading. For international rail movements the CIM consignment note will be required, and for international road haulage transit the CMR consignment note.

With the growing development of multi-modalism it is essential the shipper pre-books the consignment throughout the transit from warehouse to warehouse via a dedicated service. The booking is generally processed by major shippers using on-line computer access to the first carrier, and involves booking cargo space for the entire transit which may be by rail/ship/rail, and also for the supply of a specialist container type, if necessary. Hence, pre-planning for international distribution is very important to ensure delivery dates are met.

19.4 PROGRESS OF EXPORT ORDER AND CHECKLIST

In processing the export consignment one must bear in mind there are up to four contracts to execute. These include the export sales contract, the contract of carriage, the financial contract and finally the contract of cargo insurance. All these have to be reconciled with the processing of the export consignment.

To ensure the complex procedure of preparing the goods, packing, forwarding, shipping, insurance, customs clearance, invoice and collecting payment do not go wrong, it is suggested a checklist or progress sheet be prepared for each export order. A suggested version is given below but it must be borne in mind there are many variations in processing a given export order:

1. Manufacturer receives, in export sales office, initial export enquiry.

2. Costing department calculates approximate total weight/volume of the finished packed goods.

3. Details of weight/measurement of goods submitted to shipping department to obtain insurance/freight rates to destination delivery point. This involves obtaining quotations from freight forwarders and checking out documentation required such as export licence, certificate of origin, etc.

4. Costing department completes non-transport calculations.

5. Credit controller obtains satisfactory status report on potential customer.

6. Insurance/freight quotation submitted to costing department to formulate overall quotation.

7. Formal quotation prepared including currency, terms of delivery (Incoterms 1990) and required terms of payment. If, for example, it is DAF, CPT, CIP, it includes price of goods and related transportation. Many exporters regard the two elements as two separate profit centres and thereby have a mark up on each and formulate them into one overall quotation.

8. Quotation sent to prospective overseas buyer. It includes a validity clause.

9. Telex/fax sent asking the buyer to expedite the reply.

10. Purchase order (offer) received.

11. Export sales office checks out stock availability/manufacturing lead time/delivery schedules.

12. Export sales office rechecks credit status report. Any change from item (5).

13. Agree to accept order only if customer will pay by confirmed letter of credit.

14. Export sales office raises order acknowledgement (acceptance) to establish sales contract.

15. Export sales office despatches acknowledgement to buyer. Note that if the seller is not being paid by letter of credit, pass to item (23).

16. Await receipt of letter of credit if item (13) applies.

17. Letter of credit received.

18. Export sales office check out whether all the conditions can be met.

19. Export sales office request amendment/extension to letter of credit.

20. Export sales office awaits amendment/extension to letter of credit.

21. Export sales office receives amendment/extension to letter of credit and checks out all the conditions have now been met.

22. Export sales office confirms all the conditions have now been met and despatches acknowledgement to the buyer.

23. Export sales office issues authority for the goods to be manufactured and packed. The task of monitoring progress of manufacture of goods/packaging is handled by the Shipping Department which maintains close liaison with the Production Department to ensure the despatch date is achieved within the time-scale defined in the letter of credit/export or import licence/cargo space booked on carrier's flight/sailing/trailer.

24. Shipping Department establishes total weight/measurement of packed goods and has the completed order checked out.

25. Shipping Department raises shipping documents and export cargo shipping instructions (ECSI) noting any letter of credit conditions including any pre-shipment inspection obligations such as SGS.

26. Pre-shipment inspection completed (if applicable) and clean report of findings issued. Goods despatched to airport/seaport/ inland clearance depot, etc. in accordance with the terms of sale Incoterms 1990 and freight forwarder's/buyer's/buyer's agent's instructions. Documents to be provided include BL/AWB/CMR consignment note/packing list/export licence/certificate of origin/ certificate of insurance/commercial invoice, etc. The range and nature of the documents will vary by commodity/terms of sale/ destination country. These will be provided by the seller. The task of processing cargo through customs is likely to be undertaken by the freight forwarder, unless the seller has the goods cleared under a local export control arrangement, in which case the seller handles all the export documentation and customs clearance arrangements.

27. Await shipping documents.

28. Shipping documents received confirming goods despatched on specified flight/sailing/trailer – buyer informed.

29. Documents checked by Shipping Department – any errors found and corrected documents requested.

30. Receive corrected documents.

31. Shipping Department collates documents and letter of credit.

32. Seller raises bill of exchange signed by a director.

33. Shipping Department checks all documents against letter of credit.

34. Shipping Department presents all documents to the bank within agreed time-scale.

35. Seller awaits payment or acceptance of the bill of exchange.

36. Seller receives funds from the bank. If the funds are not in the seller's currency (i.e. sterling), the exporter should sell at spot or place against for which finance should have been arranged under (15).

37. Legal requirements followed through such as VAT.

It will be appreciated the above arrangements will vary by circumstances and many companies computerize their export consignment processing. Critical areas of variation are in the terms of payment, the method of carriage and the customs arrangements. It is important to bear in mind the seller is responsible for providing the buyer with all the requisite documents to enable the goods to be processed/imported through customs in the destination country. These must be checked out by the seller. The overall factors to bear in mind are adherence to the time-scale to ensure the goods arrive on the agreed date, and that all the documents are in order to enable the consignment to arrive in a quality condition.

As stated, many companies now computerize the processing of their export consignment and this is examined on pp. 471–9. Given below is a brief commentary on the salient documents involved.

(a) *Consular invoice.* A consular invoice may have to be prepared where the goods are consigned to countries which enforce *ad valorem* import duties. Such invoices have to be certified by the consul of the country to which the goods are consigned either at the place from which the goods are despatched, which is usual, or at the port/airport/ICD of departure.

(b) *Export invoice.* The exporter completes an export invoice which embodies the date, name of the consignee, quantity and description of the goods, marks and measurements of packages, cost of the goods, packing, carriage, freight, postage, insurance premiums, etc. The actual form of invoice varies with the method of price quotation.

(c) *The invoice.* The invoice is a document rendered by one person to another in regard of goods which have been sold. The invoice is not necessarily a contract of sale. It may form a contract of sale if it is in writing containing all the material terms. On the other hand it may not be a complete memorandum of the contract of sale and therefore evidence may be given to vary the contract which is inferred therefrom.

(d) *Certificate of origin.* Certificates of origin specify the nature of quantity/value of the goods, etc. together with their place of manufacture. Such a document is required by some countries, often to simplify their customs duties. Additionally they are needed when merchandise is imported to a country that allows preferential duties (see p. 94) on British goods, owing to trade agreements.

(e) *Contract of affreightment.* This is found in the bill of lading/CIM/CMR documentation.

(f) *Marine insurance policy/certificate.* This acknowledges that the cargo value as declared has been insured for the maritime transit.

(g) *Charter party*. This involves hire/charter of a ship.

(h) *Letter of credit*. This is a document enabling the beneficiary to obtain payment of funds from the issuer, or from an agent if the insurer complies with certain conditions laid down in the credit.

This document may be a commercial credit. It may be issued to finance international trade involving shipments of goods between countries, or non-commercial or personal credits for the use of individuals, e.g. consular letters of credit issued to tourists and holidaymakers. The commercial credit may be a bank credit, i.e. drawn on an issuing bank which undertakes due payment, or non-bank credit, which although issued through a bank does not carry any bank undertaking. The letter of credit may be revocable or irrevocable.

(i) *Mate's receipt*. Sometimes issued in lieu of a bill of lading to confirm cargo has been placed on board a ship pending issue of bill of lading.

(j) *Dock receipt*. Sometimes issued by the port authority to confirm receipt of cargo on the quay/warehouse pending shipment.

(k) *Letters of hypothecation*. Banker's documents outlining conditions under which the international transaction will be executed on the exporter's behalf, who will have given certain pledges to his banker.

(l) *Packing list*. A document providing a list of the contents of a package/consignment(s).

(m) *ATA carnet*. An international customs document to cover the temporary export of certain goods (commercial samples and exhibits for international trade fairs abroad and professional equipment) to countries which are parties to the ATA Convention and cover reimport of such goods (see p. 96).

(n) *Pre-shipment inspection certificates*. An increasing number of shippers and various organizations/authorities/governments in countries throughout the world are now insisting the goods are inspected. This includes their quality, the quantity being exported and the price(s) proposed and market price(s), and the exchange rate at the time of shipment. The organizations which undertake such work – which can extend to transhipment en route – are the Société Générale de Surveillance (SGS) and classification societies (e.g. BV – see pp. 149–54).

(o) *Certificate of shipment*. The FIATA forwarder's certificate of receipt (RCR) and forwarding certificate of transport (FCT) are becoming increasingly accepted in the trade as the recognizable documents confirming receipt of the goods. These documents are usually issued under FCA Free Carrier Incoterms 1990 involving multi-modal transport operations. Alternatively, they may be EXW (ex works). In such situations the freight forwarder would be acting as principal or road carrier.

(p) *Performance certificates*. This customs requirement involves GSP, EUR 1.

Usually there are three restraints which have to be dealt with before goods can be released to customers by the shipowner or his agent as detailed below:

(i) clearance by customs or any other relevant statutory body including the port health authority or Ministry of Agriculture, Fisheries and Food;

(ii) surrender of an original bill of lading correctly endorsed unless a waybill has been issued;

(iii) payment of outstanding charges including freight, customs duty and VAT.

In countries and ports where the consignment is delivered into and shipped out of a 'freeport' some of the above requirements may not be applicable. In many ports/CFS/CCD today customs clearance is fully computerized (see pp. 426–7).

Finally shipowners will issue an arrival notification form (ANF) to the party receiving the goods advising of goods coming forward for delivery. This ensures smooth delivery and enables the recipient to pre-plan all the necessary arrangements such as customs clearance documentation, collection, duty payment, and so on. Many ANFs are despatched over the on-line computer network.

CHAPTER 20

Information technology and electronic data interchange

20.1 INTRODUCTION

As we progress into the next millennium the ongoing rapid advances in information technology will be manifest on a global basis. Such advances will affect all areas of global trade in both service and product manufacturing industries, in particular the processing of the export consignment, the international banking payment systems and global distribution including the terminal, carriers, customs, cargo status, stowage, data bank, planning, and so on. Many of these advances are already in place and in the process of rapid improvement/development/extension. Information technology is relentless in its progress and recognizes no languages, cultures or time zone barriers. Such technology has shrunk the world in terms of communication and distribution, bringing markets closer together.

Shipping and trade are at the forefront of these changes, with shipping as the central plank on which global trade is developing. The more sophisticated the maritime network in terms of efficiency and value added network (VAN), the greater will be the acceleration of trade development. As regards distribution shipping is particularly important to the development of the global container network. Shipping, however, should not develop in isolation but must be part of the international network of global business. And it is information technology which enables all the constituents of international business to come together in a user-friendly, harmonious and completely integrated manner to produce dedicated services and procedures.

The effect the rapid advances in information technology has had on the competitive environment of the changing international marketplace and on many aspects of the business process has already been recognized. One of the best examples is provided by the European Union.

One of the main factors justifying the need for the European Single Market and for the effective economic integration of 450 million people and 15 nations has been the estimated cost to industry of a fragmented market in the order of £160 billion. This is made up of the heavy cost of national customs-related procedures, billions of pounds of losses due to the inefficiencies created by the varying product standards especially in the electronics and telecommunications industries, and the high administrative costs incurred throughout the whole trading chain, especially by small companies, discouraging them from seeking trans-border business.

A recent EU survey concluded that differing national standards and regulations are the principal barriers to EU trade and there is increasing pressure for the development of international standards, especially in the fields of communications, information technology and product data. This is already starting to provide the framework for major enterprises to redesign their business processes and organizational structures.

The same pressures driving European integration are also behind the development of other regional trading areas, notably the North America Free Trade Area (NAFTA). Others under development include Asia – the Association of South East Asian Nations (ASEAN); Africa – the Economic Community of West African States (ECOWAS); the Caribbean – the Caribbean Community and Common Market (CARICOM). South America, Africa and Australasia are all likely to follow. The objective for all of them is to generate a powerful regional economic base and to strengthen their competitive position. The adoption of advanced technology, a global high-tech distribution network and efficient working practices is an important part of this.

Already today large complex products are rarely designed, manufactured and maintained at a single location or even by a single company. Cross-border collaborative product development and global economic integration are increasingly necessary for major companies if they are to remain competitive. Seaports such as Singapore and Rotterdam have developed the distripark concept to assemble, process and distribute companies' products to serve local markets and develop a regional network (see pp. 413–16). Companies research and monitor continuously their markets worldwide to find the most suitable sources of the components from which they assemble their products so that they may remain competitive in both technology and price terms from the point of view of the total product (see pp. 428–31). Efficient global distribution and maximizing the application of computer technology play a major role in this type of company strategy. Additionally, in an environment in which instant electronic access to information is increasingly taken as the norm, the movement towards electronic commerce is starting to affect all sizes and types of business globally.

It has to be recognized that worldwide sincere governmental commitment and co-operation is essential if the rapid advances in information technology are to help open up new markets, eliminate trade barriers and improve procedures and working practices. International agreement is also required to develop global procedures and standards as well as to reduce non-tariff barriers and accelerate trade flows. This has already been recognized by the GATT Uruguay round agreement (see pp. 170–80), Incoterms 1990 (see pp. 435–7) and ICC No. 500 (see pp. 247–8). These will all inevitably affect national economies, as does the ability of major industries to choose different parts of the world in which to manufacture, assemble and trade in their products.

A more recent development has been termed electronic commerce. Traders worldwide have to compete in a global environment in which the availability of technology and advanced telecommunications means that organizations will to an ever increasing extent trade with each other electronically and the systems they use have to be open and based on international standards. SITPRO have been at the forefront of such developments (see pp. 452–4).

Electronic commerce is but part of a larger paradigm shift in the way in which business will in the future have to operate. A further example is 'concurrent engineering', the process whereby individual components of a particular product can be manufactured simultaneously in different locations and often in different countries as part of a single process. This requires organizations to use a common digital base in real time for the design, development, manufacture, distribution and servicing of products. It is termed

CAL – Continuous Acquisition and Life Cycle Support – and EDI is the vehicle for these developments. These trends are leading to the growth of the 'virtual enterprise', organizations integrating the whole business process, including all the independent component companies and services, into one single trading entity. The key to the success of this operation involving out sourcing of component units globally is the development of multi–modalism and the role EDI plays in the international distribution strategy.

Electronic data interchange (EDI) has been defined as 'the application-to-application exchange of computer-held information in a structural format via a telecommunications network'. In reality, it means that the data passes from an application on one computer into an application on another computer without printing or manual manipulation. It requires structured data – normally in a neutral data standard – to allow further processing. In other words, it permits paperless trading with no boundaries or time zones.

As we progress through the 1990s the pattern of world trade is changing, with an increasingly global supply chain. Many companies source components in one part of the world, assemble them in another and sell them in yet another. This is already starting to have a significant macro-economic impact on world trade patterns.

The development of an effective integrated global supply chain, including all the processes involved in the trade and payment cycle, has to be carefully planned, predicted and controlled. Traditional management thinking and procedures are too slow, error prone and inflexible for a global supply chain to operate competitively. This may be demonstrated by the fact that some 11–14 participants may be involved in any single export/import process: banks, exporter, forwarder, customs, port, carrier, port, customs, forwarder, importer.

Planning and co-ordinating the movement of goods and the flow of payment through such a complex system to a predictable level of certainty is virtually impossible without the discipline and control which only EDI provides.

The use of EDI can provide important cash savings and also enables a company to provide better levels of customer service and gain a competitive edge over its rivals. Looking further ahead, companies may even look to EDI to provide new business opportunities.

The benefits of EDI can be divided into three areas: strategic, operational and opportunity. They include the overall functioning of the business and affect the very business the company is undertaking. These can include a faster trading cycle, 'just in time' manufacturing, terms of trade being dictated by bargaining power and the need to respond to highly competitive market entrants.

We examine below the roles SITPRO, INMARSAT, shipping companies and port authorities are playing in the development of EDI, together with Export Master – a software house specializing in the international trade sector, particularly in the area of processing the international consignment.

20.2 SIMPLER TRADE PROCEDURES BOARD

The Simpler Trades Procedures Board (SITPRO) was set up in June 1970 to 'guide, stimulate and assist the rationalization of international trade procedures and the information flows associated with them'.

SITPRO's work falls under several headings. The central problem is that of procedures. Modern transport methods are serviced by information-handling systems which have proven to be inadequate to their task. Traditional systems are costly, complicated and prone to delays and errors, which result in delays to goods out of proportion to their speed of movement.

Procedures, therefore, have to be rationalized and simplified nationally and internationally. Their point of application in a goods movement is based on traditional cargo intervention points. However, the development of through-movement techniques requires the repositioning of official and commercial intervention points. This will in itself bring new relationships and responsibilities to the participants. Such an achievement calls for painstaking and continuous negotiations with representative organizations for which SITPRO provides an ideal and generally accepted focal point.

The work involves studies of procedures and subsequent co-operation with the relevant bodies to carry out rationalization programmes. A large part of the UK's exports are manufactured from imported raw materials and SITPRO is continuously investigating facilitation possibilities in this side of international trade.

Procedures are, however, generally represented by documents which have created their own problems and costs. Every effort has, therefore, been made to simplify existing documentation and standardize it on the United Nations ECE Layout Key. The UK now has a fully developed, aligned export documentation system, although pressure is constantly kept up for the alignment of further forms.

The aligned export documentation procedure is based on the 'master document' principle. Under the aligned one-run system, as much information as possible is entered on a master document so that all or part of this information can be reproduced into individual forms of a similar design. This method eliminates repetitive word processing and checking. The system offers the following advantages: improved accuracy and complete elimination of variations in detailed information shown on documents relating to any one consignment; quicker and cheaper production of paperwork; elimination of repetitive word processing of information onto numerous end-documents and related checking: uniformity of information presentation; easier document handling, filing and reference; and finally, masters provide a reference for all paperwork run-off. The latter eliminates the need to produce separate copies of individual documents for future reference, often with substantial reductions in filing.

An essential element in global developments is the improvement in the efficiency and openness of the actual conduct of international trade and the removal of those barriers which impede both the movement of goods to final destination and subsequent payment for them. This has to include harnessing technology – especially EDI – across the export, import and payment chains which link together to form the total process. In financial terms UNCTAD has estimated that, worldwide, trade formalities absorb 7–10% of global sales value, and that the more efficient procedures could reduce these by 25%.

Other areas in which SITPRO have played a leading role in recent years include the following:

(a) The current method of providing data to HM Customs (INTRASTAT/ESL) is less burdensome and expensive for UK companies. It emerged on the formulation of the Single European Market in 1993 with its attendant benefit of removing trade

454   *Information technology and electronic data interchange*

barriers and physical inspection of goods at international frontier points for goods originating within the European Union. This yielded reductions in transit times for the movement of goods and improved vehicle utilization (see p. 449).

(b) Major facilitation and economic benefits to trade and customs have emerged from the Customs Freight Business Review (CFBR). Its fundamental principle is for customs to supervise the majority of third world goods at traders' premises through audit-based controls using commercial records to provide the information. Benefits to traders include speed and certainty of the movement of goods, the opportunity to consolidate efficiency improvements brought about by the Single Market and to align in-house procedures into a single unified system for official reporting requirements (see pp. 92–5)

(c) SITPRO have taken the lead relevant to the UN/ECE/WP4 *ad hoc* group to develop all the documentary aspects of the transport of dangerous goods and have devised a dangerous goods note with the aim of simplyfying the movement of hazardous goods.

(d) The United Economic Commission for Europe's Trade Facilitation Committee (UN/ECE/WP4) involving SITPRO have produced a model of the international trade transaction. This provides a single diagrammatic and dynamic model including both the flows of information and the physical movement of goods for use as an inventory tool. It shows the facilitation measures available and the documents needed and provides a guide for planning the design of standard international electronic messages.

(e) Document alignment is well established, especially in the areas of banking, insurance and rail transport.

20.3 INTERNATIONAL MARITIME SATELLITE ORGANIZATION

The International Maritime Satellite Organization (Inmarsat) is an internationally owned co-operative which provides mobile communications worldwide. Established in 1979 to serve the maritime community, Inmarsat has since evolved to become the only provider of mobile global satellite communications for commercial, distress and safety applications, at sea, in the air and on land. It is based in London, and has 75 member countries.

The services that the Inmarsat satellite network can now support include direct-dial telephone, telex, fax, electronic mail and data connections for maritime applications; flight-deck voice and data transmission, automatic position and status reporting, and direct-dial passenger telephone for aircraft; and two-way data communications, position reporting, electronic mail and fleet management for land transport. Inmarsat is also used for emergency communications at times of human disaster and natural catastrophe.

Inmarsat offers several different mobile communications systems, designed to provide users with a wide variety of mobile terminals and services.

(a) Mobile terminals and services

Most current users of the Inmarsat system use Inmarsat-A terminals or their transportable derivatives. The maritime versions of these terminals, which are produced by 15 manufacturers around the world, feature dynamically driven parabolic antennas less than one metre in diameter, generally housed – on a ship – in a radome and mounted high up on the superstructure. Inmarsat-A can support high-quality direct-dial telephone, telex, fax and data services. Transportable versions of Inmarsat-A terminals fit into one or two suitcases, with folding antennas.

Inmarsat is now introducing Inmarsat-B, its successor to the Inmarsat-A system. Inmarsat-B provides a similar range of services to Inmarsat-A but, because it is based on modern digital telecommunications technologies, Inmarsat-B terminals are smaller, lighter and cheaper – with lower user charges as well.

Also being introduced is the Inmarsat-M digital telephone system. Portable Inmarsat-M terminals are the size of a briefcase and can provide direct-dial telephone, fax or 2.4 kilobits per second data connections. Maritime versions are fitted with tracking antennas with radomes about one eighth the volume of their bigger, more capable Inmarsat-A/B brothers. Terminal and user charges are also considerably less than those for the larger systems.

The Inmarsat-C system supports the smallest two-way communications terminals of all. Lightweight (only a few kilos), compact and with omni-directional antenna systems, the terminals come in fixed, mobile, transportable, maritime and aeronautical versions. Inmarsat-C supports two-way store-and-forward messages;

text or data reporting communications at a data rate of 600 bits per second.

Three types of service are available for aircraft:

(a)   Aero-C, which allows store-and-forward text or data messages, apart from flight safety communications, to be sent and received by aircraft operating anywhere in the world;

(b)   Aero-L, the low-gain real-time data-only communications service, mainly for flight-deck and airline operations purposes;

(c)   Aero-H, a high-gain service providing multiple-channel flight-deck voice and passenger telephony.

In mid-1994, more than 23 500 Inmarsat-A, 12 000 Inmarsat-C 2000 Inmarsat-M user terminals have been commissioned on land, sea and in the air for use with the Inmarsat system. About 400 aeronautical earth station terminals have been commissioned for use on aircraft.

Inmarsat has developed the world's first global paging service and in 1995 was exploring the possibilities of using its satellites for position determination and navigation applications.

Inmarsat is also working actively on its Project 21 initiative, announced in 1991, to meet the global mobile communications requirements of the next century by providing a worldwide, go-anywhere, pocket-sized telephone service by the end of the decade.

(b)   Satellites

Inmarsat uses its own Inmarsat-2 satellites, and leases the Marecs B2 satellite from the European Space Agency, its maritime communications subsystems (MCS) via several Intelsat V satellites from the International Telecommunications Satellite Organization and capacity on three Marisat satellites from Comsat General of the United States. The system is currently configured as in Fig. 20.1.

Each Inmarsat-2 spacecraft, the fourth and last of which was launched in April 1992, has a capacity equivalent to 250 Inmarsat-A voice circuits.

Inmarsat has contracted Martin Marietta Astro Space for an Inmarsat-3 series of four larger satellites for launch beginning in the second half of 1995, and is now refining its investigations into

Ocean region:	Atlantic (W)	Atlantic (E)		Indian	Pacific
Operational location:	Inmarsat-2 F4 55W	Inmarsat-2 F2, Marecs B2 15.5W 15.2W		Inmarsat-2 F1 64.5E	Inmarsat-2 178E

Spare location:	Intelsat MCS-B 50W	Intelsat MCS-A 66E	Marisat F2 72.5E	Intelsat MCS-D 180E	Marisat F1 106W	Marisat F3 182E

Fig. 20.1 Current Inmarsat satellite configuration.

the optimum design for an intermediate circular orbit (ICO) satellite system for the twenty-first century under its Project 21 initiative.

(c) Land earth stations
Land earth stations (LESs) – often referred to as coast earth stations (CES) in the maritime environment and ground earth stations (GES) in aeronautical circles – link Inmarsat's satellites with the national and international telecommunications networks. LESs are generally owned and operated by organizations nominated by the signatory countries in which they are located to invest in, and work with, Inmarsat.

Overall there are 26 land earth stations and ten ground earth stations in aeronautical circles.

20.4 MARITIME COMMUNICATIONS

Many thousands of ships and other vessels now have access to a range of communications facilities and specially developed services which are at least as good and as reliable as most people have at home or in their offices. Inmarsat offers two different categories of service, designated Standard-A and Standard-C, designed to meet the various needs of all maritime users.

(a) Standard-A
Provided mainly for larger vessels or those with sophisticated communications requirements, a Standard-A ship earth station

(SES) uses Inmarsat satellites to give high-quality connections into the world's international and national telecommunications networks.

The ship earth stations are produced by about a dozen different manufacturers and marketed through thousands of agents worldwide. Each comes equipped with an automatic, push-button telephone and a telex machine, and optional equipment is available for many other services such as facsimile, data transfer, even television.

The most obvious feature of a Standard-A SES is its radome, which encloses a parabolic dish antenna, usually of less than one metre in diameter. The antenna is motorized so that it tracks the satellite precisely, regardless of ship movement.

Standard-A ship earth stations are built to Inmarsat's performance specifications and are capable of reliable operation in the extreme weather conditions encountered at sea. Each Standard-A model is tested and type approved by Inmarsat's own engineers, and every individual Standard-A installation undergoes further checking procedures before being commissioned into the Inmarsat system and being allocated its own unique identification number, which is used for both telex and telephony.

Telephone

From wherever you are at sea, you can make a telephone call to anywhere in the world, and vice versa. The connection will be fast, the conversation will be clear and free from static and background noise, and the service is available whenever you want it, around the clock.

Making a telephone call via Inmarsat from a ship is almost as simple as dialling a call from home. A two-digit code selects the coast earth station you wish to use – usually chosen on the basis of call destination, service or price – and a single push-button selects a voice, rather than telex, call. The system then allocates a suitable circuit. Dialling is simply 00 plus the country and area codes then the subscriber number. Connection is automatic and immediate.

From most countries it is also possible to call a ship at sea via Inmarsat. In many cases these calls can be dialled automatically, in the same way as you would make a direct international call – each Inmarsat satellite region has an international dialling code. In other countries the calls can be made through an operator.

Telex

Telex is the most widely used of Inmarsat's maritime services. It offers distinct advantages in that it is economical and it provides a record of correspondence. There is also the assurance that the message has reached its destination and will command urgent attention. You can send a telex day or night, regardless of time differences or watch schedules.

Through Inmarsat, direct telex services are available from ships, and can be made to ships, on an automatic or manual basis.

Ship-to-shore telex calls are initiated by selecting an appropriate coast earth station, as with the telephone service, pressing the 'Telex' button to select a circuit then keying 00 plus the country, area and subscriber numbers.

Telex calls via Inmarsat can be made from most countries to ships at sea, generally automatically. Each satellite coverage region has its own dialling prefix. The automatic nature of the telex service gives an added economic advantage in that most coast earth station operators only charge for the amount of time actually used.

Fax

Up-to-date weather charts for the Master, mechanical drawings for the engine room, cargo loading diagrams and port and customs documentation for the deck officer, newspapers for the passengers and crew, Japanese character messages for the tuna fisherman . . . part of the everyday log of fax transmissions on the Inmarsat system.

Because the telephone connections provided via Inmarsat are clear and free from interference, they are ideal for carrying Group 2/3 fax transmissions. In many cases, the service is automatic and ship earth stations can be modified to recognize two identity numbers, so that one can be set aside exclusively for fax use. It is also possible for organizations such as shipping companies, news services and safety authorities to send faxes to groups of ships simultaneously.

Data

Inmarsat provides the only method of reliable transmission of data to and from ships at sea. Through Inmarsat satellites, huge volumes of information can be exchanged at high speed between computers ashore and those aboard ships. Many functions aboard ship – course, speed, position, fuel, cargo conditions, engine room parameters – can be monitored remotely from shipping company offices. A growing number of databases containing weather, market, news, financial and maintenance information are becoming available for the shipping industry and most ships now have micro- or minicomputers on board to take advantage of these facilities – via satellite. For instance, some ships produce their own daily newspapers for passengers and crew from a high-speed news data dump which only takes a few minutes to transmit and process.

(b)   Standard-C

Standard-C is the world's smallest, most portable commercial satellite communications system. A complete Standard-C terminal – antenna and electronics – could be carried easily in an average shopping bag. Hence for smaller vessels and other applications where size, weight, power requirements and costs matter, Standard-C provides access to the go-anywhere reliability and quality of satellite communications.

Standard-C is a text-only communications system, but it can cope with any kind of language or character set and it can interconnect, through store-and-forward switches, with the international telex, electronic mail or switched data networks. It can also handle computer-type graphics.

The normal Standard-C installation consists of a small, omni-directional antenna mounted high on a vessel's superstructure, plus an electronics package not much bigger than the average car radio. This is usually connected to a personal computer/printer, teleprinter or keyboard and VDU. Standard-C is available in most parts of the world.

Group call services

As well as connecting to the international telex, electronic mail and data services, Standard-C users can receive two special Inmarsat services. Receive-only equipment is available for vessels whose only satellite communications requirement is to have access to SafetyNET and FleetNET messages. Standard-A ship earth stations can also be augmented to receive these services.

(a)   *FleetNET.* FleetNET is ideal for messages or graphics which need to be delivered to a number of ships simultaneously. It is ideal for company messages addressed to the fleet, or news and information services for maritime subscribers.

(b) *SafetyNET*. Similar to FleetNET, this service is intended for the distribution of marine safety information and rescue co-ordination during emergencies. As well as addressing pre-designated groups of vessels, by using SafetyNET authorities can target their messages to be received only by vessels in, or entering, any area defined as a circle about a central point (say the location of an emergency) or within defined coordinates.

(c) Position reporting and determination

Inmarsat's satellite system is ideal for reporting a ship's position to anyone else who needs to know. Many ships already carry systems which automatically take position coordinates from the vessel's navigation equipment and transmit them periodically via satellite to the shipping company's central office. Aircraft are also fitted with similar systems. All of these, however, rely on separate systems – land or satellite based – to provide the actual position co-ordinates and use Inmarsat only as the data transmission path.

However, the Inmarsat system – both Standard-A and Standard-C – is also capable of providing position determination services, as well as enhancing or backing up the information extracted from dedicated navigation systems. Inmarsat is now conducting a number of trials and experiments into a broad spectrum of position determination techniques before deciding how it can best serve the navigation needs of its worldwide user community.

(d) Safety at Sea

Every Inmarsat ship earth station – Standard-A or Standard-C – is fitted with a special alert mechanism to cope with emergency situations. This is usually a single 'Distress' button or a special abbreviated dialling code.

A distress alert immediately seizes a telephone, telex or data communications channel and connects it automatically via a coast earth station to a rescue co-ordination centre for action.

Distress alerts have top priority and, because of the quality and reliability of the satellite system, connection is always made immediately, regardless of the location of the emergency or the distance to the coast earth station and rescue co-ordination centre.

All rescue co-ordination centres are interconnected, often using their own Standard-A ship earth stations, so that no matter where a call is first received it can be quickly passed to the centre responsible for dealing with the emergency.

Recognizing the efficiency and reliability of the Inmarsat system, the International Maritime Organization (IMO) has made satellite communications a cornerstone of its new Global Maritime Distress and Safety System (GMDSS). Under the GMDSS, a Standard-A or Standard-C ship earth station will satisfy regulatory communications requirements for ships operating in almost all parts of the world, apart from the extreme polar regions.

20.5 COMPUTERIZED AND EDI-RESOURCED SHIPPING COMPANIES

An example of a modern computerized advanced communication system is found in the Maersk Line. It was created with two goals in mind: the highest possible accuracy and speed. It provides fast documentation and up-to-the-minute 'cargo status' reports coupled with flexibility.

Maersk Line have a dedicated satellite base and communications network with computer centres in Copenhagen, the USA and Japan thereby providing a global data resource which is continuously available. This enables the Maersk Line to track all cargo and container movements on a 24-hour basis in a total logistics system which comprises a door-to-door global service via a large container fleet (40 ships), feeder tonnage, double-stack container trains, trucks/road vehicles, containers (125 000), dedicated rail arrangements, exclusive terminals, container yards and container freight stations. Such immediate access to data enables 'just in time' production systems and materials management to be applied by the shipper.

The Maersk Line EDI system enables shippers to reduce costs by eliminating transcription errors and simplifying the transfer of information. It also offers shippers the opportunity of participation in numerous EDI systems including DAKOSX, INTIS, ACS, TRADENET, SHIPNET and many others.

Shippers can use their own computers to gain access to the Maersk Line computer called MAGIC – Maersk Line's Advanced

Global Information Concept. It enables shippers to track the movement of their shipment from the time Maersk Line accepts the cargo until the cargo reaches the destination. MAGIC can provide container specification, consignor/consignee addresses, cut-off and pick-up times at the dedicated terminals, sailing schedules, estimated time of arrival and so on. It also permits shippers to effect on-line booking/cargo reservation and telephonic data access through the MAGIC voice. Fascimile/fax resources are also available which permit the transmission of documentation such as bills of lading or seaway bills through telefax.

Another shipping company, Hanjin Shipping, has a global computerized resource/network. It provides an 'on-line real-time' processing system connecting all networks of the company covering 62 stations in Asia, 29 stations in North America and 29 stations in Europe. It is called HANCOS – the Hanjin Shipping Computerized On-line Real Time System.

HANCOS has EDI facilities with the US computer system AMS, the Felixstowe port customs system FCP80, the Singapore Port Authority port customs system, the Australia Customs Office and many others all providing automatic customs clearance. HANCOS also provides on-line computer access for booking/data access, sailing schedules, container details, cargo tracing and estimated time of arrival to all shippers equipped with a connecting user-friendly computer network.

The Hanjin Shipping Company also offer an integrated VAN (value added network) service to all their clients. It covers all aspects of the shipping business such as vessel operation, schedules, booking, EDI shipping instructions, bill of lading data/reference, cargo tracing, freight rate details, and so on, together with details for other transportation modes via air and land which are available from affiliated companies of the business group. By 1996 the Hanjin VAN will also be linked with the major important international VAN services of other countries thereby providing a data logistics systems on a global basis to all Hanjin Shipping Company customers worldwide.

Moreover, the Hanjin Shipping Company provides a data interface and other EDI resources to connect with other external systems such as port terminals, rail companies, customs, consignors/consignees, and so on. Another facility developed by the Hanjin Shipping Company is called the mega fax system which provides customer services including arrival notice, bill of lading information, booking confirmation and vessel schedule data.

On the ship management side the Hanjin Shipping Company has developed a stowage control system called HANSCON. It encourages optimum loading of the container tonnage and also facilitates the handling of all container stowage-related duties through a PC workstation. Computerized planning of ship stowage enables forward planning of the fleet through the global/regional offices of the company and port terminals via the EDI facility.

The Hanjin also developed a database to handle dangerous cargo and has become the first global shipping line to use the computer for the International Marine Dangerous Goods Code (IMDG) (see p. 280). It handles the dangerous cargo throughout all its stages including production of the cargo manifest.

Under HANSCON booking data and data on equipment movements are brought together so that shippers can pre-book their cargo capacity through the regional offices via an on-line computer.

20.6 COMPUTERIZED AND EDI-RESOURCED SEAPORTS

(a) Southampton Container Terminals Ltd

An example of a computerized system in use at a major seaport is that of Southampton Container Terminals Ltd. It has a very high volume throughput at the terminals and requires a sophisticated system of operation and control. It is provided by Community Network Services (CNS). Over 1000 users process nearly 2.5 million customs entries a year through the CNS mainframe in Southampton. Both the Container Terminal Control and the Direct Trader Input customs systems (see p. 101) are based on the philosophy of remaining close to the end-user's requirements by providing simple easy-to-understand facilities.

The system is a real-time monitoring and control system for the container terminal. All input and output is by remote VDUs and printers. Currently some 90 VDUs and 45 printers are attached to the system. Information is available for all aspects of the terminal operation from basic container data through to final stability calculations for the vessel – a similar facility to that available on the HANSCON system discussed above. It covers the following:

1. Initial input consists of data about each container which is stored until the container physically arrives either by road or rail.

2. A model of the road vehicle or train with its associated containers is built up within the system.

3. The route of the vehicle through the terminal is controlled by the system and instructions are produced for work to be carried out on its associated containers.

4. In the case of trains, the flow of containers to and from the rail terminal is controlled by the system to meet the train schedules.

5. Containers entering the terminal are categorized automatically by the system according to voyage, port, weight, size, etc., and a directive is given for the placement of each container via a radio data system to the straddle carriers.

6. In this manner a stack of containers is built up awaiting the ship.

7. The planning manager consults this stack model and adjusts it to provide the best stack utilization and ease of access during ship loading.

8. A model of each ship is held within the system and the ship planner is responsible for transferring containers from the stack model to the ship model within the rules of ship loading and stability. A sophisticated graphical PC workstation assists the planner in this task.

9. After ship planning, the paperwork necessary for controlling the flow of containers onto the ship can be produced by the system.

10. The radio data system controls the process of ship loading and discharging and maintains a real-time update of all aspects of the operation.

11. After loading has been completed and the ship's tanks have been added to the model, the complete ship stability is calculated by the system.

12. Finally, after the ship's departure, a list of the containers loaded by each region/office of the shipping line is produced. Some lines require this in printed format, but some find it more convenient to have a directly produced telex tape linked to a telex

computer: hence the telex network. This information is transferred by EDI link via the CMS network.

13. Various statistical printouts for shifts, days, weeks or voyages are produced by the computer.

14. Charges associated with the movement of containers including demurrage charges are produced by the computer.

15. Projections of forward utilization are made to assist with management planning.

16. Transfer of handling instructions to and from mobile cargo handling equipment is via radio data transfer (RDT) for both landside and shipside operations.

The application of EDI is realized through the interface of screens and printers with other computer systems. CNS provides facilities for 40 locations within the UK and can provide a single interface to any company's internal computer system. Hence operations at ports as diverse as London, Liverpool and Immingham can be controlled centrally or through internal company facilities. At Southampton the two CNS systems (the Container Terminal Control and the customs Direct Trader Input) are linked. Cargo is monitored throughout the port including the groupage depot facility. Both containers and consignments are monitored.

External communications via EDI arise in four areas at Southampton.

(a) Firstly, many shipping lines supply their cargo manifest details to the CNS inventory system directly from their own computer systems thus minimizing the necessity for manual input. The system will be further developed to retain variance information to the line.

(b) The second area is the provision of bayplan information from and to other ports and terminals. Various shipping consortia are operating systems which transfer bayplan information from one port to the next port of call for the vessel in question worldwide. CNS has participated in the development of these messages and has successfully developed a system so that bayplan messages are supported when used by the consortia.

(c) A third area is the transfer of inventory information to and from ICDs (see p. 467). Inventory data in the form of cargo advice messages can be sent from one inventory system to the next to eliminate duplication of input.

(d) The final application concerns the statistical data required by Her Majesty's Customs (HMC) to process cargo through customs clearance (see pp. 91–100). With the recent introduction of CHIEF (see p. 94) the CNS system transfers SAD (see p. 92) information to the HMC statistical computer. The CNS system provides a personal identification number (PIN) import release facility. This enables shipping line transport departments to release cargo to their road haulage companies following customs clearance by the input of the PIN to the network. The system also provides entry data to HMC involving the SPES simplification period entry system (see p. 99) and the SPES messages which are sub-set of CUSDEC and CUSRES.

The CNS system at Southampton has a number of other capabilities which include: consignment information from exporters/hauliers and their agents; cargo advice information received to build up the export inventory; consignment status information to importers/exporters and their agents which can be provided at predefined status points; on request the despatch of consignment status messages; and finally interface with the port authority vessel traffic system (VTS) which enables ship and dangerous goods information to be automatically relayed to the port authority.

More recent extensions of the system's facilities include notification of rail requirements and transfer of TI documents (see p. 92) to ICDS via EDI; bulk transfer of transhipment information (Form C548) to HMC (see p. 94); automatic notification of container arrival; and printing of delivery notes.

(b) The Port of Singapore Authority (PSA)

The Port of Singapore has one of the largest and most technologically advanced management systems in the world. The range of facilities provided by the Port of Singapore Authority has been fully detailed in Chapter 17. Nevertheless it would be appropriate to consider here the computerized resources provided by the PSA. Overall the PSA is a market leader in the application of computer technology/EDI in port management and related resources.

(a) *CITOS – Computer Integrated Terminal Operations System.* This system directs all container handling operations and has 280 computer applications. It is involved in planning the allocation of berths, yard space, equipment and other resources. From the central yard control computer, directions for operations and equipment allocation are then transmitted to the machine operators through a wireless data transmission system in real time. As soon as arrival details are available, the berth allocation expert system allocates the appropriate berth and number of quay cranes to the arriving ship.

The stowage planning expert system helps the ship planner decide on the best stowage sequence for the ship for loading and discharging containers. The quay crane workload, the hydrostatic stability of the ship, the next port of call and the yard stacking pattern of the containers are factored into the system with great precision. With these systems, planning time is halved while more containers are handled in a shorter time. Moreover, the yard planning expert system ensures that containers are easily access- ible to avoid unproductive shuffling of boxes. The result is a shorter loading time for vessels and optimal utilization of yard space and berths. On an average day some 6000 prime movers enter or leave the port's automated gates and each is processed in less than 45 seconds. The gate automation system features a comprehensive network of CCTV cameras, electronic sensors, transponders and a container number recognition system (CNRS). This provides a paperless and speedy gate access for hauliers and freight forwarders, with security as its top priority. The gate processing system registers the container arrival at the gate, records its weight, and either assigns the location or directs the delivery of the containers, all within 45 seconds.

(b) *CICOS – Computer Integrated Conventional Operations System.* This system integrates the planning of ship and warehouse operations at the Pasir Panjang Terminal, PSA's main conven- tional cargo gateway. Operations involving a CCTV network, a voice communication network, planning systems, hand-held ter- minals and self-service terminals are all supervised from a central control room.

(c) *FAST – Freight Auto Service Terminal.* The market leader in automated teller machines for cargo operations, FAST is a self- service terminal providing a 24-hour service for hauliers bringing cargo in and out of the PSA. Overall it reduces documentation and queueing time by the hauliers using the port.

(d) *CIMOS – Computer Integrated Marine Operations System.* This system manages all the PSA's marine operations within port waters through an integration of the vessel traffic information system (VTIS) and the anchorage and channel utilization systems. It uses sophisticated radar technology, expert systems and database applications to facilitate the deployment of pilots, tugs and launches. With the use of data terminals, the status of these marine services are entered and then monitored through the Port Traffic Management System.

(e) *PORTNET.* The use of EDI in the PSA is exemplified in the PORTNET scheme, a computer system which has been extended to include the shipping community as displayed in Fig. 20.2. It has over 1400 subscribers and gives direct access to a range of business operational information and sailing schedules from the PSA database. This includes comprehensive sailing schedules with facilities to enquire by port, ETA and other data; a schedule of vessels berthing at PSA terminals; particulars of containers/cargo; tracking of containers and cargo; and a chemical database for dangerous goods. In terms of shipping information, ship chandlers, marine suppliers and bunker suppliers all have access to vessel movements, the daily shipping situation, vessel status and specification, and grid reference of vessel location.

With regard to documentation, 24-hour access is available for the electronic submission of documents such as container import status, cargo manifest, cargo/container shipment and delivery, dangerous goods declaration and vessel declaration. It also covers requests for services such as berth applications, container export schedule bookings, tugs and pilotage, and pipeline water.

PORTNET also has access to TRADENET for the processing of inward, outward and transhipment declarations to the various organizations such as customs and the Trade Development Board (TDB) and access to SNS Database Services for flight information and trade statistics, for example.

PORTNET also provides other tailor-made facilities for clients in the port environs.

Overall, PORTNET offers paperless trading and permits port users more lead time in 'just in time' operations and planning.

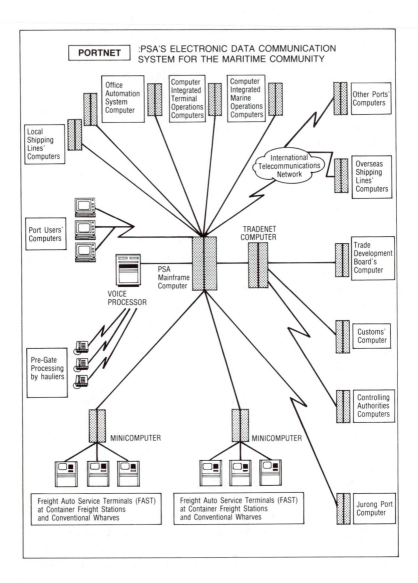

Fig. 20.2 PORTNET: The Port of Singapore Authority's EDI facility for the maritime community. (Reproduced by kind permission of the PSA.)

(f) *BOXNET*. This is a PSA interactive link with port users and dovetails the user's schedules with PSA container terminal operations so that receipt and delivery of containers can be carried out concurrently to save another trip.

(g) *TRADENET*. This is the PSA EDI network which provides access to the outward and transhipment declarations for the various governing trade agencies and authorities. The PSA and TDB have made Singapore the first country to have an electronic system which streamlines and matches the various shipping documents among trading partners. It is called MAINS – Maritime Information System.

(h) *CIHOS – Computer Integrated Hydrographic Operations System*. This system charts and updates profiles of the seabed.

(i) *CADD*. This is a simulation system used to facilitate design, research and engineering works within the PSA.

(j) *ACOS*. The automated container system shortly to be introduced will further automate existing container handling operations. A remote crane operation system is being developed to control and operate the quay cranes and yard cranes. Containers bonded and discharged will be automatically updated by the system. Also the current fleet of prime movers will be replaced by unmanned automated guided vehicles (AGVs) which receive operational instructions from the central computer. Besides checking the container recognition number it will be used for automatic seal checking and container surveying.

20.7 COMPUTERIZED EXPORT PROCESSING – EXPORTMASTER

The success of the Exportmaster software package is probably in large part due to its ability to offer a total, integrated export management and administration system. This contrasts with the smaller software systems which have generally restricted themselves to providing printing of a limited range of export documents. Exportmaster has been installed in 18% of the top 100 UK companies and is in widespread use across most industrial sectors. It has also found favour amongst non-manufacturing international traders, thanks to its module for purchasing and product sourcing operations. Since its activity system and documentary output are

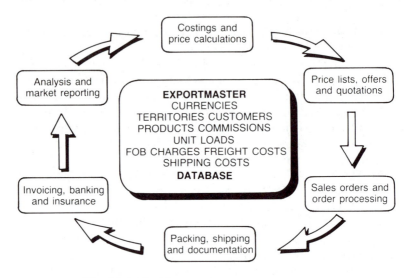

Fig. 20.3 The Exportmaster transaction cycle.

user-configurable it is not country-dependent and may be used in various countries throughout the world. (Further details are available from Exportmaster Ltd, 33 St Peter's Street, South Croydon CR2 7DG, England; Tel. 0181–681 2321; Fax 0181–667 1816.)

Exportmaster offers integrated facilities to the exporter at every stage of the export cycle, from pre-sales through order processing to shipment and banking activities. The main stages of the cycle are illustrated in Fig. 20.3.

Within the section of the cycle dealing with the shipment of the consignment, Exportmaster provides functions and facilities within six main areas:

(a) order capture and editing;
(b) processing, progress chasing and status control;
(c) documentation;
(d) costing the transaction;
(e) analysis and management reporting;
(f) communications.

(a)   Order capture and editing

Some exporters use Exportmaster for all the stages of the transaction cycle, while others employ only certain modules. Consequently, there are many different ways in which an order may be 'captured' by the system. In some cases, the details may have been entered at an earlier stage as a quotation or pro forma; once the customer has confirmed the purchase, the quotation is simply converted into an order. Other exporters will key in the order at the time of receipt, while many may download the order electronically from their main company order system. All these procedures are speeded up by the elimination of unnecessary keying by the operator through the maintenance of databases of all kinds of standard product and customer data. Orders may be re-edited at any stage.

(b)   Processing, progress chasing and status control

The main stages through which a transaction passes are shown in Fig. 20.4.

These stages and the detailed steps within them are monitored and controlled by Exportmaster's processing system. Operating like a checklist and updated both by the user and by automatic processes within Exportmaster, it monitors the status of orders, telling the user at any time what activities need to take place in connection with the order, which ones have already been carried out, which ones need to be done at the moment and which ones will need attention at a later date. Order status can be examined on-screen; alternatively, detailed action reports can be printed showing exactly which activities need to be carried out in connection with which orders. Time-critical activities, such as ensuring availability of goods to comply with a letter of credit expiry date, can be date-deadlined so that deadline reports can highlight items needing urgent attention.

As well as prompting the user to take action, the activity lines can also trigger automatic functions, such as electronic transfer of data to another system or the production of a document or documents at a particular stage of the transaction.

(c)   Export documentation

Exportmaster allows the production of hundreds of standard documents. Its main formats are the Exportmaster commercial

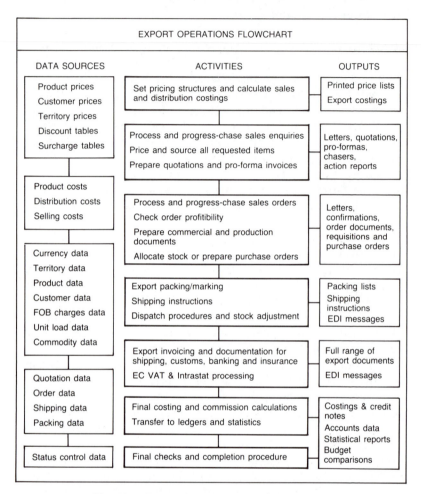

Fig. 20.4 Exportmaster transaction flowchart.

format, letter-style and SITPRO-UN aligned format (see p. 453). In addition, its User-Defined Documentation module allows users to design their own documentary output, in terms not only of appearance but also of data content and organization.

Exportmaster's documents fall into several main categories:

(a) correspondence; (b) quotations; (c) order forms (acknowledgements, works orders, delivery notes, etc.); (d) invoices;

(e) shipping documents; (f) customs documents; (g) packing lists; (h) individual pallet/case labels/documents; (i) banking and insurance documents; and (j) reports.

For each of these it extracts, classifies and reorganizes data in a different manner. The general term 'shipping documents' covers not only the obvious items such as shipping notes or certificates of origin but also more specialized paperwork such as hazard documentation. Similarly the term 'customs documents' includes items such as Common Agricultural Policy forms.

Documents are coded for ease of access. A code can denote:

(a) an individual document;
(b) a predefined list of documents for a particular eventuality (e.g. documents for an inspection procedure);
(c) a predefined list of documents applying to a customer; or
(d) a predefined list of documents applying to a destination territory.

Documents or lists can be printed:

(a) on demand by the user; or
(b) automatically when invoked by an activity status line in the processing system.

The development of laser printer technology now gives the exporter the option of printing many export documents on plain paper instead of using preprinted stationery. Laser forms software enables the printer to reproduce not only the exporter's data but also the design of the form itself.

Exportmaster allows users other options as to how to produce their documents. Instead of printing them on a local printer, they can redirect them to a modem for production at a remote despatch department or at an associated office overseas, for example. They can also produce them in the form of a file which can be further edited on a word-processing system or transmitted by electronic mail. If they install the necessary fax software on their computer network, they can transmit Exportmaster documents directly as faxes without the need to produce any paper output. They may also be transmitted as EDI messages, although, in computing terms, these are transmissions not of the documents themselves but of data for documents to be assembled or processed by the receiving system.

```
A4794       Paper goods – Education Dept.              23/06/95
```

Quantity (sales units): 1583

Unit-load shipment
Shipment weight   :13751.68   kilos
Shipment volume   :172.82   m/3

Freight: USD 3500.00 per 40' G.P. Container
Freight exchange rate: #1.00 = USD 1.50

Sales revenue in Pounds Sterling: STG 26986.26
Sales exchange rate: #1.00 = STG 1.00

Sales terms: FREE DEL'D DUTY PAID

	SHIPMENT
FREE DELIVERED DUTY PAID	**26986.26**
Duty @ 2%	529.14
FREE DELIVERED DUTY UNPAID	**26457.12**
Clearance at 55.00 per shipment	55.00
CIF REVENUE	**26402.12**
Insurance @ 0.34% on 110%	100.93
C & F REVENUE	**26301.19**
Freight @ USD2714.91 per 40' G.P. Container	1815.51
FOB UK PORT REVENUE	**24485.68**
Shipping agent's commission @ %	0.00
Shpg etc: 15.00 + 67.00 per shipment	82.00
Terminal charges: 150.00 per 40' G.P. Container	150.00
DELIVERED UK REVENUE	**24253.68**
UK haulage @ 375.00 per 40' G.P. Container	375.00
EX-WORKS REVENUE (GROSS)	**23878.68**
Comm @ 7% on FOB UK PORT to HASA01 Hasani Agency	1714.00
Comm @ 2% on EX-WORKS to LOND01 London Cfmrs	477.57
ECGD/Credit insurance @ 0.32% on total	86.36
EX-WORKS REVENUE (NET)	**21600.75**
Product cost including export packing	19967.09
NET PROFIT	**1633.66**
Net profit as % of FOB UK PORT	6.67
	%

A4794 /23/06/95   /Printed 25/10/95

Fig. 20.5 An Exportmaster consignment costing.

(d) Consignment costing

Exporters can use the system to calculate costs and profit margins on their consignments, before and after shipping. Costs can be monitored right through from the ex works to the delivered duty paid stages (see Fig. 20.5).

The costings are used for marketing decisions about pricing, sales decisions about particular orders, financial decisions, distribution decisions and negotiations. At the freight and shipping negotiation stage, the ability to undertake 'what-if?' calculations, substituting different rates and amounts and examining the effects, is especially cost-effective.

(e)   Analysis and reporting
Information from costings can be combined with data stored against each shipment for use in bespoke reporting modules which allow freight and export direct cost analysis. Reports from these modules can be particularly helpful in the areas of distribution, supplier selection and transport mode and route decisions.

Standard reports from Exportmaster's Sales Analysis module show not only what goods have been shipped to which destinations but also net profitability per product per customer after all export direct distribution costs have been taken into account.

There are many other areas in which reports can be specially produced from the Exportmaster database. For instance, a major pharmaceuticals manufacturer has a module which monitors the number of hours elapsed between receipt of an order for clinical diagnostic cultures and the departure of their flight from the selected airport, flagging orders which are falling behind a predefined standard.

(f)   Communications and EDI
Increasingly, companies operating internationally are accepting the need for their systems to communicate with one another in order to speed up transaction processing and eliminate unnecessary replication of data entry. For most exporters and importers there are three principal areas of communication:

1. third parties;
2. internal and group companies; and
3. business partners (dealers, agents, close customers).

It is with category 1, third parties, that Exportmaster's EDI module is most likely to be useful. Shipping lines, carriers and freight forwarders have established standardized messages that can be interchanged between otherwise totally incompatible systems. This opens the way to electronic paperless booking of

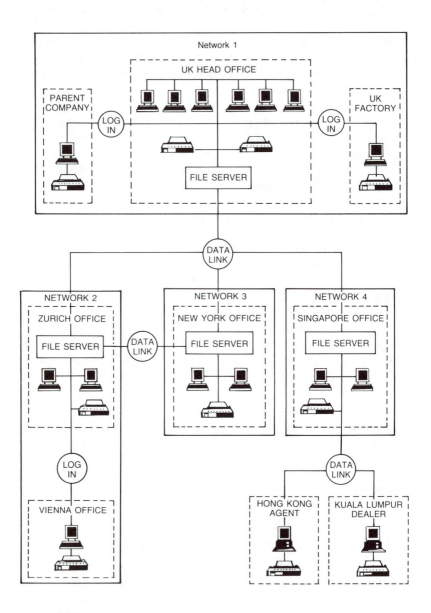

Fig. 20.6 Exportmaster Multi-National.

cargo and transport, as well as insurance and banking transactions. EDI is also used in dealings with some large retailers and in certain manufacturing sectors. The EDI module, when sending details of a shipment, extracts from the data about that shipment only those items that are required by the message. The message is then transferred to a network which deals with the mechanics of 'delivering' it to the recipient, whose system takes the data from the message and reassembles it in the format needed locally. The advantage of this approach is that all the participants can use whatever systems they choose but still be able to communicate with one another in order to process transactions.

However, for categories 2 and 3, internal and business partner communications, EDI is not always the ideal medium. The main problems are that the EDI data must conform to a particular format which can rule out vague or peculiar presentations, that only items catered for by the standard message are transmitted, and that the visual appearance of the document or message is not communicated at all. For these situations, Exportmaster offers the transmission of data and documents via communications software (modem links), electronic mail, direct fax and also the sophisticated communications and interaction system Exportmaster Multi-National (see Fig. 20.6). This system allows Exportmaster users in different locations and countries to set up their systems to operate interactively, exchanging data, orders, quotations, costings, management information and processing instructions automatically using the telephone or other communications media. This enables manufacturers and traders to link up with their overseas sales offices, factories, distributors, dealers, agents and close customers.

The operational and marketing advantages of these facilities are self-evident and it is clear that users will be looking to their international trading software to provide even more sophisticated communications capabilities over the coming years.

CHAPTER 21

Ship management

Our study of shipping would not be complete without a brief review of the more salient aspects of ship management. Broadly ship management techniques fall into five divisions – commercial, operating, technical, financial and investment disciplines.

21.1 COMMERCIAL ASPECTS OF SHIP MANAGEMENT

The shipowner's commercial policy should be to maximize gross revenue to the service within any constraints imposed on him. The latter includes liner conference or other forms of agreements and governmental legislation. Other aspects include competition, and the cost to the shipowner of the service he provides. The latter is an important point in that overall the services should be profitable, and uneconomic ones discarded unless there are compelling reasons for their operation, for example to keep out a competitor or operate a feeder service into a trunk route.

With the development of multi-modalism and through rates on a warehouse-to-warehouse or depot-to-depot basis, the maritime leg is now only one portion of the transit, although it may form the largest element in the route. Hence the shipowner must co-ordinate with other carriers and terminal operators in the formulation of the freight tariff. This includes agents, road hauliers, railway operators and port authorities. The tariffs should be so arranged as to maximize traffic flow throughout the year.

For cruise passengers the rate would be a daily tariff varying by type of accommodation provided. Much additional income can be obtained from the retail outlets on the ship such as the restaurant, bar and shop. Special attention should be given to such facilities to ensure maximum income is obtained by retailing the products most favoured by the passenger. Market research techniques should be used. Additionally income can be sought from shipboard entertainment.

On the freight side the tariffs should be based on cost plus an element of profit. The latter may not always be possible due to the market situation. This could be particularly relevant to fixture rates found in chartering.

Finally the shipowner, particularly the one who is engaged in liner-type services, should prepare a marketing plan annually. It should cover the following items:

(a) The marketing objectives of the trade/service.

(b) The nature of the service during the next 12 months giving details of ship disposition, sailing schedules, ports of call, etc.

(c) The market profile the shipping route will serve and the nature of the traffic sought.

(d) The tariffs and particularly any special concessions to attract new business and develop existing flows through possibly more favourable rebate/discounts.

(e) Any new features on the service, particularly new tonnage, additional ports of call, improved transit, better customs clearance arrangements, simpler documentation, more attractive tariffs.

(f) Budgeted forecast of carryings on the route in the next 12 months by tonnage segregated into various commodity classifications and country of origin.

(g) Any significant developments on the route foreseen in the next 12 months and how the service will benefit. For example, a new industrial complex may be opening up in a country which could generate much additional business to the route.

(h) Details of any promotional campaigns to sustain existing business and also obtain additional traffic.

(i) Technique to be used to measure route performance particularly carryings at regular intervals throughout the 12 months. This may involve regular monthly meetings with sales personnel to discuss results attained and sales strategy, particularly any new promotions.

(j) Details of the sales targets for each sales sector.

(k) The plan should stress the competitive advantages the route has over other services, and the salient points the salesforce should stress.

(l) The plan should be flexible in its approach to take account of any changed situation which may emerge in the next 12 months.

(m) It must be devised to produce a profitable service through the strategy on tariffs: selling must be towards this sole objective. Its aim must be to increase the market share on a profitable basis, particularly of those commodities which are viable or capable of becoming viable.

Overall its aim must be to provide adequate traffic to produce a profitable service. This should reflect the objectives for the forthcoming year both in terms of actual forecast carryings and the manner in which the traffic is to be secured.

21.2 OPERATING ASPECTS OF SHIP MANAGEMENT

The objective of ship management operations is to optimize the use of resources compatible with commercial requirements. Details are given below.

(a) Crew manning levels to be at a minimum compatible with safety, statutory and market needs.

(b) Critical continuous review of passage times to ensure schedules are most economically timed, bearing in mind competition, market needs, fuel cost, crew expenses, port charges, etc.

(c) Fleet size to be at a minimum compatible with market requirements and long-term development. Additional traffic flows could be conveyed on chartered tonnage.

(d) Fleet composition should be as flexible as economically practicable thereby cushioning the effect of any sharp unpredictable variation in traffic flow. Examples include OBO multipurpose, Ro/Ro vessels, Combi carriers and multi-purpose container ships.

(e) Vessels for which there is no work such as during winter or during periods of traffic recession should be placed on charter.

(f) Continuous study should be made of the net revenues resulting from individual sailings, as well as punctuality, outshipments, etc. to evaluate whether any change is necessary.

(g) A continuous review should be made of manning levels of all retail outlets on passenger ships to ensure they are profitable and/or fulfilling a market need.

(h) The merits of 'flagging out' should be examined in maritime fleets with high crew costs (see p. 73).

(i) A continuous review of bunkering ports should be undertaken to ensure the most favourable bunker prices are obtained.

(j) A commercial analysis should be undertaken to assess the suitability of the type of ships employed with regard to their configuration, age and economy.

(k) Ideally on completion of each tour of duty both the Master and chief engineer should attend a performance review with the appropriate ship manager for the specific purpose of examining the vessel's trading performance during their period of duty.

(l) The efficiency of the crew and a continuous strategy to optimize are that efficiency essential in modern crew deployment/operation today. Accordingly most high-profile shipping companies today ensure that a ship's Master and chief engineer remain permanently assigned to that particular vessel and are thus accountable for that vessel's efficiency performance on an 'on-going' basis. Moreover, when crew changeovers take place to honour crew leave commitments, most shipowners do not change the whole crew but essential key officers remain on board to brief the new crew thoroughly. Hence crew changeover is a staggered operation.

(m) Examine merits of outsourcing marine activities such as those available from Denholm Ship Management Ltd (see p. 315).

21.3 TECHNICAL ASPECTS OF SHIP MANAGEMENT

The maintenance and provision of ships form a significant cost in the shipowner's annual budget. The aim is to provide a fleet which is compatible and economical to the market requirements at the lowest possible cost having regard to safety, statutory obligations and service standards. The following points are relevant:

(a) Surveys to be conducted outside peak traffic period and to be of minimum duration compatible with market and economic circumstances.

(b) As much work as practicable prior to survey to be done during the time the vessel is in traffic use as is compatible with cost and other factors.

(c) Examine the merits of using classification societies and technical services such as those available from Lloyds Register (pp. 145–51).

(d) Vessels should be designed to keep maintenance expenditure to a minimum, likewise crew cost with modern navigational aids and shipboard labour-saving devices.

(e) A number of options exist with regard to ship surveys and these should be carefully and continuously reviewed. These include voyage survey, continuous survey, BIS notation involving 'built for in water survey', and planned maintenance systems. The latter is becoming the most popular through the harmonized ship survey programme. Surveys include sighting survey, special periodical survey – hull and equipment, continuous survey – machinery, bottom survey; tailshaft survey, auxiliary boiler survey, EO class – four yearly survey, EO annual survey, loadline annual inspection, annual general survey, and safety radio certificate (see pp. 25–33).

(f) The development of shipboard management techniques should be explored (see *Economics of Shipping Practice and Management*, Chapter 14).

(g) Competitive tendering should be adopted with regard to ship surveys. Areas requiring particular attention in the decision to award the tender to the successful shipyard include time-scale of work contracted, quality of work, industrial relations record, steaming time to and from the shipyard, payment schedule and any prolonged credit payment system, relations with the yard, currency used and the shipyard's experience in handling the type of vessel involved.

(h) Overall the technical aspects of ship management cover a range of engineering and technical support services. Full use must be made of computer technology in the application and monitoring of the technical services.

21.4 FINANCIAL ASPECTS OF SHIP MANAGEMENT

Successful ship management depends on many factors, but an important one is adequate financial control to ensure the optimum use of the shipping company's resources. To achieve this there must be disciplined budgetary control covering revenue and expenditure budgets on a service, ship, profit centre, divisional or other convenient basis.

This must be formulated with the consent of those responsible for revenue production, marketing and service managers, and covers passengers, freight, accompanied cars, catering income, chartering income and miscellaneous receipts. In the case of expenditure it will include ship maintenance, port dues, crew cost, fuel, port agents' charges, agent's passenger/freight commission, ship insurance, etc. The budget must be reviewed continuously to reflect variations in expenditure and revenue. Full use must be made of computer resources. Budgets should be produced for capital investment programmes and cash forecasts.

Today most Masters have become involved in budgetary control. The Master and his chief officers are responsible for expenditure and revenue budgets. Overall these are formulated on an annual basis and take account of cargo to be conveyed and ship operating costs including fuel, crew, maintenance, port charges, etc. This type of budgetary control is likely to become more common and is dealt with more fully in my book *Economics of Shipping Practice and Management*, Chapter 14.

The object of budgetary control is to ensure maximum profitability of service/ships and it forms a very important part of ship management today. Usually with large shipping companies it is the practice to produce one- and five-year budget business plans. It gives an indication of the future prospects of the company in financial terms and points to any defects in commercial/operating/investment policy. It should cover the following points:

(a) The shipping company's investment plans in the next five years.

(b) Traffic forecasts in the next five years by trade route and the predicted financial results by service annually.

(c) A brief commentary on each service results in the next five years and significant features which are likely to arise such as new ships, more competition, new pooling agreements under liner conference terms, expansion of flag discrimination, market developments, etc.

(d) International events which could prejudice the company's five-year developments. This could include the further development of third world countries' fleets, more infiltration by former

Eastern bloc countries into cross trades, or the expansion of national fleets enjoying operating subsidies or some other form of state aid. Overall, such developments could reduce a shipping company's share of the market and result in a reduced fleet complement or withdrawn services.

(e) Statutory developments which may result in the need for more training of sea-going personnel, the provision of improved fire prevention equipment, or more severe survey requirements for older vessels.

(f) Future plans of the company particularly within the context of new services, rationalization of ports of call, reorganization of the company structure with more decentralization, etc.

(g) Investment needs in the next five years and how these are to be financed. This may involve using the existing financial resources of the company, obtaining government aid, selling older ships, the realization of redundant estate assets, e.g. the sale of a disused office block, using loan capital, etc.

(h) Assessment of how the major competitors will develop in the next five years, and how the shipping company will combat the situation.

(i) Political events must be assessed. This may include the development of more free trade areas and the expansion of existing ones.

(j) International trade forecast for the next five years and how the shipping company will feature in such developments. For example, liner trades on some routes may expand, whilst movement of crude oil may be stabilized.

(k) Any possible takeover of another shipping company or ancillary activity, i.e. shipbroking, freight forwarding, ports, etc.

(l) Budgetary control should primarily focus on the cash flow forecast and related financial planning to ensure the company develops a viable strategy. It also covers a number of complex financial activities such as tax-based leasing which has become a major force in the debt factoring business. Another area of focus is on financial analysis to produce an assessment of the liabilities outstanding on the ship with appropriate cash flow projections.

Basically the business plan should point the way the shipping company is going in the next five years.

21.5 INVESTMENT ASPECTS OF SHIP MANAGEMENT

Ship investment today is an important function of ship management. One must bear in mind that international trade is a speculative business and subject to various fluctuations in the light of political events. For example, the development of the Far East mercantile fleets, the expansion of flag discrimination practices and flagging out have had a profound effect on trade. Moreover, it may take two to three years to construct a vessel from the time the proposal to build is originated within the shipping company to the time she is launched. The ship will have an economic operational life of between 12 and 15 years depending on her type and use. Furthermore shipping has never been a very attractive investor's proposition and has usually only produced a modest return on the capital investment.

It is against this background that one must examine much capital investment which may be for building new tonnage, converting existing tonnage or buying second-hand tonnage. The following factors must be borne in mind as criteria for investment decision-making:

(a) The actual market prospects of the trade or route both in the short term and the long term.

(b) An analysis of the existing tonnage (see p. 482).

(c) Account must be taken of existing competition and likely future developments.

(d) Any political factors relevant to ship investment facilitation. (See p. 492.)

(e) The availability of capital is a critical factor as many shipowners have difficulty in raising capital without resorting to credit or subsidy facilities. (See p. 485.)

(f) The method of financing may be through loan capital from the banks or government sources; leasing; through raising capital on the stock exchange by the issue of share capital; by utilizing existing funds through a combination of liquid assets and short-term investment; or the sale of displaced ships or other company assets such as an office block. It is usually a mixture of the foregoing.

(g) The economics of the new tonnage involves the evaluation of the direct costs such as fuel, crew, maintenance and port charges, and the indirect costs such as depreciation, loan cost, etc. Such expenditure must be related to the revenue production.

(h) New ships can provide tax relief in the form of depreciation and other fiscal benefits. (See p. 486.)

(i) An assessment should be made of the return on the investment. A return on new investment of at least between 20 and 25% should be sought.

(j) The commercial factors should be closely examined particularly within the context of maintaining the existing market share on the route and securing/attracting new profitable business to the trade.

(k) An assessment must be made of the available shipyard capacity and time-scale of the project.

(l) Finally the investment memorandum should conclude by not only outlining the financial merits of the investment in new tonnage investment etc. but also the financial effect on the shipping company if no investment took place and/or one resorted to chartering, buying second-hand tonnage, leasing or converting existing tonnage.

One must bear in mind that ship investment is very much a risk activity and of a speculative nature thereby reflecting the uncertainty of international trade and the unpredictability of future development throughout the 12–15 year life span of the ships. The investment objective must be to maintain and develop existing market shares and develop new ones to sustain and exploit investment profitability (see also *Economics of Shipping Practice and Management*, Chapter 4).

Full use should be made of computer technology and many smaller shipping companies employ independent ship management companies such as Manx Ship Management or Denholm. Ship management is all about developing services and responding to market opportunities. It is a major logistics operation and requires much capital investment with its attendant high risk.

An example of a major global container operator responding to changing market opportunities is provided by the Maersk Line – the world's largest liner operator. In early 1994 the Maersk Line extended its services into the Latin American region which thus became integrated with the line's other North American, European and Far East services which included the Arab World and Africa.

The service commenced with three chartered vessels of 1000 TEU capacity. These were later replaced with units from the Maersk Line feedership service programme comprising 15 vessels of between 1106 and 1350 TEU either in service or on order.

The decision to move into South America reflected a belief that the prospects for the continent that had been fraught with indebtedness and political instability had now improved and a new era of trading opportunities was emerging within a framework of international business confidence and strategy. This was a perception shared by many of Maersk's major multinational clients and their own moves into South America added to pressures to start the service.

Maersk's strategy focuses on meeting the requirements of these multinationals. Not only are they important clients *per se* but they are also particularly demanding, and a line able to deliver the global reach and quality they require would be unwilling to be found failing in respect of other customers.

The new operation – known as the Andean service – focuses on the west coast of South America and serves Panama, Colombia, Peru and Chile. The decision to opt for the west coast may seem rather surprising as this means eschewing major economies such as Brazil, Venezuela and Argentina. Maersk Line considered at the time that the outlook for the western seaboard was rather more promising than for the east coast. The decision was also influenced by the fact that Maersk Line already has a variety of on-carriage arrangements in respect of the east coast that enables it to offer a service to clients, there is also more competition on the Atlantic coast.

A further attraction of South America is that it is an increasingly open market, although Maersk Line will face competition from existing operators in the Magellan Conference and from a variety of individual operators ranging from Crawley Maritime to the Sung Group Pacific Steam Navigation and Lykes Lines.

The Line will bring a new value added benefit to the region through the logistic operation and multi-modal container operation. For example, shippers of perishable cargoes who previously relied on reefer trampers and palletized systems will be able to transfer to the refrigerated container with its system of temperature control. Maersk Line will also provide fixed day reliability and the use of equipment such as data loggers, not only to reduce cargo damage but also to provide a verifiable quality of service.

Undoubtedly the Andean service will bring new economic and social development to the region as the service will be fully integrated with the Maersk Line global container network.

CHAPTER 22

Political aspects

22.1 FLAG DISCRIMINATION

Our study of the elements of shipping would not be complete without a look at the main political aspects of the subject: flag discrimination, flags of convenience and subsidies.

Flag discrimination comprises the wide variety of acts and pressures exerted by governments to direct cargoes to ships of their own flag, regardless of the commercial considerations which normally govern the routeing of cargoes. It also applies to directing their port authorities to offer more favourable rates and bunker charges to the national flag vessels.

Powers against flag discrimination in its various forms are now incorporated in the Merchant Shipping Act 1974 – part III of which enables the UK government to take counteraction against foreign governments, where UK shipping or trade interests are affected, or where they are required to meet Britain's international obligations. Orders can be made to obtain information, to regulate the carriage of goods, to levy charges on ships, to refuse admittance of ships to UK ports, and to approve or disapprove agreements. The Merchant Shipping Act 1988 provided the government with further powers of retaliation against unfair trading practices from overseas competitors.

Basically, flag discrimination dislocates the competitive nature of the shipping industry, because it often diverts trade to the less efficient carrier and obscures the real cost of the service. The more important methods by which it may be exercised are as follows:

(a) *Import licences.* A number of countries including Chile, Brazil, Gabon, Malaysia, Peru, Sudan and India have used the granting of import licences to ensure carriage of cargo in ships of their own national flag.

(b) *Discriminatory customs and other dues.* Preferential rates of customs and other dues are used to influence cargoes into ships of the national flag. Discriminatory charges in harbour, lighthouse pilotage and tonnage dues, consular fees and taxes on freight revenue are other means of favouring the national flag.

(c) *Administrative pressures*. Although in many countries there may be no statutory provisions reserving cargoes to ships of the national flag, the same result is achieved by administrative pressures of one form or another.

(d) *Direct legislative control*. This is the most damaging form of flag discrimination. In the early 1990s countries such as Argentina, Brazil, Chile, Ecuador, Peru, Turkey, Uruguay, Venezuela and Egypt resorted to direct legislative control in varying degrees.

(e) *Exchange control*. The manipulation of 'exchange control' offers endless means of making shipment in national vessels either obligatory, or so commercially attractive that it has the same effect.

(f) *Bilateral trade treaties*. In all, over thirty countries have entered into bilateral trade treaties, which include shipping clauses reserving either the whole of the trade between the two countries, or as much of it as possible, to the ships of the two flags.

Many South American and developing countries who build fleets for prestige purposes and to reduce the drain on foreign exchange practise flag discrimination. They are usually subsidized in several ways as follows:

(a) up to 50% of all goods passing through their ports must be carried in their own ships;

(b) a small concession in customs charges to reduce transport costs when charging full conference rates;

(c) a customs surcharge on goods carried by foreign ships.

Additionally other countries practise flag discrimination as follows:

(a) all chartered tonnage is reserved for the national flag;

(b) all coastal services are reserved for the national flag;

(c) a freight allocation agency is set up favouring the national flag and fixing rates;

(d) unfavourable pilotage regulations are passed and there are higher bunker charges for foreign tonnage.

There is no doubt that flag discrimination is one of the most serious problems facing the industry today, but because it takes so many forms and is inspired by diverse motives, there is no simple remedy. Compromise and expediency will offer no long-term solution. What is required is determined and concerted action by governments throughout the world.

The Eighth round of the GATT trade negotiations completed and signed in Marrakesh in 1994 could signal a new era of decline in the practice of flag discrimination adopted by numerous countries (see pp. 170–80).

22.2 FLAGS OF CONVENIENCE

Shipping companies, like any other undertakings, are subject to the income and profits taxes of the state where they operate, and the level of tax is very important to the shipowner. This problem is, of course, common to all industry, but for the shipping industry it is aggravated by the enormous cost of replacement which continues to rise as building costs increase.

British shipowners in particular, and indeed owners in any maritime country subject to similar taxation, are at a serious disadvantage when competing with tax-free or virtually tax-free national merchant fleets, under flags of convenience – or open registries as they are now often termed. Two countries which featured prominently in this practice are Liberia and Panama as confirmed in Table 1.3 on p. 5.

The following points are relevant:

(a) The five major open registry countries and territories (Bahamas, Bermuda, Cyprus, Liberia and Panama) continue to increase their share of the world maritime fleet. In 1991 it stood at 35.7% involving 43.5% of the tanker fleet, 34.5% bulk carriers, 28.0% general cargo ships, 23.1% container ships and 25.8% other ships. They account for the largest share of vessels as oil tankers and dry bulk carriers (including combined carriers and general cargo ships).

(b) The average age in the mid-1990s of open registry tonnage was 15.12 years compared with the world total of 14.06 years.

To develop our evaluation of open registries we will first consider the ship register system in the mid-1990s and beyond, examine the criteria by which shipowners select their classification society and the correlation with open registries, and finally consider the rationale behind the decline in the registration of tonnage with the main land or domestic registries. We will conclude with a case study of the latest emerging open register – Malta.

Ship registers in the 1990s face a period of turmoil and change as the political and public reaction to shipping disasters forces the system of flag-state control to be overhauled. The system is supervised by the International Maritime Organization (IMO).

The flag state has a duty to survey and certify ships registered in their country according to the IMO conventions they have ratified (see pp. 127–44). The sheer scale of this work has led 125 countries (out of a total of 137) to delegate the work to classification societies and other commercial organizations. Panama uses as many as 30 different bodies. It is up to the flag state to satisfy itself that the classification society or other commercial organization undertakes the work in a competent manner.

The number of classification societies has increased in the past two decades to over 40 of which eleven are members of the International Association of Classification Societies (IACS) (see pp. 119–22). The IACS was set up in 1968 as a trade association. Overall the IACS classifies over half the world's ships but some 92% of the fleet by tonnage terms. To assure the maritime community its members are competent enough to carry out statutory surveys for flag states IACS has set up a quality system certification scheme for its members. External audits are also carried out on IACS members.

Focusing on flag states' compliance and implementation records as well as on their relationships with classification societies is one method of raising standards. The other is seaport state control.

West Europe, North America and Japan operate seaport state control and ultimately will be joined by complementary systems in Latin America and the Pacific/Asia Region. Longer term East Europe, Africa and the Middle East could follow to provide a worldwide system. However, there is no guarantee this would be more effective than the system of flag-state control it is meant to underpin.

Today there are a large number of classification societies and the criteria by which a shipowner chooses a society are complex, though many countries specify which classification society to use. Among the criteria it is acknowledged that the prime responsibility for the safe and pollution-free operation of a ship lies with its owner and operator and the flag state. Hence when a shipowner enters the specified classification society he must comply with its regulations and operate in accordance with three international requirements.

(a) *Structural integrity*. The classification society has the task of ensuring that ship maintenance and surveys are undertaken. This technical work in accord with the regulations is entrusted to the society by the state.

(b) *Safety equipment*. Every society must have the competence to undertake an annual audit of every ship in its registry to ensure safety equipment is fully operational and in accordance with international conditions.

(c) *Personnel qualifications*. All shipboard personnel must have the appropriate experience/competence and documented qualifications relative to the ship manning levels.

The guidelines by which a shipowner will select a classification society selection are given below:

(a) The administration should have a comprehensive body of laws and regulations to implement the requisite international standards.

(b) The flag state should have a recognized system of casualty investigation in place and undertake such investigations promptly and thoroughly.

(c) There should be a corporate law identifying the link between the ship and flag state.

(d) The flag state should require that every ship in its register has a 'decision-maker' available to the registry 24 hours per day.

(e) There should be provided a publicly available register of ships.

(f) The flag state should be a signatory to the principal international conventions essential to maritime safety and protection of the environment.

(g) There should be staff available who are competent to answer enquiries from owners and operators.

(h) It should have the ability to issue seamen's identity books.

(i) There should be available a current list of all ships registered in its flag.

(j)   The flag state should be committed to ensuring it does not register a ship from another registry without a deletion certificate from the previous register (see pp. 27–30).

(k)   The flag state should provide the IMO with annual details of all personnel injury records, casualties and pollution incidents occurring on or to its ships.

The decline in the numbers and size of vessels registered with the mainland or domestic registers of traditional maritime nations has been dramatic. Less than 20 years ago major maritime states like Britain, Norway and Germany all had fleets on their domestic registers large enough to rank them among the world's biggest flags. Today not one is in the top ten (see Table 1.3, p. 5). However, the Norwegian International Register (NIS) has been an outstanding success in growth terms. Its principal aim is to attract Norwegian-controlled tonnage which has been registered outside Norway.

A major attraction in 'flagging out' tonnage lies not only in the reduced manning scales/levels required (see pp. 72–7) but also in the tax allowances against new and second-hand tonnage. These two factors – reduced manning cost/scales and taxation benefits/ allowances – yield cost savings in manning levels and encourage new tonnage provision. Such factors are very powerful in the drive globally of shipowners to develop world trade, increase market share and provide more competitive tariffs.

An example of a fast-growing international registry is Malta. In September 1993 there were 937 vessels registered in Malta representing a total of 12.9 m gt. In April 1995 this had risen to 1009 ships totalling 15.5 m gt – an increase of 20% in tonnage terms. A wide range of vessel types are registered under the Maltese flag. These include container vessels, OBOs, tankers and dry cargo ships. Greek owners represent an important market together with a growing input from other European countries and the Far East. The Malta Maritime Authority is the body responsible for supervising the ship registration programme. It offers not only favourable tax advantages, but also a European profile with a stable democratic government, good telecommunications and transport links and a range of professional support services. The Malta Maritime Authority is very conscious of dispelling the poor reputation for ship safety which flags of convenience offer and have a network of 30 experienced inspectors worldwide who are available for seaport inspection of their registered tonnage. Overall the inspectors plan to survey annually some 25% of all trading vessels registered.

The number of countries considering forming an international ship register is very much on the increase. Australia, Finland, Canada, the UK, Brazil and Sweden are assessing the recent growth of the Norwegian International Ship Register (NIS) and the German International Shipping Register (ISR). Ironically both the NIS and the ISR are in decline due to the withdrawal of or reduction in the subsidies and tax incentives which were in large part responsible for their success.

The advantages to a country with a high profile and high maritime professional standards of developing an international registry are considerable. It encourages a maritime-based infrastructure in shipbuilding and repairs, education (Malta is setting up a Maritime University), income and jobs involving all levels of maritime activity, and provides the profile of a trading nation with an integrated mercantile fleet embracing both domestic and foreign tonnage.

It will be very interesting in the latter part of the 1990s to analyse the pattern of change in the registration of the world fleet.

22.3 SUBSIDIES

Subsidies distort the competitive structure of shipping and increase the cost of world shipping services, because they permit the use of vessels less efficient and more expensive than is warranted on an economic basis. However, it is difficult to see how a country like the USA can operate ships without subsidies, since the labour costs are so much higher than those of other countries. Of course, in a world where international specialization was fully used, and where no questions of national security were posed, shipowning would be undertaken only by those countries most fitted by their cost structures and efficiency to operate ships.

By the 1980s fleet subsidization was much on the increase in a variety of ways and reflected the increased tendency of nationalism and protectionism adopted by many maritime nations towards their fleet development and sustainment. Undoubtedly the

UNCTAD V conference held in Manila 1979 stimulated the development of such policies particularly by third world countries. Details of the types of subsidization are given below:

(a) Building subsidies may be a percentage of the total building cost or a fixed sum of the ship construction cost. It is usually given on certain conditions, particularly as a means of sustaining the shipyard industry in the maritime country concerned rather than allow the vessel to be built in a foreign yard at perhaps a lower cost and quicker time-scale. This policy is particularly relevant to state-owned fleets and therefore seen as part of the nation's economy and as an aid to trade development.

In the case of non-state-owned fleets, building subsidies are likewise available in similar terms or with no constraints so that a subsidy may be afforded to a vessel built in a foreign yard. It must be recognized that not all maritime nations, particularly third world countries, have their own shipyards although the situation will become less common as their industrialization develops. It must be borne in mind that few shipowners today have the funds to provide new tonnage and rarely can more than one-third be found from the shipping company's own financial resources, the rest being provided from government and/or financial institutions.

(b) Shipyard subsidies are much on the increase in a period of depression in the international shipbuilding industry. Hence governments may subsidize the shipyard both for new construction and repair work irrespective of whether the vessels are of foreign registration or of the particular maritime nation involved.

(c) A further subsidy technique is to offer interest-free or low interest loans to the shipowners for new tonnage. Again it may be subject to various conditions such as the ship being built in the maritime country shipyard. Furthermore, it may be sponsored under a 'scrap and build' policy whereby, for example, three vessels in excess of 15 years old would be scrapped and two new ones provided in their place. A similar condition could arise in building subsidies.

(d) An operating subsidy arises when the shipping company is either granted a specified sum to make good the loss incurred each year or an operating grant. The latter is usually provided annually over a specified period.

(e) A subvention arises whereby a shipping company provides a service which is essential to the economic and social well-being of a community.

(f) Subsidies also arise in the form of fleet insurance being funded by the state as found in many former Eastern bloc tonnage. It also extends to crew subsidization involving social security/ insurance contributions being state-financed.

Features of subsidies and their policies are given below:

1. It enables the maritime government to save hard currency in that if the cargo is conveyed in a foreign registered ship it would involve a hard currency out-payment. Likewise, the subsidized shipping company carries cargo for other countries and may even operate in a cross-trade situation. This earns invisible exports for the maritime country.

2. It tends to inflate the world shipping fleet capacity beyond the level which trade can support. Accordingly it destroys in some trades the commercial freedom of the seas and this is apparent when two competing companies seek the same traffic flow, one of which is subsidized and the other not so. The former can usually undercut the latter in the knowledge that if he incurs a loss on the traffic, the government will still subsidize the service.

3. It encourages uneconomic ship operation as there is no incentive in some situations to reduce costs in the knowledge the state will make good the loss and the service will not be withdrawn.

4. It develops further the policy of nationalism with fleets being built up not only for commercial reasons but also for prestige and strategic considerations. Moreover, it is a means of saving hard currency and can encourage the policy of flag discrimination in many countries.

5. It changes the financial evaluation approach when assessing the economics of a shipping service. For example, if a service is losing some £4 million annually and its invisible export contribution is £5 million, the state could decide that retention of the service is justified. Moreover, if the service were closed and it would cost some £6 million annually in hard currency for foreign carriers to convey such cargo for the maritime country, it would be justified to retain the service and subsidize it.

6. Countries having high wage scales find it increasingly difficult to compete with fleets with low wage scales relative to crew cost. Attempts have been made by industrial maritime nations to reduce their crew complement with some measure of success. Such nations, to sustain their relatively high cost fleet, often provide some form of subsidy and foster the policy of flag discrimination. Alternatively some maritime nations are encouraging their fleets to flag out (consider the NIS and ISR – see p. 497).

7. It does not usually encourage efficiency as in some cases there is no incentive to keep ship operating costs to a low level in the knowledge the state will fund it.

The practice of operating subsidized fleets tends to be on the increase particularly by developing countries anxious to save hard currency by conveying their own trade. Credit remains a dominant factor in any shipbuilding project negotiation. Banks are offering loans for new tonnage over a longer period. Governments in many countries are endeavouring to sustain their national shipyards by offering generous credit facilities and in many countries this involves substantial subsidies both to national and foreign buyers. There is also the link between national shipyards and shipping companies whereby support for the former is passed onto the latter. Government support effectively reduces the cost of capital to shipping companies and can take many forms. Recent examples are given below:

(a) Direct investment grants to shipping companies for new and/or second-hand ships. These are available in some form in France, the Netherlands, Korea and Taiwan. Also grants to shipyards may assist shipowners.

(b) Soft loans with low interest rates or moratoria financed by governments. Within the EU, finance terms more favourable than the OECD terms count against the ceiling of aid to shipbuilding set under the EU Sixth Directive on shipbuilding.

(c) The tax position of shipping companies where the government provides for accelerated depreciation allowances, low or zero corporation tax, and availability of tax-free reserves. The actual value of depreciation allowances and tax-free reserves depend on the rate of corporation tax – the higher the tax rate the greater the benefit to the company. These benefits exist in some form in many EU and Nordic countries and in Japan amongst others.

(d) The favourable tax treatment of individuals and partnerships investing in shipping.

To end our analysis we will now identify the points raised at a meeting in June 1990 of the OECD Maritime Transport Committee consisting of eight countries. The Committee concluded it would not be practical or acceptable to phase out subsidies to shipping. The OECD cited the following reasons for the continuation of subsidies:

(a) to ensure the maintenance of a national flag or nationally owned fleet for security or strategic purposes;

(b) to maintain employment of national seafarers in order to secure maritime know-how and a pool of personnel in case of need;

(c) to maintain a relatively free shipping market and preserve the freedom of shippers' choice;

(d) to make available shipping services to remote communities in the country's territory which are otherwise not commercially viable;

(e) to assist their operators in competing with other fleets who are in a favourable economic position due to non-commercial advantages granted by another state or to particular characteristics of their national economics;

(f) to increase the contribution of shipping to the balance of payments;

(g) to modernize their fleets, make them more competitive or ease structural adjustment.

It is likely that the degree of fleet subsidization and protectionism will intensify in the next few years, especially among nations endeavouring to develop their national fleet.

22.4 CONTRIBUTION OF SHIPPING TO INVISIBLE EXPORTS

Shipping revenue as an invisible export can make an important contribution to the balance of payments of the chief shipowning countries. The contribution may arise in two ways:

Table 22.1 Contribution of UK shipping industry to balance of payments (£m)

	Total revenue a+c	Revenue from abroad a	Expenditure abroad b	Net direct contribution a−b	Import savings c	Total contribution (a−b)+c
1980	3717	3121	1976	1145	596	1741
1982	3053	2407	1865	542	646	1188
1984	3002	2305	1866	439	697	1136
1986	2923	2204	1553	651	719	1370
1988	3426	2516	1570	946	910	1856
1990	3664	2579	1567	1012	1085	2097
1991	3624	2478	1557	921	1146	2067
1992	3747	2544	1594	948	1203	2151
1993	4151	2854	1767	1087	1297	2384

Reproduced by kind permission of the Chamber of Shipping.

(a) A large volume of the country's trade may be carried in its own ships, so that foreign exchange is not required to pay freight on imports. Conversely, foreign exchange is earned where freight on exports carried in the country's ships is paid by the importing country.

(b) Where a country's ships carry passengers and freight between other countries, substantial amounts of foreign exchange may be earned.

Table 22.1 shows the importance of the net contribution of British shipping to the UK balance of payments. The net direct contribution to the balance of payments is derived after deducting expenditure overseas on essential items like fuel bunkers, cargo handling and port charges. Given in Table 22.2 is an analysis of the UK-owned and registered fleet and the world trading fleet in 1995. It should be reconciled with Table 1.3 on p. 5 featuring the top ten maritime fleets.

The reasons for the decline in the UK fleet are numerous as given below.

(a) High cost of ship operation and low investment return encouraging shipowner to flag out.

(b) Little HM government support financially to aid ship investment compared with other maritime nations.

(c)   Development of flags of convenience.

(d)   Development of former Eastern bloc countries' fleets.

(e)   Adoption of liner conference code of 40:40:20.

(f)   High crew cost compared with many other maritime fleets.

(g)   Change in the pattern of world trade.

(h)   Policy by many governments worldwide to develop their maritime fleets and their overseas trade to thereby improve their external trade balance.

(i)   The decline in the UK market share of world trade.

(j)   Major technological changes especially in liner shipping whereby a modern container ship can transport more than eight times as much cargo as the general cargo ships of 1970.

(k)   Decline in liner conferences where UK tonnage was prominent and the emergence of round-the-world services and the globalization and networking of container distribution featuring major operators such as the Maersk Line.

(l)   Development of multi-modalism.

(m) Emergence of the newly industrialized economies in the Far East building up large and modern competitive fleets outside the constraints of any liner conference system, e.g. Evergreen and a number of Japanese shipping lines. This has resulted in the decline of the national flag fleets of developed countries from two-thirds of the world fleet in 1970 to less than one-third in 1994 (see p. 496).

(n)   The flagging out of tonnage (see pp. 72–7).

22.5 CONCLUSIONS

The seventh edition of this book is published more than 30 years after the first edition emerged in 1964. Throughout this period great change has taken place in the industry. The subject has become more complex and the latest edition has been completely brought up to date in all its areas. The book preserves its lucidity of presentation for an international market now extending to over 220 countries. Each new edition has become more international in its content to reflect the needs of the reader worldwide and contains more case studies. The latest edition also contains three additional chapters on multi-modalism, seaports and computer technology. It reflects the increasing role these topics have taken on in shipping today.

Table 22.2 UK-owned and world fleet (100 GRT and above) as at 31/03/95

Vessel type	UK-owned			World			UK as % of world	
	No.	000 GRT	000 dwt	No.	000 GRT	000 dwt	No.	dwt
Bulk/oil carrier	0	0	0	239	14 953	26 786	0.00	0.00
Bulk carrier	43	1 600	2 907	5 342	130 947	229 380	0.80	1.27
Total dry bulk	43	1 600	2 907	5 581	145 900	256 166	0.77	1.13
Reefer	14	104	111	1 483	7 298	7 806	0.94	1.42
Specialized carrier	24	152	89	1 306	16 568	9 537	1.84	0.93
Container (FC)	49	1 475	1 481	1 617	35 404	39 335	3.03	3.77
Ro-Ro passenger	97	632	160	2 170	9 801	2 865	4.47	5.58
Ro-Ro container	0	0	0	0	0	0		
Ro-Ro other cargo	17	136	78	849	7 058	6 016	2.00	1.30
Gen. cargo/passenger	7	10	4	338	709	362	2.07	1.10
Gen. cargo single-deck	169	236	356	9 568	10 323	22 790	1.64	1.05
Gen. cargo multi-deck	53	349	484	6 447	33 381	47 112	0.82	01.03
Gen. cargo/container	0	0	0	0	0	0	0.00	0.00
Special service	0	0	0	12	177	253	0.00	0.00
Total other dry cargo	430	3 094	2 763	24 545	133 186	147 341	1.75	1.88
Cruise ships	13	402	72	262	4 435	887	4.96	8.12
Other passenger	17	4	1	1 987	804	182	0.86	0.55
Total passenger	30	406	73	2 249	5 239	1 069	1.33	6.83

Oil tanker	132	3 617	7 072	6 672	144 853	269 561	1.98	2.62
Oil-chemical tanker	6	32	52	721	6 996	11 755	0.83	0.44
Chemical tanker	7	17	28	1 292	4 533	7 562	0.54	0.37
Other tanker	4	2	3	303	391	569	1.32	0.53
Liquified gas carrier	26	393	464	950	14 141	14 073	2.74	3.30
Total liquid	175	4 061	7 619	9 938	170 914	303 520	1.76	2.51
Trading fleet	**678**	**9 161**	**13 362**	**42 313**	**455 239**	**708 096**	**1.60**	**1.89**
Barge	28	52	89	416	825	1 115	6.73	7.98
Drilling	22	60	39	735	1 811	1 355	2.99	2.88
Dredging	116	226	358	2 090	2 926	4 037	5.55	8.87
Tugs	201	56	22	7 716	2 083	689	2.60	3.19
Off-shore supply	112	157	179	2 359	1 827	2 122	4.75	8.44
Naval craft	28	286	287	226	2 048	2 209	12.39	12.99
Other non-trading	671	563	477	26 423	18 170	12 263	2.54	3.89
Non-trading fleet	**1 178**	**1 400**	**1 451**	**39 965**	**29 690**	**23 790**	**2.95**	**6.10**

Reproduced with kind permission: Chamber of Shipping.

The last ten years in particular have seen enormous changes in the pattern of world trade and a shift to the Pacific Rim in terms of high economic growth, maritime tonnage and global trade development. This trend will continue and already manifests itself through the changes in the world fleet composition to favour the newly industrialized economies of the Far East.

The implications of the successful conclusion to the Eighth Round of the GATT trade negotiations in 1994 will be manifest in an accelerated growth in world trade especially in less developed and developing countries.

Shipping is becoming more complex in all aspects of its business. To be successful the shipping entrepreneur must be professional at all times and well qualified. The next decade will present enormous opportunities both in existing trades and in emerging markets such as those of the subcontinent and South America. Moreover, the expansion of the former Eastern bloc, the CIS and the South African trades will present more challenges to the shipping industry.

The seventh edition has been enlarged and completely updated to ensure the discriminating shipping entrepreneur and student is better equipped to meet such challenges on a professional basis. Accordingly, it is hoped it will facilitate the development of international trade through better ship management and export/import techniques and thereby raise living standards worldwide.

Shipping terms and abbreviations

Act of God	Any fortuitous act which could not have been prevented by any amount of human care and forethought.
ADR	European agreement on the international carriage of dangerous goods by road.
Affreightment	A contract for the carriage of goods by sea for shipment expressed in charter party or bill of lading.
Agent	One who represents a principal, or buys or sells for another.
ANF	Arrival notification form – advice to consignee of goods coming forward.
APT	Afterpeak tank.
Arbitration	Method of settling disputes which is usually binding on the parties concerned.
BAF	Bunker adjustment factor. Freight adjustment factor to reflect current cost of bunkers.
Balance of trade	Financial statement of balance of a country's visible trade exports and imports.
bdi	Both days included.
BIFA	British International Freight Association.
Bilateralism	Trade between two countries.
BK	Bar keel.
Bond	Guarantee to customs of specified amount of duty to be paid.
Box	Colloquial name for a container.
Break-bulk cargo	Goods shipped loose in the vessel's hold and not in a container.
Breaking bulk	Commencing discharge.
Bulk unitization	Means to consolidate multiple packages or items into a single-load device.

BV	Bureau Veritas – French ship classification society.
CABAF	Currency and bunker adjustment factor – a combination of CAF and BAF.
CAD	Cash against documents.
CAF	Currency adjustment factor – freight adjustment factor to reflect currency exchange fluctuations.
Cargo manifest	Inventory of cargo shipped.
CB	Container base.
CCC	Customs clearance certificate.
C & D	Collected and delivered.
CFS	Container freight station. Place for packing and unpacking LCL consignments.
CHIEF	Customs Handling of Import and Export Freight.
CIF	Cost, insurance and freight.
Closing date	Latest date cargo accepted for shipment by (liner) shipowner for specified sailing.
CMI	Comité Maritime International – an international committee of maritime lawyers.
C/N	Consignment note.
C/O	Certificate of origin or cash with order.
COD	Cash on delivery.
Collector's office	Customs accommodation where declaration(s) (entries) are scrutinized and amounts payable collected.
Consignee	Name of agent, company or person receiving consignment.
Consignor	Name of agent, company or person sending consignment (the shipper).
COP	Custom of port.
COT	Customer's own transport. Customer collects from/delivers to CFS/CY or other specified point.
C/P	Charter party.
cpd	Charterers pay dues.
CPT	Carriage paid to. A combined transport Incoterm.
CSC	Container Safety Convention.

CTD	Combined transport document.
CTL	Constructive total loss.
CWE	Cleared without examination. Cleared customs without inspection.
D/A	Deposit account.
DAF	Delivery at frontier. An Incoterm applicable to all modes of transport.
DDA	Duty (customs) deferment account.
DDO	Despatch money payable discharging only.
DDU	Delivered duty unpaid. An Incoterm applicable to all modes of transport.
DF	Direction finder.
Demurrage	Charge raised for detaining cargo/FCL container/trailer/ship for longer period than prescribed.
DES	Delivered ex-ship. A conventional port-to-port Incoterm of sale.
Despatch	Money paid by shipowner to charterer for earlier loading or discharging of cargo as scheduled in charter party.
DGN	Dangerous goods note.
DLO	Despatch money payable loading only.
D1/2D	Despatch money payable at half demurrage rate.
D/O	Delivery order.
D/P	Documents against payment.
DTI	Direct trader imput. Procedure for customs entry clearance.
DTp	Department of Transport.
Dunnage	Wood, mats, etc. used to facilitate stowage of cargo.
Dutiable cargo	Cargo which attracts some form of duty, that is Customs and Excise or VAT.
ECSI	Export cargo shipping instruction – shipping instructions from shipper to carrier.
EDI	Electronic data interchange. The transfer of structured data from one computer system to another.
Embarkation	Process of passengers joining a ship.

EPU	Entry processing unit. Customs office that processes customs entries.
ETA	Estimated time of arrival.
ETD	Estimated time of departure.
Exchange rate	Price of one currency in terms of another.
Export licence	Government-issued document authorizing export of restricted goods.
Faa	Free of all average.
FAS	Free alongside ship. A conventional/port-to-port only Incoterm of sale.
FCA	Free carrier (named points). Combined transport Incoterm.
FCL	Full container load.
Feeder vessel	A short sea vessel used to fetch and carry goods and containers to and from deep-sea vessels operating on basis of hub and spoke concept.
FFI	For further instructions.
FIO	Free in and out. Cargo is loaded and discharged at no cost to the shipowner.
Fixture	Conclusion of shipbroker's negotiations to charter a ship.
FO	Free overside.
FOR	Free on rail.
Forwarder's bill of lading	A bill of lading issued by a freight forwarder.
Forwarder's receipt	A document issued by a freight forwarder which provides evidence of receipt of the goods.
FOW	First open water.
Freight	Amount payable for the carriage of goods or a description of the goods conveyed.
Freight ton	Tonnage on which freight is charged.
Fwd	Forward.
Heterogeneous cargo	Variety of cargoes.
High stowage factor	Cargo which has a high bulk to low weight relationship, e.g. hay.
IATA	International Air Transport Association.
ICD	Inland clearance depot.

IMO	International Maritime Organization.
Indemnity	Compensation for loss/damage or injury.
Inland clearance depot	Customs cargo clearance depot.
Laydays	Period allotted in charter party for loading/ discharging cargo.
L/C	Letter of credit – document in which the terms of a documentary credit transaction is set out.
LEC	Local export control – a system of clearing goods/containers/trucks at exporter's premises.
LIC	Local import control – a system of clearing goods/containers/trucks at importers' premises.
LL	Load line.
LMC	Lloyd's machinery certification.
LNG	Liquefied natural gas – type of vessel.
Loading broker	Person who acts on behalf of liner company at a port.
LPG	Liquid petroleum gas.
Lump sum freight	Remuneration paid to shipowner for charter of a ship, or portion of it, irrespective of quantity of cargo loaded.
Manifest	List of goods/passengers on a vessel/aircraft/ truck.
M'dise	Merchandise.
Measurement ton	A cubic metre.
MMO	Multi-modal operator.
MSA	Merchant Shipping Act.
MV	Motor vessel.
Negotiable bill of lading	One capable of being negotiated by transfer or endorsement.
Notify Party	Party to whom arrival notification form is sent.
NVOC	Non-vessel-owning/operating carrier.
OBO	Oil bulk ore carriers – multi-purpose bulk carriers.
OEC	Overpaid entry certificate.

O/H	Overheight. A container or trailer with goods protruding above the unit profile.
OSD	Open shelter deck.
Overvalued currency	Currency whose rate of exchange is persistently below the parity rate.
PC	Passenger certificate.
Per pro	On behalf of.
P/L	Partial loss.
Pre-entered	Process of lodging with customs appropriate documentation for scrutiny prior to cargo customs clearance and shipment.
PTL	Partial total loss.
Receiving date	Date from which cargo is accepted for shipment for specified sailing.
Reefer	Refrigerated.
Removal note	Confirms goods clear of customs.
Ro/Ro	Roll-on/roll-off – a vehicular ferry service.
SAD	Single administrative document.
SHInc	Sundays and holidays included.
Shipper	The person tendering the goods for carriage.
Shut out	Cargo refused shipment because it arrived after closing date.
Slot	Space on board a vessel occupied by a container or sailing schedule allocation.
SSN	Standard Shipping Note.
Stuffing/stripping	The action of packing/unpacking a container.
TC	Time charter.
TEU	Twenty ft equivalent unit – container measurement, i.e. 1×40 ft = 2 TEU; 1×20 ft = 1 TEU.
T/L	Total loss.
TLO	Total loss only.
TSS	Turbine steamship.
ULCC	Ultra large crude carrier.
ULD	Unit load device.
UN	United Nations.
UNCTAD	United Nations Conference on Trade and Development.
Undervalued currency	Currency whose rate of exchange is persistently above the parity.

Unit loads	Containerized or palletized traffic.
VLCC	Very large crude carrier.
WTO	World Trade Organization.
WWDSHEX	Weather working days Sundays and holidays excepted. A charter party term.

NB: Readers are also recommended to study the *Dictionary of Shipping International Business/Trade Terms and Abbreviations (also incorporating Air/Travel/Tourism)*, 4th edn, 1995, 14 000 entries – by A.E. Branch, published by Witherby, London EC1R 0ET.

Index

Index